AF600442

TAKING EXCEPTION TO THE LAW

Materializing Injustice in Early Modern English Literature

EDITED BY DONALD BEECHER,
TRAVIS DECOOK, ANDREW WALLACE,
AND GRANT WILLIAMS

Taking Exception to the Law

Materializing Injustice in Early Modern English Literature

UNIVERSITY OF TORONTO PRESS
Toronto Buffalo London

© University of Toronto Press 2015
Toronto Buffalo London
www.utppublishing.com

ISBN 978-1-4426-4201-0

Library and Archives Canada Cataloguing in Publication

Taking exception to the law : materializing injustice in early modern English literature / edited by Donald Beecher, Travis DeCook, Andrew Wallace, and Grant Williams.

Includes bibliographical references and index.
ISBN 978-1-4426-4201-0 (bound)

1. English literature – Early modern, 1500–1700 – History and criticism. 2. Law and literature – England – History – 16th century. 3. Law and literature – England – History – 17th century. 4. Law in literature. 5. Justice in literature. I. Beecher, Donald, editor II. Wallace, Andrew, 1973-, editor III. Williams, Grant, 1965-, editor IV. DeCook, Travis, 1976-, editor

PR428.L37T35 2015 820.9′3554 C2014-906034-3

University of Toronto Press acknowledges the financial assistance to its publishing program of the Canada Council for the Arts and the Ontario Arts Council, an agency of the Government of Ontario.

University of Toronto Press acknowledges the financial support of the Government of Canada through the Canada Book Fund for its publishing activities.

Contents

Illustrations

Acknowledgments

The editors of this volume wish to thank our contributors for their thoughtful work, for their patience and understanding throughout the entire editorial process, and for their willingness to explore additional materials in the interests of complementarity and balance. We are appreciative of the Social Sciences and Humanities Research Council of Canada for their generous financial support in the publication of this collection. And finally we wish to acknowledge our gratitude to all those at the University of Toronto Press who collaborated in the final print production.

TAKING EXCEPTION TO THE LAW

1 Law and the Production of Literature: An Introductory Perspective

GRANT WILLIAMS

Recent scholarly work on the interconnections between legal and literary matters has compelled Renaissance studies to view the subfield of early modern Law and Literature as much more than a boutique interdisciplinary jurisdiction, an academic niche of peculiar technical legalese interesting only to law experts and historians.[1] This volume of essays originates from the realization that English Renaissance studies must confront the profound relevance and broad appeal of legal questions to understanding early modern literary activity. Accordingly, the volume's contributors do not hail from law departments, but – with a single exception – belong to literature departments. This volume then is not so much a contribution to the subfield of early modern Law and Literature as a bellwether of the degree to which the entire field of English Renaissance literary studies is absorbing and profiting from the findings, insights, and issues raised by this exciting interdisciplinary inquiry.

In English Renaissance literary scholarship, an intellectual emphasis on the law seems long overdue, considering the proportional influence that the curriculum of the premodern university has exercised on scholarship's interrogation of literature's epistemological foundations and implications. The degrees at Oxford and Cambridge were organized around four faculties. Theology and the philosophically minded liberal arts, the first two faculties, have always been regarded as crucial intellectual spheres for studying literary production, and over the 1980s and 1990s the concentration of feminism and gender studies on textual bodies led to a surge in studying the four bodily humours, disease, and anatomy, all of which fall under the rubric of the third faculty, medicine.[2] Yet only now has the fourth faculty finally come into its own. I don't mean to imply that the university monopolized society's legal machinery, since only the civil law, the Roman law tradition, was taught at Oxford and Cambridge, whereas the Inns of Court dealt primarily with the English law, the basis of the common law tradition; however, the fourth faculty, a quarter of the university's curricular disposition, helps us to sense the disciplinary weight that the law exerted on the period's conceptualizations of knowledge and vocational culture.

English Renaissance literary studies can no longer appeal to an ignorance of the law, because, on one level, the field of Law and Literature has brought to our attention just how engrossed the period's literary works are with legal questions. The scholarly mode of what Law and Literature calls "law in literature" has demonstrated the rich potential of mining from literary stores jurisprudential topics, discourses, and even types of legal thinking, in addition to mimetic and parodic representations of juridical apparatuses, such as statutes, trials, and punishments.[3] The "law in literature" mode does not merely recover forgotten allusions for interesting footnotes or unpack minor themes planted only for the scrutiny of lawyer-readers, but testifies to the law's explicit cultural and intellectual prominence in English Renaissance society. An exemplary work in this regard is R.S. White's study, which makes the case for the natural law's astonishing complexity and ubiquity. Foreign to modern and postmodern sensibilities, the natural law signified an "innate form of knowledge, imprinted on the human mind," deriving from God, nature, or reason, but easily compromised by the likes of sin, the emotions, and ignorance.[4] Interposed between the inaccessibility of the divine law and the fallibility of man-made rules, this all-encompassing category covers the endless intellectual work – if not rationalization – of separating the universality and justness of the natural order of things from society's flawed and corrupt renderings of this order. White's scholarship reveals the natural law forming the basis of Renaissance literary theory and literature, from More's *Utopia* and Sidney's *Arcadia* to Milton's *Paradise Lost*.[5] The period's incessant concern with poetic justice, towards which so many narratives pursue resolution, bespeaks the natural law's fundamental influence upon shaping literary content.[6] The mode of "law in literature," however, does not privilege only massive frames of cultural reference as evinced, say, by Brian C. Lockey's *Law and Empire in English Renaissance Literature*. Legal matters can interpenetrate literature in subtler, less apparent ways too. Exemplary in this regard is Charles Ross's *Elizabethan Literature and the Law of Fraudulent Conveyance*. Fraudulent conveyance refers to a debtor's action of removing his or her property from the reach of creditors. As narrowly technical as it may appear, this type of fraud may broadly speaking underlie the motivation of abducting nubile women, a situation that drives the plot in many major early modern literary texts, such as Sidney's *Arcadia*, Spenser's *The Faerie Queene*, Shakespeare's *The Merry Wives of Windsor*, and *The Merchant of Venice*.[7] In Ross's account, these literary representations of the particular fraud raise fascinating ethical questions about debt, one of the most common legal concerns in early modern culture.

The profundity and persistence of the law as a literary topic may also be gauged by Shakespeare's frequent reference to various judicial matters throughout his corpus. B.J. and Mary Sokol's *Shakespeare, Law, and Marriage* meticulously identifies and glosses the sheer bulk of marriage law in Shakespeare's plays and his two narrative poems, elucidating the various legal aspects of the institution, from what makes a marriage valid to issues of arranged marriages, wardship, dowries, solemnization, separation, divorce, and death.[8] Their work, another good example of the approach of "law in literature," lays bare only one strand of the extraordinary Shakespearean wealth of legal topics and allusions, which has long captivated the Law and Literature movement so much so that the argument could be made that Shakespeare studies in the first half of the twentieth century – and not just the seminal scholarship arising out of the American law schools in the 1970s – paved the way for the movement's inception.[9] And today such Shakespeare scholarship shows no sign of abatement.[10] So impressively wide ranging is Shakespeare's knowledge of legal matters that some eighteenth- and nineteenth-century scholars conjectured that he had received technical training as a lawyer.[11]

Law and the Production of Literature: The Author's Rhetorical Education

The law, however, should not be conceived as merely a bountiful "topic" within Renaissance literary studies. Recent work indicates that legal questions inform not just the literary signified – the topic or theme – but more significantly the literary signifier, the literary speech act, literary agents, and literary institutions. In short, the law is intimately and inescapably implicated in many dimensions of literary production. That is why Renaissance literary studies today cannot plead ignorance of the law. To avert that shortsightedness, we can map out the different vectors of the legal that contribute to producing literary texts, just as book history has mapped out the various collaborators in the manufacture of the printed artefact from author, through printer and distributor, to reader. I don't mean to suggest that Robert Darnton's famous model of the social relations around the life cycle of the book overlaps neatly with law's influence on literature; it doesn't: legal networks within literary culture are ever changing and proliferating, pulling in unforeseen stakeholders.[12] But I do mean to offer a brief survey to make the simple point that early modern literary studies cannot ignore the extensive macro and micro effects of legal matters on producing literature.

Any such survey cannot avoid beginning with the author's schooling. Tudor authors acquired their learning from the pedagogical agenda of rhetoric, which literary scholars have long formalized and aestheticized, downplaying the fact that this humanist revival of letters essentially drew upon the classical judicial-political oratory promoted by the influential Roman lawyers Cicero and Quintilian.[13] Literate Englishmen spoke, wrote, and read through rhetorical conventions and protocols emerging from and designed for legal thinking and communication. Legal education often did not end there. A remarkable number of Elizabethan and Jacobean authors, poets, and playwrights attended the Inns of Court, London's law schools: Thomas More (Lincoln's Inn), George Gascoigne (Gray's Inn), Sir John Davies (Middle Temple), Abraham Fraunce (Gray's Inn), Thomas Lodge (Lincoln's Inn), Thomas Middleton (Gray's Inn), John Donne (Lincoln's Inn), John Marston (Middle Temple), Thomas Carew (Middle Temple), Frances Quarles (Lincoln's Inn), George Wither (Middle Temple), John Webster (Middle Temple), and Francis Bacon (Gray's Inn), to name but a few. Whether or not they eventually practised law, young gentlemen lived, studied, and forged social connections at the Inns of Court, what Charles I's Privy Council described as "Seminaries and Nurseries wherein the Gentrie of the Kingdome and such serve his Majesty in the Common Wealth are bredd and trayned upp [*sic*]."[14] The Inns immersed youths in a legal community with its own religious rituals, symbols, and entertainments that sought to legitimate the common law as representing the constitutional authority of the sovereign.[15] That homosocial world with its unique material semiotics would have left a lasting impression on its young members, who afterwards dispersed throughout England's various educational, political, religious, and commercial sectors. The lasting impression may not have always been edifying, though. One relatively obscure Stuart poet, Francis Lenton, warns that the youth culture of the

Inns fostered indolence and wild behaviour among its students, who for the first time in their lives were no longer under strict adult supervision. In his collection of satirical portraits of various urban dwellers, Lenton, presumably speaking from first-hand knowledge, describes "A yong Innes a Court Gentleman" as having his educational priorities mixed up: he "holds it a greater disgrace to be Nonsuit with a Lady, than Nonplus in the Law" and "when he should bee mooting in the Hall, he is perhaps mounting in the Chamber, as if his father had onely sent him to Cut Capers," "mooting" being the debating exercise that would help prevent one from being at a loss for words or nonplussed on the law's stage.[16]

Considering the legal orientation of literacy and higher education, early modern scholars cannot overlook the overt and subtle ways in which the period's literary texts implement compositional strategies calibrated to the cultures of jurisprudence. Scholars have long understood that early modern literary texts are inherently rhetorical ones, marshalling tropes, schemes, commonplaces, and arguments to achieve persuasive effects; but only now are the legal ramifications of literature's rhetoric being fully spelled out. Lorna Hutson's *The Invention of Suspicion* has gone far in demonstrating the extent to which Cicero's judicial oratory, particularly through his treatise *De Inventione* and its mediation through a new English participatory jury system, taught a generation of dramatists to construct characters with psychological and historical depth.[17] By imitating moral writers like Theophrastus or by imitating rhetoricians like Cicero, early modern authors would have practised forms of charactery with the figures of *descriptio*, *notatio*, and *ethopoeia*.[18] Lenton's aforementioned collection *Characterismi: or, Lentons leasures* (1631) belongs to this very same rhetorical-legal genre.

Falling under the rhetorical canon of style, figures of speech, in general, provide another fertile area of enquiry into the production of literature, since they convey legal assumptions about the manipulation of language. Clearly such assumptions motivated Abraham Fraunce, an Inns of Court man who composed both a manual on logic with illustrations from the common law and a handbook of figures, mostly collected from Sidney's *Arcadia*.[19] Patterning one's discourse with oratorical ornament implies that one's interlocutors are persuaded not only by reason but also by the capacity of language to stir the affects; and in order to activate that capacity, one must observe rules and past precedents – this angle on literary praxis proceeds through a kind of conceptual pathway somewhere between statutory and common law. For English rhetorical treatises, there is also a sort of natural law encoded in figures insofar as writers may follow proper linguistic usage or commit linguistic abuse. Tellingly, corrupted figures were known as vices, suggesting that there is a law of the figure – just as there is a law of genre.

Moreover, judicial oratory's agonistic epistemology, what Thomas O. Sloane has called rhetoric's "inventive contrarianism," is diffused throughout the production of early modern literary texts.[20] Arguing on either side of a question would have been intellectually cultivated by a learning exercise foundational to the pedagogy of the Inns of Courts: mentioned by Lenton, "mooting" was the improvisational activity of debating hypothetical cases, which students practised to hone their skills as lawyers. Karen Cunningham, among other scholars, has unpacked how mock trials trained the early modern law student's verbal and performative imagination, inviting scholars to forge rich connections with London's stage.[21] Mooting has obvious implications not only for the prevalent dialogue form, such as Thomas Wilson's *Discourse on Usury*, but also for the argumentative structures in poetry, romance, and drama. The moots highlight the polemical process through which a writer fashions his exempla, commonplaces, and arguments, imagining simultaneously an opponent who struggles to refute his thesis and a judge who will be persuaded by his efforts. Sidney's influential *Defence of Poesy*, which painstakingly follows the arrangement or *dispositio* of a judicial oration, is designed to be judged by an educated jury, no matter how symbolic, and furnishes strong evidence for the jurisprudential orientation of English poetics.[22] Shelley's famous line about poets being unacknowledged legislators enters English poetics via Sidney and George Puttenham, both of whom regard the poet as the first lawmaker and by implication the poem as the first law.[23] George Puttenham's *The Art of English Poesy*, the other extensive Elizabethan statement on poetics, similarly defends literature from detractors but also elaborately aligns the efficacy and knowledge of poetry with the figures of speech, a move that, as said before, has legal ramifications, especially for this author, who, like Abraham Fraunce, was admitted to the Inns of Court.[24] Early modern English poetics would reach its legalistic height in Jonson's and Dryden's neoclassical prescriptions, which emerge from a Renaissance European history of conceiving and applying Aristotelian descriptions of poetry as regulations to follow in the composition of literature.

Law and the Production of Literature: The Printing Press and the Theatre

Once the author had penned his manuscript, the period's main literary institutions, the printing press and the theatre, would fully enter the picture if they had not entered before, further shaping the literary text according to various legal constraints and pressures. As Adrian Johns has extensively argued, piracy, which "came to stand for a wide range of perceived transgressions of civility emanating from print's practitioners," was rampant within the book trade, prompting printers and booksellers to be "manufacturers of credit" and, we might add for good measure, "manufacturers of legitimacy," since allegations of piracy, whether spurious or well founded, could at any point stigmatize a print product.[25] To forestall these allegations, paratexts, such as title pages, dedicatory epistles and poems, prefaces, and errata pages, strove to convince readers of a book's lawfulness. But ultimately, the actual regulation of piracy in the London book trade was conducted less by the government than by the Stationers' Company, the London guild of printers and booksellers: "The vast majority of incidences that came to light were dealt not by the legal system, but by the Stationers' own private court."[26] However, Johns's sharp division between the legal system on the one hand and the Stationers' own court on the other falls into the intellectual trap of jurisdictional bias, whereby the law appears as a sovereign, unitary entity. Peter Goodrich has effectively exploded this bias by investigating throughout history what he terms "minor jurisprudences," that is, the alternative jurisdictions and courts forming the legal unconscious of an all-powerful universal law;[27] taking a page from Goodrich's book, we should acknowledge that the Stationers' Company was one such important jurisdiction of potentially many that extended into literature. Joseph Loewenstein's *The Author's Due: Printing and the Prehistory of Copyright* in effect makes such an acknowledgment. Loewenstein locates the regulatory dynamics of the book trade within the Stationers' Company, rather than simply ascribing regulation to a top-down view of state power, and thereby effectively contests the Foucauldian thesis that the state's disciplinary control alone constructed the category of the author in order to hold someone accountable for the generation of discourse. According to Loewenstein, intellectual property law leading up to eighteenth-century copyright emerges out of the economics and politics of the book trade, particularly with respect to conflicts over monopolization. The state granted the Stationers' Company exclusive right over the production of printed material and the power to enforce this right through different mechanisms, including a registration process, a court, and a kind of impromptu police force; however, regular stationers would often come into conflict with the lucrative patents awarded by the Crown not only to privileged stationers but also to individuals outside the guild altogether. One significance of Loewenstein's work is that it radically revises our conceptions of early modern authorship and early modern print products, turning them into sites, neither natural nor universal, of jurisdictional and economic struggle.

Lowenstein's work on intellectual property law puts into practice the "law of literature," an area in Law and Literature that examines the "miscellany of laws regulating literature, some statutory, some judge-made, some criminal, others civil."[28] Another related field of enquiry into how the early modern "law of literature" has a bearing on authors and playwrights encompasses censorship and libel. In response to the rapid expansion of the printing trade and the establishment of professional theatrical troupes, the Tudor government laid down mechanisms for controlling the circulation of ideas deemed subversive to the state. Chief among these mechanisms were licensing systems that delegated the administration of censorship practices to state-recognized parties. All printers had to be members of the Stationers' Company, and all books were required to be licensed before they could be entered into the Stationers' register, the ledger recording which stationers had permission to print a given manuscript or book.[29] Acting troupes were required to be licensed too, and it is from such a licence in 1574 that the first mention was made of using the office of the Master of Revels to see and allow a play before it could be performed in public.[30] But censors were hardly marching to the beat of a single drummer. As Richard Dutton argues, the Master of Revels operated less as a repressive arm of the state than as a conciliatory broker between the court on the one hand and the acting troupe and the playwright on the other hand.[31] Cyndia Clegg marshals a similar argument with respect to Elizabethan press censorship, which was not implemented by an authoritarian state in a systematic and consistent manner but by multiple and competing interests responding ad hoc to isolated incidents and specific texts.[32]

What we discover in contemporary studies on Tudor and Stuart censorship is what we have found to be the general case of recent early modern scholarship on the law: the legal apparatus is not a totalizing, oppressive instrument wielded from above but a cultural player that resists facile political categorization.[33] M. Lindsay Kaplan's monograph *The Culture of Slander in Early Modern England* admirably spells out the stakes of this perspective. Taking issue with the repressive model of censorship assumed by Annabel Patterson and others, Kaplan aims for a more "complex and contestatory account" of power relations between censorship and literature.[34] The defamatory discourse that she studies when looking at slander and slander law attests to the "incredible instability of the categories of legitimate and illegitimate speech" and allows readers to recognize greater agency and resistance on the part of writers.[35] Such scholarship pulverizes monolithic views of omnipotent institutionality, suggesting that slander law resembles less a disciplinary state mechanism than a means of negotiation and even a mode of aesthetic and social production. A spectacular version of this argument is Shuger's reversal of the repression model in which censorship, she argues, polices not dangerous truths but dangerous lies and thus yields substantial social benefits.[36] Such scholarship problematizes, as Andrew Hadfield astutely observes, liberal humanist truisms about the freedom of expression and at the same time provides a historical corrective to overly zealous appropriations of Foucault's theory of disciplinary power and new historicist analyses of subversion within containment.[37]

As with the printing press, the institution of the theatre cannot be understood without reflecting upon its involvement and implication in legal apparatuses. London playhouses were built beyond the city's walls, in the impoverished suburbs known as the Liberties, where their theatrical troupes fell outside the jurisdiction of the city's mayor along with its sheriffs and the Common Council. Throughout the Tudor and Stuart periods, puritanical and Anglican writers, as is well known, cried for their closure, condemning them as hubs of pestilence and ungodly, subversive activity. Playhouses existed in a place of liminality or rather a state of exception.[38] They tried to escape the civic law even as they operated within the legal ambit. London playhouses shared with the law more than those superficial similes routinely prompted by the chiastic cliché of the stage being compared to a courtroom and a courtroom being compared to a stage.[39] Between the two social spaces there exist deeply set institutional homologies, to which recent scholars bear witness.[40] The impetus behind many dramatic plots involves accumulating evidence, whether testimony, omens and signs, or inferential character traits, in order to assert criminal behaviour. The handkerchief, the terms of bonds, and daggers are just some of the memorable props that over the course of well-known Shakespearean plays are transformed into evidence before our eyes. The early modern theatrical construction of character, aptly explicated by Luke Wilson, owes a significant debt to juridical and mercantile discourses, which treat the individual as his own "autonomous economic agent."[41] Conversely, the proceedings of the law court revolve around subjects following scripts and performing roles, with jury members assessing intentions and formulating interpretations of those performances.[42]

The heady correspondences between stage and courtroom are not accidental since in the West the origins of ancient Greek drama have been connected to the advent of trial by jury within Athenian law;[43] this parallel culture, as Subha Mukherji after Lorna Hutson observes, was transmitted to the Renaissance by way of Roman oratorical treatises and commentaries on Terence's comedies, instilling in playwrights "the perception of structural affinity between theatrical and legal practice," which allowed them "to address actual legal issues of evidence, interpretation, and judgement – the commonest preoccupations of plays interested in the law."[44] Undergoing at the same time secularization and modernization, "[t]heater and law," as Dennis Kezar contends, "were not simply relevant to each other in the early modern period; they participated with each other and defined an institutional co-presence."[45] In Kezar's volume, his essay on *The Witch of Edmonton* and Ernest B. Gilman's on *The Tempest* reveal that a play's interrogation of the law on the stage often means questioning the very foundations of theatre itself. Theatre both interpellates the audience as a jury who casts judgment on the protagonists' actions and meta-theatrically indicts them for taking pleasure in the plight of others.

Law and the Production of Literature: The Reader and the Spectator

Early modern literary production thus ends with the reader and the spectator, the terminal points of the communication circuit. Literature was not just written by members of the Inns of Court but was also written for them. Donne's and Marston's erotic verse no doubt targeted this readership, and many books too, such as Gerard Legh's popular treatise on heraldry and Bartholomew Griffin's poems, were dedicated to the gentlemen of the Inns.[46] From a perspective wider than a narrow demographic bracket, the rhetorical curriculum of the grammar school and the university brings us full circle because it teaches students how to decode as well as encode writing. Of course, exposure to the law and its apparatuses arose from everyday business as well. As Timothy Stretton observes in this volume, the Elizabethan period saw over a million claimants seeking litigation in England's courts, and even though most of these claims revolved around debt, the magnitude of the citizenry's immersion in the legal apparatus and its procedures could not help but encourage one to perceive his or her world through the mediation of juridical premises, arguments, and cases. The broad participation of the populace in seeking recourse from the law interpellated individuals as juridical subjects, generating identifications and counter-identifications with law-abiding figures and creating fantasies of vindication and vengeance in addition to prompting cynical and guilty responses towards authority structures. The law was not a schoolbook abstraction but a dispersion of imaginary postures and desires propagated by early modern juridical subjects, whom writers could easily captivate with legal controversies and conflicts.

Juridical readers not only produced literature through their choices and responses as consumers but were also produced by it. Exciting and influential work done over the last decade suggests that early modern playwrights and poets encouraged their audiences to read people's characters forensically. Luke Wilson postulates that Shakespearean tragedy and Jonsonian comedy, as well as the popular trope of Nobody/Somebody, evince routines of practical reasoning for determining purposive action. Such practical reasoning, redeployed from legal processes of thought elaborated in notable trial and contractual cases of the period, makes the modern move of separating the deed from the intention in order to follow a method for ascertaining the motivations behind apparently inexplicable behaviour. According to the praxis of the institutions of theatre and the law, intentions do not come first but need to be retroactively posited and then intelligibly reconstructed around feelings, desires, and plans. Both courtroom and stage thus weave together enabling fictions to rationalize why a character acts in a certain way, thereby creating the phenomenon of interrogating interiority, which we know so well from Hamlet's soliloquies. Building upon Wilson's scholarship, Lorna Hutson identifies the way in which this forensic reading of character entered the theatre via legal channels. She demonstrates that during the sixteenth-century, newly formed justices of the peace had to learn how to examine suspects through marshalling rhetorical invention, that is, finding arguments of suspicion. The new English participatory jury system required that the jury reach its judgment by basing its hypothetical construction of the suspect's intention on the existing evidence supplied to the court. Suspicion had to engage actively with material evidence, while acknowledging the inscrutability of the suspect's interiority. Together Wilson and Hutson show how our modern proclivity to attribute psychological depth and motivation to characters arises from the institutional co-presence of the early modern stage and courtroom: "our conviction of the characters having minds at all is an optical illusion generated by the text; the diffusion of judicial rhetoric through the education system facilitated the kind of writing which produces the illusion that behind speech is consciousness."[47]

Taking Exception to the Law

From the author's rhetorical education and the text's construction through the institutions of the press and the stage to the reader and spectator, this brief survey is not meant to define once and for all the discrete planes upon which law and literature interact with one another; its purpose is to raise the basic point that English Renaissance literary studies cannot plead ignorance of the law because at various turns legal discourses, mechanisms, and practices facilitate, enable, constrain, impede, and mediate the production of literature. One might even argue as well that early modern literature possesses at times a legal unconscious, whose invisible influences and dramatic effects, sudden eruptions and nuanced symptoms, continually require identification, explication, and exploration. Nonetheless, this is not to say that legal production does not have a literary unconscious. Both Elliott Visconsi's *Lines of Equity* and Victoria Kahn's *Wayward Contracts* have shown the arresting ways in which seventeenth-century literature and poetics directly contribute to their culture's legal imaginary, even their legal machinery.[48] Under the aegis of cultural studies the law's sway quickly broadens outward to the production of culture itself – just as literature, poetry, and drama do. Of course, the danger of acknowledging the permeability of boundaries between culture and literature or between law and literature is that one can bring upon oneself the accusation of dissolving disciplinary objects altogether. In a lively piece of interdisciplinary soul searching, Julie Stone Peters notes the jurisdictional shift occurring in the field of Law and Literature: the field is starting to cover the area "law, culture, and the humanities"(451), going the way of its parent, literary studies, which shies away from valorizing the putatively restrictive categories of "literature" and "aesthetics." Make no mistake: as methodologically diverse as its essays are, this volume proceeds with the confidence that literature can still be meaningfully triangulated with the law and culture. In fact, it has no ambition to collapse the boundary between the legal and the literary either, and registers the importance of preserving this tension in the first part of its title, an early modern expression for "disapproving of" or "finding fault with." Its essays accordingly pay their due to literary anti-jurisprudence. "Exception," in the title's phrase, euphemistically signifies an objection, which, according to some of the volume's contributors, Shakespeare's plays take to a particular legal instrument. Despite his impressive grasp of legal matters, Shakespeare's continued engagement with the law – as one contemporary scholar notes – betrays a strong anti-jurisprudential stance.[49] Witness, for example, the locus classicus *Measure for Measure*, a play that puts on trial the overly rigorous and outrageously literal application of the statute to social behaviour, given the hypocrisy of the puritanical judge, the complicated guilt of the accused, and the foundational trust that the judicial authorities must cultivate in the citizenry for enabling their decision-making capacity. In this volume, John Staines's chapter argues that *King Lear*, along with Foxe's martryology *Acts and Monuments*, incites readers and audiences to see the unjustness in using torture, a common Continental method of extracting the truth from criminals, while Timothy Stretton's chapter reveals the ways in which *The Merchant of Venice* exposes the failings of the conditional bond to compel the debtor to make good on his promise.

Shakespeare hardly holds the monopoly on developing a critical anti-jurisprudence, however. This volume is collectively concerned with showing how a range of writings in the period take exception to the law. It corroborates the flexibility of the category "literary" in contemporary English studies, covering a range of sixteenth- and seventeenth-century literary works, from Shakespearean drama, Spenserian romance, and Miltonic epic to educational treatises, crime pamphlets, autobiography, and the parodic writings of the Inns of Court. The volume's mixture of classical and popular genres offers a corrective to overprivileging canonical voices when it comes to studying Law and Literature. Indeed, taking exception to the early modern law may occur in less prominent literary venues and through subtler means. David Stymeist's chapter reveals the way in which the popular crime pamphlet created a public space that represented the legal system from a vantage point at times distinct from, if not resistant to, the ideological agendas of Church and State. Another non-canonical literary venue is raised in Debora Shuger's chapter on Archbishop Laud's prison notebooks. Shuger discovers in his diary a refreshingly critical and thus unusual "outside" perspective on the common law, which since the early modern period has enjoyed a privileged position over the non-common-law traditions. Tudor and Jacobean writers were fascinated with questions of the law and knew that their readers would be too, no doubt in part because of a social preponderance of suits and court battles. Early modern literature provided a safe haven, where writers and readers could question and even challenge at length juridical authority figures, real or imagined; other discourses obviously did not have the same freedom to interrogate these figures, who in the non-democratic polity of pre-Enlightenment England were the direct deputies of state, sovereign, and God.

Treating the literary text as an exception or an objection to legal instruments, processes, and judgments is nothing new in the interdisciplinary field of Law and Literature. Since the field first arose in U.S. law schools during the 1970s, it justified the importance of lawyers reading literature on the grounds that literary texts bring to the study of law something that it inherently lacks.[50] Over time, the literary supplement has rescued legal practice and scholarship from a series of disciplinary deficits, which commentators have grouped into three main phases: literature's humanism can counteract the impersonal, perfunctory professionalism of lawyers through cultivating sympathy and moral awareness; its understanding of hermeneutics and literary theory can prise open the law's literal and unreflective formalism with new interpretive methodologies; and its orientation around narrative can expose the law's marginalization of different class, racial, and gender positions by attending to the stories occluded by the dominant epistemology and culture.[51] This interdisciplinary field has for some time recognized that the literary exception, operating outside, apart from, and exterior to juridical apparatuses, furnishes the legal discipline with contextual complexity about language, society, and history.

As much as early modern literary texts regularly take exception to the law, scholars need to be wary of buying into the view that literature holds an idealistic moral or humanistic authority over legal matters. Law and Literature has for good reason questioned the methodological assumption that the legal discipline should encompass an autonomous and homogeneous terrain and possess innate deficits that can be filled by an entirely exteriorized literary praxis. In an influential 1999 article,

Jane Baron has criticized literary scholars for working with a caricatured version of the legal discipline. Whereas, within actual legal scholarship, the law displays a multidisciplinary richness, "a dazzlingly complex array of social, cultural, linguistic, and normative practices," in Law and Literature it often comes across as an autonomous code starkly "instrumental, analytic, rational, non-emotional, technical, mechanical, and – above all – doctrinal."[52] Literary scholars must be careful to avoid using the logic of such traditional stereotypes, which can sponsor ingenuous missions to rescue the law from itself through an exaggeratedly elevated literary history. During the last decade early modern studies in Law and Literature have, however, refrained from the impulse to galvanize narratives of literary triumphalism over juridical discourses. They have effectively eroded the caricatures observed by Baron. One hallmark of this scholarship is a complication, if not a wholesale rejection, of the assumption that the law exerts a homogeneous top-down force on society, as previously mentioned with reference to Foucault's notion of disciplinary power. As Bradin Cormack's *A Power to Do Justice* teaches us, the law neither circumscribes a "stable constitutional reality" nor impresses itself upon subjects as an abstract and unified entity, but realizes itself through jurisdictional variation, a jurisdiction being the administrative delimitation of generic or geographic boundaries. Sixteenth- and seventeenth-century literature, according to Cormack, bears witness to an early modern jurisdictional crisis, in which an earlier era concerned with protecting English secular courts against the Church's legal authority clashed with the development of a rationalized and centralized common law. Thanks in part to this crisis, the early modern law manifests itself in local, extemporaneous, and provisional actions, "unfolding into doctrine only as and through unruly practice."[53] Another caricature eroded by recent scholarship is that the law lacks the imaginative resources indigenous to the literary domain. In *Imaginary Betrayals* (2002), for instance, Karen Cunningham reads trials and plays alongside one another, allowing her to explore the dialogical relations between the two realms, because both law and literature, according to her argument, engage in similar imaginary practices about treason. Early modern culture from plays to the state's prosecution of treason trials would portray the traitor not as an individual with an ideological axe to grind but as a peculiar type of subjectivity whose every act and thought were inherently seditious. In her analysis of this dramatic construction of the traitor, Cunningham recognizes the creative, mimetic, and disputative nature of the law. Scholarship like Cunningham's and Cormack's pushes beyond traditional conceptions of disciplinarity and methodology by revealing how the law and literature not only cross-pollinate one another but also invaginate one another as in Cormack's claim that the improvisational nature of the law points to its fundamental literariness. Recent scholarship has proposed nuanced configurations of how literature and the law actively contest, compete, collaborate, and interpenetrate one another. The sensitivity to subtle formulations of disciplinarity stems from the multidisciplinary direction taken by legal studies and literary studies. The multiplication of theories and historical approaches militates against discursive coherence so much so that, in each of those disciplines, it has thus become more and more challenging to identify a distinct methodological object, let alone demarcate clear borders around such an object. How then can the filial field of Law and Literature conduct itself with methodological simplicity or coherence when the parent disciplines have already complicated, even overdetermined, what they study? Cormack's idiom offers a healthy perspective on why collections of essays on Law and Literature, including this one, strike one as heterogeneous: the varied jurisdictions of the field yield an unruly scholarly practice, not reducible to patent doctrines. That has not stopped vigorous efforts over the last few decades to latch onto a singular way in which law and literature may be distinguished from one another.[54] As important and difficult as it is to hammer out their differences, there exist multiple configurations and entanglements between these two disciplinary zones, each of which is already riven with inconsistencies, complexities, and pluralities. There exists a plasticity to their connections. Scholars do not come upon legal and literary objects prefabricated, discursively coherent, and branded with the seal of a discipline's approved purity, especially in the early modern period, when the practices of literature and the law were under no obligation to observe the strict division of labour characterizing the contemporary university's administrative and historical exigencies of compartmentalization. As cultural products, legal instruments and literary texts do not consistently occupy two definitively demarcated and separate jurisdictions or epistemological fields. As Subha Mukherji observes, recent early modern scholarship has cultivated a receptivity to the interactive, intersecting, and intermeshing discourses and practices between the two areas, apparent in the major studies written since Luke Wilson's groundbreaking work *Theaters of Intention*.[55]

This volume of essays wants to acknowledge the gains made by early modern Law and Literature over the last decade by simultaneously alluding to another signification of "exception" in its title. "Taking exception to the law" is never a complete removal to a transcendent plane or domain. In this sense, the title resonates with Cicero's much-abused dictum, "the exception confirms the rule in cases not excepted."[56] By exception, one may typically refer to something that deviates from a norm or a proposition; what the famous expression means, though, is that an exception to a rule implies the existence of the said rule. Exceptions to the law, in other words, may already exist within the legal dialectic of rule and that which is excepted from the rule. A wonderful example of Elizabeth's reign as a legal exception occurs in *The Faerie Queene*'s Legend of Justice, when Spenser is discussing the Amazonian warrior Radigund: "But vertuous women wisely vnderstand, / That they were borne to base humilitie, / Vnlesse the heauens them lift to lawfull soueraintie."[57] Elizabeth is a divinely lawful exception to the rule that women are subordinated to male governance. According to Spenser's logic, her exceptionality, rather than threatening the smooth running of the law, only reconfirms the order of things. In the case of the volume, the title imparts the caveat that literature does not transcend legal practices, jurisdictions, and instruments but holds an immanent relationship to them. Since you cannot have rules without exceptions and cannot have exceptions without rules, literature's exceptional status serves only to prove the validity of the law, to entangle itself further in the statutory – a proposition that many humanist readers might not want to countenance. Perhaps the fantasy of entirely removing oneself from the domain of the rule-bound underlies the phenomenon of escapist fiction – as though daydreaming and desiring occur in an imaginary zone outside legal operations and shielded from the legal gaze. Theoretically speaking, Lacan's psychoanalytic insights into language effectively puts the lie to the utterly private, extralegal sphere of any symbolic act, whether reading, writing, talking, or thinking.[58] We can contend that there are no definitive exceptions to the law insofar as any such areas only make exclusionary sense through being inscribed within a culture of jurisprudential institutions, procedures, and structures in the first place. To express this point in other terms, one can say that there exists no pure generic ground from which literature can judge the law. Invoking Derrida's classic exposition on the law of genre, the legal scholar Peter Goodrich makes this argument with reference to legal textuality, but it operates equally well for literature. Given that genre is for Derrida "precisely a principle of contamination, a law of impurity, a parasitical economy," the law of genre is at once the genre of the law that inhabits every literary inscription.[59]

And yet taking literary exception to the law, as the title indicates, still raises a literary objection. By enfolding the exceptional status of literature within the law, the title's wording is not intended to signal the conceptual stalemate of a clever paradox or to announce an ultimate deconstructive reading of Law and Literature, whereby each blurs irretrievably into the other. Notwithstanding their diverse methodologies, Wilson's *Theaters of Intention*, Cunningham's *Imaginary Betrayals*, Hutson's *The Invention of Suspicion*, and Cormack's *Power to Do Justice* are exemplary in this regard, refusing to totalize the interface between law and literature, while still preserving literary difference.[60] Their understanding of that interface resists the oversimplification of the oppositional, realizing that the connections that they trace cannot be confined to a single, flat linguistic plane. Although to my knowledge Actor Network Theory (ANT) has not been widely implemented by practitioners in Law and Literature, the theory's inherent critique of linguistic and discursive determinism and concomitant resistance to social reductionism can effectively summarize the scholarly pitfalls early modern scholarship in the field wants to avoid.[61] As Bruno Latour, a major advocate of ANT, laments, "language has become," for structural and post-structural thinkers, "a law unto itself, a law governing itself, and its own world" – in short, Derrida's law of genre as conceived by proponents of linguistic determinism. Indeed, early modern law extends well beyond the jurisdiction of language.[62] Despite an emphasis during the 1980s on hermeneutics, scholars in Law and Literature have also avoided this trap by recognizing that the law forges relations and connections that involve referents themselves, that is, for example, matter, objects, technologies, instruments, actions, bodies, and environments.[63] Generally speaking, ANT proves instructive for articulating the subtlety and complexity with which these scholars approach the historical multi-connectedness between authors, print artefacts, the royal court, poetics, educational practices, patronage, theatre, etc., on the one hand, and, on the other hand, property, various law courts, jurisprudential procedures, lawyers and judges, legal instruments, the Inns of Court, criminals, etc. There can be no single interdisciplinary interface, because law and literature do not demarcate finished geometrized disciplinary territories, but instead, bearing out the conclusions of ANT, trace ever anew the literary-legal webs of relations, flows, and hybridizations, which are continuously assembling and disassembling the early modern social. Today, we can take the "and" interposed between law and literature as signifying an ongoing circulation between two open sets, operating according to the principle of Deleuze and Guattari's rhizome, the actual inspiration for Latour's concept of the network.[64] Rhizomes, which unfold through an open series of multiple "ands" that accumulate connections and dimensions without possessing a beginning and an end, capture the complexity that the leading scholars strive for when mapping out legal-literary networks. Although none of the essays in this volume can be said to put into practice ANT per se, taken together they represent the proliferating connections that such legal-literary networks multiply in their ever-changing production of culture. "Taking exception to the law" recognizes the jurisdictional possibilities of the literary exception, attempting to articulate less a single interdisciplinary relationship than an ongoing process of connectivity, which produces the multiple, the provisional, and the intersectional.

Materializing Injustice: Contributors

Early modern literature frequently represents and thematizes illegalities, those violations of state or church codes perpetrated by upstarts, cony-catchers, frauds, hypocrites, thieves, and traitors; but it also scrutinizes the inequities originating from juridical vehicles and processes themselves. It takes exception to the law's limitations, inequities, and failures. The essays in this volume focus their attention accordingly on literature's record of the injustices produced by legal instruments, discourses, procedures, and institutions. Its objections do not seek to overthrow the principle of juridical adjudication and administration in society – if that anarchical project were at all possible or indeed imaginable in early modern culture. Literature speaks out against the juridical on the basis of its particular failings but does so because it shares with it the same fundamental concern: to see justice carried out. The essays in this volume examine the ways in which literature addressing the law's failings strives to contribute to the process of early modern justice: they tacitly enlarge the generic scope of Hutson's argument that an English participatory judiciary, not Foucault's disciplinary power, offers the epistemological model for understanding Renaissance drama, because common people during the period became increasingly involved in the pursuit of justice through serving on juries and testifying, bringing about the valorization of evidence, rather than the appeal to authority or rank, as a means of making legal judgments.[65]

In examining early modern literature taking exception to the law, the volume, however, does not want to suggest that the literary holds a morally superior position to the juridical enterprise. Literature has no special access or privileged proximity to justice, since as the introduction has argued at length, it is implicated at various levels in legal questions and mechanisms. Its engagement with justice thus does not occur on a plane of idealism operating above social reality. The volume tries to avoid reproducing two interrelated idealizations of literature, one pejorative and the other noble: the idealization of literature in which literary representations exist in a fictional, fake, and irrelevant world divorced entirely from the law's real and pragmatic operations; and the concomitant idealization of literature in which literary ideals, not tethered to the mundane and dirty, can gain an ethereal or ethical vantage point over the law. Needless to say, early modern literature is more than capable of idealizing justice as in *The Defence of Poesy*, where Sidney argues that the lawyer approaches justice through a limited negation insofar as the law uses the threat of punishment to deter men from misbehaving, while the poet approaches it positively and constructively insofar as poetry cultivates in readers the love of this supreme virtue.[66] Spenser's *The Faerie Queene* etherealizes justice too, especially with the sublimated figure of Astraea, who, withdrawn to the heavens, presumably looks down on Artegall's earthly struggles.[67] The traditional way of rationalizing the law's deficiency is to appeal to an ideal, which lawmakers, lawyers, and judges fail to live up to. If only the law were adequate to the truth of justice or if only the heavenly virtues of mercy helped to balance judicial rigour, then jurisprudence could deal with crime in such a way that would lead to social harmony. When the law fails, the legal apparatus needs to redouble its efforts, stretching further and striving harder for the transcendent nobility of Astraea.

But readers need not buy into such a narrative that reduces law and literature to a fatuous metaphysical hierarchy. As we will find in Judith Owens's chapter on Artegall and wardship, cultural contexts are capable of grounding the most abstract of Spenser's conceptualizations of justice. This virtuous yet elusive quality, along with freedom, happiness, and dignity, inspires interminable idealistic and metaphysical ruminations on the universal, leading us far from historical and cultural specificity. The present volume's historicist-oriented essays are not focused on determining once and for all the nature of early modern justice and equity, but direct their enquiries at the myriad failures of justice materialized in the law. As much as taking exception to the law in the period may trigger idealistic indignation, it also regularly uses the law against itself, extending other legal networks and activating other jurisdictions. As it takes exception to the law, literature participates in legal cultures. If literature poses a critical difference from the law, it can be understood as a material one. This means that, rather than holding a transcendent position above it, literature is immanent within its operations.

This volume proceeds with the understanding that such materializations may tell us more about early modern legal-literary cultures than the idealizations of justice do. Throughout the volume, injustice assumes diverse yet intersecting material forms, but broadly speaking we can isolate four specific legal materializations for the purposes of grouping the essays: injustice is materialized through legal instruments such as statutes, bonds, and writs; it is materialized through juridical administration, whether the circumstances, language, or procedures of the trial; it is materialized through educational institutions and pedagogical discourses; and finally, it is materialized through the Tyrant's deployment of the law.

Stretton, Strain, Cormack

Timothy Stretton's chapter, "Conditional Promises and Legal Instruments in *The Merchant of Venice*," attends to the period's distrust of bonds and indentures to guarantee the payment of a debt. His analysis reveals the social paradox of securing someone's word with a written contract: trust is indispensable for the smooth running of economic interactions, but it remains permanently invisible, a thing which shows itself only in its effects, its past performances. The bond answers our anxieties by materializing this invisible interpersonal trait. Paradoxically enough, the early modern period, as Stretton notes, regarded the unprecedented proliferation of such legal instruments as an index of fraudulence and oath-breaking. Ratcheting up the stakes to gain more security, early modern subjects had recourse to the particular and popular legal instrument of the conditional bond, which built into the written contract a form of penalty that would come into effect if the debtor did not satisfy his end of the bargain. As Stretton argues, *The Merchant of Venice* abounds in promises with such conditions, most notably Shylock's stipulation of the pound of flesh and Bassanio's and Gratiano's wedding rings as requisite of Portia's and Nerissa's fidelity. The play's brilliance may be found in another economy circulating around the conditional bond. Whereas we are all familiar with promises being manipulated by deceitful debtors, Shakespeare reveals the creditor's manipulation of the promise through the penalty. Rather than serving as a prompt to fulfil a contract, the condition provides the creditor with the compensation of surplus pleasure in humiliating and punishing the forfeited debtor. The bond is thus forged not out of any goodwill to foster trust but out of a desire to expose untrustworthiness, which yields to the creditor a perverse enjoyment. And yet far from portraying a cynical world in need of serious legal reform, Shakespeare's play recognizes the limits of the legal instrument and searches for a supplemental trust, which both exceeds and makes possible the discourse of the contract. To renew her faith in Bassanio after he gives up the wedding ring, Portia must gesture beyond the letter of the law. Such supplemental trust is not available to Shylock, whose distrust appears to be a reflexive posture of his alienation in the Venetian community. Stretton's reading of the play locates the effectiveness of the bond in the parties, "the right hands," that use it, but to what extent is this just another suspect hypostatization of something that we can never secure?

The period's literature bears witness to the law's material failure in terms of not only a fundamental deficiency but also a disturbing surplus – as Virginia Lee Strain reveals in her chapter, "The 'Snared Subject' and the General Pardon Statute in Late Elizabethan Coterie Literature." Her chapter focuses on the Elizabethan general pardon statute – an annual parliamentary ritual following the granting of the Queen's subsidy – and the parodic version of it created by the members of Gray's Inn during their Christmas revels. The reading of the statute officially performed the Queen's pardoning of subjects who had accidentally – or one can say inevitably – offended one of the numerous statute laws, multiplying to absurd proportions during the era. For the fledgling lawyers, the statute appears to have subsumed the entire symbolic universe to the point that its unmanageable, ubiquitous regulations are in need of regulation themselves. In the revels, the parody of the general pardon statute, a supplemental vehicle of the Queen's mercy, indicates the degree to which statute law with its dense rhetorical qualifications and contradictory exceptions only serves to ensnare subjects further when purporting to extricate them from the judicial system's ludicrous excesses in the first place. While ostensibly freeing the subject from the morass of laws, the pardon materializes an unproductive intensification of state power and legal control over every aspect of the citizenry's life. Strain also argues that through the hyperbolic humour of the mock pardon the Inns of Court revellers signal their commitment and mastery of legal culture and expose the dangers posed by lawmakers and their products to society at large. This parody exemplifies what the volume means by literature taking exception to the law.

The uncontrollable vicissitudes of the law's materiality are also explored at length in Bradin Cormack's chapter, "Paper Justice, Parchment Justice: Shakespeare, *Hamlet*, and the Life of Legal Documents." Cormack argues that *Richard III*, *I Henry IV*, and *Hamlet* supplant one reality with another in the form of legal instruments. Shakespeare's detailed attention to "the material technologies that make the law" originates in a desire to interrogate the ways in which the juridical apparatus of the late sixteenth and early seventeenth centuries exercised the power to make the world. Legal instruments in the plays are evidence not so much of Shakespeare's legal training, then, as of his "conceptual investment" in a different version of the poet's world-making abilities, familiar to humanist poetics, which, as previously mentioned, has deep roots through rhetoric in the Western legal tradition. There are affinities too between Cormack's observation on the potential of legal documents to create something out of nothing and Victoria Kahn's insights on poetics in her study *Wayward Contracts*. Cormack's chapter builds towards an argument on how the circulation of paper and parchment technologies in *Hamlet* invite reflection upon the fragility of human bodies under the law, given the cured, stretched, and meticulously prepared animal skins subtending legal authority.

His chapter, along with Stretton's and Strain's, attests to the early modern period's dense bureaucratizing and administrative materiality in which the King's very authority dissolves into endless paper trails/trials. This dimension of the law's excessive materiality can be explained by the polymath Robert Burton, who also laments the impenetrable cacophony of the legal machine: "A vast confusion of Vowes, Wishes, Actions, Edicts, Peticions, Law-suits, Pleas, Lawes, Proclamations, complaints, Grievances, are daily brought to our Eares."[68] Burton notes that the profusion of legal instruments does not lead so much to any kind of "justice" as to a sort of tribunal "labyrinth,"[69] one of Burton's favourite tropes for describing the subject's disorientation in the endless proliferation of early modern print media and the concomitant expansion of disciplinary knowledge. The experience of being caught in a labyrinth of arcane statutes was addressed by what Quentin Skinner calls "neo-Roman" political theory, a system of thought that counteracted the threat posed to individuals and society by the law's increasing powers. For thinkers in this tradition, freedom means that people should not be subject to laws that lack the approval of all the people (approval, in practice, through their representatives). The experience of Egeon of Syracuse in *The Comedy of Errors*, sentenced to death for ignorantly breaking a law about which he had no knowledge, illustrates an unjust subjection to law, and neo-Roman thinkers affirmed the necessity of transparency and consent in order for freedom and justice to exist.

In drawing attention to both the deficit and the surplus of the law's materiality, these three chapters provide us with two experiences of what we can call after Lacan the Real of the law – the point at which the legal machinery's idealizing impulses break down to reveal the vacuity and density of a medium inhospitable to subjectivity.[70] Anticipating the post-Enlightenment's general distrust of institutionality and authority structures, early modern literature does not merely conceive of the law as a site of the subject's potential imaginary completion, as it is under the fantasy of misfired idealism, but penetrates beneath its hypnotic surface to see it for what it is: a Kafkaesque domain breeding continuous confusion, guilt, and betrayal, while providing no way of egress from its inescapable materialities.

Shuger, Stymeist, and Kreps

The next three chapters show how literature materializes injustice through the law's faulty administration in trials gone awry. If the trial is a forum for determining the elusive commensurability between past injuries and "just" deserts, then the period's literature often laments the deep problems preventing the courtroom from effecting justice. In Debora Shuger's chapter, "The Prison Diaries of Archbishop Laud," we encounter a string of inequitable legal practices that Laud had to endure during his trial: the presentation and recording of evidence, the choosing and questioning of witnesses, the absence of oath-taking, the arbitrary powers of the bench, and the suppression of key written documents were all prejudicial to the defendant's guilt. The underlying source of these inequities seems to come from the common law approach to legal proceedings. Common law jury trials were generally championed as an escape from continental *inquisitio* trials, which the English associated with the excesses of the so-called Inquisition, and especially the use of torture as a means for establishing incriminating evidence. Experienced as a high ecclesiastical officer, Laud was accustomed to the canon and civil law's procedural framework of *inquisitio*, which sought to demonstrate the truth less from the testimony of character witnesses than from the accused's testimony under oath and before a judge. Instead, Laud was tried, much to his chagrin, under the common law, the procedural framework of which was *accusatio*. *Accusatio* fostered an adversarial approach to court proceedings, placing the onus on private citizens to accuse and prosecute the suspected individual. Under the common law, evidence was a prosecutory instrument for winning the case, not the means by which the parties sought to discover the truth. Laud's trial and his account of it highlight the competing regimes for reading the materiality of evidence in the early modern period and find injustice where we would least expect it: in the common law procedure itself.

In David Stymeist's chapter, "Criminal Biography in Early Modern News Pamphlets," criminal trials leave something more generally to be desired. Stymiest argues that pamphlets lend a perspective on criminals quite different from that of the courtroom's narrative of crime and punishment. The crime pamphlet reached a large audience through the relatively inexpensive costs of its production and through the accessibility and topicality of its form and subject matter. Although it capitalized on the sensationalist violence of murder and execution and did not hold back from moralizing on the criminal's actions, its reportage introduced to a wide, popular readership the subgenre of crime biography. It is within the pamphlet's depictions of the criminal as a biographical subject that the reader encounters a surplus of subjectivity, not reducible to limited judiciary narratives. By providing a backstory to the criminal's life and actions, the biography allows readers to find points of identification with the criminal, identifications not available to spectators of the state trial and scaffold speech, where the criminal was routinely interpellated as a disciplinary object of guilt. In these micronarratives, the law does not loom in a transcendent realm above the early modern landscape but materializes itself in the lives of subjects, exposing its inconsistencies and at times its idealistic posturing. Criminal biography effectively renders visible what the legal system fails to take into account, situating the criminal within a greater horizon of class, gender, and economic relations that permitted readers to regard crime as belonging to a social totality, not simply arising from a causal chain initiated by personal motivation.

As Barbara Kreps's chapter, "Two-Sided Legal Narratives: Slander, Evidence, Proof, and Turnarounds in *Much Ado About Nothing*," suggests too, the course of true "law" never did run smoothly. Shakespeare's dramatic world owes its linguistic and narrative legerdemain to the moot courts where the members of the Inns of Court rehearsed trial procedures. Implicit in their proceedings was the development of rhetorical skills that pivoted on debating both sides of a question and that necessitated interpreting "evidence" and "testimony" from a number of narrative perspectives. In *Much Ado*, Hero's helplessness before her accusers arises in part from her female position outside the male-dominated rhetorical institution of argumentation. But the play's main concern with justice centres on language games by which evidence can be abused for malicious purposes. Shakespeare's focus on verbal manipulation reveals the dilemma of legal argumentation – and even the law itself, taken in the widest sense possible as the symbolic, that is, the regulated, ordered cultural system into which early moderns were born. The dilemma of the law is like Benedict's relationship to Beatrice: you can't live with it and you can't live without it. You can't live with the law for all of the strife and grief it causes, but at the same time you can't live without it because it makes possible and maintains the basis of personal interaction. The law impedes the smooth running of social relationships but also mediates those relationships in the first place. The play's primary juridical irony is that a representative of the common law through sheer accident stumbles upon the evidence that vindicates Hero of infidelity. What is most troubling about the plot is not that the community's informal legal apparatus errs in incriminating an innocent person but that the judicial representatives finally arrive at justice through a circuitous route of bumbling stupidity. In the play, the legal apparatus does not appear as a necessary force of truth, fate, or divinity, but as a dead letter whose contingencies and slippages are of the same order as Dogberry's mindless malapropisms or as the farcical motions of comedy itself. When the subject remains seduced by the imaginary dialectic between idealism and realism, misfired justice appears merely as an ideal just out of reach on desire's horizon; but when the subject gets too close to the legal machinery, he catches sight of the disturbing underside of the law, the empty and inscrutable substrate in which our fantasies of justice dissolve and our judicial desires become alien.

Hanson and Owens

The next two chapters materialize the inequities in and around educational apparatuses. Questions of a just society begin on the rudimentary level of providing the citizenry with opportunities of learning. How the younger generation, who embody the future, is schooled has a direct bearing on what we imagine fair social relationships should look like. But so much can get in the way of achieving that fantasy. Elizabeth Hanson's chapter, "No Boy Left Behind: Education and Distributive Justice in Early Modern England," contends that the modern sentiment that a just society apportions to its members equitable access to schooling shares a strong genealogical connection with sixteenth-century humanist pedagogy. Hanson uses contemporary debates over universal education to launch an inquest into how this humanist pedagogy contributed to bringing education within the jurisdiction of distributive justice. Her analysis concentrates on Erasmus's *De Pueris Instituendis* and Richard Mulcaster's *Positions Concerning the Training Up of Children*, two formative pedagogical treatises, which reveal subtle responses to the challenges of teaching and the limits of learning. Hanson charts her course through taking issue with Richard Halpern's Marxian claims on humanism and adjusting Pierre Bourdieu's sociological ones on cultural capital. Whereas Halpern finds in Erasmus and Mulcaster the emergence of a "discourse of capacities" that divides the world into "intellectual haves" and "intellectual have nots," Hanson discerns the ways in which these two humanist pedagogues were "haunted by a question of justice" that they "could not fully articulate, let alone resolve." For Erasmus, the privilege of schooling is not exclusively limited to students with cognitive competence, for he opens the school's doors to those who do not have talent as well as those who do. Though not as generous, Mulcaster's position recognizes the restriction of resources affecting the number of students, while valorizing the importance of symbolic – if not actual – diversity in the classroom. Whereas Bourdieu argues for emergent social forms such as cultural capital, Hanson wants to highlight the way in which residual social forms contributed to the link between schooling and distributive justice: humanist schooling expanded into the clerical jurisdiction of providing charity for the poor, and it is on this basis that English humanist learning could be said to foster a new belief in human potential.

Judith Owens's chapter, "Warding off Injustice in Book Five of *The Faerie Queene*," also wrestles with articulating the opportunity of education, but as it relates to imagining a just commonwealth, not an equitable society – one feudal and noble, not modern. Book V responds to the contemporary abuses in administering the institution of wardship, the legal guardianship of a minor and his estate until he comes of age. During the Tudor period, the Court of Wards and its officers were accused of profiteering at the expense of their charges, whose education was often neglected. With Artegall, the knight of justice, Spenser appears to eliminate the abuses stigmatizing the institution of wardship, recognizing its importance in nurturing a true commonwealth. Artegall receives a principled though detached tutelage from Astraea, the goddess of justice. Spenser also portrays a variant on wardship's martial configuration in feudal times. Medieval wardship was chiefly implemented to raise up warriors; Artegall's education improves upon the chivalric code of trial by combat, which operates according to the logic of "might is right." Unlike the typical knight, he learns to privilege moral strength over physical throughout his adventures.

For all his associations with the ideal of justice, however, this paragon falls short of the mark. Ironically, the ward of Astraea does not quite possess virtue sufficient to advance the British commonwealth under the reign of the Faerie Queene. Owens locates Artegall's insufficiency in the emotional detachment with which he administers justice – an emotional detachment characterizing his guardian's tutelage and colourfully embodied in his own squire, the animated iron golem bequeathed to him by Astraea and possessing no desires and emotions to distract it from its relentless pursuit of lawbreakers. There is something just not good enough in Artegall's justice. In contrast, his brother Arthur, whose wardship emphasized affective bonds, holds out more promise than does Artegall for fulfilling the British commonwealth. But as with any ideal in Spenser's epic poem, Arthur's union with the Faerie Queene exists well beyond the narrative.

Staines, Visconsi, and Stevens

The final three chapters of the volume grapple with the ways in which legal and ecclesiastical mechanisms stigmatized as tyrannical and autocratic materialize injustice. It is through negating these mechanisms that literature offers a kind of salutary resistance to authoritarian political regimes and their violent means of establishing order. Taking exception to the law – long before Enlightenment revolutions – may be seen to have substantial political and ethical consequences. In his chapter, "Torture and the Tyrant's Injustice from Foxe to *King Lear,"* John Staines asks the question of why judicial torture disappeared from England in the early seventeenth century. Even though English law, unlike Continental jurisprudence, did not need to wrack the accused with pain because it did not require a confession to convict him or her of a capital felony, the Tudors still had recourse to torture when protecting their authority from potential threats. However, by the time of James and Charles this legal practice had become virtually extinct. Staines argues that one contributing factor to judicial torture losing favour with the state was the political campaign waged by narratives of tyranny within both Protestant and Catholic writings. In particular Foxe's influential *Acts and Monuments* uses evocative woodcuts to expose torture's sadistic and impotent underside. The judicial technique is depicted not so much as a tool for getting at the truth as an expression of a tyrant's cruelty, desperate frustration, and lack of control over his emotions. In these woodcuts, the tyrant's intemperance offsets the victim's stoic resistance by which the martyr remains true to his or her conscience. Readers are moved to sympathize with the victim, identifying with depicted onlookers who are often protesting and even resisting the "legal" proceedings. *King Lear* seems to be informed by the same discourse in the gruesome scene where a servant stands up to his master Cornwall after the latter enucleates Gloucester. By folding torture into tyranny, Foxe and other early modern writers helped to phase out the practice in England and, in doing so, participated in the larger political project of questioning the authority of monarchy, a questioning which would ultimately lead to the English Revolution.

The objection to torture expressed by Foxe and others in the period dovetails in many ways with the critique of religious executions and violence, against which Foxe was again a strident opponent. The sixteenth-century experience of violent persecution and the opposition to the coercion of religious uniformity set the stage for the seventeenth-century political discourse of toleration, examined by Elliott Visconsi's chapter, "The Literatures of Toleration and Civil Religion in Post-Revolutionary England." Visconsi argues that the constitutional language of American civil religion emerges out of the Stuart literature of the Restoration. The American revolutionaries of the eighteenth century saw the colonies as continuing the English constitution while fighting the perpetuation of "Stuart-style tyranny." Seventeenth-century

English arguments for permitting religious diversity came to be predominantly grounded in appeals to public peace and political sociality. For writers such as Roger Williams and John Milton, the principles of Christianity forbade any defence of it, except by the sword of the spirit, that is, the word of God. Only threats to civil peace warranted the state's use of physical force. The period witnessed the development of "civil religion" – the non-sectarian religion fostered to stabilize the social order – and this could operate as a subtly coercive force as well, elevating peace, but at the expense of individual conscience and the beliefs of minority groups. The period's literature takes issue with Erastian views of subordinating religion to the state and advocates, along with religious pluralism, a separation between the two. Theological beliefs should not be permitted to undermine civic peace. While the emergent sphere of privatized religion ameliorated much of religious violence, which we see in Foxe's martyrology, Visconsi points out that the ethos of civil religion paved the way for new forms of violent exclusion under the aegis of the modern nation state.

Paul Stevens's chapter, "Obnoxious Satan: Milton, Neo-Roman Justice, and the Burden of Grace," intriguingly raises Milton's misgivings over a point of injustice at the heart of the theological concept of grace. Extending Quentin Skinner's archaeological work on recovering the dead ends of history, Stevens argues for the importance of understanding that Milton, among a number of seventeenth-century writers, insisted that dependence of any sort constituted an injustice akin to what Skinner calls "unfreedom." Informed by neo-Roman theories of the law, Milton takes exception not only to the overt slavery suffered from direct coercion but also to the condition of subjection that exists when an individual falls under someone else's jurisdiction, whether or not any threat is acted upon. Satan in *Paradise Lost* experiences God's grace as precisely this sort of subjection: as a tyrannical imposition of dependency in which Satan and the rest of creation are ineluctably reliant on the will of God. Like Queen Elizabeth's general pardon, albeit in a theologically profound form that cuts to Satan's very sense of self, divine forgiveness is experienced by him as the "tyranny of grace." Satan's obsession with selfhood and individual agency – his pride – cannot endure the infinite debt created by God's magnanimity, a debt whose impossible repayment plunges him into the despair at having to express endless gratitude. Stevens wants to suggest that when grace is conceived as absolute dependency it provokes a similar existential anxiety in Milton, as evinced in *Samson Agonistes* and his correspondence with his own father.

In an effort to break the impasse between the self-abnegation that clouds the doctrine of grace and the personal anti-Augustinian virtue that subtends Roman views on justice, Milton conceives of another dimension to the doctrine that Stevens finds in the Son's intervention on behalf of a fallen humanity. Rather than being understood as an intolerable burden imposed by an overwhelming external force that negates one's agency and identity, grace becomes depicted as working alongside human agency, as a process whereby the divine assists in human flourishing, which Stevens terms as "grace as growth." We have a relationship of mediation and mutuality, rather than a relationship of radical difference, in which an external power demeans and subjugates us.

NOTES

1 "Law and Literature" will be capitalized in the introduction, when referring to the interdisciplinary field.

2 Two representative and influential books on the body in early modern literature are Gail Kern Paster, *The Body Embarrassed: Drama and the Disciplines of Shame in Early Modern England*, and Michael Carl Schoenfeldt, *Bodies and Selves in Early Modern England: Physiology and Inwardness in Spenser, Shakespeare, Herbert, and Milton*.

3 The "law in literature" is contrasted with "the law as literature." Whereas the latter mode employs hermeneutic tools from literary studies to interpret legal texts, the former leverages legal knowledge to decipher, for example, statutes, trials, and punishments mimetically and parodically represented in literature. For an explanation of this distinction, see Jeanne Gaakeer, "Law and Literature," and Ian Ward, *Law and Literature: Possibilities and Perspectives*, pp. 4–15. For work on "law as literature," see Sanford Levison, *Interpreting Law and Literature: A Hermeneutic Reader*.

4 R.S. White, *Natural Law in English Renaissance Literature*, p. 2.

5 R.S. White, *Natural Law in English Renaissance Literature*, p. 16

6 R.S. White, *Natural Law in English Renaissance Literature*, p. 3.

7 Charles Ross, *Elizabethan Literature and the Law of Fraudulent Conveyance*, p. xii.

8 The Sokols have also published *Shakespeare's Legal Language: A Dictionary*.

9 See, for instance, Edward J. White, *Commentaries on the Law in Shakespeare, with Explanations of the Legal Terms used in the Plays, Poems and Sonnets, and a Consideration of the Criminal Types Presented*, and D. Plunket Barton and James M. Beck, *Links between Shakespeare and the Law*. Julie Stone Peters, "Law, Literature, and the Vanishing Real: On the Future of an

Interdisciplinary Illusion," p. 443, refers to the institutionalization of Law and Literature occurring in the 1970s. Subha Mukherji, "'Understood Relations'": Law and Literature in Early Modern Studies," p. 706, attributes the founding of the Law and Literature movement to James Boyd White's 1973 *The Legal Imagination*, as does Ian Ward, *Law and Literature: Possibilities and Perspectives*, p. 23.

10 For some recent work in this area, see Paul Raffield and Gary Watt, *Shakespeare and the Law*; Bradin Cormack, Martha C. Nussbaum, and Richard Strier, eds, *Shakespeare and the Law: A Conversation among Disciplines and Professions*; and Andrew Zurcher, *Shakespeare and Law*.

11 A sound historical overview of early debates over Shakespeare's legal expertise can be found in Mark Andre Alexander, "Shakespeare's Knowledge of Law." The debates up to Alexander himself are fuelled by the authorship issue in Shakespeare studies.

12 Robert Darnton, "What is the History of Books?" pp. 67–8, proffered a synoptic model of the life cycle of the book in order to gain distance on the profusion of disconnected scholarly work arising from different disciplinary backgrounds.

13 On the law's foundational relationship to humanist education, see Thomas O. Sloane, *On the Contrary: The Protocol of Traditional Rhetoric*, p. 106.

14 Quoted in Wilfrid Prest, "Legal Education of the Gentry at the Inns of Court, 1560–1640," p. 20.

15 This argument is expertly sustained by Paul Raffield, *Images and Cultures of Law in Early Modern England: Justice and Political Power*, pp. 1–2.

16 Francis Lenton, *Characterismi: Or, Lentons Leasures Expressed in Essayes and Characters, Neuer before Written on*, f4v–f5r.

17 Lorna Hutson, *The Invention of Suspicion: Law and Mimesis in Shakespeare and Renaissance Drama*, p. 7.

18 For an introduction to the origins of charactery in early modern writing, see Donald Beecher, "Introduction," pp. 31–56.

19 Abraham Fraunce, *The Lavviers Logike* and *The Arcadian Rhetorike: Or the Præcepts of Rhetorike made Plaine by Examples*.

20 Thomas O. Sloane, *On the Contrary: The Protocol of Traditional Rhetoric*, p. 3.

21 Karen Cunningham, *Imaginary Betrayals: Subjectivity and the Discourses of Treason in Early Modern England*, pp. 23–39.

22 For an analysis of Sidney's defence as a classical oration, see Kenneth Orne Myrick, *Sir Philip Sidney as a Literary Craftsman*, pp. 46–83

23 Philip Sidney, *The Defence of Poesy*, p. 5, sees Solon, the first famous lawgiver, as essentially a poet; and George Puttenham, *The Art of English Poesy*, p. 97, claims that poets were the first lawmakers.

24 George Puttenham, *The Art of English Poesy*, pp. 221–40.
25 Adrian Johns, *The Nature of the Book: Print and Knowledge in the Making*, pp. 32–3. So concerned with the issue of legitimacy, Henry Chettle's *Kind-Harts Dreame* is produced, according to his preface, to vindicate the author of the charge that he forged *Greene's Groatsworth of Wit*. The text proper too can be read as an act of legitimating the author-printer Chettle.
26 Adrian Johns, *The Nature of the Book: Print and Knowledge in the Making*, p. 62.
27 Peter Goodrich, *Law in the Courts of Love: Literature and Other Minor Jurisprudences*, pp. 2–3.
28 Anthony Julius, *Law and Literature: Current Legal Issues*, p. 13.
29 Cyprian Blagden, *The Stationers Company a History, 1403–1959*, pp. 40, 43–4.
30 Richard Dutton, *Mastering the Revels: The Regulation and Censorship of English Renaissance Drama*, p. 32.
31 Richard Dutton, *Mastering the Revels: The Regulation and Censorship of English Renaissance Drama*, p. 47.
32 Cyndia Susan Clegg, *Press Censorship in Elizabethan England*, p. 222.
33 See Cyndia Susan Clegg, *Press Censorship in Elizabethan England*; Janet Clare, *"Art made Tongue-Tied by Authority": Elizabethan and Jacobean Dramatic Censorship*; Richard Dutton, *Mastering the Revels: The Regulation and Censorship of English Renaissance Drama*; and Debora Shuger, *Censorship and Cultural Sensibility: The Regulation of Language in Tudor-Stuart England.*
34 M. Lindsay Kaplan, *The Culture of Slander in Early Modern England*, p. 2.
35 M. Lindsay Kaplan, *The Culture of Slander in Early Modern England*, p. 9.
36 Debora Shuger, "Civility and Censorship in Early Modern England," p. 95.
37 Andrew Hadfield, "Introduction: The Politics of Early Modern Censorship," p. 6.
38 Steven Mullaney, *The Place of the Stage: License, Play, and Power in Renaissance England*, p. 21.
39 Constance Jordan and Karen Cunningham, eds, "English Law in Shakespeare's Plays," for example, turns to the double simile: "Like the law courts, Shakespeare's theatre was a place of trial and testing and law, like theatre, relied on narratives that posited and analyzed conceptions of motive, character, intention, and origin" (p. 1). Their introduction also pursues much deeper connections.
40 See, for example, Dennis Kezar, "Introduction," pp. 2–3; Subha Mukherji, *Law and Representation in Early Modern Drama*, p. 3; and Karen Cunningham, *Imaginary Betrayals*, pp. 2–3.
41 Luke Wilson, *Theaters of Intention: Drama and the Law in Early Modern England*, p. 171.

42 Luke Wilson, *Theaters of Intention: Drama and the Law in Early Modern England*, pp. 165–72, has instructively defamiliarized this term "performance" by tracing its origin in legal contracts to its later transference to the aesthetic field.
43 See Theodore Ziolkowski, *The Mirror of Justice: Literary Reflections of Legal Crises*, in which he historicizes the linkages between the origins of ancient Greek drama and the development of jury trial.
44 Subha Mukherji, *Law and Representation in Early Modern Drama*, p. 3.
45 Dennis Kezar, "Introduction," p. 2.
46 Bartholomew Griffin, *Fidessa, More Chaste then Kinde*, and Gerard Legh, *The Accedens of Armory*.
47 Lorna Hutson, *The Invention of Suspicion: Law and Mimesis in Shakespeare and Renaissance Drama*, p. 7.
48 Visconsi's book examines the origins of law in later Stuart England by concentrating on how literary texts incite readers to reflect upon the first principles of government. Literature in his account becomes the powerful means of civilizing a nation in the aftermath of the Revolution, in which the English people were widely seen to have degenerated into barbarity. This period breaks with earlier attempts to civilize through literature insofar as literature no longer addresses a strictly aristocratic readership but reaches out to a general public more broadly conceived.

Kahn's book demonstrates how seventeenth-century contract theory constituted a kind of poetics. The domain of aesthetics with questions of the role of language and representation in affecting subjectivity impact the period's conceptions of political obligation and understandings of the complex relationship between common law and the natural law.
49 Anthony Julius, "Introduction," pp. 1–2.
50 There were of course numerous books and articles written on law and literature, but the field came into its own only in the 1970s.
51 Jane B. Baron, "Law, Literature, and the Problems of Interdisciplinarity," pp. 1063–6; Julie Stone Peters, "Law, Literature, and the Vanishing Real: On the Future of an Interdisciplinary Illusion," pp. 444–8.
52 Jane B. Baron, "Law, Literature, and the Problems of Interdisciplinarity," p. 1059.
53 Bradin Cormack, *A Power to do Justice: Jurisdiction, English Literature, and the Rise of Common Law, 1509–1625*, p. 1.
54 Richard Posner's *Law and Literature: A Misunderstood Relation* kindled significant debate in the field on account of its extreme position of seeing the two disciplines as not sharing anything in common when it came to interpretation. Since Posner's initial position, which he has nuanced over

the years, the scholarship on the relationship between the two disciplines has proved quite extensive. The following list is only a sampler, not a survey: Lenora Ledwon, *Law and Literature: Text and Theory*; Willem J. Witteveen, "Law and Literature: Expanding, Contracting, Emerging"; Kostas Myrsiades and Linda S. Myrsiades, *Un-Disciplining Literature: Literature, Law, and Culture*; Jane B. Baron, "Law, Literature, and the Problems of Interdisciplinarity"; Julie Stone Peters, "Law, Literature, and the Vanishing Real: On the Future of an Interdisciplinary Illusion"; and Subha Mukherji, "'Understood Relations': Law and Literature in Early Modern Studies."

55 Subha Mukherji, "'Understood Relations': Law and Literature in Early Modern Studies," p. 714: "It is time, then, to go beyond the polarities of whether literature and the law are different or similar, or whether one is largely critical of the other or not; and to address without embarrassment the diversity that is both the condition and the character of their dialogue. In our interdisciplinary studies, we must be true to the nuances and range of interdisciplinary practice – institutional as well as discursive – in any given period." Mukherji, "'Understood Relations': Law and Literature in Early Modern Studies," pp. 709–10, has in mind the scholarship of Victoria Ann Kahn, *Wayward Contracts: The Crisis of Political Obligation in England, 1640–1674*; Lorna Hutson, *The Invention of Suspicion: Law and Mimesis in Shakespeare and Renaissance Drama*; Subha Mukherji, *Law and Representation in Early Modern Drama*; and Bradin Cormack, *A Power to do Justice: Jurisdiction, English Literature, and the Rise of Common Law, 1509–1625.*

56 Cicero, *Pro Balbo*, xvi, 32.

57 Edmund Spenser, *The Faerie Qveene*, 5.5.25.7–9.

58 As Lacan cryptically says, the unconscious is the discourse of the Other; that is, the signifier, which belongs to society and precedes us, determines our intimate selves, from our identities to our desires. See Anthony Wilden, *The Language of the Self*, for an introduction to Lacan's take on language.

59 Quoted in Peter Goodrich, *Law in the Courts of Love: Literature and Other Minor Jurisprudences*, pp. 116–17.

60 Bradin Cormack, "Practicing Law and Literature in Early Modern Studies," p. 91; Frances E. Dolan, "Early Modern Literature and the Law," p. 352; and Subha Mukherji, "'Understood Relations': Law and Literature in Early Modern Studies," p. 714.

61 Alain Pottage, *Law*, "Introduction," pp. 18–19, recognizes ANT's importance for understanding the role of objects and hybrids of subjects and objects in the production of the law.

62 Bruno Latour, *We Have Never been Modern*, p. 63.

63 Take, for instance, Luke Wilson, *Theaters of Intention*, p. 1, where he begins with an emphasis on "artefacts" and objects, which opens up nonlinguistic connections reminiscent of ANT's interest in quasi-objects.

64 Bruno Latour, "On Recalling ANT," p. 15, says that he based his view of the network on the Deleuzian concept of the rhizome. See Gilles Deleuze and Félix Guattari, *A Thousand Plateaus: Capitalism and Schizophrenia*, pp. 3–25.

65 Lorna Hutson, *The Invention of Suspicion: Law and Mimesis in Shakespeare and Renaissance Drama*, p. 6.

66 Sidney, *The Defence of Poesy*, p. 15.

67 Ross, *Elizabethan Literature and the Law of Fraudulent Conveyance*, p. 88, notes how "the sheen of Arthur's higher purpose" graces "the often dirty business of administering justice that clouds Artegall's deeds." Ross's chapter on Spenser argues that Artegall's witnessing of Duessa's execution marks the end of the era of menacing intrigue around Mary, Queen of Scots, right around the time when the bill against fraudulent conveyance was, interestingly enough, gaining traction.

68 Robert Burton, *The Anatomy of Melancholy*, p. 5.

69 Robert Burton, *The Anatomy of Melancholy*, p. 49.

70 As Žižek, *The Sublime Object of Ideology*, pp. 36–7, argues, we do not obey the law on the basis of rationality but on the basis of belief's tautological nature, and as soon as we lose this belief "the very texture of the social field disintegrates"; we submit because we do not ultimately understand the incomprehensible, traumatic, irrational character of the law.

BIBLIOGRAPHY

Alexander, Mark Andre. "Shakespeare's Knowledge of Law." Shakespeare Oxford Fellowship: http://www.shakespeareoxfordfellowship.org/shakespeares-knowledge-of-law/. 1 May 2013.

Baron, Jane B. "Law, Literature, and the Problems of Interdisciplinarity." *Yale Law Journal* 108, no. 5 (1999): 1059–85.

Barton, D. Plunket, and James M. Beck. *Links between Shakespeare and the Law*. London: Faber & Gwyer, 1929.

Beecher, Donald. "Introduction." *Characters: Together with Poems, News, Edicts, and Paradoxes Based on the Eleventh Edition of A Wife Now the Widow of Sir Thomas Overbury*. Ottawa: Dovehouse Editions, 2003. Publications of the Barnabe Riche Society. 11–108.

Blagden, Cyprian. *The Stationers' Company a History, 1403–1959*. London: Unwin, 1960.

Burton, Robert. *The Anatomy of Melancholy*. Ed. Thomas C. Faulkner, Nicolas K. Kiessling, and Rhonda L. Blair. Vol. 1. Oxford: Clarendon Press, 1989.

Chettle, Henry. *Kind-Harts Dreame*. London, 1593. Early English Books Online. Web. 7 May 2013.

Cicero, Marcus Tullius. *De Inventione, De Optimo Genere Oratorum, Topica*. Ed. H.M. Hubbell. London: Heinemann, 1960.

– *Pro Balbo, with Introd., Notes, Vocabularies, and Translation by the Editors of "Cicero De Amicitia."* London: Univ. Corr. Coll. P, 1900.

Clare, Janet. *"Art made Tongue-Tied by Authority": Elizabethan and Jacobean Dramatic Censorship*. Manchester; New York: Manchester UP, 1990.

Clegg, Cyndia Susan. *Press Censorship in Caroline England*. Cambridge; New York: Cambridge UP, 2008.

– *Press Censorship in Jacobean England*. Cambridge; New York: Cambridge UP, 2001.

– *Press Censorship in Elizabethan England*. Cambridge; New York: Cambridge UP, 1997.

Cormack, Bradin. *A Power to Do Justice: Jurisdiction, English Literature, and the Rise of Common Law, 1509–1625*. Chicago: U of Chicago P, 2007.

– "Practicing Law and Literature in Early Modern Studies." *Modern Philology* 101, no. 1 (2003): 79–91.

Cormack, Bradin, Martha C. Nussbaum, and Richard Strier, eds. *Shakespeare and the Law: A Conversation among Disciplines and Professions*. Chicago: U of Chicago P, 2013.

Cunningham, Karen. *Imaginary Betrayals: Subjectivity and the Discourses of Treason in Early Modern England*. Philadelphia: U of Pennsylvania P, 2002.

Darnton, Robert. "What is the History of Books?" *Daedalus* 111, no. 3 (1982): 65–83.

Davis, Cushman Kellogg. *The Law in Shakespeare*. 1884. New York: AMS Press, 1972.

Deleuze, Gilles, and Félix Guattari. *A Thousand Plateaus: Capitalism and Schizophrenia*. Minneapolis: U of Minnesota P, 1987.

Dolan, Frances E. "Early Modern Literature and the Law." *Huntington Library Quarterly* 71, no. 2 (2008): 351–64.

Dutton, Richard. *Licensing, Censorship, and Authorship in Early Modern England: Buggeswords*. Basingstoke, UK; New York: Palgrave, 2000.

– *Mastering the Revels: The Regulation and Censorship of English Renaissance Drama*. Basingstoke, UK: Macmillan, 1991.

Fraunce, Abraham. *The Arcadian Rhetorike: Or the Præcepts of Rhetorike made Plaine by Examples*. London, 1588. Early English Books Online. Web. 1 May 2013.

– *The Lavviers Logike*. London, 1588. Early English Books Online. Web. 1 May 2013.

Gaakeer, Jeanne. "Law and Literature." *IVR Encyclopaedia of Jurisprudence, Legal Theory and Philosophy of Law*. http://ivr-enc.info/index.php?title=Law_and_Literature. 16 April 2009.

Goodrich, Peter. *Law in the Courts of Love: Literature and Other Minor Jurisprudences*. London; New York: Routledge, 1996.

Griffin, Bartholomew. *Fidessa, More Chaste then Kinde*. London, 1596. Early English Books Online. Web. 1 May 2013.

Hadfield, Andrew. "Introduction: The Politics of Early Modern Censorship." *Literature and Censorship in Renaissance England*. Basingstoke; New York: Palgrave, 2001. 1–13.

Hutson, Lorna. *The Invention of Suspicion: Law and Mimesis in Shakespeare and Renaissance Drama*. Oxford; New York: Oxford UP, 2007.

Johns, Adrian. *The Nature of the Book: Print and Knowledge in the Making*. Chicago: U of Chicago P, 1998.

Jordan, Constance, and Karen Cunningham, eds. "English Law in Shakespeare's Plays." In *The Law in Shakespeare*. Basingstoke, UK; New York: Palgrave Macmillan, 2007. 1–19.

Julius, Anthony. "Introduction." *Law and Literature: Current Legal Issues*. Ed. Michael D.A. Freeman and A.D.E. Lewis. Vol. 2. Oxford; New York: Oxford UP, 1999. xi–xxv.

Kahn, Victoria Ann. *Wayward Contracts: The Crisis of Political Obligation in England, 1640–1674*. Princeton, NJ: Princeton UP, 2004.

Kaplan, M. Lindsay. *The Culture of Slander in Early Modern England*. Cambridge; New York: Cambridge UP, 1997.

Kezar, Dennis. "Introduction." *Solon and Thespis: Law and Theater in the English Renaissance*. Notre Dame, IN: U of Notre Dame P, 2007. 1–16.

Latour, Bruno. "On Recalling ANT." In *Actor Network and After*. Ed. J. Law and J. Hassard. Oxford: Blackwell and the *Sociological Review*, 1999. 15–25.

– *We Have Never Been Modern*. Cambridge, MA: Harvard UP, 1993.

Ledwon, Lenora. *Law and Literature: Text and Theory*. New York: Garland, 1996.

Legh, Gerard. *The Accedens of Armory*. London, 1562. Early English Books Online. Web. 1 May 2013.

Lemon, Rebecca. *Treason by Words: Literature, Law, and Rebellion in Shakespeare's England*. Ithaca, NY: Cornell UP, 2006.

Lenton, Francis. *Characterismi: Or, Lentons Leasures Expressed in Essayes and Characters, Neuer before Written on. by F.L. Gent.* London, 1631. Early English Books Online. Web. 1 May 2013.
Levison, Sanford. *Interpreting Law and Literature: A Hermeneutic Reader*. Evanston, IL: Northwestern UP, 1988.
Lockey, Brian. *Law and Empire in English Renaissance Literature*. Cambridge: Cambridge UP, 2006.
Loewenstein, Joseph. *The Author's Due: Printing and the Prehistory of Copyright*. Chicago: U of Chicago P, 2002.
Mukherji, Subha. *Law and Representation in Early Modern Drama*. Cambridge; New York: Cambridge UP, 2006.
– "'Understood Relations': Law and Literature in Early Modern Studies." *Literary Compass* 6, no. 3 (2009): 706–25.
Mullaney, Steven. *The Place of the Stage: License, Play, and Power in Renaissance England*. Ann Arbor: U of Michigan P, 1995; 1988.
Myrick, Kenneth Orne. *Sir Philip Sidney as a Literary Craftsman*. Lincoln: U of Nebraska P, 1965.
Myrsiades, Kostas, and Linda S. Myrsiades, eds. *Un-Disciplining Literature: Literature, Law, and Culture*. New York: Peter Lang, 1999.
Paster, Gail Kern. *The Body Embarrassed: Drama and the Disciplines of Shame in Early Modern England*. Ithaca, NY: Cornell UP, 1993.
Peters, Julie Stone. "Law, Literature, and the Vanishing Real: On the Future of an Interdisciplinary Illusion." *PMLA* 120, no. 2 (2005): 442–53.
Richard Posner. *Law and Literature: A Misunderstood Relation*. Cambridge, MA: Harvard UP, 1988.
Pottage, Alain, and Martha Mundy. *Law, Anthropology and the Constitution of the Social*. Cambridge; New York: Cambridge UP, 2004.
Prest, Wilfrid. "Legal Education of the Gentry at the Inns of Court, 1560–1640." *Past & Present* 38 (1967): 20–39.
Puttenham, George. *The Art of English Poesy*. Ithaca, NY: Cornell UP, 2007.
Raffield, Paul. *Images and Cultures of Law in Early Modern England: Justice and Political Power, 1558–1660*. Cambridge; New York: Cambridge UP, 2004.
Raffield, Paul, and Gary Watt. *Shakespeare and the Law*. Oxford; Portland, OR: Hart, 2008.
Ross, Charles. *Elizabethan Literature and the Law of Fraudulent Conveyance: Sidney, Spenser, and Shakespeare*. Aldershot, UK; Burlington, VT: Ashgate, 2003.
Schoenfeldt, Michael Carl. *Bodies and Selves in Early Modern England: Physiology and Inwardness in Spenser, Shakespeare, Herbert, and Milton*. Cambridge; New York: Cambridge UP, 1999.

Sheen, Erica, and Lorna Hutson, eds. *Literature, Politics, and Law in Renaissance England*. Basingstoke, UK; New York: Palgrave Macmillan, 2005.

Shuger, Debora K. *Censorship and Cultural Sensibility: The Regulation of Language in Tudor-Stuart England*. Philadelphia: U of Pennsylvania P, 2006.

– "Civility and Censorship in Early Modern England." In *Censorship and Silencing: Practices of Cultural Regulation*. Ed. Robert Post. Santa Monica, CA: Getty Research Institute Publications, 1998. 89–110.

Sidney, Philip. *The Defence of Poesy*. In *Sidney's "The Defence of Poesy" and Selected Renaissance Literary Criticism*. Ed. Gavin Alexander. London; New York: Penguin, 2004. 3–54.

Sloane, Thomas O. *On the Contrary: The Protocol of Traditional Rhetoric*. Washington, DC: Catholic U of America P, 1997.

Sokol, B.J., and Mary Sokol. *Shakespeare's Legal Language: A Dictionary*. London; New Brunswick, NJ; Somerset, NJ: Athlone Press, 2000.

– *Shakespeare, Law, and Marriage*. Cambridge; New York: Cambridge UP, 2003.

Spenser, Edmund. *The Faerie Qveene*. Ed. A.C. Hamilton. Rev ed. New York: Longman, 2006.

Visconsi, Elliott. *Lines of Equity: Literature and the Origins of Law in Later Stuart England*. Ithaca, NY: Cornell UP, 2008.

Ward, Ian. *Law and Literature: Possibilities and Perspectives*. Cambridge; New York: Cambridge UP, 1995.

– *Shakespeare and the Legal Imagination*. London; Charlottesville, VA: Butterworths; Lexis Law Pub., 1999.

White, Edward J. *Commentaries on the Law in Shakespeare, with Explanations of the Legal Terms used in the Plays, Poems and Sonnets, and a Consideration of the Criminal Types Presented. also a Full Discussion of the Bacon-Shakespeare Controversy*. 2d ed. St Louis, MO: The F.H. Thomas Law Book Co., 1913.

White, James Boyd. *The Legal Imagination; Studies in the Nature of Legal Thought and Expression*. Boston: Little, Brown, 1973.

White, R.S. *Natural Law in English Renaissance Literature*. Cambridge; New York: Cambridge UP, 1996.

Wilden, Anthony. *The Language of the Self; the Function of Language in Psychoanalysis*. Baltimore: Johns Hopkins Press, 1968.

Wilson, Luke. *Theaters of Intention: Drama and the Law in Early Modern England*. Stanford, CA: Stanford UP, 2000.

Wilson, Thomas. *A Discourse upon Usury, by Way of Dialogue and Orations, for the Better Variety and More Delight of all Those that Shall Read this Treatise*. Ed. R.H. Tawney. New York: Kelley, 1963.

Witteveen, Willem J. "Law and Literature: Expanding, Contracting, Emerging." *Cardozo Studies in Law and Literature* 10, no. 2 (1998): 155–60.

Ziolkowski, Theodore. *The Mirror of Justice: Literary Reflections of Legal Crises*. Princeton, NJ: Princeton UP, 1997.

Žižek, Slavoj. *The Sublime Object of Ideology*. London; New York: Verso, 1989.

Zurcher, Andrew. *Shakespeare and Law*. London: Arden Shakespeare, 2010.

2 Paper Justice, Parchment Justice: Shakespeare, *Hamlet*, and the Life of Legal Documents

BRADIN CORMACK

Introduction: Indicting Law

In a short scene in Shakespeare's *Richard III*, performed just after Richard as Lord Protector has had Hastings executed on charges of witchcraft, a scrivener enters, according to a stage direction in the 1597 Quarto, "with a paper in his hand."[1] The paper belongs to a group of props that move across act 3 as signs of the political and theatrical process through which a duke transforms himself into a king.[2] These include the "rotten armour, marvellous ill-favoured" that Richard and Buckingham wear to persuade the Mayor they are in danger (3.5.0.2–3), the head of Hastings brought preposterously onto stage as though in evidence of the very treachery that has led to his execution (3.5.19.1), and the prayer book that Richard carries when, supported between two bishops, he appears before the citizens of London to finagle their consent to his coronation (3.7.95–8).[3] (One might include in the list even the strawberries that, at Richard's request, the Bishop of Ely sends for but which never arrive [3.4.31–3, 3.4.46–7]. These act as a kind of ghost prop whose failure to appear on stage nicely answers the ambiguity of their plot significance: are the strawberries an emblem, a ploy, a red herring?)

In contrast to these other bits of political machinery, the Scrivener's paper is strikingly institutional in form and function. As such, it is a more frightening because more ordinary instrument of tyranny:

> Here is the indictment of the good Lord Hastings,
> Which in a set hand fairly is engrossed,
> That it may be today read o'er in Paul's –

And mark how well the sequel hangs together:
Eleven hours I have spent to write it over,
For yesternight by Catesby was it sent me;
The precedent was full as long a-doing;
And yet, within these five hours, Hastings lived,
Untainted, unexamined, free, at liberty.
Here's a good world the while! Who is so gross
That cannot see this palpable device?
Yet who so bold but says he sees it not?
Bad is the world, and all will come to nought
When such ill dealing must be seen in thought. (3.6.1–14)

Engrossment is the textual form given a legal document as one expression of its authority. The Scrivener's knowing point about the time it took him to copy a "precedent" copy that itself took time to write is simple enough: the arguments responding to Hastings's arrest and justifying his execution – a few moments earlier, Richard has given the case in brief to the Mayor of London (3.5.39–44) – are out of sync with the material "sequel" of composition, which means in turn that the "sequel" the document records, namely, the causal story about Hastings's guilt and execution, is merely an instance of the tyrant's "charades."[4] The law is a process, and the special point here is that the legal and narrative process to which the proclamation loudly pretends as the very ground of its authority is here exposed as a conceptual object produced by the document, rather than only recorded in it.

Especially notable is the fact that the Scrivener refers to the paper he is carrying as an "indictment." Like the strawberries, armour, and bishops, the proclamation to be read at Paul's has its source in Thomas More's *History of Richard III*, as printed in Edward Hall's history of the civil wars. There, however, the Scrivener's sceptical role is played by "one that was scolemayster at Paules," who, true to his pedagogical office and distinctly humanist scepticism, exposes the fraud to his fellow citizens by "comparying the shortnesse of the tyme with the length of the matter."[5] In Shakespeare's source, furthermore, the suspicious document is referred to simply as a "proclamacion," which Richard orders to be read in London after Hastings's death has led to rumour and suspicion there. Both of Shakespeare's alterations intensify More's brief analysis of legal chicanery. First, with the figure of a scrivener rather than a schoolmaster, Shakespeare underlines the relation of law to its own mediation: the law, we are allowed to hear, is words on paper or parchment, written by particular people, literally so by scriveners, for particular ends. Second, in the use of "indictment," Shakespeare looks to the specifics of legal textuality in order to define the institutional trick being performed. *Indictment* is a technical word for the document containing a formal accusation (also an indictment), usually as found by a Grand Jury and so presented to the court. The important point for the present argument is that an indictment does not follow but precedes the trial, as happens, for example, in *The Winter's Tale*, where Leontes opens the process against Hermione by crying, "Read the indictment" (3.2.11), an act the Officer then performs. In no way can a personal indictment ("the indictment of the good Lord Hastings") be synonymous with a proclamation meant to justify a judicial sentence and execution after the fact.[6]

What should we make of Shakespeare's legal solecism? Now, More's text speaks of the proclamation as both a material and a rhetorical artefact, as being both "fayre writen in Parchement in a fayre sette hande" and "curiously endyted," that is, carefully composed. Here, then, is the origin of Shakespeare's peculiar word choice, which has transformed a generic verb form in his source (*endite* can mean "to put into words") into a noun form, "indictment," which word carries, however, a specific and unavoidable technical resonance that is not really apposite to the plot. But rather than seeing the verbal and conceptual flexibility as the choice of a writer who, as Samuel Johnson has it, "attends more to his ideas than to his words," we may understand Shakespeare's choice as an experiment productive of a semantic effect that is both thematically appropriate and analytically complex.[7] For Shakespeare's lexical recasting of his source gives extra force to Richard's attempt to gloss over Hastings's murder, by offering a verbal emblem for the tyrant's fraudulent distortion of law. A document, and word, that should stand at the beginning of a trial for treason instead follows the execution of judgment: reversing normal process, the Scrivener's paper substitutes, *literally* substitutes, a new reality for the one it suppresses, with the deceitful "indictment" making the execution of sentence cause of the charge, rather than its outcome. (This is the force, equally, of the Scrivener's saying that "within these five hours" Hastings "lived ... / Untainted, unexamined, free, at liberty," a four-part sequence that puts in reverse order the legal process that leads from confinement through examination to attainder and so to death, but which here has been suppressed in favour of an execution that must, preposterously, generate the evidence in support of it.)[8] As used by the

Scrivener, "indictment" is the play's one-word argument for the temporal scheming the scene as a who'le unfolds. Heard with its technical force intact, Shakespeare's "indictment," rooted in his source but adjusted to its dramatic context, goes off in the play text like a depth charge.

Insofar as they point to Shakespeare's imaginative engagement with the material technologies that make the law, the small shifts that make a schoolteacher into a scrivener and a proclamation into an indictment tell us a good deal about what Shakespeare extracts from the law when he deploys its language inside his own linguistic artefacts. As Tim Stretton demonstrates in this volume, in his essay on *The Merchant of Venice* and the differences among kinds of legal bonds, the law is a discipline that effects its ends by manipulating linguistic forms and by making evident the consequences of small differences in language and form.[9] Generally speaking, Shakespeare is most engaged by law, I think, when tracing out the semantic differentiations that one finds in both poetry and the law. It is in this meeting of law and poetry as twin arts for *making* something in language, for using language to produce an effect in the world, that we can most accurately speak of a poetics of law or a legal poetics.[10]

My essay contributes to the larger project of articulating this version of the interdisciplinary encounter by considering in particular Shakespeare's engagement with the law's materiality, as this finds expression in his exploitation of the language around some very basic documents – the paper and parchment of my title – that allowed the law to function. The argument will be that Shakespeare turns to the material life of law, with sometimes surprising attention to technical matters, as a way to explore the character of justice inside a legal system whose ongoing effect was to change the order of the real by offering a set of textual and technical substitutions *for* the real, this as a second reality, the one through which, namely, the law becomes able to exercise its peculiar authority. In this encounter between, as it were, complementary reals, the image or possibility of ideal justice does not so much shatter as fade away, an irrelevancy in respect of the procedural forms that institute the law by shifting the parameters of the real. In such a legal-administrative dynamic, the dramatist's attention to legal textuality may begin with the familiar opposition between true justice and mere legalism, but it cannot stop there. Even as Shakespeare exposes the law's textual substitutes to critique, I would suggest, the imaginative engagement with the law's forms discovers in the law's poetic capacities a version of the dramatic fiction's own aspiration, in language, to encounter the world as world.

A minor caveat: in positing that Shakespeare is interested in the technical side of legal documents, I am not supposing that he was deeply read in law. On the contrary, my sense is that Shakespeare enters the law, as he enters all the disciplines that inform his writing, through an encounter with its language in which language itself remains primary, and in which the law's words are turned through their various registers and functions as a way to test their analytical potential. As I have begun to suggest, a good way to track Shakespeare's thinking about law is to follow him in these experiments, by listening for those places in the plays where a word brought under pressure opens the play's argument to an unexpected analytical perspective.

History and the Legal Real

A good example of Shakespeare's thinking about documents and substitution comes in act 3, scene 1 of *1 Henry IV*, a familiar scene in which Hotspur, Mortimer, and Glendower meet to finalize their pact and prospectively divide the kingdom among themselves. The scene depends upon a map, but it opens with a legal bond: "These promises are fair, the parties sure," Mortimer says (3.1.1). In Shakespeare's rendering of the historical agreement, Mortimer further notes for his fellows that "our indentures tripartite are drawn," and now need only to be "sealèd interchangeably – / A business that this night may execute" (3.1.77–9).[11] This is a document, then, in triplicate, one for each party. Since the detail comes from Holinshed, who also speaks of a "tripartite indenture" among the rebels, it is not immediately evident that Shakespeare was thinking much about the instrument as such; and indeed editors do not have much to say about the technical detail.[12] It is notable, however, that while Holinshed's indenture is "sealed with their seales," it is not "interchangeably" so sealed. Although this word sounds generic, it is in fact a term of art, absorbed, perhaps for its up-to-date flavour, from the contemporary instruments with which Shakespeare was most familiar. Thus William West notes in his formulary of legal instruments and precedents that an indenture is a deed on which the parties to the deed "haue to euery part thereof interchangeably, or seuerally set their seuerall Seales."[13] That technical language was also internal to the indenture: the Bargain and Sale for Shakespeare's purchase of the Blackfriar's Gatehouse in March of 1613 ends, for example, by recording that the "said parties to theis indentures interchaungeablie have sett their seales."[14]

Especially significant as evidence for Shakespeare's conceptual investment in the legal instrument is the fact that, thirty lines on, he comes back to Holinshed's word in a part of the scene that is wholly his invention. The earlier and later usages illuminate one another. Irritated by Glendower and using as pretext for a quarrel the portion of land he has been assigned, Hotspur famously swears to change the course of the River Trent where it divides his portion from Mortimer's, in order to prevent the river from flowing north, a course that, as he has it, deprives him of land that might otherwise belong to his northern holdings.[15] Critics have noted how the scene wittily upsets norms of cartographic representation, with Hotspur imagining altering not "the *map* so as to increase the value or nature of his property," but rather "the land itself."[16] As John Gillies nicely puts it, by seeking to change the lines on the land, rather than the lines on the map, Hotspur is able "solemnly [to abide] by the letter of the cartographically expressed agreement while increasing his own territory" at the others' expense.[17] So far so good. Equally interesting is the relation of Hotspur's cartographic and fluvial fantasies to the scene's other technological fantasy, namely, the instrument that purports to effect the division in the first place. An indenture – its name relates etymologically to teeth – is a deed between two or more parties executed in as many copies (or "parts").[18] Originally, these copies were written out on a single piece of parchment top to bottom, and then cut one from the other along a serrated or, more commonly for the Elizabethan period, sinuous line, this as a way to verify the authenticity of the document when the parties brought the copies back together and reassembled the original whole. That half-submerged materiality is the aspect of the indenture that Shakespeare activates in the quarrel scene, when he has Hotspur boast that, once his dam changes the Trent's course, the river "shall not wind with such a deep *indent*, / To rob me of so rich a bottom here" (3.1.101–2, my emphasis).

When Hotspur, at "here," points to the map and, at "*such* a deep indent," even traces thereon the sinuous line that he supposes to be doing him injury, he converts the rich plains of Lincolnshire to a place on the map (a "here" that is textually there). But he also changes the map and the land it represents into versions of the indenture itself, as though the insight issuing from Shakespeare's pun were that a loss of parchment and a loss of land might be continuous. In Hotspur's telling, a notched parchment, in its relation to a notched map, has notched his right in the land. If Shakespeare thus casts England as a space that, puzzle-like, fits together like a document, the point issuing from the joke is not only that, as Phyllis Rackin argues in relation to *Richard II*, writing replaces the "enduring, immanent value of land and sea" with a "fluctuating, mediated value of the market, represented by legal documents,"[19] but also that, under a documentary order, the real itself begins to lie *in* documents, with the thing that the document subtends beginning to disappear into the aspect of its own vehicle. The land in *Henry IV* becomes an indenture as one emblem for what the law in fact is doing all the time, as an ordinary and not fully visible aspect of its power, which is to substitute for the real a version of the real that allows the law to effect its ends, even as it sponsors the possibility that this may, after all, be the only real that ends up mattering. Shakespeare's improvisation on Holinshed invents the metaphor of a parchment England to reflect the accelerating reality at common law that what matters – what is material at law – is not, say, the land you live on, but the land that gets onto parchment or paper to be imagined, conveyed, inherited, forfeited *there* or, in Hotspur's terms, "here."

There is something both terrible and grand about the law construed in this way. As Stretton suggests in relation to written versus oral bonds, Shakespeare attends closely to legal writing because writing in law, as in many other spheres, was becoming ever more present as a way to imagine relations and stabilize authority.[20] I think a related point is that in the legal instruments whose forms organized the world in the law's own image Shakespeare found a figure, not inappropriate for his own fiction-making, of a textual culture that could be said to be in immediate relation to a world, for exactly the reason that its world is not quite the real one. The law looks mimetic, but in fact it is heterotopic, in the sense adopted by Michel Foucault (though Foucault is hardly thinking of the law) when he writes of heterotopia as a second and orderly real, "meticulous" and "well arranged," whose power resides in the fact that, precisely not our "messy, ill constructed, and jumbled" real, it is nevertheless continuously in relation to it.[21]

For a more complex example of the reality effect that I am locating in Shakespeare's engagement with legal textuality and legal substitution, we can turn to *Henry VIII*, whose contemporary title, *All Is True*, gestures towards its representation of an increasingly formalized machinery for truth. This is a play stuffed with paper as an emblem of court bureaucracy and court intrigue, a play populated by scribes, by secretaries (including Gardiner and Cromwell), and by chancellors: by Wolsey, More, and, perhaps most interestingly, by "Sir Gilbert Perk," who in the Gentleman's report of Buckingham's trial for treason in act 2 is referred to, not as the Duke's secretary, but as his "chancellor," a minor chancellor, that is, to mirror the major ones working for the King (2.1.21). Henry's chancellors matter because they have in England a double function that constitutes the play's political centre. The Lord Chancellor is keeper of the King's possibly compromised conscience and, even more important, he is supervisor of his records: the grants, charters, commissions that issued under the great seal, and also the Chancery writs or forms of action through which cases were initiated at common law.[22] "I love a ballad in print, alife, for then we are sure they are true," Mopsa says in *The Winter's Tale* (4.4.258–9). *All Is True* might be said to duplicate in a political register Mopsa's unwitting analysis of the place of textuality in authorizing the true.

The relation of documents to authority is nicely captured in the plot detail that sees Wolsey fall from power by mistakenly including a paper "schedule" or "inventory" of his accumulated riches among the "Papers of state" he has prepared for the King (3.2.105.1, 3.2.122, 3.2.126).[23] If Wolsey is trapped by the same machinery of governance that has worked to consolidate his power as the person who controls the King's writing and textual instruments, this is a matter, first, of his confusing administrative levels, with a private legal paper, an account "drawn together / For mine own ends" (3.2.212–13), circulating inappropriately among public ones.[24] Second, we might say that Wolsey's fate is sealed also because the "secret" paper he passes to Henry reveals something untoward generally about the syntax of the legal and documentary culture he oversees. In her study of legal records, Cornelia Vissman notes that the non-syntactic order of the *list* reflects the fact that "Lists do not communicate, they control transfer operations."[25] Vissman's insight is suggestive for the kinds of meaning that documents might carry not so much through their content as in their form. For Wolsey's list as such makes clear to the King the true force of the counsellor's work on behalf of his master: "What piles of wealth hath he accumulated / To his own portion," Henry says, denouncing the "inventory thus *importing* / The several parcels of his plate, his treasure, / Rich stuffs, and ornaments of household" (3.2.108–9, 3.2.125–7, my emphasis). What kind of meaning is implied here by Henry's "importing," a word with which Shakespeare makes the list the vehicle both of a deduced meaning and of the material transfer of goods behind that meaning?

The list spells treachery because it is too personal, certainly, but also because, in the very way it signifies, a list given over to undigested "piles" of matter erases the very syntax that underwrites the orders and hierarchical relations that separate, say, a master and servant in the first place, or, more pertinently, allow a master to remain visible in his documents and delegates. Rather than only reflecting Wolsey's treachery, the list or inventory may be seen also as the textual genre that makes the treachery possible. It is Shakespeare's emblem for a documentary culture that, in Wolsey's hands, has formally misplaced the King in the textual substitutes it imagines for him.

A similar analysis of legal textuality is behind Queen Katherine's response to the law being used against her in the courtroom scene in act 2, scene 4. There, an exchange of formalities at the trial's opening works to thematize the relation of textual authority to the world of bodies and speech:

> SCRIBE (TO THE CRIER): Say, "Henry, King of England, come into the court."
> CRIER: Henry, King of England, &c.
> KING HENRY: Here.
> SCRIBE: Say, Katherine Queen of England, come into the court.
> CRIER: Katherine, Queen of England, &c.
> The Queen makes no answer, rises out of her chair, goes about the court, comes to the King, and kneels at his feet: then speaks. (2.4.6–10.3)[26]

In the formulaic repetitions that transform script into speech (so that speech can in turn be converted to record), the scene offers a brief analysis of the difference between text and non-text as sites for the real. Shakespeare takes the core of the exchange from Holinshed, but it is in the dynamic play between the scribe's language and the actor's body that the drama most powerfully represents both the law's need for a textualized reality and the ineradicable difference between that reality and the one it replaces. Metatheatrical pleasures aside, the scene is most impressive, first, for Katherine's silent refusal to enter the domain of writing that the Scribe instantiates and, second, for the movement on stage through which she registers an alternative presence to the one the law demands in the only apparently innocent "here" it solicits from her.[27] In her tongue's silence and her body's movement across the stage, Katherine may be understood to be teaching her husband something about the law his minister oversees. She suggests, namely, that, against the King's own deep interests, Wolsey's England has become a place in which the King must be absent in order to be real, or at least held at some distance from the legal words ("here") that, in this bureaucratized reality, now signify his presence.[28]

The play's most direct analysis of this textual gap that constitutes the new Tudor reality comes in its treatment of Wolsey's fall, just after the King gives Wolsey the paper evidence of his disloyalty and angrily leaves the room. Suffolk and Norfolk re-enter and, in the King's absence, command the Lord Chancellor, at "the King's pleasure," to render up the great seal that is the chief instrument of the King's documentary presence:

> WOLSEY: Stay –
> Where's your commission, lords? Words cannot carry
> Authority so weighty.
> SUFFOLK: Who dare cross 'em,
> Bearing the King's will from his mouth expressly? (3.2.233–6)

In a perceptive essay on the relation of historical and theatrical truth in the play, Anston Bosman points to the exchange as exemplary of the "competing truth claims of auditory versus scriptorial authority."[29] The testy exchange on the relative authority of spoken and written authority puts pressure not just on Suffolk and Norfolk's request, but on the very idea of legal writing as an instrument of royal power. Each side expresses a half-truth about what the King's authority means under a regime in which the King has also a documentary life. Wolsey appropriately asks for the sign of the authority capable of undoing the authority that has been delegated to him, conveniently forgetting that he holds the seal that would normally authorize that commission; Suffolk points out that writing, especially royal writing, is a substitute for the authority of oral utterance, conveniently forgetting that, well, he is not the King. In the absence of the King's asking for the seal himself, the conundrum is that neither of the King's two ways of being present can overpower the other. And the King himself cannot ask for the seal, since that would intolerably expose the gap between his royal presence and the instrument that, in *its* presence, constitutes it: the King must remain off stage in order both to remain himself and to make the seal mean what it means.

The play's representation of the bureaucratic self's alienation from itself is given further nuance in an extraordinary scene in which the now fallen Wolsey meets his servant Cromwell. To Wolsey's "Why how now,

Cromwell?" the stricken Cromwell replies, "I have no power to speak, sir" (3.2.373–4). This sentence takes on charged significance in light of the earlier exchange between Wolsey and Suffolk, since for a fluttering instance Cromwell's private grief as Wolsey's beloved servant takes the form precisely of the formal incapacity of a delegate who lacks the commission to speak on behalf of another: "I have no *power* to speak, sir." In one reading of the oral/written distinction over which Wolsey and Suffolk quarrel, writing depends on the speech for which it is always a substitute. According to the secretaries, however, and especially Cromwell's formula, Shakespeare offers a powerful "repudiation of a pristine orality" (Bosman's phrase), in favour of a speech that depends always on the writing that makes speech possible: on the play script, of course, but also the warrant that allows a sergeant to arrest someone (1.2.197.1–227), the commission that finds its force in its delivery, and, most generally, the written law that girds any expression of justice.[30] In his analysis of Tudor legal textuality, Shakespeare represents the phenomenon whereby the thing that had seemed authentic (speech, Cromwell's sincere grief, an ordinary material life beyond law) is revealed as already shaped to the textual reality that somehow replaced it.

Documenting Character in *Hamlet*

For my chief example of Shakespeare's interest in the legal text's substitutive intrusion upon the real, I want to turn at greater length to *Hamlet*, taking my cue from Alan Stewart's dramaturgical analysis of letters in the play and, especially, from Timothy Hampton's reading of the play in relation to early modern diplomacy.[31] Seeing Claudius as a modern monarch who, in contradistinction to his warrior brother, depends on negotiation and diplomacy to settle disputes and rule his kingdom, Hampton brilliantly places diplomatic letters and their bearers – Cornelius and Voltemand, Rosencrantz and Guildenstern – at the heart of the play's cultural-political argument, both as signs of a shift towards new forms of authority and governance and as a powerful backdrop for the play's representation of theatrical speech. The "sending outward ... of diplomatic representation and royal authority" is recalled, as Hampton says, "in the motif of theatrical representation," which similarly gets sent out into the world, this time to "catch the conscience of the diplomatically savvy king." On the one hand, theatre thus "emerges as the alternative to diplomacy"; on the other, diplomacy starts to look even more like theatre, as in the scene in which Hamlet, aboard the ship taking him to England and his death, rewrites his uncle's diplomatic letter:

> Being thus benetted round with villainies –
> Ere I could make a prologue to my brains,
> They had begun the play – I sat me down,
> Devised a new commission, wrote it fair. (5.2.30–3)

Hamlet's perverse diplomatic act is cast here, Hampton notes, as rewriting "someone else's [play] script" and in that way making the prince his own author.[32]

The documents that Hampton shows to be such critical actors in the play merit our further attention. There are two: the letter that Claudius sends to Norway in act 1, and the letter to England that Claudius prepares in act 3 and sends in act 4. Hampton points out that, whereas the first shows Claudius using diplomacy to "assert the unity of his state" against a potential external threat, the second shows him using foreign relations to deal with "the enemy within," this being a piece of statecraft that is equally "central to the project of state-building."[33] Hampton is certainly right here, but I think the twinned letters in the play depend as well on a difference in their executive and, ultimately, legal function. This difference, furthermore, is one that makes the play's diplomatic representations legible in terms not only of international law but of domestic law as well, specifically, the paper and parchment technologies supporting legal centralization.

The letter that Rosencrantz and Guildenstern are to deliver to England is purportedly a request for unpaid tribute, but in reality it contains, for that "faithful tributary" of Denmark, the "exact command" to behead the prince (5.2.40, 20).[34] This letter is repeatedly referred to as a *commission*, a word that operates as a synonym generally for command or order but also in a stricter sense that is powerfully relevant to the play's political and theatrical arguments. Carried to England by the two messengers, the commission is for that reason theirs – "I your commission will forthwith dispatch," Claudius tells them (3.3.3) – but more narrowly (and in light of the letter's true function) it is England's commission, since it is England that is asked, ordered, to carry out the King's business. In act 5, scene 2, when Hamlet gives Horatio the original letter as proof of the King's intention towards him and then tells the story of how he substituted for his companions' "grand commission" a "new commission" sending them to their deaths (5.2.19, 5.2.33),

Shakespeare presents the legal instrument under two aspects: as content (Claudius's and Hamlet's letters are both bearers of death) and as a material form. On the one hand, Claudius's letter is materially present on stage, in Hamlet's hand and then in Horatio's. On the other, Hamlet's letter is materialized in his description of those signs of authentication that disguise his forgery and, coextensively, make it the legal instrument it becomes when it is received as such:

> I had my father's signet in my purse,
> Which was the model of that Danish seal,
> Folded the writ up in the form of th'other,
> Subscribed it, gave't th'impression, placed it safely,
> The changeling never known. (5.2.50–4)

The legal instrument is presented here as matter, as a piece of writing whose meaning is the material form that facilitates the execution of a content. The interesting point is that, according to the scene's logic, Hamlet's forgery is not so much an accidental possibility besetting the state as it is the perfection of the state's material-textual routinization of justice.[35] Designed *in order* to be decoupled from its origin and in that way to carry the sovereign's will outwards (this is the function of legal letters), Hamlet's forged commission can be seen to be not just cleverly indistinguishable from its authentic companion, but in a deep sense identical with it. Just as the reproduction of kingship is constitutive of kingship (this is the problem, and promise, of the heir), so too the reproduction of authority is constitutive of authority (this is the problem, and promise, of the document).

What about the genre, and content, of the commission? Technically speaking, a commission at English law was an ad hoc grant of authority under the Great Seal. In John Cowell's definition from 1607, a commission is at common law "as much as (*delegatio*) with the Civilians, ... and is taken for the warrant or letters patents, that all men exercising iurisdiction ordinarie or extraordinarie haue for their power to heare or determine any cause or action."[36] As an instrument of judicial centralization, the commission expresses the centre's authority, but it does so by dispersing it, by using a subordinate authority in the sense of acknowledging it towards a given end and in that sense also controlling it. In *Hamlet*, Claudius's and Hamlet's letters assign to England a precise jurisdiction over particular bodies, as an expression of England's place in the machine of imperium and of its subordinate relation to the imperial centre.

Understood as a legal instrument granting England jurisdiction over a Danish matter, the commission stands in interesting tension with the play's first letter, which Claudius sends to Norway in act 1. This letter directs the old King to "suppress" his nephew, young Fortinbras (1.1.30), who, according to Horatio's prescient analysis, intends "by strong hand / And terms compulsative" to retake land that thirty years before passed to Denmark with old Hamlet's defeat of old Fortinbras and the latter's consequent forfeit "of all those his lands / Which he stood seized of to the conqueror" (1.1.101–2, 1.1.87–8).[37] Whatever lands are meant here – and the play simply does not make clear, as editors mostly want, that only Norway's personal lands are being referenced – this historic victory has placed Norway in a subordinate position to Denmark similar to England's. And it is that relationship, along with his hereditary lands, that young Fortinbras successfully challenges when he enters Denmark and asserts his "rights of memory" (5.2.343) over Hamlet's lands. The salient point is that, in the case of this letter, Claudius expresses his central authority, not by ceding jurisdiction, but rather by holding onto it: by asking, or ordering, one party, Norway, to direct another, Fortinbras, to do something; and, second, by emphasizing at length the jurisdictional limits of the messengers' delegated authority in relation to his own. Claudius says:

> we have here writ
> To Norway, uncle of young Fortinbras ...
> to suppress
> His further gait herein ...
> and we here dispatch
> You, good Cornelius, and you, Voltemand,
> For bearers of this greeting to old Norway,
> Giving to you no further personal power
> To business with the King, more than the scope
> Of these dilated articles allow. (1.2.27–39)[38]

If the English letter bodies forth Claudius's power in an instrument that assigns jurisdiction to a subordinate power, here Claudius embodies his power in a limited greeting, which functions as pure command that another complete a task on his behalf.

The best word for this kind of document is Claudius's own *writ*: "we have here writ / To Norway." Half-punningly, Claudius's verb activates "writ" as noun and thus the object of his writing. Like *commission*, *writ* is a generic term that also points in a more technical register to a particular legal instrument and so to a domestic form submerged in the international one. As the very cornerstone of the common law system and as the primary machine for judicial centralization, the legal writ (*breve* in Latin, *brief* in law French) was "a thin strip of parchment containing a letter in the name of the king, usually written in Latin, and sealed with the great seal."[39] The so-called original writs issued from Chancery, the judicial writs from one of the central courts; together the original and judicial writs shaped legal process as an elaborate exchange of letters. On behalf of the plaintiff who requested it, the original writ initiated the case in the King's name, by ordering a recipient, usually the sheriff, to do something; or more precisely by ordering that recipient to order a third person (the responding party) to do something (return goods, surrender land, appear in court, etc.). The first point of interest for the present argument is that this written command did not give jurisdiction by direct grant. Instead, the recipient was directed to execute it and then return the writ to King's Bench or to Common Pleas (the writ was for this reason said to be *returnable*), whereupon that court gained jurisdiction over the case, in the sense of being able now to send out judicial writs making further inquiries into the case.[40] And so the case went forward, step by step, to a writ of final process, whereby judgment was executed. The writ, then, is quite different from the commission. In the case of the writ, the King or court authorizes another to do something, but in such a way as firmly to hold judicial authority at the centre; formally speaking, the writ has a double character as a command and as returnable: it goes out in order to come back. This is in contradistinction to the commission, which, because it assigns a *power*, goes out, if all goes well, in order to stop there, enabling something at its jurisdictional destination.

This legal dynamic is suggestive for *Hamlet* because Claudius's writing to Norway closely follows both the form and itinerary of the English writ. Hampton perceptively notes that Voltemand's name etymologically invokes, through the pairing of *volvere* and *mandare*, "the sending and returning of orders" in the diplomatic sphere.[41] I would suggest that Shakespeare's passage layers onto that international context a domestic one; that even more than a diplomatic exchange Voltemand's name emblematizes, in its evocation of command and return, the legal writ as it operated in English common law. This play on writs is appropriate, of course, because the quarrel between Claudius and Fortinbras concerns the tenure of land, specifically those lands, in Horatio's formulation, of which old Fortinbras had once been "seized," *seisin* being the term, very particularly, for possession at English common law. In a curiously English lawsuit, Voltemand is a document, a writ or returnable command. We may note in this regard that some common law writs, including the so-called prerogative writs, contain "*mandamus*" as the King's word for "we command"; and also that when Claudius calls the letter his "greeting" to Norway (1.2.35), even that word has a specific resonance, since it is the term that begins all writs (which are, after all, letters): "The king to the sheriff of Nottinghamshire, greeting [*salutem*]."[42] Most pertinently, Claudius's letter shares the tripartite structure of the writ, as a monarch's command to a subordinate authority to command another to do something, this in order to redress some injustice: "The king to the sheriff of Middlesex greeting. Command A. that justly and without delay he render to B. the manor of N."[43]

If, through Voltemand, Claudius can thus be said to play plaintiff to Fortinbras's respondent in a common law suit, we may hear in that dynamic a final ripple in Shakespeare's domesticization of the international scene. In one sense, Claudius is insisting that Fortinbras is in the process of violating a historic and legal *right* that he, Claudius, has in the land won by his brother. In another, he is complaining against a *wrong* or *trespass* that Fortinbras is effecting or about to effect. Now, Fortinbras's name is original to the play and, of course, translates as "strong in arm" or, since the French *bras* is grammatically invariable, as "strength in arms" or "force in arms." In the common law context I am describing, this sounds like a multilingual joke on the "*vi et armis*" formula originally pertaining in writs of trespass.[44] The connection to trespass is relevant to the legal context of the play's quarrel since in Shakespeare's time one particular writ of trespass, the writ of ejectment, was overwhelmingly favoured as the means, at law, to try title to land.[45] The "*vi et armis*" formula included in that writ, as in writs of trespass generally, originally designated a given trespass as being the kind of wrong that required royal justice, the act having been done "by force and arms and against the king's peace": *vi et armis/by force and arms/fortinbras*. Just as Shakespeare invents a legal messenger whose name embodies the common law writ as a returnable command, so too he makes the personal object of the King's complaint into the very wrong being addressed.[46]

Why might Shakespeare be interested in these admittedly arcane legal jokes? The parchment technologies for extending royal authority – by commission, by writ, by conferring jurisdiction, by consolidating jurisdiction – are useful to Shakespeare, first, I think, as an analytical tool for conceptualizing the play's pre-eminent instance of a royal command, namely, the Ghost's double injunction to Hamlet: "If thou didst ever thy dear father love / ... Revenge his foul and most unnatural murder"; "Remember me" (1.5.23–5, 1.5.91). Famously, Hamlet responds to the injunction, in Jonathan Goldberg's formulation, by "receiv[ing] the Ghost's *words* as a scriptive command":[47]

> Yea, from the table of my memory
> I'll wipe away all trivial fond records,
> All saws of books, all forms, all pressures past,
> That youth and observation copied there,
> And thy commandment all alone shall live
> Within the book and volume of my brain
> Unmixed with baser matter. (1.5.98–104)

In an influential argument, Peter Stallybrass, Roger Chartier, and their collaborators have shown how Hamlet's desire to prepare in his memory a clean surface for the writing that now most matters to him implicates the technologies of erasable table books and of commonplacing.[48] I would suggest, further, that this moment of inscription and reinscription works in the play's overall argument to emblematize quite specifically the legal metamorphosis of *royal* utterance into royal writing. Hamlet's memorialization of his father's speech makes that speech into a letter like Claudius's letters, with the prince its sole recipient. In that sense, Hamlet's later concern with the authenticity of the command's origin – "The spirit that I have seen / May be the devil, ... / I'll have ground / More relative than this" (3.1.600–6) – analogizes the problem posed by the forged letter and the diplomatic letter as bearer of the sovereign will. Monarchs effect their ends in writing, but that means also that, removed from the command that coordinates their sovereignty, they come structurally to depend upon a process of authentication that they can only partly control. Is it because letters so constitute royal authority, I feel driven to ask, that Shakespeare has the dead King tell his son (well before the end of his speech), "methinks I scent the morning's air. / *Brief* let me be" (1.5.58–9, my emphasis)? In the play's documentary imaginings, I mean, is the King himself a dead letter?

Certainly, Hamlet's mental conversion of the Ghost's injunction into royal writing is shaped by the play's broader documentary plotting. For in light of the two letters that Claudius sends out as an expression of *his* power, we are licensed to ask whether, in so addressing his son, old Hamlet has issued something more in the manner of a writ or of a commission. That question seems especially pertinent because in the gap between the two kinds of letter there lies a curiously technical source for Hamlet's dilemma and for his delay in taking it upon himself to execute the King his father's will. A letter like the one to England would bestow jurisdiction upon him and orient him to judicial action; a letter like the one to Norway would make him more like a sheriff and orient him, not to that kind of action, but instead to the kind of forensic activity that he undertakes when he uses the play to inquire into Claudius's guilt. Understood as a royal letter, but ambivalently of one or another kind, the Ghost's injunction offers Hamlet two proximate but ultimately incompatible legal subjectivities, with the conflict between these generating the plot that then torments him. Reading forward to *All Is True*, and especially to Shakespeare's sense there that Cromwell's "power" to speak might be like the power bestowed through delegation, we might say that Hamlet delays in part because, lacking clarity as to the formal nature of the document delivered him, he is unable to secure his own agency vis-à-vis the King his father's will and in that way assume a power to act that, by its nature, is textually instituted.[49] If *Hamlet*'s dramatization of the prince's subjectivity remains for readers and audiences its most startling effect, it is surely salutary to note that this most "modern" of the play's achievements derives in part from its attention to the legal subjectivity pertaining to an agent who, addressed by law and pulled by text towards his or her action, discovers in that encounter simultaneously what it is to be textual and what to be real.[50]

At a second and more general level, then, Shakespeare's playful take on legal textuality directs us to the play's conception of textual life, including the kind of life that playwrights themselves market in. Characters in *Hamlet* resemble documents, I would argue, as a way to reflect on the ordinary but similarly mysterious phenomenon through which, at law, documents make persons.[51] At the beginning of act 5, *Hamlet* offers what is perhaps the paradigmatic instance of the legal substitutions that, as I have argued, subtend Shakespeare's analysis of legal documentation. Just before taking up Yorick's skull, Hamlet takes up another bony remainder and, supposing it to be a lawyer's, asks after the meaning of the writing that makes the law and is the law:

> There's another [skull]. Why might not that be the skull of a lawyer? Where be his quiddits now, his quillets, his cases, his tenures, and his tricks? ... H'm! This fellow might be in 's time a great buyer of land, with his statutes, his recognizances, his fines, his double vouchers, his recoveries ... Will his vouchers vouch him no more of his purchases, and double ones too, than the length and breadth of a pair of indentures? The very conveyances of his lands will scarcely lie in his box; and must th'inheritor himself have no more, ha! (5.1.95–109)

These documents, for securing mortgages and for conveying, recovering, and securing land, can all be said to be in the service of possession or, in Hamlet's plain saying, of *having*; and the joke is that what the ambitious lawyer now *has* is land just in the dimension of the two parts of the parchment indenture that had served his getting.[52] The parchment assigns, in a way quite other than intended, the land the possessor can really call his own, an irony that Hamlet emphasizes by juxtaposing the legal writing that transmits and secures the land with the matter literally underneath it: "Is not parchment made of sheepskins?" he asks, to which Horatio replies, "Ay, my lord, and of calf-skins too." "They are sheep and calves [i.e., fools] that seek out assurance in that," Hamlet says (5.1.111–14). This nice quibble is the first part of the scene's densest joke on the law, one that Shakespeare has split into two, withholding its full force across fifty or so lines. "That the body at death should cover the same acreage as a legal document is apt," Margreta de Grazia notes, since animal man has a skin, too.[53] "How long will a man lie I'th'earth ere he rot?" Hamlet asks the Clown later in the scene. Barring the pox, "some eight year," comes the reply, "or nine year. A tanner will last you nine year." And why the tanner, Hamlet asks. "Why sir, his hide is so tanned with his trade that a will keep out water a great while" (5.1.159–66).

So there we are. According to the Clown, it is skin that makes the man last as a man and the tanner as a tanner, skin that differentiates the human being and the human artisan from the other thing they are on their way to becoming. In his father's trade, Shakespeare thus finds an emblem not only for his perversely documentary mode of plotting and characterization, but more generally also for his own work in writing.[54] In the same way that a life might be remade in a record, or a stretch of land become the document organizing it, in the same way that a secretary's human speech might approximate the speech allowed him by the written authority to which he is subject, in the same way that

Voltemand may be a writ and Fortinbras an injury (and a dead king, even, his own brief), so here the human body is fully a textual body, this through a root continuity between the life forms that are served by the law and those that make the law what it is. At issue in Shakespeare's law, therefore, is not just the technical mastery that skilfully substitutes a textual real for a material one, but also, more fundamentally, an unregistered commonality among the world's surfaces. In size, in substance, the real and the textual fuse. That is a tempting thought for the craftsman who makes persons from pen and paper, even if, of course, it also carries a dark warning. In spite of the conjuring trick that the law is, and that textuality is, the skins we variously learn to trust do fall away. In *Hamlet*'s telling, however, that dark sentiment about legal forms and life forms is not entirely without hope. What stays behind, all we have seen, at least for a while, are the bones, which leads me to ask if there may be in bones, not skin, the hint of a new justice. In a play where action occurs under the sign of the writ or commission that makes action possible, and where the technical appropriation of the real seems to make law's promise and its deceptions indistinguishable, this justice on the far side of the document or skin may be construed as a poetic justice, a made justice coextensive with the interpretive work – which Hamlet's graveside suppositions and wordplay themselves instantiate – that makes the hard things in the body, the resistant bits in the text, animate again.

NOTES

This essay was written with the assistance of a National Endowment for the Humanities research fellowship at the Folger Shakespeare Library. For their insights and suggestions, I am grateful to Kathy Eden, Barbara Mowat, Stephen Orgel, Georgianna Ziegler, and to Donald Beecher, Travis DeCook, Andrew Wallace, and Grant Williams and the participants in their conference on justice at Carleton University in June 2010.

1 William Shakespeare, *The First Quarto of King Richard III*. Unless otherwise noted, citations to Shakespeare's plays are to William Shakespeare, *The Complete Works*, and appear in the text.

2 On the life of props on the early modern stage, see Frances Teague, *Shakespeare's Speaking Properties*; Andrew Sofer, *The Stage Life of Props*; Jonathan Gil Harris and Natasha Korda, eds, *Staged Properties in Early Modern English Drama*. On scrolls or paper as props, especially in relation to the

circulation, reading, and printing of their content, see Tiffany Stern, *Documents of Performance in Early Modern England*, pp. 174–200.

3 Buckingham tantalizingly refers to the two bishops as "Two props of virtue for a Christian prince" (3.7.96), that is, as Richard's moral stays. Since the contraction of theatrical property to prop is not recorded until the nineteenth century, we cannot say that the pun that seems so evident to us was operative. I would suggest that this use of "prop" is, however, at very least an instance of Shakespeare's linguistic invention, his way of bringing words in contact with one another to supercharge their meanings. *Properties* was the usual term for stage objects, and in Buckingham's plan the point is that the clergymen are indistinguishable in function from the book that is manifestly stage property, both in Shakespeare's theatre and in Richard's: "And look you get a prayer book in your hand, / And stand between two churchmen, good my lord" (3.7.47–8). It is to the point here that earlier Richard has said of Hastings that, in trusting his counsel, he "Made him my book" (3.5.26). Persons can be books and to that extent, perhaps, properties. The bishops support the prince by being the kind of support, and stage prop[erty], the book is.

4 John Jowett, ed., *The Tragedy of King Richard III*, p. 266.

5 Edward Hall, *The Pitifull Life of Kyng Edward the V*, in *The Union of the Two Noble and Illustrate Famelies*, fol. xvir. The passage is printed in Shakespeare, *King Richard III*, ed. Antony Hammond, Appendix III, p. 354. On Shakespeare's debt to More, see Hammond's introduction, pp. 74–80.

6 Jowett accurately notes that the indictment must be a "document accusing Hastings to explain why he has been executed" and not, "as the term might suggest, the basis for a trial" (p. 266), but he does not further explore the gap between Shakespeare's meaning and the normative one.

7 Samuel Johnson, ed., *The Plays of William Shakespeare*, vol. 2, pp. 288–9.

8 On the preposterous, see Patricia Parker, "Hysteron Proteron," pp. 133–45.

9 Tim Stretton, "Conditional Promises and Legal Instruments in *The Merchant of Venice*," pp. 71–99 in this volume.

10 For the intimate relation between early modern law, especially contract, and the "history of poetics" in the sense of a "productive capacity ... to create new artifacts," see Victoria Kahn, *Wayward Contracts*, p. 15.

11 On the history of the Tripartite Indenture, see R.R. Davies, *The Revolt of Owain Glyn Dwr*, pp. 166–9. On Shakespeare's Glendower, see David J. Baker, "Glyn Dwr, Glendouer, Glendourdy, and Glendower," pp. 43–57.

12 Raphael Holinshed, *The Chronicles of England, Scotlande, and Irelande*, p. 521. The relevant passages are given in Shakespeare, *The First Part of King Henry IV*, ed. A.R. Humphreys, Appendix III, pp. 170–1.

13 William West, *The First Part of Simbolegraphy*, sig. B5v. Note that "Interchangeably" translates the Latin *alternatim*, for an example of which see West, sig. B6r.

14 Folger Shakespeare Library manuscript Z.c.22 (p. 45). This is reproduced in Heather Wolfe, ed., *"The Pen's Excellencie,"* pp. 73–4.

15 On Hotspur's plans for the River Trent in relation to the work of Aconcio of Trent, an Italian engineer who in the mid-century was known for land salvage, see William Jones, "The Turning of Trent in *I Henry IV*."

16 Garrett A. Sullivan, Jr, *The Drama of Landscape*, p. 94. See also David Read, who interestingly notes that the conspirators' insistence that they "see" the river on the map makes it possible for them to take a "schematic rendering" as "irrefutable evidence of the river's winding" ("Topographical Understanding," p. 479).

17 John Gillies, *Shakespeare and the Geography of Difference*, p. 47.

18 See West, *The First Part of Simbolegraphy*, sig. B6r: "These deeds indented … may be made tripartite, that is of three parts, or quadrupartite, quinquepartite, or of as many parts as shall be needfull." Note, however, that in early modern England, a tripartite indenture usually involved only two parties, with the third copy of the agreement to be retained by the court. It is possible that this convention that makes the court a record holder also informs the play. In changing the site of the rebels' meeting from the house of the Archbishop of Bangor (as given in Holinshed, p. 521, who notes further that the rebels were represented their by deputy) to Glendower's castle, Shakespeare creates an inequality among the parties. Hotspur makes clear that he cannot leave Wales until, with the sealing of the indenture, he can take his copy of the agreement with him. Glendower, presumably, retains his at home. Is there a sense, then, in which, with respect to the all-powerful tripartite indenture, Glendower is structurally occupying the position of party and court, and that it is this status that makes Hotspur so eager to challenge his primacy? (For an illustrated example of a tripartite indenture whose third part or "foot" (it met, horizontally, each of the other two parts of the indenture) has been retained by the court, see Wolfe, ed., *"The Pen's Excellencie,"* pp. 68–70.

19 Phyllis Rackin, "Anachronism and Nostalgia," in *Stages of History*, p. 101.

20 On the emergence of authority as a textual effect, see also Robert Weimann, *Authority and Representation*.

21 Michel Foucault, "Of Other Spaces," p. 27.

22 On the function generally of the Lord Chancellor, see J.H. Baker, *Introduction to English Legal History*, pp. 114–21. The most prominent document in *All is True* is the royal commission, which operates as the sign of the King's

bureaucratized power and, more narrowly, of Wolsey's authority as a delegate who is out of control (e.g., 1.2.21; 2.2.6; 3.2.321).

23 In making the wayward inventory cause of Wolsey's fall, Shakespeare and Fletcher draw on a different moment in Holinshed involving Thomas Ruthall, Bishop of Durham. See Holinshed, *The Chronicles of England*, p. 796; and Jay Halio, "Introduction," *Henry VIII*, p. 16.

24 Note that this tension between public and personal administrative levels is repeated in the structure that sees Buckingham fall when the King's chancellor turns the lord's chancellor (as well as his surveyor) against him (2.1.20–4).

25 Cornelia Vissman, *Files: Law and Media Technology*, p. 6.

26 I have restored F's "&c" here, which the Oxford edition expands to "come into this court." That written symbol sits interestingly at the limit between speech and writing, signifying speech that cannot, however, be understood except via the sign as writing rather than speech.

27 The divorce court is not Henry's, of course, but it is Wolsey's. Since Shakespeare follows Holinshed in having Campeius [Cardinal Campeggio] present from Rome the "commission" naming himself and Wolsey as judges in the matter of the divorce (2.2.104), it is worth asking what it means for commissions with different origins to operate within a single space. At the beginning of the trial scene, Shakespeare varies from Holinshed, who notes that the commission was read aloud, in having Henry request that the commission from Rome not be read, since "on all sides th'authority [is] allowed' (2.4.1). As Gordon McMullan notes in his edition of *King Henry VIII*, this change works dramatically to avoid a "tedious recital of the commission," but surely the point is that Shakespeare, his ear attuned to what a commission is, has also found a way to prefigure the jurisdictional dispute with Rome that the play all but leaves out.

28 For this process of so displacing the King in the realm of Tudor legal writing, see Jonathan Goldberg, *Writing Matter*, who notes that, with the invention of the dry stamp, which enabled the facsimile reproduction of the King's signature, "the sign manual [becomes] the manipulable signature placed into the secretary's hand in an act of deauthenticating authentication that allows the circulation of power always to be in another hand" (p. 264). On the rise of the sign manual in relation to household governance, see David Starkey, "Court and Government," pp. 46–55.

29 Anston Bosman, "Seeing Tears," p. 464. Reading Wolsey's fall as emblematic of the decline of the seal's importance relative to the sign manual, Bosman locates Wolsey's authority in orality, seeing him here as only

gradually ceding the authority of speech, as figured by the seal, to that of script, as figured in the "hand." I am not quite convinced by this reading of the scene, since to my mind it effectively reverses the logic of an exchange that pitches Wolsey's documentary formalism against the others' naive realism.

30 Bosman, "Seeing Tears," p. 465.

31 Alan Stewart, *Shakespeare's Letters*, esp. chapters 6–7; Timothy Hampton, *Fictions of Embassy*, pp. 138–62.

32 Hampton, *Fictions of Embassy*, p. 149, p. 156.

33 Hampton, *Fictions of Embassy*, p. 146, p. 152.

34 Stewart, *Shakespeare's Letters*, pp. 262–3, perceptively relates Claudius's deceitful letter to the Bellerophon Letter from the *Iliad*.

35 On Hamlet's forgery in relation to technologies of memory and erasure, see Stewart, "Rewriting Hamlet," chapter 7 in *Shakespeare's Letters*, pp. 261–94.

36 John Cowell, *The Interpreter*, Q4v.

37 I vary here from the Oxford text, substituting Q1's "seized of" for F's "seized on."

38 I vary from the Oxford text, substituting F's spelling of Voltemand (F also uses Voltumand) for Q2's Valtemand.

39 Baker, *Introduction to English Legal History*, p. 67

40 For the range of writs, see Baker, *Introduction to English Legal History*, pp. 63–79.

41 Hampton, *Fictions of Embassy*, 148. Hampton similarly relates Cornelius to the gemstone carnelian, which was used for making signet rings.

42 A Praecipe writ, as cited in Baker, *Introduction to English Legal History*, p. 615.

43 A writ of Formedon in the descender, as cited in Baker, *Introduction to English Legal History*, p. 615.

44 On writs of trespass, see Baker, *Introduction to English Legal History*, pp. 71–5.

45 On ejectment as a way to try comnon law title, see Baker, *Introduction to English Legal History*, pp. 341–3.

46 I would note that the play may be imagining Fortinbras's territorial incursions into Denmark also as a kind of entry (*ingressus*). In that reading, he and Claudius could be read as plaintiff and respondent in an assize of novel disseisin.

47 Jonathan Goldberg, "Hamlet's Hand," p. 311.

48 Peter Stallybrass et al., "Hamlet's Tables." See also H.R. Woudhuysen, "Writing-Tables."

49 On the critical history of Hamlet's delay in relation to character and plot, see Margreta de Grazia, *"Hamlet" without Hamlet*, esp. pp. 158–75.

50 The legal roots of Hamlet's modernity are theorized with great acuity by de Grazia in her discussion of land and property in relation to Hamlet's more general dispossessions. See *"Hamlet" without Hamlet*, ch. 5. For a dazzling account of how changes in the forensic plot generated mimetic depth on stage, quintessentially in Shakespeare, see Lorna Hutson, *The Invention of Suspicion*.

51 On the relation between literary character and social, including legal, personhood, see Elizabeth Fowler, *Literary Character*.

52 As a technological form and format, indentures of course could vary in size, from very small to very large. The pair of indentures in Hamlet suggests the largest and most impressive instruments associated with the sale of property. For example, the indenture for the Bargain and Sale for Shakespeare's purchase of the Blackfriar's Gatehouse in 1613 measures 482 by 600 mm; the indenture for the Bargain and Sale for James Burbage's purchase of seven rooms at Blackfriars in 1596 measures 660 by 745 mm. Doubled along the indentured axis, these make for "plots," respectively, of 894 by 600 mm and 1320 by 745 mm. For the relevant images, see Wolfe, ed., *"The Pen's Excellencie,"* p. 73, p. 79.

53 De Grazia, *"Hamlet" without Hamlet*, p. 146.

54 On Shakespeare's theatricalization of his father's trade, see Anston Bosman, "Shakespeare in Leather."

BIBLIOGRAPHY

Baker, David J. "Glyn Dwr, Glendouer, Glendourdy, and Glendower." In *Shakespeare and Wales: From the Marches to the Assembly*. Ed. Willy Maley and Philip Schwyzer. Farnham, UK: Ashgate, 2010. 43–57.

Baker, J.H. *An Introduction to English Legal History*. 3rd ed. London: Butterworths, 1990. 114–21.

Bosman, Anston. "Seeing Tears: Truth and Sense in *All is True*." *Shakespeare Quarterly* 50, no. 4 (1999): 459–76.

– "Shakespeare in Leather." In *The Forms of Renaissance Thought: New Essays in Literature and Culture*. Ed. Leonard Barkan, Bradin Cormack, and Sean Keilen. London: Palgrave, 2010. 225–45.

Cowell, John. *The Interpreter*. Cambridge, 1607.

Davies, R.R. *The Revolt of Owain Glyn Dwr*. Oxford: Oxford UP, 1995.

de Grazia, Margreta. *"Hamlet" without Hamlet*. Cambridge: Cambridge UP, 2007.

Foucault, Michel. "Of Other Spaces." Trans. Jay Miskowiec. *Diacritics* 16, no. 1 (1986): 27.

Fowler, Elizabeth. *Literary Character: The Human Figure in Early English Writing*. Ithaca, NY: Cornell UP, 2003.

Gillies, John. *Shakespeare and the Geography of Difference*. Cambridge: Cambridge UP, 1994.

Goldberg, Jonathan. "Hamlet's Hand." *Shakespeare Quarterly* 39, no. 4 (1988): 307–27.

– *Writing Matter: From the Hands of the English Renaissance*. Stanford, CA: Stanford UP, 1990.

Hall, Edward. *The Pitifull Life of Kyng Edward the V. The Union of the Two Noble and Illustrate Famelies of Lancastre and York*. London, 1548.

Hampton, Timothy. *Fictions of Embassy: Literature and Diplomacy in Early Modern Europe*. Ithaca, NY: Cornell UP, 2009.

Harris, Jonathan Gil, and Natasha Korda, eds. *Staged Properties in Early Modern English Drama*. Cambridge: Cambridge UP, 2000.

Holinshed, Raphael. *The Chronicles of England, Scotlande, and Irelande*. 2nd ed. London, 1587.

Hutson, Lorna. *The Invention of Suspicion: Law and Mimesis in Shakespeare and Renaissance Drama*. Oxford: Oxford UP, 2007.

Johnson, Samuel, ed. *The Plays of William Shakespeare*. London, 1765.

Jones, William. "The Turning of Trent in *I Henry IV*." *Renaissance News* 17, no. 4 (1964): 304–7.

Kahn, Victoria. *Wayward Contracts: The Crisis of Political Obligation in England, 1640–1674*. Princeton, NJ: Princeton UP, 2004.

McMullan, Gordon, ed. *King Henry VIII*. Arden Shakespeare 3rd Series. London: Thomson Learning, 2000.

Parker, Patricia. "Hysteron Proteron: or the Preposterous." In *Renaissance Figures of Speech*. Ed. Sylvia Adamson, Gavin Alexander, and Katrin Ettenhuber. Cambridge: Cambridge UP, 2007. 133–45.

Rackin, Phyllis. *Stages of History: Shakespeare's English Chronicles*. Ithaca, NY: Cornell UP, 1990.

Read, David. "Topographical Understanding in the 'Henriad.'" *Modern Philology* 94, no. 4 (1997): 475–95.

Shakespeare, William. *The Complete Works*. Ed. Stanley Wells and Gary Taylor. 2nd ed. Oxford: Clarendon, 2005.

– *The First Part of King Henry IV*. Ed. A.R. Humphreys. Arden Edition 2nd series. London: Methuen, 1960.

– *The First Quarto of King Richard III*. Ed. Peter Davison. New Cambridge Shakespeare Early Quartos. Cambridge: Cambridge UP, 1996.

– *Henry VIII: The Oxford Shakespeare*. Ed. Jay Halio. Oxford: Oxford UP, 1999.

– *King Richard III*. Ed. Antony Hammond. Arden Edition 2nd series. London: Methuen, 1981.

– *The Tragedy of King Richard III*. Ed. John Jowett. Oxford: Oxford UP, 2000.

Sofer, Andrew. *The Stage Life of Props*. Ann Arbor: U of Michigan P, 2003.

Stallybrass, Peter, et al. "Hamlet's Tables and the Technologies of Writing in Renaissance England." *Shakespeare Quarterly* 55, no. 4 (2004): 379–419.

Starkey, David. "Court and Government." In *Revolution Reassessed: Revisions in the History of Tudor Government and Administration*. Ed. Christopher Coleman and David Starkey. Oxford: Clarendon, 1986. 29–58.

Stern, Tiffany. "Scrolls." In *Documents of Performance in Early Modern England*. Cambridge: Cambridge UP, 2009. 174–200.

Stewart, Alan. *Shakespeare's Letters*. Oxford: Oxford UP, 2008.

Sullivan, Garrett A., Jr. *The Drama of Landscape: Land, Property, and Social Relations on the Early Modern Stage*. Stanford, CA: Stanford UP, 1998.

Teague, Frances. *Shakespeare's Speaking Properties*. Lewisburg, PA: Bucknell UP, 1991.

Vissman, Cornelia. *Files: Law and Media Technology*. Trans. Geoffrey Winthrop-Young. Stanford, CA: Stanford UP, 2008.

Weimann, Robert. *Authority and Representation in Early Modern Discourse*. Ed. David Hillman. Baltimore: Johns Hopkins UP, 1996.

West, William. *The First Part of Simbolegraphy*. London, 1603.

Wolfe, Heather, ed. *"The Pen's Excellencie": Treasures from the Manuscript Collection of the Folger Shakespeare Library*. Washington, DC: Folger Shakespeare Library, 2002.

Woudhuysen, H.R. "Writing-Tables and Table Books." *electronic British Library Journal* (2004): article 3.

3 Conditional Promises and Legal Instruments in *The Merchant of Venice*

TIM STRETTON

But indeed, words are very rascals, since bonds disgraced them.
Feste the Clown, *Twelfth Night* (3.1.18–19)[1]

Promises pervade *The Merchant of Venice*, sometimes to the point of comic absurdity. Throughout the play, characters keep, seek to enforce, or break a variety of oaths, vows, and obligations they have made to others or to themselves, a process that strengthens, strains, or ruptures an array of different bonds – personal, familial, financial, and religious.[2] Scholars seeking unities behind these disparate promises and their consequences used to invoke a familiar series of binary oppositions: Christian sacrifice versus economic self interest, charity versus usury, unconditional love versus self-love, frugality versus prodigality, the noble values of Belmont versus the mercantile greed of Venice, and so on. Others have highlighted oppositions arising from contemporary legal developments, pitting common law courts against equity courts, and customary bargaining against newer forms of contractual thinking associated with the common law action of *assumpsit* debated in *Slade's case* (1597–1602).[3]

Each of these pairings provides significant insights into the structure and themes of the play and its characters' motivations, but each is undone by niggling inconsistencies.[4] In the early stages of the trial scene, for example, Portia appears to represent mercy against Shylock's legalism, embodying a New Testament emphasis on forgiveness to his Old Testament demand for vengeance. Yet, for all her talk of mercy, Portia does not attempt to dispense it, and as the scene unfolds her reliance on strict legalism exceeds Shylock's. The rigour of her uncompromising commitment to the keeping of promises is brought home in the final act of the play, where she holds Bassanio to account for having broken his vow never to part with her ring.[5] These same aspects of Portia's behaviour, along with her partiality, also preclude a simple alignment of her character with equity and Shylock's with the common law. Furthermore, a growing number of scholars now argue that the equity dispensed in the Court of Chancery, which served to mitigate the harsh effects of strict applications of common law, does not feature anywhere in the play (except perhaps in its absence).[6] Other binaries prove equally problematic under scrutiny, and it is a mark of Shakespeare's artistic vision that the play's apparent incoherence over the status of promises defies neat categorizations or reductive allegorical readings.[7]

In this chapter I want to suggest that this incoherence is deliberate and brings into relief an unresolved debate about promises, obligations, and law that was raging in Elizabethan society at the time of the play's composition and first performance. That debate found perhaps its shrillest voice in litigant complaints about the misuse of parchment and paper bonds that survive in the records of Chancery, the Court of Requests, and the Equity side of Exchequer, with the result that English equity and its jurisdictions are indeed relevant to understanding how audiences received *The Merchant*, even though the play never explicitly refers to them. Investigating the nature of these disagreements not only confirms and illuminates the topicality of the bond plot of act 4 and the ring plot of act 5, but also helps explain the intriguing parallels between them. Yet, while *The Merchant* holds up the role of law courts and of particular legal instruments to scrutiny, ultimately it shifts our attention to the personal responsibility involved in making and keeping promises and in deciding how to respond when they are broken. Shakespeare emphasizes that solutions to the dilemma of promise keeping cannot come simply from without, through bonds or symbolic tokens such as rings, but ultimately must come from within, through individual integrity and compassion. Our focus, I want to suggest, should centre on litigants rather than on laws.

Expressions of anxiety about the perceived reluctance of English men and women to keep their word rose appreciably in the sixteenth century. Some commentators worried that upheavals in religion were undermining personal promises as well as religious vows and oaths. John Christopherson noted in 1554 that "when fayth toward god was in manner utterly abolished fayth toward man was banished therwith," while the puritan divine William Perkins reflected in 1596 that "It is an hard thing to find a man that will stand to his word and lawfull promise."[8] The techniques of casuistry and dissimulation practised by Jesuit priests and church papists added further weight to apprehensions about whether or not a person's word could be trusted.[9] In the secular world, prosecutions for perjury – which was made a statutory offence in 1563 – were rising and the common law practice of compurgation, or wager of law, was rapidly falling out of favour.[10] This defence, in which debtors could escape liability for their debts if they could find twelve acquaintances willing to swear that their oaths were trustworthy, was being corrupted by the cynical employment of professional oath-takers.[11] In the words of the influential legal authority Edward Coke, "experience now proves that men's consciences grow so large that the respect of their private advantage rather induces men to perjury."[12]

In society, as in the play, one response to the perceived problem of deceit and broken promises was a dramatic rise in the use of bonds or "bands," as well as "bills obligatory," deeds, indentures, and other written instruments under seal. As an epigram on avarice reflected,

> The faithfull Abr'am for his Heritage
> Did rest content with promise of a Land:
> Whereto the faithless Bastards of our Age,
> Words nought availe without performance Band.[13]

In the 1570s Edward Bicknoll employed a familiar proverb when he reported how "the lawyer teacheth us this lesson, to trust few or none upon their words, words are but wind, bind every man's bargain sure by writing."[14] Thousands upon thousands of English men and women now secured their debts and other obligations with bonds, sharing the pragmatism of Demetrius in *A Midsummer Night's Dream* when he spurns Lysander's assurance that "I will keep my word with thee" by saying "I would I had your bond, for I perceive / A weak bond holds you; I'll not trust your word' (3.2.267–9). Bonds could be used for an astonishing array of purposes and, because they were under seal, constituted powerful evidence in the event of a dispute, but they were relatively expensive, and therefore usually reserved for weightier matters. Their use in late Elizabethan England was unprecedented, yet it was dwarfed by an even larger growth in oral promises marked by public rituals and exchanges of tokens.[15] The English were making oral *and* written promises in record numbers.

In the 1580s and 1590s disputes over these obligations drove the most dramatic litigation boom in English history. One speculative estimate suggests that English and Welsh courts were hearing over one million civil suits a year by 1588, most of them concerning debt, which accounted for around 90 per cent of actions nationally and 60–70 per cent of actions in the central common law courts.[16] In local courts actions on oral promises predominated, reflecting the greater flexibility demanded by individuals engaged in small-scale private bargaining in a rapidly expanding economy. Of the debt actions dominating litigation in the central common law courts of Queen's Bench and Common Pleas, however, 90 per cent involved written instruments. Most of these were conditional bonds of the same general form as Shylock's, in which one party agreed to pay another party a stated sum of money – the penalty – unless they met a specified condition by a certain date. In terms of total numbers, suits over bonds and other legal instruments increased by over 500 per cent between 1560 and 1606.[17]

At the time Shakespeare penned *The Merchant* the country was awash with lawsuits, the vast majority of which centred on allegations of broken promises or hard dealing. In the central courts thousands of creditors were putting bonds in suit at common law to claim agreed penalties, and thousands of debtors and sureties were bringing counter suits in equity courts, claiming that the common law actions against them were unconscionable or even fraudulent. Like Shylock and Antonio, many creditors were also debtors, and the messy implosion of the credit system, based as it was on increasingly complex chains of largely non-transferable loans, raised the spectre of a crisis of trust and a crisis of credit in both senses of the word – the lending of money and personal worth and trustworthiness – that provide an obvious context for the play's legal themes. It is worth observing in this context that *The Merchant* does not simply set a moneylender against a debtor, but instead brings into its frame a moneylender (Shylock), a debtor (Bassanio), a debtor's surety (Antonio), and a supplier of capital (Tubal), reflecting the everyday intricacies of myriad agreements transacted in late Elizabethan England.

The astonishing ubiquity of bonds prompted Shakespeare to include them in a number of his plays and sonnets, often in the form of metaphors.[18] In act 1 of *The Merchant*, Portia describes how her Scottish suitor "borrowed a box of the ear of the Englishman and swore he would pay him again when he was able. I think the Frenchman became his surety, and sealed under for another" (1.2.66–9), an employment of the language of debt, credit, sureties, and bonds that foreshadows the economic entanglements about to connect Bassanio, Shylock, and Antonio. In act 2, Salarino remarks that Venus's pigeons fly faster "To seal love's bonds new made than they are wont / To keep obligèd faith unforfeited!" (2.6.6–7), providing a similar amplification of the play's focus on conditional bonds and forfeitures.

The dramatic expansion of debt-related and other litigation (and of the legal profession) spawned a growing cynicism about legal instruments and opportunistic lawsuits for private gain. Writing in 1593, the Puritan Phillip Stubbes looked back to a simpler age when lawyers "studyed not to coyne quirkes & quiddities, nor to hammer clauses, and provisoes to circumvent and deceyue one another," lamenting that "A man's bare word or naked promise then, was better than any bands, bills, or writings now." By contrast, "Now adays we must have, if not, so many skinnes of parchment, yet so many lynes as they had wordes, and a great sort moe, and yet all will not serve neyther, but mayster Lawyer (forsooth) will finde you a hundred holes in it."[19] Lawyers themselves made related complaints on behalf of their clients, and the adversarial pleadings from surviving common law and equity cases can be read as a vibrant and often acrimonious public debate about the best means for enforcing promises – whether they were written or spoken, sworn or unsworn – as well as the circumstances in which individual litigants and officials felt that strict law should be mitigated, not by mercy, but by equity.

In the contest between what might be characterized as the objectivity of common law (which looked to the cause) and the subjectivity of equity (which looked to the person), debtors and sureties railed at the unfairness of strict bonds and excessive penalties, while creditors lauded the certainty that bonds could bring and accused their defaulting opponents of sour grapes or of making up stories after the event. Rather than pick sides in this debate, Shakespeare exposes the problems inherent in each of these approaches.[20] Again and again the play demonstrates how the form of promises can shape or even transform them in important ways, but that no particular form can guarantee that a promise is kept. In Elizabethan England, an increasingly common solution to this familiar dilemma was to make one promise conditional upon another, yet as the play reveals, this approach brings its own perils if individuals allow conditions to eclipse or subvert the promises they are intended to secure.[21]

To begin with written promises or obligations, in act 1 of *The Merchant* Antonio's and Shylock's negotiations over their loan agreement are couched in the language of speaking and hearing. Shylock says, "May I speak with Antonio?" (1.3.26) and a few lines later Bassanio asks, "Shylock, do you hear?" (1.3.47). Further into the scene Shylock says, "You come to me, and you say, / 'Shylock, we would have moneys' – you say so" (1.3.111–12), followed by "What should I say to you? Should I not say / 'Hath a dog money?'" (1.3.116–17), before accusing Antonio of being deaf to his kind offer: "you'll not hear me" (1.3.136). In act 3, however, once Shylock realizes that Antonio has defaulted, his language shifts abruptly, dismissing speech and hearing in favour of sight and privileging written words and agreements over spoken words and oral promises. He repeats three times in as many lines that Antonio should "look to his bond" (3.1.39–42). In response to Antonio's plea, "Hear me yet, good Shylock," he responds, "I'll have my bond. Speak not against my bond. / I have sworn an oath that I will have my bond" (3.3.3–5). Antonio pleads again, "I pray thee hear me speak," and again Shylock refuses him: "I'll have my bond; I will not hear thee speak: / I'll have my bond, and therefore speak no more" (3.3.11–13 and see 3.3.17). In act 4 he says to Graziano, "Till thou canst rail the seal from off my bond / Thou but offend'st thy lungs to speak so loud" (4.1.138–9), before swearing to Portia, "There is no power in the tongue of man / To alter me. I stay here on my bond" (4.1.236–7), oblivious, it seems, to the power in the tongue of a woman that will be his undoing.

Free-flowing talk created the men's agreement, but writing it down has frozen it, the dry ink of a conditional bond abruptly cutting short the easy, if tense, banter of their negotiations. In English law, as in the law of Shakespeare's Venice, the written bond took precedence over the spoken promise, because it provided a more reliable proof of what it asserted, a hierarchy of reliability reinforced in the play's treatment of written and spoken communication more generally. When Bassanio wins Portia's hand in the casket game he tells her that he stands "As doubtful whether what I see be true / Until confirmed, signed, ratified by you" (3.2.147–8).[22] In another example, it is a letter that confirms that Antonio's heavily laden argosies have arrived safely in port, after the "news on the Rialto," the "gossip Report," and the "good news ... heard in Genoa" all alleged they had sunk (3.1.1, 3.1.6, 3.1.88–9). Shylock's transformation, from a moneylender open to negotiating with

Antonio into a closed-eared creditor anxious for his pound of flesh, is driven by his desire for vengeance, having sworn to his countrymen even before his daughter Jessica's elopement "That he would rather have Antonio's flesh / Than twenty times the value of the sum / That he did owe him" (3.2.285–7 and see 1.3.41–2). However, the change is also a product of the ability of writing to transform promises, both in general ways and in ways specific to conditional bonds in England at the time of the play's composition.

First of all, Shylock's language makes it clear that in his mind the bond does not merely symbolize the agreement; it constitutes it. He does not say to Antonio, "remember our agreement"; he says, "look to your bond," thinking of the parchment itself.[23] Without the actual bond no common law debt suit was possible, and if the seal had come off, whether deliberately or by accident, the law considered it cancelled. Portia confirms this when she asks Shylock to "Take thrice thy money. Bid me tear the bond" (4.1.229 and see 3.2.298). The character Susanna discovers this fact to her cost in George Chapman's *Two Wise Men and all the Rest Fooles* (1619) when she tries to get the usurer Antonio to honour his sealed bill promising payment of £10 to her kinsman. Antonio declares, "If it be mine I will discharge it," but when she hands it to him he rips off the seal and says, "I owe him nothing, nor will pay thee any thing," adding for good measure, "Be gone; Thy tongue is left thee to raile at large, but thy meanes be short to revenge thy selfe by law."[24] At this time bonds and other forms of legal "specialty" had no intrinsic value at common law, for example, if they were stolen.[25] The tension between the value of a document and the value of what it represented (and the harm it could cause) is apparent in Thomas Kyd's *The Spanish Tragedy* (1592), when Hieronymo "rents and tears" the legal documents of three suitors, as he would rend and tear those who murdered his son, and seems puzzled at the men's incredulous responses, saying to one, "I gave it never a wound, / Shew me one drop of bloud fall from the same."[26]

Second, Shylock is evoking legal procedure concerning bonds. As a sealed legal instrument, a bond put in suit at common law could not normally be answered with oral testimony, only with the same or another legal instrument.[27] Testimony relating to whether a condition had been met could be presented, but dispute over the agreement itself or excuses or justifications for failing to perform conditions were inadmissible, even in instances of fraud; for example, "if the writer deceive a man in the making or dating of a bond, without the lenders privitie, his mony is lost although he had no such meaning" (although victims of this particular kind of sharp practice could plead *non est factum suum,* "this is not my deed").[28] In the words of Christopher Saint German in *Doctor and Student,* "as the defendant is charged by a sufficient writing ... so he must be discharged by sufficient writing."[29] In the case of conditional bonds sufficient writing meant an acquittance proving that the bond had been satisfied – if the bond was not proof itself, through being torn or defaced or lacking a seal. If, as in Antonio's case, the bond had not been satisfied, then the penalty was due and there was literally no possibility of speaking or having a court of common law hear any arguments or excuses.

Third, conditional bonds of the type depicted in the play effectively substituted one promise for another. If drawn up in England, Antonio's bond would have read as follows (and almost certainly in Latin): "Know all men that I, Antonio, am firmly bound to Shylock to have him cut off an equal pound of my fair flesh taken from nearest my heart three months from today." That was the legally binding agreement the two men made. On the reverse, or underneath this text, the two would have subscribed the condition (most likely in English): "The condition of this obligation is that if Antonio pays Shylock three thousand ducats on or before the due date then this obligation shall become void."[30] Conditional bonds took this form for reasons of procedural and evidentiary simplicity, but this resulted in hundreds of thousands of Elizabethans making promises to each other that that they did not envisage keeping, consenting to pay a substantial and sometimes exorbitant penalty when they were really agreeing to pay "such sum or sums as are / Expressed in the condition" (1.3.143–4). Few critics have realized the significance of this inversion of common logic, an inversion so familiar to Shakespeare's audience that it would have given an extra piquancy to Antonio's jovial acceptance of such a morbid agreement.[31]

Finally, the penalty itself transformed Antonio's and Shylock's agreement, because it was out of all proportion to the money owed, or to the loss or damage that the failure to pay would have caused Shylock. The pound of flesh penalty obviously had no direct equivalent in English (or Venetian) law, and critics have rightly emphasized its symbolic as well as its dramatic value, yet it would be a mistake to dismiss the instrument and the law used to judge it as completely alien to an English audience.[32] I would argue that the metaphorical device of an unnecessarily harsh penalty fell on receptive ears in the 1590s, when bond forfeitures had been running high and litigants in equity courts regularly complained that the scale of penalties was excessive in comparison to the harm caused by default. One bond from the 1570s, for example, had a penalty of £80 for a debt of £20 and many others resulted in the forfeiture of real estate.[33] Furthermore, failure of debtors or their sureties to pay penalties increasingly resulted in imprisonment for debt, a punishment of the bodies or flesh of defaulters as well as their purses.[34] Where bonds were used for loans, the usual penalty was double the amount lent, even though the most common loan period, as in Antonio's case, was only three months. The high level of penalties provided an obvious incentive for sharp practice, especially given the above-mentioned reluctance of common law judges to admit oral evidence.

Other aspects of common law procedure induced further cynicism among those who had borrowed money. If debtors met their obligations in full but neglected to cancel their bonds or request acquittances, then those bonds remained in force. This made it possible for unscrupulous creditors to claim the penalties on bonds even in instances where the debts had been settled, effectively amounting to triple payment.[35] Common lawyers saw nothing wrong with this practice: if a debtor repaid a debt without ensuring that the original bond was cancelled then they were victims of their own foolishness and should receive no relief at common law or in equity for having to pay the penalty as well.[36] Litigants in equity courts saw it differently, and balked at having to pay penalties on top of settled debts.

In common with Antonio, many debtors accepted that they had failed to satisfy bond conditions. They requested, as Portia requests on Antonio's behalf, that instead of the penalty, their creditors accept something less, most commonly the original sum owing, plus something in addition "for forbearance" in recognition of the payment being late. Katherin Taylor, for example, offered to recompense her opponent "if he be injured to the value of one penny" contrary to the terms of the original condition attached to a bond, rather than pay the agreed penalty of £200.[37] Others requested that equity justices look beyond the wording of bonds to what had actually transpired between the parties and to distinguish valid excuses for non-payment (illness, a delayed harvest, being robbed on the day of payment or having repaid most but not quite all of the monies owed) from malicious attempts to evade obligations.[38]

Pleas of this kind met with some success in Chancery and Requests, but fell on deaf ears in Queen's Bench and Common Pleas, and the upshot of the widespread failure to meet conditions or to cancel bonds was that creditors suing at common law could hope to make legal gains equivalent to 100, 200, or even 500 per cent or more per annum, without infringing the laws against usury or charging even permitted rates of interest.[39] This is a key reason why *The Merchant*, a play that features a notorious usurer, contains no usury. Against his usual practice, Shylock does not charge interest on his loan. Furthermore, no character disputes that a bond detailing a loan with a penalty for default is legal and not in strict terms usurious, because, as Shylock makes clear through the story of Laban's sheep, the risk exists that no gain will be made.[40] In the biblical story Jacob negotiated to keep all of Laban's lambs born "streaked and pied" (1.3.75) and then used a trick to make the ewes conceive parti-coloured lambs. He was able to keep them because the result was thought "A thing not in his power to bring to pass, / But swayed and fashioned by the hand of heaven" (1.3.88–9). The risk in Shylock's case is that Antonio will repay the loan on time, leaving him with nothing.[41] The central issue, therefore, is not usury but forfeiture.[42]

The penalties resulting from forfeitures were far more lucrative than gains from legal (or even illegal) rates of interest, and as Antonio explains, Shylock hates him and seeks his life in part because "I oft delivered from his forfeitures / Many that have at times made moan to me" (3.3.22–3). English men and women living in the 1590s were all too familiar with Shylock-like characters "that live by forfeitures of bandes and poore men's pledges," the minister William Burton decrying their "cruell and craftie Bandes and Obligations" and the "merciles pledges and forfaitures" that they "swallow[...] up."[43] In a Chancery case from 1586, for example, a surety being sued on bonds by a London goldsmith for penalties amounting to £300 accused his adversary not only of usury, but also of admitting that he deliberately sought to engineer defaults on the bonds leading to forfeiture, "for that he would be revenged" on the original debtor.[44] Yet for all of its highlighting of the inflexibility of bonds and the strictness of common law procedure, the play does not appear to present Chancery's equity as the solution. In the 1590s Chancery and other equity courts were subject to as much criticism as the common law courts, with commentators as well as defendants complaining of the spurious nature of many equity actions. The need for equitable relief could also be difficult to prove, and equity actions were often expensive and time consuming.[45] Furthermore, the fact that gaining justice in the face of the double promises of a conditional bond required two legal actions, with two sets of lawyers' fees and court costs, only added to many debtors' bewilderment at the state of the common law of bonds.[46]

Common law justices refused to hear oral testimony relating to bonds because it would be an incitement to perjury, to coercion, and to exercises of legal discretion that would work, as Richard Posner has noted, to the particular disadvantage of foreigners and outsiders such as Shylock.[47] They defended judgments that resulted in debtors having to repay debts they had already settled, because, as justices Stamford and Bromley explained in 1541, "it is better to suffer a mischief to one man than an inconvenience to many men, which would subvert a legal rule."[48] Various characters apart from Shylock use similar logic to endorse legal rules and the strict enforcement of legal instruments. Portia (disguised as Balthazar) rejects out of hand Bassanio's plea to save Antonio – "To do a great right, do a little wrong" (4.1.211) – by saying, "There is no power in Venice / Can alter a decree establishèd. / Twill be recorded for a precedent, / And many an error by the same example / Will rush into the state" (4.1.213–17). Even Antonio acknowledges that "The Duke cannot deny the course of law, / For the commodity that strangers have / With us in Venice, if it be denied, / Will much impeach the justice of the state" (3.3.26–9). As Alice Benston has pointed out, Portia's intervention proves necessary not so much to save Antonio as to save the law and uphold the legal system at the point where complacent Venetians are considering overriding or jettisoning it, with the Duke announcing that "Upon my power I may dismiss this court" (4.1.103).[49] As we shall see, the play makes clear the need for mercy to temper law, but not necessarily for mercy dispensed by a judge.

Portia's recognition of the importance of strict adherence to law develops around another legal instrument, her father's will. When she first appears on stage she declares that her "little body is aweary of this great world" (1.2.1–2). The source of her unhappiness is the prospect of marriage and the difficulty of making correct decisions. She reflects that, "If to do were as easy as to know what were good to do, chapels had been churches," before concluding that, "It is a good divine that follows his own instructions" (1.2.11–13). As the play demonstrates so well, making promises or commitments is easy. It is keeping them after circumstances change that proves difficult. Society's solution to this uncertainty is law, which aims to hold people to their commitments and to privilege reason over passion. To quote Portia again, "The brain may devise laws for the blood, but a hot temper leaps o'er a cold decree. Such a hare is madness, the youth, to skip o'er the meshes of good counsel, the cripple' (1.2.15–18). The terms of the will make Portia's receipt of her inheritance conditional on her marrying according to her father's stipulations. At first she is resentful that her own will is "curbed by the will of a dead father" (1.2.21–2), but over the course of the scene she comes to appreciate the will's ability to shield her from unworthy suitors who are unwilling to "give and hazard all" they have (2.7.9).[50] By the successful conclusion of the casket plot Portia has become persuaded of the virtues of "The law," "the cold decree," and "the meshes of good counsel," and she spends much of the remainder of the play supporting law and the sanctity of contract, convinced (in her mind at least) that law can be manipulated to advantage as long as it is not broken.

In the darker moments of the bond plot it might be possible to paint Shakespeare as harking back to a simpler age before written promises, embodied in signed and sealed legal instruments, supplanted oral promises grounded in personal relations and marked by symbolic gestures, such as handshakes, the exchanging of rings or halves of a broken coin, and the drinking of alcohol.[51] However, rather than mythologize a linear move from oral to written promises, and from personal to impersonal economic relations, Shakespeare exposes the complexity of these changes, in a world where newer forms of obligations coexisted with older ones and where both could inspire ethical dilemmas about human trust. In the final act he demonstrates how many of the same problems associated with written promises enshrined in bonds can also attach to spoken promises marked by exchanged tokens.

As a number of critics note, in the ring plot Portia is guilty of applying a legalistic interpretation to promises as strict and unforgiving as Shylock's in the bond plot, and there are pronounced similarities between the two episodes.[52] In a telling inversion, having made arguments before Shylock resembling those of a *plaintiff* in an equity action, Portia resembles a *defendant* in an equity action as she refuses to accept any of Bassanio's excuses for having given away the ring he had vowed on his life to keep. In doing so, she emphasizes the "virtue" (5.1.198) or power of the ring as firmly as Shylock had asserted the authority of the sealed bond. Much of the sexual comedy in this final scene comes from the fact that Portia and Nerissa set so much store by their husbands' promises to keep hold of their gold rings that they lead Bassanio and Graziano to believe that the loss of the rings will result in the women's sexual infidelity (with all the innuendo about their other "rings").[53] Yet how absurd, Graziano and Bassanio suggest, that the symbol of a promise should become more important than the promise itself; that Bassanio's promise never to relinquish the ring should be more important to

Portia than her promise "to have him to her wedded husband, forsaking all others." As Graziano exclaims, "What, are we cuckolds ere we have deserved it?" (5.1.264).

In marriages outside of the playhouse rings symbolized unions, but they did not embody or replace them. They were key elements in the ritual of marriage, just as the exchanged tokens accompanying oral economic transactions were key elements in publicizing those agreements and burning their details into the memories of their makers and witnesses.[54] However, while they could possess great symbolic or sentimental power, rings or other tokens did not constitute those agreements and no legal implications flowed from their loss.[55] Graziano, for example, is bewildered by the fuss Nerissa makes "About a hoop of gold, a paltry ring" (5.1.146), and she concedes that "the posy or the value" (5.1.150) of the ring is immaterial. To provide an analogy, English land transfers traditionally depended upon the practice of "livery of seisin," in which the actual passing of possession from one holder to the next was achieved not by the written deeds recording the transaction, but by a symbolic ritual performed on the land, most commonly involving the handing over of a clod of earth with a stick in it.[56] The ritual was essential, "since it was the notoriety of the transaction that testified to its authenticity" and because it made clear the precise moment of transfer, but on completion the buyer simply discarded the stick and clod of earth.[57] Portia and Nerissa pervert the logic of the marriage contract by turning their promises to remain faithful into conditions attaching to the keeping of rings, a move just as bizarre as making the payment of a debt a condition to prevent a promised sacrifice of a pound of flesh.[58] The association is hardly accidental – to Elizabethans, "bands" meant wedding rings as well as conditional bonds (and shackles) – and the women's at times playful insistence on harsh penalties and the strict enforcement of conditions parodies Shylock's reliance on his bond in the previous act, both in the illogical fixation on the symbols of agreements, whether made of gold or parchment, and in the privileging of ancillary conditions that directly or indirectly threaten death as the price for default.[59]

In both the bond plot and the ring plot the form of key obligations transforms what is agreed, and the transformation risks undermining the very things promised. Failure to pay a debt almost results in murder, and failure to hold on to a ring appears to provide a licence for adultery. These manipulations are deliberate, with Shylock setting out to use a promise about a debt to achieve revenge and Portia deftly using the ring promise to test Bassanio's loyalty, educate him about his new wife's virtues, and ensure his future fidelity.[60] Other examples of promises or undertakings to which (more or less) unrelated conditions attach pepper the play.[61] Graziano promises to love Nerissa, but only if Bassanio wins Portia. Bassanio makes the forgiving of Antonio's debts conditional upon Antonio witnessing him die. In her famous legal sleight of hand, Portia makes the cutting out of Antonio's heart conditional upon the failure to spill a drop of blood or to take one iota more or less than a pound of flesh.[62] Antonio, the intended victim of the bond's brutish condition, promises Shylock half of his share of the Jew's patrimony, but only on condition that he convert to Christianity. And the near tragedy of the play arises from the additional condition that Shylock places on the bond through the vow he takes to enforce it, which he argues precludes him from showing mercy: "I have an oath in heaven. / Shall I lay perjury upon my soul?" (4.1.223–4). Again and again in the play conditions alter the nature of the promises they support, whether they are incorporated into written instruments, come in vows to a God, or take the form of a customary exchange of tokens. It is revealing, for example, that when Nerissa chides Graziano for giving away her ring she tells him he should have kept his promise, if not for her sake, "yet for your vehement oaths" (5.1.154).

Conditions themselves are not the problem. After all, Elizabethan Protestants believed that the bond of conscience "is conditionall, according to the tenour of the covenant of grace; for we are bound to beleeve in Christ if we would come to life everlasting."[63] In the absence of unconditional love, which Samuel Ajzenstat has argued is effectively unobtainable, it often takes conditions, rituals, tokens, or (reasonable) penalties to hold people to their promises and to provide a means for dealing with them if they fail.[64] However, conditions work best when they are in reasonable alignment with the core promises they support. The wildly disparate promises found in the play's conditional bond invert this logic – Antonio legally agreeing to sacrifice a pound of flesh, rather than legally agreeing to repay a loan – bringing into stark relief the not dissimilar disparities between agreed promise and agreed penalty found in countless conditional bonds that were familiar through personal experience not just to audience members, but also to theatre managers, owners, and players, including Shakespeare himself.[65]

The manner in which so many oaths, vows, conditions, tokens, rituals, and writings threaten to overwhelm the promises they are intended to support helps to shape and enrich the play's recurrent theme that things are rarely what they seem. This makes for excellent theatre, but for poor human relations. Shakespeare's implicit message appears to be that promises *should be* what they seem. In an echo of Antonio's reflection that "The devil can cite Scripture for his purpose" (1.3.94), Lorenzo laments "How every fool can play upon the word!" (3.5.37) and expresses his frustration at "Yet more quarelling with occasion!" by pleading with Lancelot: "I pray thee understand a plain man in his plain meaning" (3.5.47–9).[66] Lawyers and litigants are especially guilty of distortion and obfuscation, with Bassanio remarking in the casket scene, "The world is still deceived with ornament. / In law, what plea so tainted and corrupt / But, being seasoned with a gracious voice, / Obscures the show of evil?" (3.2.74–7).

In contrast to debt actions, actions of *assumpsit* did centre on the plain meaning of the actual thing promised – the word is commonly translated as "he has undertaken" – and scholars rightly acknowledge *assumpsit* as the precursor to modern contract law.[67] Shakespeare was aware of *assumspit* and addresses it in *The Comedy of Errors*, however, the action of *assumpsit* was not available for written instruments such as Shylock's bond, and debt suits on bonds or other obligations remained "the commonest single class of actions in the Common Pleas rolls" until at least the eighteenth century.[68] Furthermore, contracts to be enforced through *assumpsit* could contain penalties identical to those in conditional bonds.[69] In discussing *assumpsit*, it is therefore important not to be anachronistic, for example by championing Slade's Case (1597–1602) as ushering in almost overnight a "modern" approach to contracts.[70]

It is certainly possible that some members of the audience, if not Shakespeare himself, may have wondered why the regard for the intentions of the negotiating parties found in actions of *assumpsit* could not somehow be applied to debt actions on bonds: that Shylock could be held to his initial "kind" offer to Antonio – "I would be friends with you, and have your love, / Forget the shames that you have stained me with, / Supply your present wants, and take no doit / Of usance of my moneys" (1.3.133–6).[71] However, reading the play's legal themes as a demand for a more sustained focus on intentions in the law of contract resolves only some of its inconsistencies, given the preponderance of rash promises and the transformative effects of risk.[72] For, while *The Merchant* highlights the limitations of bonds, it does not call for their abolition or replacement. Indeed, the comic resolution of the play is achieved through what appears to be an endorsement of the very forms of contract that have been the subject of so much scrutiny in the bond and ring plots. Bassanio agrees to be bound to Portia and at her insistence Antonio agrees to be surety, declaring, "I dare be bound again, / My soul upon the forfeit," in a new obligation that Portia seals by giving the ring to Antonio to give to Bassanio (5.1.250–1). This conditional "bond" marked by a ring reaffirms Portia's and Bassanio's commitment to each other and by inviting Antonio into the circle of their marriage makes him happy for the first and only time in the play.[73]

A key difference between this new "bond" and Shylock's bond is that Bassanio swears on his soul and Antonio offers his soul rather than his body as the forfeit. Aside from its implications for love and friendship, this switch holds echoes of the legal idea that the law consists of two parts, "the flesh and soule."[74] As William West explained in 1594 (translating the law French of Edmund Plowden), "The letter of the law is the body of the law and the sense and reason of the law is the soul of the law."[75] Both are essential to justice.[76] As English litigants were learning in record numbers, the legalism of the common law produces difficulties, if it is too rigid, but so too does the judicial discretion required by equity, if it is too unfettered. In the language of the play, society needs both law *and* mercy, and they work best when they are complementary rather than being in competition, as they often were in Elizabethan England. The dilemma citizens and legal institutions face is in getting the balance right and in finding the best way to live up to cherished ideals.[77] Beginning in the late seventeenth century, reformers addressed the very concerns raised in the play by introducing equitable principles into common law practice, moving away from the strict enforcement of penalties agreed between the parties to compensating actual losses.[78] It is telling that despite these changes, parties continued to use bonds as securities for promises, much in the way Portia suggests that Shylock should use his: to underpin and provide certainty for transactions between reasonable parties and to ensure compensation for actual losses, but not to exact vengeance or make easy profits.[79]

The Merchant provides a critique of law and legal instruments, but does not demand that its audience choose between law and equity, or indeed between natural law and positive law, status and contract, debt law and *assumpsit*, Belmont and Venice, or friendship bonds and commercial bonds.[80] The play's ultimate concern, I would argue, is with practice more than with jurisdictions (or eras, ideologies, or pure principles) and with human frailties more than structural deficiencies.[81] Over and above its explorations of mercy at law, the play emphasizes the need for a greater spirit of mercy in individuals. As Portia observes in her most famous phrase, "The quality of mercy is not strained" and therefore cannot be forced upon anyone (4.1.179). It needs to come from within, in this case from Shylock himself, rather than from the judicial bench or from a particular law or jurisdiction. For as Antonio observes, Shylock "stands obdurate" and "no lawful means can carry me / Out of his envy's reach" (4.1.8–9). With the exception of the Duke's bestowal of a pardon, mercy in the play is personal rather than legal. When Portia asks, "What mercy can you render him, Antonio?" (4.1.373), Antonio responds by giving up his share of Shylock's goods for the benefit of Jessica and Lorenzo, even though at this point in the play he believes he is penniless. Character after character asks to be pardoned, from Portia's "pardon me, Bassanio" and Nerissa's "pardon me, my gentle Graziano" (4.1.419–20) to Bassanio's repeated requests to Portia to "pardon me" (4.1.433; 5.1.218–21, 5.1.239).

Bassanio's final plea for forgiveness is perhaps the most revealing, given its return to the language of hearing: "Nay, but hear me. / Pardon this fault, and by my soul I swear / I never more will break an oath with thee" (5.1.245–7). Portia does hear and (eventually) pardon him, and as we have seen, one of the reasons why Shylock is "Uncapable of pity, void and empty / From any dram of mercy" (4.1.3–4) is that he refuses to hear. He will not hear Antonio or respond to Portia's pleas that he forgive the penalty for reasons of mercy or have a doctor standing by because "'Twere good you do so much for charity" (4.1.256), or the Duke's expectation that "touched with human gentleness and love" he might "Forgive a moiety of the principal" as well as the forfeiture (4.1.24–5). He insists instead on looking to his bond and to Antonio himself, exclaiming, "Jailer, look to him. Tell not me of mercy. / This is the fool that lent out money gratis. / Jailer, look to him" (3.3.1–3). In another context Shylock even tells Jessica "But stop my house's ears" (2.5.33). The consequences of Shylock's deafness are clear and reverberate in Lorenzo's musings in act 5 about music and the movement of planets in the heavens: "Such harmony is in immortal souls, / But whilst this muddy vesture of decay / Doth grossly close it in, we cannot hear it" (5.1.62–4). As he concludes, "The man that hath no music in himself, / Nor is not moved with concord of sweet sounds, / Is fit for treasons, stratagems, and spoils ... Let no such man be trusted" (5.1.82–4, 5.1.87).

Shylock refused to listen, but so too did those many Elizabethans ruthlessly pursuing bond penalties in an England where, as in Venice, "creditors grow cruel" (3.2.315). The perceived disintegration of neighbourliness embodied in countless lawsuits could aptly be described as "this muddy vesture of decay," and Shylock was far from alone in being deaf to pleas to show more compassion when deciding whether or not to sue; and having sued, whether enforcing his penalty was the best way to have his original loan repaid.

In evaluating *The Merchant's* legal contexts, then, the play's most pressing unspoken question is not which courts are best at resolving bond disputes, common law or equity, but why these and other courts are bursting at the seams with lawsuits. Why are more disputes not being resolved amicably or at least settled out of court? In contrast to Shylock, the play implies, creditors holding forfeited bonds should "Tarry a little" (4.1.300) and speak with and listen to their adversaries, instead of hotfooting it to their lawyers.[82] For while the play endorses the need for law, Portia reminds Shylock "That in the course of justice none of us / Should see salvation. We do pray for mercy, / And that same prayer doth teach us all to render / The deeds of mercy" (4.1.194–7).[83] The law, in other words, works best when teamed with Christian forgiveness. Or as William Perkins warned, men who "have nothing in their mouthes but Justice, Justice and have banished mercie, yet let them know, that Justice will not stay where mercie is not."[84]

In *The Merchant* the responsibility for this wedding of law with forgiveness rests with litigants more than with judges. Shylock is oblivious to mercy as he attempts to use a legal instrument to cause harm and exact revenge, the very things laws are intended to prevent. But as we have seen, Portia, too, is guilty of failing to show mercy to Shylock. "The flaw," to quote Randy Lee, "is not in the law itself, but in what people do with the law through their ignorance and arrogance and through their hate and near-sightedness."[85] Like Shylock, Portia "understands that the law is something to be used ... rather than supinely to yield to."[86] In common with a litigant or lawyer she employs whatever legal or other means is best suited to achieving her purposes, insisting upon the letter of the law at some points and on its spirit at others. The inconsistencies that result from her selective use of rhetoric and the equivalent of "forum shopping" are born of pragmatism rather than principle. Where most critics used to excuse her "understandable unscrupulousness" by considering the results of her actions, many now rightly find her "disingenuous use of the law" deeply unsettling.[87] Law-weary Elizabethans were capable of both responses. It seems likely, however, that most would have applauded her skills at navigating perplexing legal terrain and turning the tables on a cynical exploiter of bond forfeitures, excusing her legal trickery in light of her expressed motivation to achieve "a good deed in a naughty world" (5.1.90).

The Merchant of Venice illustrates the extent to which the effectiveness of legal systems and legal instruments depends on the parties who use them. In the wrong hands "inky blots and rotten parchment bonds" can cause great harm, but so too can other methods of making promises. In the right hands they can bring security and certainty to transactions of many types.[88] And the right hands are well-intentioned, reasonable, and merciful hands.

NOTES

1 Quotations from Shakespeare plays are from *The Norton Shakespeare* and are cited in the text.

2 Jill Phillips Ingram, *Idioms of Self-Interest: Credit, Identity, and Property in English Renaissance Literature*, pp. 110–14; Conal Condren, *Argument and Authority in Early Modern England: The Presupposition of Oaths and Offices*, p. 245.

3 See, for example, Maxine MacKay, "*The Merchant of Venice*: a Reflection of the Early Conflict Between Courts of Law and Courts of Equity," pp. 371–5; O. Hood Phillips, *Shakespeare and the Lawyers*, pp. 91–118; W. Nicholas Knight, "Equity, *The Merchant of Venice*, and William Lambarde," pp. 93–104; B.J. Sokol, "*The Merchant of Venice* and the Law Merchant," pp. 60–7; Daniela Carpi, "Law, Discretion, Equity in *The Merchant of Venice* and *Measure for Measure*," pp. 2317–30.

4 Lawrence Danson, *The Harmonies of* The Merchant of Venice, pp. 12–13, 17.

5 Richard H. Weisberg, *Poethics and Other Strategies of Law and Literature*, pp. 100–4; S.A. Cohen, ""The Quality of Mercy": Law, Equity and Ideology in *The Merchant of Venice*," pp. 35–53.

6 Thomas C. Bilello, "Accomplished with What She Lacks: Law, Equity, and Portia's Con," pp. 11–32; B.J. Sokol and Mary Sokol, "Shakespeare and the English Equity Jurisdiction: *The Merchant of Venice* and the Two Texts of *King Lear*," pp. 417–39; Theodore Ziolkowski, *The Mirror of Justice: Literary Reflections of Legal Crises*, pp. 177–81; E.F.J. Tucker, "The Letter of the Law in *The Merchant of Venice*," pp. 93–101; Richard A. Posner, *Law and Literature*, p. 148.

7 William Kerrigan, *Shakespeare's Promises*, pp. 94–5; Constance Jordan and Karen Cunningham, eds, *The Law in Shakespeare*, pp. 5–7; Peter G. Platt, *Shakespeare and the Culture of Paradox*, esp. p. 79; Walter Cohen, "*The Merchant of Venice* and the Possibilities of Historical Criticism," p. 775; Kiernan Ryan, *Shakespeare*, p. 19.

8 John Christopherson, *An Exhortation to All Menne to Take Hede and Beware of Rebellion* (1554), sig: Aa7v; William Perkins, *A Discourse of Conscience Wherein is Set Downe the Nature, Properties, and Differences Thereof: As Also the Way to Get and Keepe Good Conscience* (1596), p. 83.

9 Perez Zagorin, *Ways of Lying: Dissimulation, Persecution, and Conformity in Early Modern Europe*; Jonathan Michael Gray, "Vows, Oaths, and the Propagation of a Subversive Discourse," pp. 731–56; cf. John Spurr, "A Profane History of Early Modern Oaths," pp. 37–63.

10 J.A. Guy, *The Court of Star Chamber and its Records to the Reign of Elizabeth I*, 53–60; M.D. Gordon, "The Invention of a Common Law Crime: Perjury and the Elizabethan Courts," pp. 145–70.

11 J.H. Baker, *An Introduction to English Legal History*, pp. 74, 322–3.

12 J.H. Baker and S.F.C. Milsom, *Sources of English Legal History: Private Law to 1750*, p. 441.

13 William Gamage, *Linsi-woolsie. Or Two Centuries of Epigrammes* (1621), sig: Dv.

14 As quoted in Spurr, "A Profane History of Early Modern Oaths," p. 55.

15 Craig Muldrew, *The Economy of Obligation: The Culture of Credit and Social Relations in Early Modern England*, pp. 204, 240.

16 Muldrew, *Economy of Obligation*, pp. 204, 236; Craig Muldrew, "The Culture of Reconciliation: Community and the Settlement of Economic Disputes in Early Modern England," pp. 915, 921–2; C.W. Brooks, *Pettyfoggers and Vipers of the Commonwealth: The Lower Branch of the Legal Profession in Early Modern England*, p. 69.

17 Brooks, *Pettyfoggers*, pp. 68–9 (my calculation based on his figures).

18 Natasha Korda, *Labors Lost: Women's Work and the Early Modern English Stage*, p. 57.

19 Phillip Stubbes, *A Motive to Good Workes Or Rather, To True Christianitie Indeede* (1593), pp. 43–4.

20 Ziolkowski, *The Mirror of Justice*, 174–5; Daniel Kornstein, *Kill all the Lawyers? Shakespeare's Legal Appeal*, p. 75.

21 See Samuel Ajzenstat, "The Ubiquity of Contract in *The Merchant of Venice*," pp. 262–78.

22 See also Weisberg, *Poethics*, p. 95.

23 A.G. Harmon, *Eternal Bonds, True Contracts: Law and Nature in Shakespeare's Problem Plays*, p. 13.

24 George Chapman, *Two Wise Men and all the Rest Fooles: or A Comicall Morall, Censuring the Follies of this Age* (1619), pp. 68–9; for a historical example, see J.H. Bettey, ed. *Case Book of Sir Francis Ashley, J.P. Recorder of Dorchester 1614–1635*, p. 88.
25 William Blackstone, *Commentaries on the Laws of England*, vol. 4, p. 234.
26 Thomas Kyd, *The Spanish Tragedy* (1592), 3.13.134–5; and see Bassanio's reference to his letter from Antonio: "The paper as the body of my friend, / And every word in it a gaping wound / Issuing life-blood" (3.2.263–5).
27 Oral testimony could be heard on the question of whether or not a condition had been satisfied; Baker, *Introduction to English Legal History*, p. 324.
28 Anon., *The Death of Usury, or, the Disgrace of Usurers* (1594), p. 22; Simpson, *History of the Common Law*, pp. 98–9; Baker, *Introduction to English Legal History*, p. 324. Common law rules also prevented a defendant from testifying in his or her own cause.
29 Christopher Saint German, *The Dialogue in English betweene a Doctor of Divinitie and a Student of the Lawes of England* (1593), fol. 22v.
30 A.W.B Simpson, "The Penal Bond with Conditional Defeasance," pp. 392–422; A.W.B Simpson, *A History of the Common Law of Contract: The Rise of the Action of Assumpsit*, pp. 88–126; Baker, *Introduction to English Legal History*, p. 323; William O. Scott, "Conditional Bonds, Forfeitures and Vows in *The Merchant of Venice*," p. 286.
31 Exceptions include Scott, "Conditional Bonds," and Amanda Bailey, "Shylock and the Slaves: Owing and Owning in *The Merchant of Venice*," pp. 1–24.
32 Posner, *Law and Literature*, pp. 142–4.
33 *Agnes Whight* v. *Edward Elam*, The National Archives, Kew, Surrey (hereafter TNA) REQ 2/164/176.
34 Bailey "Shylock and the Slaves," esp. pp. 2, 4–5, 12, 14, 18, 24; David Hawkes, *The Culture of Usury in Renaissance England*, pp. 145–55; J.H. Baker, *Oxford History of the Laws of England*, vol. 6, *1483–1558*, pp. 383–4.
35 The amount of the loan plus the penalty of double the amount of the loan. W.J. Jones, *The Elizabethan Court of Chancery*, p. 444.
36 Anon., "The Replication of a Serjeant at the Laws of England," p. 100.
37 *Katherin Taylor* v. *Jonas Waters*, TNA REQ 2/279/8.
38 See, for example, TNA C33/87, fols 29v–30; W.H. Bryson, *Cases Concerning Equity and the Courts of Equity 1550–1660*; Tim Stretton, "Written Obligations, Litigation and Neighbourliness, 1580–1680."
39 Muldrew, *Economy of Obligation*, p. 114.
40 Usury involved charging to lend money without risk to the lender; Eric Kerridge, *Usury, Interest and the Reformation*, pp. 5–21.

41 See Leah Woods Wilkins, "Shylock's Pound of Flesh and Laban's Sheep," pp. 28–30; cf. Bailey, "Shylock and the Slaves," pp. 8–10.
42 Bailey, "Shylock and the Slaves," p. 3.
43 William Burton, *An Exposition of the Lords Prayer Made in Diverse Lectures* (1594), p. 148; *Davids Thanksgiving for the Arraignement of the Man of Earth* (1598), pp. 71–2.
44 *John Barney* v. *Giles Sympson*, TNA C2/Eliz/B11/31, m.1.
45 Jones, *Chancery*, 425–6; Bryson, *Cases Concerning Equity*, vol. 1, pp. 330–1.
46 Bryson, *Cases Concerning Equity*, vol. 1, pp. xxii–xxiii.
47 Posner, *Law and Literature*, p. 148.
48 As quoted in Simpson, *History of Contract*, p. 403.
49 Alice N. Benston, "Portia, the Law, and the Tripartite Structure of *The Merchant of Venice*," pp. 373–9.
50 Ingram, *Idioms of Self-Interest*, pp. 105–6.
51 Harmon, *Eternal Bonds*, pp. 12–13.
52 See, for example, Weisberg, *Poethics*, p. 102; Ingram, *Idioms of Self-Interest*, p. 112; Bailey, "Shylock and the Slaves," p. 23.
53 Lisa Jardine, *Reading Shakespeare Historically*, pp. 59–60, 62–3.
54 Condren, *Argument and Authority*, p. 235.
55 On the symbolic power of the rings in the play, see Subha Mukherji, *Law and Representation in Early Modern Drama*, pp. 37–8; Karen Newman, *Essaying Shakespeare*, pp. 59–76; Craig Muldrew, "Hard Food for Midas; Cash and Its Social Value in Early Modern England," p. 117.
56 Baker, *Introduction to Legal History*, pp. 305–6.
57 Harmon, *Eternal Bonds*, pp. 12–13; M.T. Clanchy, *From Memory to Written Record: England 1066–1307*, p. 260.
58 Bassanio's dizzy joy as he promises Portia he will die if his ring parts from his finger (3.2.175–85) mirror's Antonio's positive mood when he agrees to the deadly terms of Shylock's "merry jest" (1.3.145–74).
59 Bailey, "Shylock and the Slaves," p. 22.
60 For further reflection upon harsh penalties such as death or the equal division of goods between the state and the intended victim, see "Shylock's Penalty" in Charles Ross, *Elizabethan Literature and the Law of Fraudulent Conveyance*, pp. 113–31.
61 It is the frequency, not the presence, of conditional promises that is unusual; see, for example, Joel B. Altman, *The Improbability of Othello: Rhetorical Anthropology and Shakespearean Selfhood*, pp. 25, 33–5, 136–8, 148, 198, 203, 289, 369–70.
62 I owe this observation to Rory Leitch.
63 Perkins, *Discourse of Conscience*, p. 34; Scott, "Conditional Bonds," p. 305.

64 Ajzenstat, "The Ubiquity of Contract," p. 263.
65 Knight, "Equity, *The Merchant of Venice* and William Lambarde," pp. 98–102; D.L. Thomas and N.E. Evans, "John Shakespeare in the Exchequer," pp. 315–8; Hotson, *Shakespeare versus Shallow*, pp. 4–5, 9.
66 On the play's ambivalence towards plain speech, see Platt, *Culture of Paradox*, pp. 81–3.
67 David Harris Sacks, "The Promise and the Contract in Early Modern England: Slade's Case in Perspective."
68 Barbara Kreps, "Playing the Law for Lawyers: Witnessing, Evidence and the Law of Contract in *The Comedy of Errors*," pp. 262–71; Baker, *Introduction to English Legal History*, p. 324.
69 See, for example, R.A. Foakes and R.T. Rickert, eds, *Henslowe's Diary*, p. 240.
70 Simpson, "Penal Bond with Conditional Defeasance"; David Ibbetson, "Sixteenth Century Contract Law: *Slade's Case* in Context," pp. 295–317; Luke Wilson, *Theaters of Intention: Drama and the Law in Early Modern England*, pp. 81–2.
71 Charles Spinosa, "Shylock and Debt and Contract in 'The Merchant of Venice,'" pp. 65–85.
72 On the cultural significance of the rise of *assumpsit*, see Sacks, "Slade's Case"; Paul Raffield, "*The Comedy of Errors* and the Meaning of Contract," pp. 207–29; Wilson, *Theaters of Intention*, pp. 76–82.
73 Benston, "Portia, the Law and the Tripartite Structure of *The Merchant of Venice*," pp. 383–5.
74 Knight, "Equity, *The Merchant of Venice*, and William Lambarde," p. 97.
75 William West, *Three Treatises of the Second Parte of Symbolæographie* (1594), Part 2, sig. A4v.
76 Bradin Cormack, *A Power to Do Justice: Jurisdiction, English Literature, and the Rise of the Common Law, 1509–1625*, esp. pp. 82–3.
77 Kornstein, *Kill all the Lawyers*, p. 75; Mark Fortier, *The Culture of Equity in Early Modern England*, p. 128; Nevill Coghill, "The Basis of Shakespearean Comedy," p. 217.
78 Mike Macnair, "Common Law and Statutory Imitations of Equitable Relief under the Later Stuarts," pp. 118–21, 125, 127.
79 Tim Stretton, "Contract, Debt Litigation and Shakespeare's *The Merchant Of Venice*," pp. 123–4.
80 See Danson, *The Harmonies of* The Merchant of Venice, pp. 17–18; Platt, *Culture of Paradox*, pp. 76, 79, 95–119.
81 Jan Lawson Hinely, "Bond Priorities in the *The Merchant of Venice*," pp. 238–9.

82 Scott, "Conditional Bonds," 301; Kornstein, *Kill all the Lawyers*, p. 67.
83 Grace Tiffany, "Law and Self-Interest in *The Merchant of Venice*," pp. 384–400.
84 William Perkins, *Hepieíkeia: or, a Treatise of Christian Equitie and Moderation* (1604), p. 17.
85 Randy Lee, "Who's Afraid of William Shakespeare?: Confronting our Concepts of Justice and Mercy in *The Merchant of Venice*," p. 19.
86 Posner, *Law and Literature*, p. 150; Karlone Szatek, "*The Merchant of Venice* and the Politics of Commerce," esp. pp. 347–8.
87 Bilello, "Accomplished with What She Lacks," p. 13; Ajznenat, "Ubiquity of Contract," p. 273; and see how Posner changed his analysis of Portia between the 2nd and 3rd editions of *Law and Literature*.
88 *Richard II* (2.1.64), referring to Richard's cynical use of blank charters.

BIBLIOGRAPHY

Manuscript Sources

Agnes Whight v. *Edward Elam*. The National Archives, Kew, Surrey (TNA). REQ 2/164/176.

John Barney v. *Giles Sympson*. TNA C2/Eliz/B11/31.

Katherin Taylor v. *Jonas Waters*. TNA REQ 2/279/8.

TNA C33/87, fols 29v–30.

Printed Sources

Ajzenstat, Samuel. "The Ubiquity of Contract in *The Merchant of Venice*." *Philosophy and Literature* 21, no. 2 (1997): 262–78.

Altman, Joel B. *The Improbability of Othello: Rhetorical Anthropology and Shakespearean Selfhood*. Chicago: U of Chicago P, 2010.

Anon. *The Death of Usury, or, the Disgrace of Usurers*. Cambridge, 1594.

Anon. "The Replication of a Serjeant at the Laws of England." In *Christopher St. German on Chancery and Statute*. Ed. J.A. Guy. London: Selden Society, 1985. 99–105.

Bailey, Amanda. "Shylock and the Slaves: Owing and Owning in *The Merchant of Venice*." *Shakespeare Quarterly* 62, no. 1 (2011): 1–24.

Baker, J.H. *An Introduction to English Legal History*. 4th ed. London: Butterworths/LexisNexis, 2002.

– *The Oxford History of the Laws of England, Vol. VI: 1483–1558*. Oxford: Oxford UP, 2003.

Baker, J.H., and S.F.C. Milsom. *Sources of English Legal History: Private Law to 1750*. London and Edinburgh: Butterworths, 1986.
Benston, Alice N. "Portia, the Law, and the Tripartite Structure of *The Merchant of Venice*." *Shakespeare Quarterly* 30, no. 3 (1979): 367–85.
Bettey, J.H., ed. *Case Book of Sir Francis Ashley, J.P. Recorder of Dorchester 1614–1635*. Dorset Record Society 7, 1981.
Bilello, Thomas C. "Accomplished with What She Lacks: Law, Equity, and Portia's Con." *Law and Literature* 16, no. 1 (2004): 11–32.
Blackstone, William. *Commentaries on the Laws of England*. Oxford: 1765–69. Facsimile ed. Vol. 4. Chicago: U of Chicago P, 1979.
Brooks, C.W. *Pettyfoggers and Vipers of the Commonwealth: The Lower Branch of the Legal Profession in Early Modern England*. Cambridge: Cambridge UP, 1986.
Bryson, W.H. *Cases Concerning Equity and the Courts of Equity 1550–1660*. 2 vols. London: Selden Society, 2001.
Burton, William. *Davids Thanksgiving for the Arraignement of the Man of Earth*. London: 1598.
– *An Exposition of the Lords Prayer Made in Diverse Lectures*. London: 1594.
Carpi, Daniela. "Law, Discretion, Equity in *The Merchant of Venice* and *Measure for Measure*." *Cardozo Law Review* 26 (2005): 2317–30.
Chapman, George. *Two Wise Men and all the Rest Fooles: or A Comicall Morall, Censuring the Follies of this Age*. London: 1619.
Christopherson, John. *An Exhortation to All Menne to Take Hede and Beware of Rebellion*. London: 1554.
Clanchy, M.T. *From Memory to Written Record: England 1066–1307*. 2nd ed. Oxford: Blackwell Publishers, 1993.
Coghill, Nevill. "The Basis of Shakespearean Comedy." In *Shakespeare Criticism 1935–1960*. Ed. Anne Ridler. Oxford: Oxford UP, 1970. 201–27.
Cohen, S.A. "'The Quality of Mercy': Law, Equity and Ideology in *The Merchant of Venice*." *Mosaic* 27, no. 4 (1994): 35–53.
Cohen, Walter. "*The Merchant of Venice* and the Possibilities of Historical Criticism," *English Literary History* 49, no. 4 (1982): 765–89.
Condren, Conal. *Argument and Authority in Early Modern England: The Presupposition of Oaths and Offices*. Cambridge: Cambridge UP, 2006.
Cormack, Bradin. *A Power to Do Justice: Jurisdiction, English Literature, and the Rise of the Common Law, 1509–1625*. Chicago and London: U of Chicago P, 2007.
Danson, Lawrence. *The Harmonies of* The Merchant of Venice. New Haven, CT: Yale UP, 1978.
Foakes, R.A., and R.T. Rickert, eds. *Henslowe's Diary*. Cambridge: Cambridge UP, 1961.

Fortier, Mark. *The Culture of Equity in Early Modern England*. Aldershot, Hampshire: Ashgate, 2005.

Gamage, William. *Linsi-woolsie. Or Two Centuries of Epigrammes*. London: 1621.

Gordon, M.D. "The Invention of a Common Law Crime: Perjury and the Elizabethan Courts." *American Journal of Legal History* 24, no. 2 (1980): 145–70.

Gray, Jonathan Michael. "Vows, Oaths, and the Propagation of a Subversive Discourse." *Sixteenth Century Journal* 41, no. 3 (2010): 731–56.

Guy, J.A. *The Court of Star Chamber and its Records to the Reign of Elizabeth I*. London: Her Majesty's Stationery Office, 1986.

Harmon, A.G. *Eternal Bonds, True Contracts: Law and Nature in Shakespeare's Problem Plays*. New York: State U of New York P, 2004.

Hawkes, David. *The Culture of Usury in Renaissance England*. New York and Houndsmills, Basingstoke: Palgrave Macmillan, 2010.

Hinely, Jan Lawson. "Bond Priorities in *The Merchant of Venice*." *Studies in English Literature, 1500–1900* 20, no. 2 (1980): 217–39.

Hotson, Leslie, *Shakespeare versus Shallow*. London: The Nonesuch Press, 1931.

Ibbetson, David. "Sixteenth Century Contract Law: *Slade's Case* in Context." *Oxford Journal of Legal Studies* 4, no. 3 (1984): 295–317.

Ingram, Jill Phillips. *Idioms of Self-Interest: Credit, Identity, and Property in English Renaissance Literature*. New York and London: Routledge, 2006.

Jardine, Lisa. *Reading Shakespeare Historically*. London and New York: Routledge, 1996.

Jones, W.J. *The Elizabethan Court of Chancery*. Oxford: Oxford UP, 1967.

Jordan, Constance and Karen Cunningham, eds. *The Law in Shakespeare*. New York and Houndsmills, Basingstoke: Palgrave Macmillan, 2007.

Kerridge, Eric. *Usury, Interest and the Reformation*. Aldershot, Hants: Ashgate, 2002.

Kerrigan, William. *Shakespeare's Promises*. Baltimore and London: Johns Hopkins UP, 1999.

Knight, W. Nicholas. "Equity, *The Merchant of Venice* and William Lambarde." *Shakespeare Survey* 27 (1974): 93–104.

Korda, Natasha. *Labors Lost: Women's Work and the Early Modern Stage*. Philadelphia: U of Pennsylvania P, 2011.

Kornstein, Daniel. *Kill all the Lawyers? Shakespeare's Legal Appeal*. Princeton, NJ: Princeton UP, 1994.

Kreps, Barbara. "Playing the Law for Lawyers: Witnessing, Evidence and the Law of Contract in *The Comedy of Errors*." *Shakespeare Survey* 63 (2010): 262–71.

Kyd, Thomas. *The Spanish Tragedy*. Ed. T.W. Ross. Berkeley and Los Angeles: U of California P, 1968.

Lee, Randy. "Who's Afraid of William Shakespeare?: Confronting our Concepts of Justice and Mercy in *The Merchant of Venice*." 32 *University of Dayton Law Review* (2006–2007): 1–28.

MacKay, Maxine. "*The Merchant of Venice*: A Reflection of the Early Conflict Between Courts of Law and Courts of Equity." *Shakespeare Quarterly* 15 no. 4 (1964): 371–5.

Macnair, Mike. "Common Law and Statutory Imitations of Equitable Relief under the Later Stuarts." In *Communities and Courts in Britain, 1150–1900*. Ed. Christopher Brooks and Michael Lobban. London and Rio Grande: Hambledon P, 1997. 115–31.

Mukherji, Subha. *Law and Representation in Early Modern Drama*. Cambridge: Cambridge UP, 2006.

Muldrew, Craig. "The Culture of Reconciliation: Community and the Settlement of Economic Disputes in Early Modern England." *Historical Journal* 39, no. 4 (1996): 915–42.

– *The Economy of Obligation: The Culture of Credit and Social Relations in Early Modern England*. New York: St Martin's Press, 1998.

– "Hard Food for Midas: Cash and Its Social Value in Early Modern England." *Past and Present* 170, no. 1 (2001): 78–120.

Newman, Karen. *Essaying Shakespeare*. Minneapolis: U of Minnesota P, 2009.

Perkins, William. *A Discourse of Conscience Wherein is Set Downe the Nature, Properties, and Differences Thereof*. Cambridge: 1596.

– *Hepieíkeia: or, a Treatise of Christian Equitie and Moderation*. Cambridge: 1604.

Phillips, O. Hood. *Shakespeare and the Lawyers*. London: Methuen, 1972.

Platt, Peter G. *Shakespeare and the Culture of Paradox*. Ashgate, 2009. Farnham, Surrey, and Burlington, VT, 2009.

Posner, Richard A. *Law and Literature*. 3rd ed. Cambridge, MA, and London: Harvard UP, 2009.

Raffield, Paul. "*The Comedy of Errors* and the Meaning of Contract." *Law and Humanities* 3 no. 2 (2009): 207–29.

Ross, Charles. *Elizabethan Literature and the Law of Fraudulent Conveyance: Sidney, Spenser, and Shakespeare*. Aldershot, UK; Burlington, VT: Ashgate, 2003.

Ryan, Kiernan. *Shakespeare*. Houndsmills, Basingstoke: Palgrave, 2002.

Sacks, David Harris. "Slade's Case in Perspective." In *Rhetoric and Law in Early Modern Europe*. Ed. Victoria Kahn and Lorna Hudson. New Haven, CT: Yale UP, 2001.

Saint German, Christopher. *The Dialogue in English betweene a Doctor of Divinitie and a Student of the Lawes of England*. London: 1593.

Scott, William O. "Conditional Bonds, Forfeitures and Vows in *The Merchant of Venice*." *English Literary Renaissance* 34, no. 3 (2004): 286–305.

Shakespeare, William. *The Merchant of Venice. The Norton Shakespeare.* Ed. Stephen Greenblatt et al. 1st ed. New York: W.W. Norton, 1997.

– *Richard II. The Norton Shakespeare.* Ed. Stephen Greenblatt et al. 1st ed. New York: W.W. Norton, 1997.

– *Twelfth Night. The Norton Shakespeare.* Ed. Stephen Greenblatt et al. 1st ed. New York: W.W. Norton, 1997.

Simpson, A.W.B. *A History of the Common Law of Contract: The Rise of the Action of Assumpsit*. Oxford: Oxford UP, 1975.

– "The Penal Bond with Conditional Defeasance." 82 *Law Quarterly Review* (1966): 392–422.

Sokol, B.J. "*The Merchant of Venice* and the Law Merchant." *Renaissance Studies* 6, no. 1 (1992): 60–7.

Sokol, B.J., and Mary Sokol. "Shakespeare and the English Equity Jurisdiction: *The Merchant of Venice* and the Two Texts of *King Lear*." *Review of English Studies* ns 50, no. 200 (1999): 417–39.

Spinosa, Charles. "Shylock and Debt and Contract in *The Merchant of Venice*." *Cardozo Studies in Law and Literature* 5 (1993): 65–85.

Spurr, John. "A Profane History of Early Modern Oaths." *Transactions of the Royal Historical Society* 6th ser. 11 (2001): 37–63.

Stretton, Tim. "Contract, Debt Litigation and Shakespeare's *The Merchant Of Venice*." *Adelaide Law Review* 31, no. 2 (2010): 111–25.

– "Written Obligations, Litigation and Neighbourliness, 1580–1680." In *Remaking English Society: Social Relations and Social Change in Early Modern England*. Ed. Steve Hindle et al. Woodbridge, Suffolk and Rochester NY: Boydell and Brewer, 2013. 189–209.

Stubbes, Phillip. *A Motive to Good Workes Or Rather, To True Christianitie Indeede*. London, 1593.

Szatek, Karlone. "*The Merchant of Venice* and the Politics of Commerce." In *The Merchant of Venice: New Critical Essays*. Ed. John W. Mahon and Ellen Macleod Mahon. London and NY: Routledge, 2002. 325–52.

Thomas, D.L., and N.E. Evans. "John Shakespeare in the Exchequer." *Shakespeare Quarterly* 35, no. 3 (1984): 315–18.

Tiffany, Grace C. "Law and Self-Interest in *The Merchant of Venice*." *Papers on Language and Literature* 42, no. 4 (2006): 384–400.

Tucker, E.F.J. "The Letter of the Law in *The Merchant of Venice*." *Shakespeare Survey* 29 (1976): 93–101.

Weisberg, Richard H. *Poethics and Other Strategies of Law and Literature*. New York: Columbia UP, 1992.

West, William. *Three Treatises of the Second Parte of Symbolæographie*. London, 1594.

Wilkins, Leah Woods. "Shylock's Pound of Flesh and Laban's Sheep." *Modern Language Notes* 62 (1947): 28–30.

Wilson, Luke A. *Theaters of Intention: Drama and Law in Early Modern England.* Stanford, CA: Stanford UP, 2000.

Zagorin, Perez. *Ways of Lying: Dissimulation, Persecution, and Conformity in Early Modern Europe*. Cambridge, MA: Harvard UP, 1990.

Ziolkowski, Theodore. *The Mirror of Justice: Literary Reflections of Legal Crises.* Princeton, NJ: Princeton UP, 1997. 177–81.

4 The "Snared Subject" and the General Pardon Statute in Late Elizabethan Coterie Literature

VIRGINIA LEE STRAIN

As one of the most extensive surviving accounts of Inns of Court revelling, the *Gesta Grayorum* (1688) has inspired a number of studies on the intimate relationship between early modern legal and literary culture.[1] The text documents the elaborate Christmas revels mounted by the members of Gray's Inn from December 1594 to March 1595, and that involved the coronation of a fictional Prince of Purpoole, processions through London, orations, masques, dances, and other devices. These revels are best known to literary historians for what was almost certainly the first performance of *The Comedy of Errors*.[2] According to the report in the *Gesta Grayorum*, the large crowd that had assembled for one of the evenings of entertainments would not make room for the professional actors onstage. The play could not be performed until the numbers were thinned by the departure of the contingent from the Inner Temple (another Inn of Court) and not until dancing had exhausted some of the revellers' energies. The evening thus earned the nickname "The Night of Errors."[3] The "pattern of error and reform" that Andrew Zurcher identifies as a structural principle behind the revels, however, began long before this infamous debacle.[4]

Although the Prince of Purpoole's rule was ostentatiously established with more than one hundred followers in attendance on the very first "grand night," the plans to hold a mock parliament as well fell by the wayside as "some special Officers" were missing "without whose Presence it could not be performed" (20). This excuse may in fact be pretence and may signal dramatic compression that is intentionally or unavoidably clothed as disorganization or error.[5] In any case, the organizers proceeded by enacting two bills: "The one was, a Subsidy... towards the Support of His Highness's Port and Sports. The other was [...] his gracious, general and free Pardon" (20). These bills were chosen with special care by the members of Gray's Inn: ratified by nearly every Elizabethan parliament, the subsidy and the general pardon stand in synecdochically for a full session during the legal revels. The subsidy, the government's major source of tax revenue, was the primary reason for calling a parliament in the first place. After the subsidy was formally accepted at the end of a session, the general pardon was declared and operated most immediately as a kind of royal thanks. The pardon's tribute to the "love" and "affection" of the Queen's subjects was a decorous nod to their financial generosity.[6] This is the last we hear of the subsidy in the *Gesta Grayorum*, but the general pardon, including its formulaic preamble, was studiously replicated and reinterpreted by the revellers. Its lengthy items and exceptions were read out by the mock Prince's mock Solicitor and enclosed the subsequent entertainments within a parody of the statute's regulatory intentions and language. The detailed attention given by the revellers to their fabricated general pardon invites closer scrutiny of the historical model on which it was based and of the context in which this occasional measure became a fixture of the Elizabethan parliament.

The first part of this essay proceeds by investigating the "mischief" (in early modern legal terminology) that led to the development of the Elizabethan general pardon. The pardon's rhetoric, legal writings, and coterie literature from the period all represent the English subject as unjustly "snared" by statute law. These pervasive anxieties over the condition and application of the statutes resonate especially in John Donne's *Satyres*, which are heavily inflected by his experiences in the 1590s as a member of Lincoln's Inn and as a secretary to the Lord Keeper, Sir Thomas Egerton. In two of these satires, the speaker polarizes victimization-by-statute and statute-writing, which comes to represent the genuine legal, political, and social authority to which Donne and his coterie readers aspired.

Through the tactical extension of royal mercy, the Elizabethan general pardon was intended to mitigate the dangers that the law itself posed to the English people. At the same time, the pardon's contents also provided direction for the local execution of law and social policy. The second part of this essay treats in depth the Gray's Inn Christmas revels in which these two faces of the pardon come into focus. As it migrates to Gray's Inn Hall, the form of the general pardon explodes with excesses that invert and subvert its socio-political and regulatory utility, exposing an internal clash between the universal extension of royal mercy and the simultaneous extension of the law into every aspect of the subject's life. In parodying the structure and terms of this statute, the revellers deliberately undermine the corrective potential of a significant legal-political mechanism in order to illuminate its exploitative potential. In addition, the revellers' parody exaggerates the distortions to the statute form itself when it is twisted to accommodate contemporary political ends. The revels thus dramatize a structural threshold within the system, discovering within the relationship between legal instrument and lawmaker a point where the law's flexibility jeopardizes its integrity and functionality.

To the degree that it is possible, this article attempts to correct the general neglect of lawmaking and parliamentary writings within the fields of early modern law and literature, and politics and literature. Oliver Arnold has recently taken New Historicists to task for this oversight: "the new historicist map of early modern political culture has very seldom stretched beyond crown and court," with the result that the field has "discovered the crackle of art and psychic complexity in Elizabeth's speeches and James's many writings, but this ocean of parliamentary discourse remains unexplored."[7] A topic that should bridge legal and political cultural studies, lawmaking has instead fallen into the fissure produced by disciplinary divisions. The topic of the general pardon statute presents its own particular reasons for deflecting critical attention. It is conceivable that the very idea of a *general pardon* – which at various times included the forgiveness of offences ranging from treason, to homicide, to heresy, to violations of regulatory statutes – has been taken to be a particularly absurd extension of the revellers' fiction by modern readers of the *Gesta Grayorum*. This article places the revellers' parody within the context of the historical discourse on snaring statutes, the conventions of statute-writing, and the specific form of the Elizabethan general pardon.

The "Snared" Subject

The preamble of the Elizabethan general pardon statute refers to the sovereign's "m[er]cifull Disposicyon" towards her subjects, but this image of the queen is predicated on an unsettling (or, alternatively, a very funny) characterization of all her subjects as not only "lovinge" (loyal, dutiful), but also as legal offenders in need of a reprieve from legal punishment. The character of these legal offenders is redeemed, however, not only by their love for their sovereign but by the misfortune that triggered their entanglement with the law. They are presented as accidental offenders, devoid of criminal intention, stumbling into trouble: "Subject[es] have many and sundry waies by the Lawes and Statut[es] of this Realme, fallen into the daunger of div[er]se greate Penaltyes and Forfeytures ... wherewith her sayde Subject[es] stande now burthened and chardged." The Queen's mercy, it is expected, will inspire not the reform of conscience so much as a more attentive consideration of the law's extensive stipulations: she is "most graciouslie inclyned ... to dischardge some [part] of those greate Paynes Forfeytures and Penalties ... trustinge [her subjects] wilbe thereby the rather moved & induced from henceforthe more carefully to observe her Highnes Lawes and Statut[es]."[8] Speakers of the House traditionally thanked the Queen in return for her pardon during their closing speeches, assuring her that her subjects were "most graciouslie incited (by this your Majestie's clemencie) to a more dilligent and carefull observacion of your Highnes' lawes then heretofore wee have accustomed."[9] "[C]arefully to observe" the law is of course synonymous with obeying the law, but the phrasing of the statute preamble and the speaker's remarks implicate a legal system that required the subject's active ("dilligent and carefull") endeavour to keep clear of its punitive grasp. The general pardon statute's subsequent itemization of pardonable offences thus reveals the system's failings over and above the offender's. The statute was a tacit admission of and response to the law's continuing imperfections despite Parliament's best legislative efforts.

Numerous parliamentary speeches and legal reform writings shed light on the "swaruing [snaring] penalties that lye vpon many subiects" and that are implicated in the general pardon preamble.[10] The sheer volume of statutes that had accumulated by the end of the sixteenth century was a problem in itself, bewildering both subjects and legal representatives alike, and signalling (by the end of Elizabeth's reign) an increasingly restrictive social policy.[11] Condensing the number of laws through amendment and abridgement was repeatedly promoted by Elizabeth's first Lord Keeper, Nicholas Bacon, and those that came after him in largely unsuccessful attempts to mitigate the burden and confusion of statute law. In his opening remarks to the third Elizabethan parliament, he instructed Members, "yow are to looke whether there be too many lawes for any thinge, which breedeth soe many doubtes that the subiect somtime is to seeke howe to observe them and the counsellor howe to give advise concerninge them" (PPE 1:137–9). In the eighth parliament, Lord Keeper John Puckering cautioned Members "not to spend the tyme in devising of new lawes and statutes; wherof there is already so great store … that … it were more convenient by abridgment and explanacion to make them lesse difficill for the practise of them, then by addicion of newe, to increase the danger of the quiet subiect" (PPE 3:18).

In the same session, Francis Bacon (MP for Middlesex) found an opportunity to support Puckering's opening remarks and to echo his late father's: "scarce a whole year would suffice, to purge the statute-book [or] lessen the volume of laws; – being so many in number that neither common people can half practice them, nor the lawyer sufficiently understand them."[12] In a House of Commons speech from 1601, he urged "the repeal of divers statutes, and of divers superfluous branches of statutes … The more laws we make the more snares we lay to trap ourselves."[13] And again, in 1607, he complained that "this continual heaping up of laws without digesting them maketh but a chaos and confusion, and turneth the laws many times to become but snares for the people."[14] According to this parliamentary refrain, the law itself was an obstruction to justice. New legislation compounded with half-remembered and impenetrable older statutes to lie in wait for the English subject, unaware of his or her transgressions and likely unprepared to extricate himself or herself from the law's punishment.

Anxieties over the dangers to the subject from statute law focused in particular on the state of the penal laws, whose obsolete crimes or punishments could be turned into weapons through interpretation and application. It was a topic that would inspire a powerful rhetorical response from Francis Bacon throughout his legal-political career. In his essay "Of Judicature," for example, he depicts the strict application of the law as an injustice that would debilitate rather than reform subjects. While cautioning judges against both "hard constructions and strained inferences" in legal interpretations, he warns that "there is no worse torture then the torture of lawes; specially in case of Lawes penall": "[Judges] ought to haue care that that which was meant for terrour, be not turned into rigour; and that they bring not vpon the people that shower whereof the Scripture speaketh; Pluet super eos laqueos: For penall lawes pressed, are a showre of snares vpon the people."[15] Here, Bacon portrays the English subject's vulnerability before a legal process directed by a tyrannical judge. Later, in "A Proposition … Touching the Compiling and Amendment of the Laws of England," he vividly imagines the potential of these statutes to transform into mechanisms of social repression during "bad times" (i.e., under pressure from some kind of social, political, or economic crisis): "there are a number of ensnaring penal laws, which lie upon the subject; and if in bad times they should be awaked and put in execution, would grind them to powder."[16] Bacon was not alone in his concern with the state of these laws and the threat they posed to the English people. His professional and sociopolitical rival, Sir Edward Coke, similarly worried about the existence and enforcement of laws and punishments that were out of date: "certaine of our penall statutes ... time hath antiquated as unprofitable, and remaine but as snares to intangle the subjects withall."[17] Barbara Shapiro and Julian Martin both report that "[s]peeches which deplored the confusion produced by the tangle of penal laws" were made throughout the 1590s and 1601 parliaments.[18]

Literary historians, for their part, have yet to register the continuity between this legal-political discourse on the law's dangerous imperfections and the representation of statute law in literature from the period. I will examine this relationship in coterie works that characterize the subject's personal vulnerability before the law in contrast to the legal, political, and social pre-eminence embodied by statute-writing. John Donne's *Satyres* present young gallants as particularly susceptible to ensnarement within the statutory culture described above. For this very reason, statutes emerge as an expression, and statute-writing as a practice, of the authentic or fully realized social, legal, and political power to which the satiric speaker and his coterie audience aspire.

Statutes are not mentioned until the last two lines of Donne's "Satyre II," but they conclude a catalogue that progresses from the least to the most effectual forms of writing. Poets, playwrights, and those "who write to Lords, rewards to get ... like singers at doores for meat," are all outdone by barristers like "Coscus," who are becoming rich by buying up the property of "heires melting with luxurie."[19] Although Coscus will soon "compasse all the land, / From Scots, to Wight; from Mount, to Dover strand" through "parchments ... large as his fields" (ll. 77–8), the last two lines present statute-writing as an alternate form of legal-political power and as a weapon that could, if deployed correctly, forestall the progress and success of Coscus and his kind. "Satyre II" concludes with the courtier-speaker's complaint that "my words none drawes / Within the vast reach of th'huge statute lawes" (ll. 111–12), suggesting that the splenetic and detailed description of human faults and legal abuses found in the satire is generically related to statute law. Indeed, both satirist and legislator enjoyed a privileged liberty of speech and a "vast reach" when it came to the scrutiny of social, economic, and political conditions, and the morality of personal conduct. The "reformation of manners" was a preoccupation of each.[20]

That the Satirist's words are not statutes, however, reveals their poetic impotence; he is, in the end, one more of those poets who are "poore, disarm'd … not worth hate" (l. 10). His complaint becomes one last refraction of his social, economic, and finally political marginalization. Nevertheless, the speaker succeeds here in breaking down the binary opposition between gallant and lawyer that structures the rest of the poem, and with it the seemingly inevitable degeneration of the former's lifestyle and influence that correlated with the gains in the latter's. Studies on the Inns of Court emphasize social and class tensions between gentlemen's sons (who treated the Inns as finishing schools that would prepare them for a life at court) and serious law students (who were pursuing advancement through a profession).[21] Donne's speaker disrupts this dynamic by introducing a third term in the form of the legislator, a position to which the gallant may still aspire: although his words are not law, the speaker implies that his credentials as a satirist qualify or prepare him for the job of lawmaker. Donne increases the stakes of his satire by projecting the tensions among Inns students onto an arena of national political consequence.

"Satyre IV" likewise ends with an expression of the speaker's desire to see his verse adopted as a form of law ("some wise men shall, / I hope, esteeme my writs Canonicall" [ll. 243–4]), registering his frustrated ambition and worsening circumstances despite (or as a direct result of) his progress from the Inns of Court milieu to the Royal Court. The comparison drawn between satire and statute within "Satyre II" blows up into outright competition in "Satyre IV," in which the speaker paints himself and his fellow wits as unfairly targeted by the law. From the beginning, he aligns himself and his friends with the kind of hapless subject that is represented in the general pardon's preamble as innocently stumbling into trouble. We hear of "Glaze" or "Glare," who went "To'a Masse in jest, catch'd, was faine to disburse / The hundred markes, which is the Statutes curse, / Before he scapt" (ll. 8–11). A joke is taken too seriously, and statutory regulations impinge upon the gallants' penchant for (harmless?) jests and caprice. Glaze's case is then compared to that of the speaker, whose "destinie" finds him guilty of the "sin" of going to court and punishes him as if he were "As vaine, as witlesse, and as false as they / Which dwell at Court, for going once that way" (ll. 11–16). The law (man-made statute or destiny's) is unable to discriminate between irony and earnestness in the way that a witty satirist can. The satirist's judgment is more refined or subtle, and therefore potentially more equitable, than the law. The speaker implicitly defends Glaze and himself based on their non-serious intentions and the fact that their offences are isolated incidents, in light of which their respective punishments are excessive and unjust: Glaze must dole out a hundred marks, and the speaker is shadowed at court by an insufferable parasite.

The speaker's decision to take one anomalous action, however, paves the way for habitual misconduct. His so-called punishment quickly leads to more inadvertent offences the longer he remains at court. Socially trapped by the parasite, the speaker is forced to listen as his companion's conversation implicates him in gossip that rapidly progresses from "triviall household trash" (l. 98) to outright slander. That slander, in turn, degenerates into a form of treason, exaggerating (one hopes) the ease with which an individual (merely visiting court, merely listening to the wrong person – and unwillingly) may accidentally come within the law's grasp, imagined here as a form of monstrous ingestion:

> He [the parasite] like a priviledg'd spie, whom nothing can
> Discredit, Libells now 'gainst each great man ...
> I more amas'd then Circes prisoners, when
> They felt themselves turne beasts, felt my selfe then
> Becoming Traytor, and mee thought I saw
> One of our Giant Statutes ope his jaw
> To sucke me in; for hearing him. (ll. 119–36)

Given the new nature of his offence (treason) and the developing nature of his offensiveness (the speaker becomes characterized over the poem as a repeat offender), the speaker's punishment (the continued presence of this unshakable parasite) no longer seems unjust.

In order to uphold the fiction of the unfair law, the speaker reimagines his punishment as a fine so exorbitant that it would compensate not merely for a bad act or a bad character, but for original sin or the inherited weaknesses of human nature itself: "since I am in / I must pay mine, and my forefathers sinne / To the last farthing" (ll.137–9). But, we are told, "the'houre / Of mercy" (ll. 140–1) arrives, through which this incalculable fine is reduced to a comparably negligible payoff. The parasite requests, and receives, money before finally moving on to prowl for more benefactors:

> [He] tries to bring
> Me to pay a fine to scape his torturing,
> And saies, Sir, can you spare me; I said, willingly;
> Nay, Sir, can you spare me a crowne? Thankfully I
> Gave it, as Ransome ...
> But he is gone, thankes to his needy want,
> And the prerogative of my Crowne. (ll. 141–50)

The speaker can only escape the court parasite – and thus the jaws of "Giant Statutes" – through a "Ransome." At the turn of the seventeenth century, a "ransom" was an "action or means of freeing oneself from a penalty; a sum of money paid to obtain pardon for an offense or imposed as a penalty … a fine." A "ransom" was also, as it is today, a "sum or price paid or demanded for the release of a prisoner or hostage."[22] In Donne's "Satyre IV," both senses of the word resonate to implicate the parasite's tenacious attachment to the speaker and the law's aggressive hold (through giant statute jaws) on the English subject. The speaker's "Ransome" is paid by "the prerogative of my Crowne," playing on the name of the coin and comparing his release from the parasite's conversation to the Queen's mercy when it was extended to forgive statutory infractions or to rescue the subject from the law's unjust operations.

Donne uses the dynamics of the statute culture described above by legal experts and statesmen to shape the character – the moral judgment and the desires – of his satiric speaker. Over-identifying with the snared subject, the speaker is unable to make the leap from versifying to lawmaking. With much more gusto, the Gray's Inn revellers indulge downright in this legislative fantasy through their version of the general pardon statute. The historical menace from "Giant Statut[e] ... jaw[s]" was most successfully, or at least most publically, offset by the Elizabethan general pardon. But the pardon simultaneously encumbered the subject from another direction. The revellers approach the pardon as a device for social regulation that extended deep within the subject's life, conflicting with its ostensibly merciful project of forgiving infractions and fines. Through their interpretation of the statute's lists of pardonable offences and exceptions, the revellers display an acute knowledge of the structural and rhetorical dimensions of legislation that, in turn, would testify to their credentials for office-holding.

The Gray's Inn Revels and the Mock General Pardon Statute

While the rhetoric of the real statute's preamble expressed the hope that the Queen's clemency would inspire the better attention and obedience to her laws, the enlarged list of pardonable offences and the tone of linguistic and conceptual playfulness in the Prince of Purpoole's statute seemingly establish a culture of permissiveness. The list is organized by alliteration and rhyme more frequently than by legal categories of offence. Thus, alongside real and serious crimes are placed near-crimes and non-crimes: "Frauds" are grouped with "Fictions, Fractions, Fashions," and "Fancies"; "Conspiracies" with "Concavities." "Suppositions" are forgiven alongside "Suppositaries" (22), recalling a very old joke from George Gascoigne's *Supposes*, played at the Gray's Inn Candlemas revels some thirty years earlier. The revellers' expanded list of pardonable offences parodies the rhetorical flare-ups evident in the speeches of statesmen as well respected as Nicholas Bacon, who, in his first closing speech to Parliament, enlarged the role of magistrates in the following terms: "yee are to forsee the avoyding of all manner of frayes, forces, ryottes and rowtes, and the discoveringe and revealinge in tyme of all manner of conspiracyes, confederacyes and conventicles" (PPE 1:49). The revellers' statute mocks the lawyer's and the parliamentarian's well-known tendency towards verbosity and synonymity in the vain pursuit of comprehensiveness. In his study of "the way in which the commons debated the language of lawmaking itself," Seth Lerer tracks the critique of excessive amplification that was believed to breach parliamentary decorum and threaten the effectiveness of legislation.[23] Philip J. Finkelpearl writes that the revellers' pardon was "a gigantic, self-defeating 'amplificatio,' a parody of the attempt of legal documents to embrace all categories and possibilities."[24] In the case of the revellers' statute, however, I would argue that rhetorical effects of comprehensiveness do succeed in instituting an alarming form of legal comprehensiveness. The wordplay exposes the Prince's law as an instrument that enables the ensnarement of the subject and the state's aggressive sprawl into the subject's life. The superficial linguistic associations among major, minor, and imagined infractions (of decorum and of law) position minor offences on a continuum with major felonies: it is a slippery slope from the one to the other, greased by excesses of legal-political rhetoric. At the same time that the mock pardon's rhetorical excesses apparently stress a radical policy of permissiveness, that is, they also implicate the law's far-reaching application to "All, and all manner of" (22) subjects and their activities. No aspect of public or personal behaviour – including one's "Washings, Clippings and Shavings" (22) – was conceivably or actually beyond the reach of legal regulation. The mock pardon overwrites the law only to strategically illuminate the law's comprehensive jurisdiction over social life and personal conduct. Through their comical list of pardonable offences, then, the revellers bring the two faces of the general pardon – the lessening of the subject's statutory penalties and the increasing legal circumscription of the subject – into open conflict. That list is followed by satiric exceptions to the pardon that bring into focus the complexities of lawmaking in general and the distinct contradictions of a statute of general pardon in particular.

At the same time that the Queen's mercy ostensibly ransomed her subjects en masse through the real general pardon, the statute also defined the unpardonable in a list of exceptions through which the deliberate transgressions of subjects were itemized. That is, these exceptions highlighted intentional rather than accidental offences and were explicitly included in order that they would receive the full attention of the law. This list of exceptions conventionally included serious felonies and the infractions of officers side by side with pressing social problems identified in Parliament or by the Privy Council.[25] Through the statute's lists of pardonable and unpardonable offences, judges and local office-holders were guided as to which infractions to forgive and which to punish; they were guided as to the execution of which laws within an overgrown system of statutes best reflected the central government's social policy. Despite its practical utility for magistrates, however, the general pardon introduced complications into the conventional statute form.

In his (serious, technical) *Reading of the Statute of Uses*, presented to the same community of Gray's Inn in 1600, Francis Bacon divided statutes into three parts: "The statute consisteth … upon a preamble, the body of the law, and certain savings and provisoes. The preamble setteth forth the inconvenience; the body of the law giveth the remedy; and the savings and provisos take away the inconveniences of the remedy."[26] "Provisoes" were built into the lawmaking process to circumvent the contradictions and uncertainties attendant upon legal innovations. Bacon explains: "For new laws are like the apothecaries' drugs; though they remedy the disease, yet they trouble the body: and therefore they use to correct them with spices. So it is not possible to find a remedy for any mischief in the commonwealth, but it will beget some new mischief; and therefore they spice their laws with provisos to correct and qualify them."[27] Bacon's elaboration on "provisoes" is a product of his concern with legal reform and with method – legal, rhetorical, philosophical, and scientific. Indeed, the reforming and refining mechanism of the statute proviso closely resembles a key stage of his philosophical method. As Daniel Coquillette notes, the "final step of 'negation' or 'definition by exception' [that] was to become an important part of Bacon's philosophical method" was already present in his early legal works.[28] The statutes are larded with hypothetical clauses beginning with "Provided that" and "Provided alwaies." As with amplification, however, these "strings of qualifiers that distinguish the rhetoric of act and statute" incited anxieties about their potential to backfire. Lerer quotes a parliamentarian from 1571 who argues that provisos "have bene oft the overthrow of that which was truly ment, wherein the cunninge adversary ... subtilly insert more ... to the hindrance of the whole."[29] This potential for legislative confusion (accidental or deliberate) was augmented by the form of the general pardon. And, as with their own take on legal-parliamentary amplification, the Gray's Inn revellers' version of the proviso implicates what was "truly ment" or enabled by the device on a political level.

In the historical general pardon, the conditional provisos occur chiefly in the form of "exceptions" through which the statute explicitly doubles back upon itself. This statute was an assertion of the sovereign's prerogative power, of her authority to designate the exception through mercy; and the pardon was one enormous exception, ostensibly a universal liberation from the rule of law. Thus, the statute's provisos constituted exceptions to an exception. In the 1594–5 revels, the fictional pardon's exceptions are further qualified – there are exceptions to the exceptions to the exception – derailing sense and exposing the awkwardness of the Crown's improvisation on a legal form that cannot comfortably frame a general pardon: "Except, All such Persons as shall shoot in any Hand-Gun, Demy-Hag, or Hag-Butt, either Half-shot, or Bullet, at any Fowl, Bird, or Beast; either at any Deer, Red or Fallow, or any other thing or things, except it be a Butt set, laid, or raised in some convenient place, fit for the same purpose" (26). Taken in a general sense, this provision amounts to a caution not to shoot unless you have a good shot. Taken in a more technical or legal sense, the provision warns subjects that they are prohibited from hunting unless, of course, it is legal. In the Gray's Inn Christmas revels, the exceptions multiply until the statute form collapses upon itself, inverting the pardon's apparent intention. The revellers expose and mock the actual Elizabethan statute's inversion of a basic legal intuition about the nature of rules inherent in the very idea of a general pardon from the rule of law. They expose and mock, too, the inversion of a legal and commonplace intuition about the nature of clemency produced by a general pardon that was, in reality, heavily restrictive.

Though the real provisos were supposed to qualify and refine new or amended legislation, the revellers' exceptions ultimately undo the apparent magnanimity of the Prince of Purpoole's statute. This is vividly evident in the very last exception. While "all, and all manner of Treasons, Contempts, [and] Offences" are initially forgiven, the Prince's Solicitor concludes with a bald negation in which "All, and all manner of Offences, Pains, Penalties, Mulets, Fines, Amerciaments and Punishments, Corporal and Pecuniary, whatsoever" (27) are finally excluded from the pardon. Once the reader gets past this blatant about-face, a more technical sleight of hand becomes evident. Whereas the beginning of the statute emphasizes the pardon of offences, the final exception emphasizes the enforcement of punishments, particularly (though not exclusively) the pecuniary kind. If the real statute is presented as a generous release from the "burthen" of "greate Penaltyes and Forfeytures" inflicted for inadvertent infractions, here in the Prince of Purpoole's statute the penalties for those infractions still apply and with them – and this is the joke – the Crown's income from the judicial process. K.J. Kesselring explains that Henry VIII's first general pardon proclamation was intended to allay public resentment inspired by the perception that Henry VII and his chief financial officers had exploited legal processes for profit at the expense of English subjects.[30] Future pardons "provided appropriate expressions of gratitude for taxation because the king willingly forfeited the financial proceeds of his justice" and "freed people of the fines that potentially attended a host of business transactions and from the costs of often protracted litigation on these matters."[31]

While all the Tudor monarchs except Mary enhanced their public image as merciful and magnanimous rulers through the general pardon, Elizabeth turned what had been an occasional measure into a regular feature of Parliament and thus into a constituent aspect of the spectacle of her royal justice.[32] In legal writings and in his first masque-like device, Francis Bacon links the Queen's virtue as a sovereign to the protection she provided subjects from excessive penalties and snaring statutes. In *Of Tribute; or, Giving That Which Is Due* (1592), the speaker in "Praise of His Sovereign" addresses, among many other matters of state, the Queen's moderate methods of raising revenue: "[t]here shall you find … no extremities taken of forfeitures and penal laws, a means used by some kings for the gathering of great treasures … Yea further, there have been … a course taken by her own direction for the repeal of all heavy and snaring laws."[33] In his Dedication to the Queen in *The Maximes of the Law* (1596/7), he lauds the "purpose for these many yeares, infused into your Maiesties breast, to enter into a generall amendment of the states of your lawes," including the removal of "the swaruing penalties that lye vpon many subiects." This project is "greater than wee can imagine … of highest merit and beneficence towards the subiect … because the imperfections and dangers of the lawes are couered vnder the clemency and excellent temper of your Maiesties gouernment."[34] In the absence of systemic law reform, the Queen's mercy, embodied in the general pardon statute, provided a necessary supplement to the law. The general pardon was "an act of grace, a gift from the royal prerogative"[35] for the benefit of her subjects whose welfare was threatened by the postlapsarian system of man's laws.

The members of Gray's Inn also used the general pardon as a vehicle for self-promotion, though to very different effect. On the one hand, their mock statute demonstrated a mastery of legal-political forms and discourse that the revellers were able to wield for their sport. The compressed mock parliament was an opportunity to showcase expertly honed skills for service to the state. Their festivities advertised the revellers' ability to fit themselves into the system and roles of central power relations in a blatantly literal way. As substitutes for legal-political substitutes, as representations of representatives, they broadcasted their finesse as officials in a culture "predispos[ed] to delegate authority."[36] As mock lawmakers, they showed their commitment to the system's continuity through the reiteration and propagation of law. On the other hand, the Gray's Inn statute uncovers "the imperfections and dangers of the lawes," specifically the dangers posed by the lawmakers themselves. The reconstruction of the general pardon parodies the rhetoric, complications, and contradictions of an accepted improvisation of power through which the traditional statute form was manipulated to accommodate political ends that could exploit the subject. Through their parody of legal forms and processes, the revellers thus highlight the unavoidable creative dimension of legal-political administration that resulted from the contribution of individuals making, interpreting, reproducing, reforming, and executing the law. The mock general pardon ultimately points to the officer's or statesman's character as the enabling or limiting condition of an effective justice system.

NOTES

1 The Inns of Court are the historical educational institutions and professional societies of the English common law. For a full account of the current state of research on the Inns of Court, see Jayne Elizabeth Archer, Elizabeth Goldring, and Sarah Knight, eds, *The Intellectual and Cultural World*. Future work will no doubt benefit from the new three-volume guide to surviving dramatic records of the Inns of Court (1407–1642) from the Records of Early English Drama, Alan H. Nelson and John R. Elliott Jr, eds, *Inns of Court*.
2 On *The Comedy of Errors* in connection with the revels or the Inns of Court, see Margaret Knapp and Michal Kobialka, "Shakespeare and the Prince of Purpoole"; Douglas Lanier, "'Stigmatical in Making'"; Elizabeth Rivlin, "Theatrical Literacy"; Lorna Hutson, *The Invention of Suspicion*, especially chapter 4; Andrew Zurcher, "Consideration, Contract and the End of *The Comedy of Errors*"; Barbara Kreps, "Playing the Law for Lawyers"; Lorna Hutson, "The Evidential Plot"; Bradin Cormack, "Locating *The Comedy of Errors*"; and Richard C. McCoy, "Law Sports and the Night of Errors."
3 D.S. Bland, ed., *Gesta Grayorum*, p. 32. This text is cited parenthetically in the text hereafter.
4 Zurcher, "Consideration," p. 33.
5 Zurcher reads error during the revels as strategic and only as a pretence. No parliament was ever really intended; the "Night of Errors" was more or less scripted. On theatrical confusion, see also William N. West, "'But this will be a mere confusion,'" pp. 217–33. On the script and the rhetoric of interruptions and Inns-of-Court revels, see Ann Hurley, "Interruption."
6 David Dean, *Law-Making and Society*, p. 55. See also K.J. Kesselring, *Mercy and Authority*, pp. 56–73. *A Treatise Concerning Statutes, or Acts of Parliament: and The Exposition Thereof*, attributed to Christopher Hatton, distinguishes between those statutes whose benefits "seem to proceed from subjects only to the Prince, as those of … Subsidies, and some other of like nature," and those whose benefits "seem to proceed from the Prince only, as Pardons and Priviledges, Confirmations of Customes, and such like" (3–4).
7 Oliver Arnold, *The Third Citizen: Shakespeare's Theater and the Early Modern House of Commons*, pp. 24–5.

8 35 Eliz. c. 14.

9 Proceedings in the Parliaments of Elizabeth I, 27. Hereafter this text is cited parenthetically in the text by PPE followed by the volume and page number.

10 Francis Bacon, *The Elements of the Common Lawes of England*, sig. A4^r. Henceforth this work is cited as Maximes.

11 On the increasing number of exceptions to the general pardon and the increasingly restrictive nature of Elizabethan governance, see Kesselring, *Mercy and Authority*, p. 69.

12 Quoted in Daniel R. Coquillette, *Francis Bacon*, p. 29.

13 Bacon, *The Letters and Life*, p. 19.

14 Bacon, *The Letters and Life*, p. 336.

15 Francis Bacon, "Of Judicature," *Essaies*, pp. 213–14.

16 Francis Bacon, "A Proposition to His Majesty by Sir Francis Bacon … Touching the Compiling and Amendment of the Laws of England," in *Works*, p. 367.

17 Edward Coke, *Selected Writings*, p. 97.

18 Julian Martin, *Francis Bacon*, p. 107; Barbara Shapiro, "Codification," p. 437.

19 John Donne, 'Satyre II,' in *Complete English Poems*, ll. 79. All references to Donne's Satyres are to this edition and will appear in the text.

20 On the traditions of "free" speech and criticism within the Inns of court and within parliament, see Arthur Marotti, John Donne, *Coterie Poet*, pp. 33–4.

21 See Marotti, *John Donne, Coterie Poet*, pp. 25–43, esp. p. 40; Wilfred Prest, *The Inns of Court*, pp. 40–6; and Ronald J. Corthell, '"Coscus onely breeds my just offence.'"

22 "ransom, n.," *OED Online*, March 2010, Oxford UP, web, 8 June 2010.

23 Seth Lerer, "An Art of the Emetic," 173. Francis Bacon was quite articulate about the self-defeating work of legal verbosity: "The loquacity and prolixity used in the drawing up of laws I do not approve. For it does not at all secure its intention and purpose; but rather the reverse. For while it tries to enumerate and express every particular case in apposite and appropriate words, expecting greater certainty thereby; it does in fact raise a number of questions about words; so that, by reason of the noise and strife of words, the interpretation which proceeds according to the meaning of the law (which is juster and sounder kind of interpretation) is rendered more difficult" (qtd in Donald Veall, *The Popular Movement for Law Reform*, p. 64).

24 Philip J. Finkelpearl, *John Marston of the Middle Temple*, p. 42.

25 Dean, *Law-Making and Society*, pp. 34–5; See also the later Elizabethan Acts of General Pardon: 27 Eliz. c. 30, 31 Eliz. c. 16, 35 Eliz. c. 14, 39 Eliz. c. 28, 43 Eliz. c. 19.

26 Francis Bacon, *Reading on the Statute of Uses*, in *The Works of Francis Bacon*, ed. James Spedding, Robert Leslie Ellis, and Douglas Denon Heath, p. 417. According to Coquillette, Bacon's *Reading on the Statute of Uses* 'was the closest thing to a modern theory of statutory interpretation until Jeremy Bentham's *A General View of a Complete Code of Laws, Pannomial Fragments*, and *The Promulgation of Laws*, two centuries later' (Coquillette, *Francis Bacon*, p. 59). This particular passage echoes Sir Thomas Egerton's earlier treatise on statute interpretation: see *A Discourse upon the Exposicion [and] Understandinge of Statutes; with Sir Thomas Egerton's Additions*.

27 Ibid., pp. 417–18. In the Preface to *The Maximes of the Law* (contemporaneous with the Gray's Inn Christmas revels), Bacon would explain that his novel method for the "cleere and perspicuous exposition" of legal rules entailed 'opening them with distinctions' (*Maximes*, sig. B4^{v}). A few years later, in *The Advancement of Learning*, he would criticize the traditional form of rhetorical induction, 'For to conclude upon an enumeration of particulars without instance contradictory is no conclusion, but a conjecture' (p. 221).

28 Coquillette, *Francis Bacon*, p. 41. On the relationship between Bacon's legal practice, statecraft, and natural philosophy, see Martin and Coquillette. By contrast, the work of Markku Peltonen argues that the various projects that captured Bacon's attention cannot be synthesized, as recent studies have sought to do: 'Politics and Science,' pp. 279–305.

29 Lerer, *Air of the Emetic*, p. 173

30 Kesselring, *Mercy and Authority*, p. 60.

31 Ibid., p. 61.

32 Ibid., p. 67.

33 Francis Bacon, "Of Tribute; or, Giving That Which Is Due," in *Francis Bacon: A Critical Edition*, p. 40.

34 *Maximes*, sig. A4^{r}.

35 Dean, *Francis Bacon*, p. 56.

36 Hindle, *State and Social Change*, p. 5.

BIBLIOGRAPHY

Archer, Jayne Elizabeth, Elizabeth Goldring, and Sarah Knight, eds. *The Intellectual and Cultural World of the Early Modern Inns of Court*. Manchester: Manchester UP, 2011.

Arnold, Oliver. *The Third Citizen: Shakespeare's Theater and the Early Modern House of Commons*. Baltimore: Johns Hopkins UP, 2007.

Bacon, Francis. "The Advancement of Learning." In *Francis Bacon: A Critical Edition of the Major Works*. Ed. Brian Vickers. Oxford: Oxford UP, 1996. 120–299.

– *The Elements of the Common Lawes of England*. London, 1630.

– *The Essaies of Sr Francis Bacon Knight, the Kings Solliciter Generall*. London, 1612.

– *Francis Bacon: A Critical Edition of the Major Works*. Ed. Brian Vickers. Oxford: Oxford UP, 1996.

– *The Letters and Life of Francis Bacon*. Vol. 3. Ed. James Spedding. London, 1868.

– *The Works of Francis Bacon*. Vol. 4. Ed. James Spedding. London, 1826.

– *The Works of Francis Bacon*. Vol. 7. Ed. James Spedding, Robert Leslie Ellis, and Douglas Denon Heath. London, 1879.

Bald, R.C. *John Donne: A Life*. Oxford: Clarendon P, 1970.

Bevington, David. "The Comedy of Errors in the Context of the Late 1580s and Early 1590s." In The Comedy of Errors*: Critical Essays*. Ed. Robert S. Miola. New York: Garland Publishing, 1997. 335–53.

Bland, D.S., ed. *Gesta Grayorum or the History of the High and Mighty Prince Henry Prince of Purpoole, Anno Domini 1594*. Liverpool: Liverpool UP, 1968.

Bullough, Geoffrey. "Donne, The Man of Law." In *Just So Much Honor: Essays Commemorating the Four-Hundredth Anniversary of the Birth of John Donne*. Ed. Peter Amadeus Fiore. University Park: Pennsylvania State UP, 1972. 57–94.

Coke, Edward. *The Selected Writings of Sir Edward Coke*. Vol. 1. Ed. Steve Sheppard. Indianapolis: Liberty Fund, 2003.

Coquillette, Daniel R. *Francis Bacon*. Edinburgh: Edinburgh UP, 1992.

Cormack, Bradin. "Locating *The Comedy of Errors*: Revels Jurisdiction at the Inns of Court." In *The Intellectual and Cultural World of the Early Modern Inns of Court*. Ed. Jayne Elizabeth Archer, Elizabeth Goldring, and Sarah Knight. Manchester: Manchester UP, 2011. 264–85.

Corthell, Ronald J. "'Coscus onely breeds my just offence': A Note on Donne's 'Satire II' and the Inns of Court." John Donne Journal 6, no. 1 (1997): 25–31.

Dean, David. *Law-Making and Society in Late Elizabethan England: The Parliament of England, 1584–1601*. Cambridge: Cambridge UP, 1996.

Donne, John. *Complete English Poems*. Ed. C.A. Patrides. London: J.M. Dent, 1994.

Egerton, Thomas. *A Discourse upon the Exposicion [and] Understandinge of Statutes; with Sir Thomas Egerton's Additions*. Ed. Samuel E. Thorne. San Marino, CA: Huntington Library, 1942.

Finkelpearl, Philip J. *John Marston of the Middle Temple: An Elizabethan Dramatist in His Social Setting*. Cambridge, MA: Harvard UP, 1969.

Hatton, Christopher. *A Treatise Concerning Statutes, or Acts of Parliament: and The Exposition Thereof*. London, 1677.

Hindle, Steve. *The State and Social Change in Early Modern England, c. 1550–1640*. Houndmills, Basingstoke, Hampshire: St Martin's Press, 2000.

Hurley, Ann. "Interruption: The Transformation of a Critical Feature of Ritual from Revel to Lyric in John Donne's Inns of Court Poetry of the 1590s." In *Ceremony and Text in the Renaissance*. Ed. Douglas F. Rutledge. Cranbury: Associated University Presses, 1996. 103–21.

Hutson, Lorna. "The Evidential Plot: Shakespeare and Gasgoigne at Gray's Inn." In *The Intellectual and Cultural World of the Early Modern Inns of Court*. Ed. Jayne Elizabeth Archer, Elizabeth Goldring, and Sarah Knight. Manchester: Manchester UP, 2011. 245–63.

– *The Invention of Suspicion: Law and Mimesis in Shakespeare and Renaissance Drama*. Oxford: Oxford UP, 2008.

Kesselring, K.J. *Mercy and Authority in the Tudor State*. Cambridge: Cambridge UP, 2003.

Knafla, Louis A. "Mr. Secretary Donne: The Years with Sir Thomas Egerton." In *John Donne's Professional Lives*. Ed. David Colclough. Cambridge: D.S. Brewer, 2003. 37–73.

Knapp, Margaret, and Michal Kobialka. "Shakespeare and the Prince of Purpoole: The 1594 Production of The Comedy of Errors at Gray's Inn Hall." *Theatre History Studies* 4 (1984): 71–81.

Kneidel, Gregory. "Coscus, Queen Elizabeth, and the Law in John Donne's 'Satyre II.'" *Renaissance Quarterly* 61, no. 1 (2008): 92–121.

– "Donne's *Satyre I* and the Closure of the Law." *Renaissance and Reformation / Renaissance et Réforme* 28, no. 4 (2004): 83–103.

Kreps, Barbara. "Playing the Law for Lawyers: Witnessing, Evidence and the Law of Contract in *The Comedy of Errors*." *Shakespeare Survey* 63 (2010): 262–71.

Lanier, Douglas. "'Stigmatical in Making.'" In *The Comedy of Errors: Critical Essays*. Ed. Robert S. Miola. New York: Garland Publishing, 1997. 335–53.

Lerer, Seth. "An Art of the Emetic: Thomas Wilson and the Rhetoric of Parliament." *Studies in Philology* 98, no. 2 (2001): 158–83.

Marotti, Arthur. *John Donne, Coterie Poet*. Madison: U of Wisconsin P, 1986.

Martin, Julian. *Francis Bacon, the State, and the Reform of Natural Philosophy*. Cambridge: Cambridge UP, 1992.

Maule, Jeremy. "Donne and the Words of the Law." In *John Donne's Professional Lives*. Ed. David Colclough. Cambridge: D.S. Brewer, 2003. 19–36.

McCoy, Richard C. "Law Sports and the Night of Errors: Shakespeare at the Inns of Court." In *The Intellectual and Cultural World of the Early Modern Inns of Court*. Ed. Jayne Elizabeth Archer, Elizabeth Goldring, and Sarah Knight. Manchester: Manchester UP, 2011. 286–301.

Nelson, Alan H., and John R. Elliott Jr., eds. *Inns of Court*. Woodbridge: Boydell and Brewer, 2010.

Peltonen, Markku. "Politics and Science: Francis Bacon and the True Greatness of States." *Historical Journal* 35, no. 2 (1992): 279–305.

Prest, Wilfred. *The Inns of Court under Elizabeth I and the Early Stuarts, 1590–1640*. London: Longman, 1972.

Proceedings in the Parliaments of Elizabeth I, vol. 2. Ed. T.E. Hartley. Wilmington, DE: M. Glazier, 1981.

Rivlin, Elizabeth. "Theatrical Literacy in *The Comedy of Errors* and the *Gesta Grayorum*.' *Critical Survey* 14, no. 1 (2002): 64–78.

Shakespeare, William. *The Norton Shakespeare*. Ed. Stephen Greenblatt et al. New York: W.W. Norton, 1997.

Shapiro, Barbara. "Codification of the Laws in Seventeenth Century England." *Wisconsin Law Review* 2 (1974): 428–65.

Veall, Donald. *The Popular Movement for Law Reform, 1640–1660*. Oxford: Clarendon P, 1970.

West, William N. "'But this will be a mere confusion': Real and Represented Confusions on the Elizabethan Stage.' *Theatre Journal* 60 (2008): 217–33.

Zurcher, Andrew. "Consideration, Contract and the End of *The Comedy of Errors*." In *Shakespeare and the Law*. Ed. Paul Raffield and Gary Watt. Oxford: Hart, 2008. 19–37.

5 The Prison Diaries of Archbishop Laud[1]

DEBORA SHUGER

William Laud, archbishop of Canterbury since 1633, began his prison diaries in March of 1641, when Parliament had him confined to the Tower on charges of high treason; the last entry is dated 3 January 1645, the day Laud received word that the Lords had passed the bill of attainder sentencing him to death. The diaries, which include a detailed narrative of his 1644 trial, exist in two manuscript versions. In the original diary, Laud wrote each day's events on one of the facing pages, initially leaving the other page blank; he then used the blank pages to add comments and context, filling out the narrative in preparation for his closing statement but also with an eye to future publication.[2] The diaries stop a week before Laud's death, and it may have been during this week that Laud had a copyist rewrite the original manuscript, this time weaving together both sides of the page to create a single continuous account, in the hope that it would be translated into Latin after his death to inform "the judgment of the learned in all parts of Christendom" (3:120). This second manuscript must have been prepared in haste, since when it resurfaced during the Restoration it was judged too defective to print. Shortly thereafter, however, William Sancroft found the original at St John's, Oxford; the promised edition failed to materialize because in 1677 Sancroft found himself archbishop of Canterbury; at his death sixteen years later, he left the half-finished project to Henry Wharton, who in 1696 finally brought out the prison diaries under the lamentable title, *The History of the Troubles and Trial of the Most Reverend Father in God, William Laud*. The narrative, which fills over six hundred pages in the nineteenth-century edition of Laud's collected works, is one of the unacknowledged masterpieces of English prose.

The charges against Laud included attempting "to subvert the fundamental laws and government of the kingdom," "to introduce an arbitrary and tyrannical government against law," and to corrupt "the true religion here established" (3:398, 4:300). As these suggest, the proceedings belong among the post-Reformation religio-political *causes célèbres* that fill the first two volumes of *State Trials*. Yet in crucial respects, Laud's trial stands alone. The difference has to do with the nature of Laud's defence: in contrast to the other post-Reformation state trials where religion played a key role, Laud based his defence on fact rather than law; that is, whereas in most such trials the accused fought conviction by alleging procedural iniquities,[3] Laud argued that he was not, in point of fact, guilty. Yet he does now and then comment on procedural matters – on the justice, or lack thereof, of the proceedings – and, as the rest of this essay will attempt to show, these comments repay consideration.

Throughout most of the Caroline period, Laud had sat on both Star Chamber and High Commission, courts whose quasi-criminal proceedings did *not* use common law forms but something akin to canon and civil law procedure – the procedure, that is, of the Continental *ius commune*.[4] Laud's own trial, however, was at common law – and its workings often seem to have taken him by surprise. The diaries give Laud's summary of and response to each day's hearing – recounting the evidence and arguments presented by both sides, but also, in "crochets," what he wished he had remembered to say, or what he thought but decided against saying (4:51). His comments on the procedural aspects of the trial thus express ad hoc reactions to the day's events, not a thought-out position on the common law. Yet, taken together, these comments present a fairly serious critique of its criminal procedure – a critique from the unusual (and perhaps for this period unique) "outside" perspective of someone accustomed to canon and civil law suddenly confronted with English exceptionalism. Both then and now, accounts of the common law tend to be inside jobs. Moreover, since common law won the day (Star Chamber and High Commission were abolished in the 1640s, most other non-common law courts soon thereafter), it gets all the good press, and indeed virtually all the coverage. Most of the new Law and Literature scholarship, at least for the early modern period, gives similarly short shrift to non-common law traditions, which it tends to dislike on instinct. Laud's perspective is thus highly unusual, and for that reason alone of *prima facie* interest.

Whether Laud *had* a common law trial, of course, remains to be seen. As archbishop, Laud was a peer, which moved his trial into the House of Lords, whose members served as both judge and jury. The exigencies of civil war resulted in the Commons, rather than the King's attorney, conducting the prosecution; four MPs, all common lawyers, served as prosecutors, each presenting a portion of the case to the Upper House. What catches Laud's attention, however, is not this unusual set-up, but a cluster of rules and procedures that clearly strike him as deeply problematic. First, the Commons is not just conducting the prosecution but basically running the entire trial. The judges (i.e., the members of the House of Lords) have only a passive role; they can neither call witnesses nor cross-examine them; nor can they summon records or investigate allegations. In their deliberations, they must rely on notes provided them by the prosecution: notes that time and again laid out the evidence against the accused but omitted his response (4:416).

Moreover, not only is the prosecution calling all the shots, but the men in charge of the prosecution included several of Laud's bitterest personal enemies. The Commons appointed Alexander Leighton (4:14) and William Prynne (4:24), both of whom had previously been sentenced in Star Chamber for writing violently abusive libels against Laud, to build the prosecution case. Prynne, whom the Commons put in charge of the evidence, was a busy beaver throughout, serving, in Laud's words, as "relater, and prompter, and all, never weary of anything, so he might do me mischief" (4:47). He apparently concealed the existence of the Elizabethan and Jacobean coronation books that would have proven Laud's innocence of one of the gravest charges – that of tampering with the oath administered to Charles at his coronation (4.213). To support the charge of "popery," Prynne introduced in evidence a paper itemizing, he claimed, the rich furnishing of Laud's private chapel at Aberguilly; at the reading of which paper, Laud recounts, "I was a little troubled. I knew I was not then so rich as to have such plate, or furniture; and therefore I humbly desired sight of the paper. So soon as I saw it, I found there was nothing in it in my hand but the endorsement, which told the reader plainly that it was the model of reverend Bishop Andrewes his chapel." That is, the paper included a note in Laud's handwriting stating that the furnishings were those of Lancelot Andrewes's chapel at Winchester. Laud showed the endorsement to the Lords, noting in his diary (in crochets) that "it would have made any man ashamed but Mr. Prynne, who had delivered upon oath that it was a paper of my chapel furniture at Aberguilly, contrary to his conscience, and his own eyesight of the paper" (4:251).

Prynne had been Laud's bitterest enemy for two decades, his appointment eliciting the latter's dry observation that "it will not be the greatest honor to these proceedings, that he [Prynne] ... should now be thought the only fit and indifferent man to be trusted with the witnesses and the evidence against me" (4:47–8). Nor was Prynne the only one who prosecuted in the spirit of no-holds-barred partisanship. At least two of the charges against Laud had been investigated by the Commons shortly before his trial, and in both instances the enquiry had determined that the charge was false. The members of the prosecution team had been in the Commons when these determinations were made, yet they revive both allegations at Laud's trial – without ever even mentioning the Commons' prior investigation (4:219, 4:330–1).[5] With the exception of Samuel Browne (4:402), the MPs appointed by the Commons to present the case against Laud approach their task in the spirit of hostile *parties* rather than as officers of the court.

The prison diaries also comment on the fact that Laud had no legal representation, and was barred even from seeking legal advice until the last day of the trial, when the focus shifted from issues of fact to those of law. Until then, he had to conduct his own defence, although confined to the Tower, without access to his papers or to potential defence witnesses (4:50). Furthermore, although he had advance notice of the general charges, these turn out to be uselessly vague; the treason charge thus accuses him of attempting to subvert the "fundamental laws" of the kingdom; its failure to indicate what these laws were elicits Laud's barbed protest that, since "men's lives [are being] called this way in question, 'tis very requisite that these 'fundamental laws' were known to all men, that so they may see the danger before they run upon it; whereas now the common laws of England have no text at all," so that even experienced lawyers "cannot in many points assure a man what the law is. And by this means, the judges have liberty to retain more in *scrinio pectoris* than is fitting, and which comes a little too near that 'arbitrary government' so much and so justly found fault with; whereas there is no kingdom (that I know) that hath a settled government but it hath also a text ... of the laws written, save England" (3:399). What makes an arbitrary power tyrannical is precisely its uncertainty: if there is no set (i.e., written) definition of what the law is, you cannot know in advance whether doing such-and-such will violate it. This had been the common lawyers' argument against the royal prerogative, so Laud here is (quite brilliantly) turning the tables.[6]

Laud has advance notice only of the vague general charges. As he several times points out, he has seen neither the specific charges nor the evidence allegedly supporting them until the day on which the prosecution presented that portion of the case (4:38, 4:43), and that he had to answer the same day, with no time given him to gather counter-evidence or locate defence witnesses (4:46). Even if he could identify a potential defence witness, he had no authority to summon the person, although the diaries imply that if such a witness happened to be present in the House, Laud could request that he testify (4:46). He could, of course, ask the court to summon a witness on his behalf, but such requests rarely met with success. Moreover, the prosecution, which could summon witnesses, often failed to do so. Instead, Laud notes, they frequently relied on hearsay testimony, which the court allowed even on occasions when the alleged speaker was alive, nearby, and presumably could have been called (4:122–4, 4:171). Thus to support the charge that Laud pressured a church court to overturn its ruling on a matter of altar policy, the prosecution introduces a witness who testifies that "Mr. Morgan, a man inward with the judge [Chief Justice Finch], 'told him [the witness], that the judge told him [Mr. Morgan], that the little man [Laud] had put a spoke in their cart; and thereupon,' as he [the witness] conceives, 'the petty jury was changed.'" To which Laud responds with understandable outrage that this "is the witness's report of Mr. Morgan's report, that the judge had said so of me: but why is not Mr. Morgan produced to clear this" (4:122). We hear nothing further of Mr Morgan, but the next witness testifies that he was told that "upon petition to Sir Wi. Portman for some assistance, the Bishop of Bath [Piers] laid all upon me [Laud]," whereupon Laud asks the obvious question: "Why is not the Bishop [Piers] that is said to lay all upon me brought into the court, that he may clear himself and me, if he said it not; or that I may make him ashamed, if he said it?" (4:123–4). Piers is not called. The diaries indicate that the court consistently dismissed these objections to treating hearsay as evidence.

The least expected of Laud's difficulties with the procedures governing his trial, and the last to be considered, was the court's refusal to allow oath-taking as a form of proof. When he hears the charge of popery, his first instinct is to deny it under oath with his hand on the Bible; turning to his judges, he thus declares, "I do here offer my corporal oath (please it the Lords to give it me), in the strictest form that any oath can be conceived, that I am wholly innocent of this charge" (3:413). The offer is refused, but later, in crochets, the diaries include just such an oath as being the only possible proof the charge allows – the charge in this case being that he had had dealings with the papal nuncio, George

Con. Since one cannot prove a negative,[7] all Laud can do is flatly deny that any such contact took place, but in the margins of the diary he adds "*in verbo sacerdotis*, this is true" (4:332). The unavailability of the oath looms large in the surreal final moments of the trial, when the prosecution introduces a dream Laud allegedly had years before about dying on the gallows. Whether or not Laud dreamt this had, obviously, no legal significance, but he clearly found the allegation profoundly upsetting. As before, since the court will not allow him to be sworn, Laud uses the diary to take the oath that, in his eyes, should have constituted presumptive proof of innocence: "But once for all, and to satisfy any man that desires it, that is all true which I have here set down concerning this dream, and upon my Christianity and hope of future salvation, I never had this dream nor any like it" (4:367).

What is one to make of this Kafkaesque trial? Since the trial notes taken by the Clerk of the Parliaments, John Browne, corroborate Laud's version, dismissing the prison diaries as self-serving fiction, which had been my first instinct, does not seem an option.[8] Yet perhaps what they accurately record was a highly irregular show trial: an unfortunate episode, to be sure, but the sort of thing that happens in times of crisis. This second hypothesis, however, also failed inspection. Laud's trial, it turns out, was not an aberration but followed standard common law criminal procedures.

To see this, one need only look at the portions of John Langbein's *The Origins of the Adversary Criminal Trial* dealing with early modern England. These reveal that in the sixteenth and seventeenth centuries, criminal defence was almost always a "do-it-yourself activity," since in capital cases the accused could not have counsel except on controverted points of law (48).[9] However, except in major state trials, neither was there a lawyer for the prosecution; instead, the victim of the alleged crime or (in murder trials) the victim's kin prosecuted the case (11). A Frenchman visiting England in the early nineteenth century was thus appalled to discover that the English did not have a cadre of experienced and reasonably impartial court officers either to investigate or prosecute crimes, both tasks being "committed entirely to the hands of the injured party," whom he also terms "the avenger" (11–12). Moreover, Langbein notes, the Marian pretrial statutes lent whatever official support there was to the prosecutor-avenger, since these required the JP to take pretrial depositions from the accused, the accuser, and any witnesses brought by the accuser, writing down "as much thereof as shall be material to prove the felony." The statutes make no mention of defence witnesses nor do they ask the JP to include any exculpatory evidence in his report. Instead, the primary role of the "public officer" becomes helping "the private prosecutor to build his case," or as the Frenchman quoted above put it, the English authorities "make no efforts to obtain proofs of the crime, confiding its punishment entirely to the hatred or resentment of the injured party" (40–3). The prosecutorial bias of common law criminal procedure was exacerbated by the fact, Langbein adds, that in most felony cases, the accused would be jailed until trial, making it virtually impossible for him to prepare a defence, especially since the prisoner was not allowed to see the indictment; it was not until his arraignment, when the indictment was read aloud to the court, that the accused knew either the specific charges against him or the nature of the prosecution evidence (27–8, 49–51). Furthermore, while the prosecution had "compulsory process to require the appearance of its witnesses, the accused did not," nor could defence witnesses testify under oath (51–2).

The common law proceedings in criminal cases that Langbein describes bear an unmistakable resemblance to the practices that astounded and dismayed Laud during his trial (except for the business about oaths, which Langbein does not mention). One has little doubt that the archbishop would have endorsed Langbein's conclusion that English criminal justice from the Middle Ages on suffered from "a truth deficit" brought on by its "privatization of criminal investigation" (333, 338).

Langbein's book, which is only a few years old, affords a powerful counterweight to the "I ♥ common law" reflex that still dominates Anglo-American scholarship. Yet its overlap with Laud seems curious. Why should their critiques so closely resemble each other? Since most work on English law takes a very different tack, the points both make could not have been obvious. Assuming that Langbein's account is fundamentally correct, why did earlier legal historians not notice these problematic aspects of the common law? Why could Laud see what they could not? The answer, I suspect, has to do with the fact that in 1974 Langbein published *Prosecuting Crime in the Renaissance*, which dealt not only with England, but also with Germany and France, whose criminal courts used a procedural framework close to that Laud encountered in Star Chamber and High Commission. Both Laud and Langbein, like the aforementioned Frenchman, approach the common law criminal trial from a perspective shaped by long-standing familiarity with the *ius commune*. *Ius commune* criminal procedure is a large topic; however, for our purposes, a single key text (written *mirabile dictu* in English) will help to clarify how this alternative tradition bears on Laud's complex response to the common law, but also how it bears on wider, although related, issues of legal justice and political freedom.

In 1591 Richard Cosin, a canonist/civilian and ally of Archbishop Whitgift, published a long (and long-winded) treatise, the *Apology for Jurisdiction Ecclesiastical,* defending the High Commission – the "supreme court" of England's post-Reformation ecclesiastical justice system – against criticisms levelled by Puritan common lawyers, in part by launching a counter-critique of the common law's criminal procedures, which makes many of the same points Langbein does. Cosin, however, embeds these particulars within a history of Western legal development intended to show that the West evolved two distinct types of criminal procedure, and that the common law employs a variant of the earlier type, known as *accusatio,* which went back to Roman law and remained the dominant form on the Continent through the early thirteenth century. The defining feature of the *accusatio,* Cosin explains, is that responsibility for both the initial accusation and the subsequent prosecution falls to private persons.[10] In the alternative type of criminal procedure, the type widely adopted on the Continent after 1215, the court and its officers take over both functions.[11] In England, only the appeal[12] was technically an *accusatio;* common law criminal trials were, in theory, public prosecutions, which is why the indictment was always in the prince's name (*Rex* v. John Doe); but, as both Cosin and Langbein recognize, the actual prosecution was left in private hands, normally either those of the victim or the victim's kin, so that in essence common law trials remained a type of *accusatio.*

On the Continent, according to Cosin's narrative, *accusatio* turned out to have two fatal defects: it discouraged legitimate prosecution, most decent people being reluctant to accuse their neighbours, and it provided too convenient a weapon for retaliating against personal enemies. Hence throughout most of Europe, beginning in the early thirteenth century, the courts adopted a new procedural framework known as *inquisitio,* in which officers of the court took over responsibility for investigating and prosecuting criminal wrongdoing. In the inquisitorial trial, the key player was not the victim-accuser but the judge, who examined the witnesses (the lawyers for both sides playing a subordinate role) and investigated the allegations, guided by an official dossier reporting the court's own pretrial investigation.[13] In the sixteenth century, a modified version of *inquisitio* procedure was adopted both by High Commission and Star Chamber – the courts on which Laud sat.[14]

"Inquisitio" has an alarming ring (having something to do with the Inquisition). The procedural framework, however, has no intrinsic connection to heresy trials, and in fact remains to this day standard criminal procedure in dozens of countries, including France, Germany, and Japan. Moreover, as Thomas Barnes points out in his 1961 "Star Chamber Mythology" – and as Laud's comments on his own trial imply – the *inquisitio* format of the Star Chamber gave crucial "procedural advantages ... to defendants ... which were not yet enjoyed by defendants in criminal cases in common law courts: the right to counsel and the right to call witnesses to give testimony on oath on the defendant's behalf." Moreover, Barnes adds, "at each stage of the [Star Chamber] proceedings, all public, the defendant and his counsel were apprised of the prosecution's case." The bill, which the defendant saw from the outset, included not only the offence "but also all the allegations of fact to support it." Whereas in common law trials, the defendant had access only to the "brief and uninformative indictment," in courts using the *inquisitio* model, the accused "from the outset had a knowledge of the specifics involved." Early modern inquisitorial courts, Barnes concludes, seem far more concerned than their common law counterparts to "safeguard the procedural rights of [the] defendant."[15]

Barnes does not deal with the admissibility of hearsay or oaths. Other studies, however, indicate that "the *ius commune* ... limited a witness to testifying about events that he had perceived directly. Testimony based on the statements of other people had no evidentiary value."[16] Wigmore's classic 1904 "The History of the Hearsay Rule" concludes that the English common law courts regularly allowed hearsay evidence through the mid-seventeenth century, but he also notes that hearsay was "occasionally excluded." Although Wigmore does not comment on the fact, his sole example of such an exclusion comes from a 1632 Star Chamber case – a case, in fact, on which Laud sat – which suggests that the English courts using inquisitorial procedure generally followed the *ius commune* norm.[17] As to the admissibility of oath-taking, this had been used by common law as a form of proof, but only for actions of debt, and even this had faded away by the mid-seventeenth century; in the *ius commune*, however, it was a standard form of proof in cases where there was probable suspicion but no compelling evidence of guilt. It was how the radical Puritan John Udall cleared himself when charged by High Commission with having written the Marprelate tracts. (He refused to take a similar oath concerning his authorship of *A Demonstration of Truth*, which he indeed had written.)[18] Inquisitorial procedure also required that the accused testify under oath to questions posed by the court concerning the matter under investigation (the *ex officio* oath), although this requirement is not usually seen as "safeguard[ing] the procedural rights of a defendant." Nonetheless, like the *ius commune*'s exclusion of hearsay and its purgatory oath, the requirement that the accused answer under oath to the court's potentially self-incriminating questions supports Langbein's basic point: namely, that inquisitional procedure was designed to elicit *truth*. That was the main benefit of making criminal investigation a public rather than a private function: the trial was conducted by persons who "had a duty to seek the truth" and the investigative authority to do so.[19]

While all this greatly illuminates Laud's response to the procedural aspects of his trial, it raises an unexpected problem: for if Langbein is right, why then didn't England adopt the *inquisitio*? Langbein's own answer is "the great European blunder, the medieval law of torture" (338–9). This, however, cannot be the whole answer, since the English courts that used *inquisitio* procedures never tortured anyone.[20] Yet this notwithstanding, early modern English persons show zero enthusiasm for replacing the accusatory procedures of common law with something closer to the *inquisitio* model. Rather the opposite – especially among religious dissidents. At least from Archbishop Whitgift's crackdown on the crypto-Presbyterian classis movement in the mid-1580s, Puritan activists regularly objected to the inquisitional procedures used in their trials: above all to the self-incriminating *ex officio* oath, the reliance on written depositions rather than oral testimony, and the fact that the court did not have to wait for an accuser to bring charges but could itself initiate a criminal enquiry. So in his initial questioning by the Privy Council in 1590, Udall insists that no man should be put to answer except after "presentment before justices, or things of record, or by due process, or writ original," citing 42 Edw. III, cap 5, and refuses to "swear to accuse myself or others." During his subsequent trial at High Commission, he denies that a sworn deposition read in court constituted valid evidence, demanding to confront his accuser, despite the judge's explanation that the statement was verified by two sworn witnesses, both LL.D.s, to be the deponent's true answer.[21] In his 1637 Star Chamber trial, the equally radical John Lilburne likewise demands to be brought "face to face" with his accusers. He too refuses the "oath of inquiry," informing the court that he would rather die than swear to answer questions that might incriminate him.[22]

These are typical protests. Throughout the post-Reformation period, religious dissidents, Catholic mission priests as well as hot Protestants, objected principally and specifically to what they describe as unjust and un-English inquisitional procedures. One of the Long Parliament's first steps was to abolish Star Chamber and High Commission. Since the English "inquisitorial" courts didn't use torture and apparently gave the accused more protection than at common law, what was the problem?

The problem pretty clearly has something to do with Langbein's observation noted above: that *inquisitio* procedure, in contrast to the common law alternative, was designed to get at truth: to secure, that is, the innocent against false accusations, but not to protect the guilty from detection. It was precisely this truth-seeking aspect of the *inquisitio* which Cosin singles out for praise. Moreover, it was also what, in his view, justified requiring the potentially self-incriminating (but also potentially self-exculpating) *ex officio* oath. The need for (and hence right to) protection against self-incrimination, Cosin argues, applied only to adversarial proceedings, where the prosecutor was a hostile party with all the attendant temptations to seek victory rather than justice, since the accused "ought not to be driven to furnish up his adversary's intention."[23] In the *inquisitio*, however, one had a dispassionate judge-prosecutor acting merely "for discharge of his duty according to the trust reposed in him, and not of malice or to pull any private benefit from the party," and why should not such a judge urge the accused "to tell the whole truth of the matter ... as well for the public benefit's sake of the commonweal" as also, if innocent, "for his own good and escaping of punishment"?[24] Why shouldn't all "good means" (i.e., excluding torture) be used "for the discovery of the whole truth"?[25]

Udall and Lilburne, however, did not want truth. They were both guilty. They wanted to confront the witnesses against them because these were confederates who had, under pressure, made damaging revelations, but who also might well shrink from betraying their erstwhile comrades in open court. They demanded to see their accuser, insisting that there could be no case unless a private individual brought charges – the point, Cosin explains, being to prevent the court from initiating an enquiry without having to wait for the common law's victim-avenger. He suspects, with considerable justification, that most of these procedural demands were merely the "cautels and frustratory shifts" of offenders seeking to wriggle off the hook.[26] Thus at one point, Udall, who normally objects to any deviation from common law process, demands the protection of the *ius commune*'s exceedingly high standard of proof in capital cases, which, he notes, required the testimony of two eyewitnesses to the crime itself for conviction.[27] Udall, however, fails to mention that *ius commune* also regarded the defendant's confession as full proof, which was why (since few crimes have two eyewitnesses) the Continental courts had recourse to torture. Udall's enthusiasm for the two-witness rule does not imply a principled stance on the laws of evidence; he simply, and reasonably enough, wants the court to have a standard of proof that will make it possible for him to avoid conviction despite being guilty.

That is to say, Udall is asking for something along the lines of modern adversarial criminal procedure, with its exclusion rules, dismissal on technicalities, right to confront hostile witnesses, protection against self-incrimination, etc. If, as Langbein notes, the modern adversarial criminal trial is truth-averse, it is so in part because its bedrock procedures, like the QWERTY keyboard, were designed to be suboptimal; the procedures, that is, were meant to hamper somewhat the detecting and punishment of lawbreakers so that dissidents who violated laws they believed unjust might have a fighting chance. Four of the ten amendments that make up the original U.S. Bill of Rights have to do with protecting suspected criminals: partly from witch-hunts and railroading, but also partly from the long arm of the law.[28] Nearly half the Bill of Rights concerns the rights of criminal defendants, a concern that cannot be unrelated to the way men like Udall and Lilburne appealed to common law criminal procedure to defend the liberties of free-born Protestant Englishmen from the unjust edicts of a godless and tyrannical State.[29]

Laud, however, was not guilty; or, as the *DNB* puts it, "Laud's trial was a travesty of justice. He was manifestly innocent of the charges of treason and the advancement of popery that were leveled against him."[30] Laud's objection to the common law procedures at his trial was that they did not allow him to prove his innocence. The court never specified what the "fundamental laws" he allegedly violated were; it didn't check to see if hearsay testimony was corroborated by the persons who supposedly made the incriminating statements; it didn't allow him to summon defence witnesses or to impeach prosecution ones; he didn't have time or access to materials to prepare his defence; the entire prosecution team was composed of political enemies, and the MP managing the prosecution, William Prynne, had published rabid libels against Laud and been sentenced by courts on which Laud was among the judges; several witnesses had also had previous legal run-ins with

Laud and so were actually hostile parties; the prosecution, which prepared the written summary of the testimony for the Lords, frequently left out Laud's answers; and there was no "purgatory oath" – which, before fingerprinting, wiretaps, and the like, would often be only proof one *could* make.

Although the purgatory oath remained *verboten*, most of the common law procedures that dismayed Laud were subsequently altered. The changes make it easy to forget the heavy prosecutorial bias of the early modern common law criminal trial, so that Laud's prison diaries, which preserve one of the only surviving common law trial narratives from this period, offer a rare corrective to the patriotic-populist celebration of the common law that goes back to John Fortescue's praise of the English jury and becomes such a marked feature of "Whig" historiography.[31] (The Elizabethan diplomat and statesman Sir Thomas Smith, by contrast, thought judicial combat fairer than the common law criminal trial, since, if neither gave justice better than even odds, at least the former put accuser and accused at equal risk.)[32] Yet, Laud's procedural objections assume throughout that criminal justice seeks to determine the truth of the charges brought against the accused: to determine, that is, whether or not the accused broke the law(s) he is alleged to have broken. This seems blandly irreproachable, until one realizes that the procedural objections of Lilburne and Udall imply a quite different model of criminal justice, one in which the object is decidedly not truth; instead both demand procedures capable of balancing the interest of the State in punishing lawbreakers with the protection of individual conscience from the State. They seek to handicap *Rex* so that John Doe might contest on something approaching a level playing field. Laud never defends arbitrary government; rather, he takes almost a classical republican position on the supremacy of law and the rule of law, insisting to his judges, "I have ever been of opinion that human laws bind the conscience, and have accordingly made conscience of observing them" (4:59). Dissidents like Lilburne and Udall, by contrast, wanted the procedures of man's law to correct for the fact that the substance of man's laws might be against the law of God, and accordingly one should make conscience of breaking them.

NOTES

1 All quotations have been modernized to conform to modern Canadian punctuation and spelling.

2 *The Works of the Most Reverend Father in God, William Laud*, vol. 4, pp. 370–83. Further references to these volumes will be given parenthetically in the text.

3 See the 1590 trials of John Udall; the 1637 trial of Prynne, Burton, and Bastwick; and the several trials, beginning in 1637, of John Lilburne in Thomas Bayly Howell, ed., *A Complete Collection of State Trials and Proceedings for High Treason and Other Crimes and Misdeameanors from the Earliest Period to the Year 1793*, vols 1–3.

4 "Civil law" in this context refers to the modernized Roman law adopted by most of Continental Europe. The *ius commune* refers to the shared inheritance of canon law and Roman law that formed the basis of a common system of legal thought and practice in most of Western Europe from the High Middle Ages.

5 The charges are those concerning Laud's alleged omission of *populus elegerit* in the coronation oath and whether he had knowingly sheltered an English-born Catholic priest. As Laud explains, with regard to the latter charge, "The statute of 27 Eliz. makes it 'felony without benefit of clergy, to maintain or relieve any Romish priest born in England … knowing him to be such.' Now they [the Commons] had laid in their Article, that I had given maintenance to Monsieur S. Giles, a popish priest at Oxford, knowing him to be such. But when, upon examination of S. Giles, they found him to be a Frenchman, and so not within the statute … they cast about how to make S. Clara [who was an English-born Catholic priest] and Mr. S. Giles to be one man. And though they could find no shadow of proof … yet against their own knowledge and conscience, they give that in evidence to reach my life any way" (4:330–1).

6 The force of his objection comes home in the end in Laud's conviction by bill of attainder (4:352, 4:389); there was a written, statutory definition of treason, but it became evident during the trial that Laud was not remotely guilty on its terms, so the Commons fell back on the claim that the statutory definition of treason left in force a common law catch-all offence of high treason. Laud comments on the ominous arbitrariness of this in his final recapitulation, noting that since none of the particulars of which he was accused was "treason by law" (the reference is to the treason statute of 25 Edw. III), none, in fact, even felonies, for the court to decide that various misdemeanours added together can equal high treason "will devour all the safety of the subject of England, which now stands so well fenced by the known law of the land" (4:381). It was the fact that the common law was (allegedly) *known* that had made it seem a bulwark of the liberties of the subject. See Edward Hake, *Epieikeia: a dialogue on equity* (ca 1585), pp. 80–3; William Blackstone, *Commentaries on the Laws of England*, bk 3, chap. 22.

7 That is, Laud could, in principle, show that on Monday he was in place X (and so not dealing with Con), and on Tuesday he was in place Y (and so not dealing with Con), etc., but these are affirmative proofs; and even if he could show that on each of a hundred days he was doing something that precluded any meeting with Con, the possibility remains that they met on the hundred-first or hundred-second day.

8 William Lamont, *Marginal Prynne, 1600–1669*, pp. 119–20. Browne, Lamont notes, was a Puritan and disliked bishops on principle, so the fact that his notes support Laud's version and not the wildly different version given in Prynne's *Canterbury's Doom* (1646) is even more telling.

9 John Langbein, *The Origins of the Adversary Criminal Trial*, page references given parenthetically in the text.

10 Hence in the *ius commune*, accusers were not considered witnesses but parties, and as such forbidden to testify.

11 As Cosin explains, "the means to bring any crime and offence into question before judges … are either by prosecution of some party, or else upon the office of the judge." *An Apologie: Of and for Sundrie Proceedings by Iurisdiction Ecclesiasticall*, pt. 2, p. 6; see also pt. 2, pp. 18, 30.

12 A medieval form of trial, where the proof was by battle; see Blackstone, *Commentaries*, bk 4, chap. 23.

13 Langbein, *The Origins of the Adversary Criminal Trial*, vol. 2, p. 333.

14 For the substance of this and the previous paragraph, see Cosin, pt 2, pp. 18–59. It was also later adopted (again, with modifications) by the UCLA committee charged with investigating faculty misconduct, which is where I first encountered it.

15 Thomas Barnes, "Star Chamber Mythology," pp. 9–10. See also William Lambarde, *Archeion* (ca 1591), p. 85.

16 Richard Fraher, "Conviction According to Conscience," p. 34.

17 John Wigmore, "The History of the Hearsay Rule," p. 444.

18 *State trials*, vol. 1, pp. 1271–2. The 1630–1 records of High Commission, where Laud was one of the judges, show the oath being used to clear ministers charged with simony and adultery (S.R. Gardiner, ed., *Reports of Cases in the Courts of Star Chamber and High Commission*, p. 247, p. 254, p. 259). In his 1637 Star Chamber trial, John Lilburne first tells the judges that he will take an oath if that will clear him of the charges, but when the judges offer "that if they [Lilburne and co-defendant] yet would submit and take their oaths [of purgation], their lordships would accept thereof, and not proceed to censure against them," he refuses (*State trials*, vol. 3, pp. 1325, 1327).

19 Langbein, *The Origins of the Adversary Criminal Trial*, vol. 1, pp. 332–3, 338–9.

20 See John Langbein, *Torture and the Law of Proof: Europe and England in the Ancien Régime*, pp. 73–140. No English court could or did authorize the use of torture. On the rare occasions when suspects were tortured, it was by order of the Privy Council. Of the eighty-one instances where the Council did authorize torture between 1540 and 1640, only two date from the fourteen years of Charles's reign, the period of Laud's ascendency.

21 *State Trials*, vol. 1, pp. 1274–5, 1281.

22 *State Trials*, vol. 3, pp. 1317–23.

23 Cosin, pt 2. p. 36.

24 Cosin, pt 3, pp. 44–5; he also notes that in *civil* suits, the common law forced defendants to confess under oath to their own harm (as in the U.S., the privilege against self-incrimination applies only to criminal cases), and he finds it incomprehensible that the law would make it harder for a defendant to weasel out of a debt than a murder (pt. 2, p. 36, p. 49; pt 3, pp. 43–4).

25 Cosin, pt 2, p. 6; pt 3, p. 44.

26 Cosin, pt 3, pp.179–82.

27 *State Trials*, vol. 1, p. 1302.

28 The relevant articles are the fourth (no unreasonable search and seizure), fifth (due process, no self-incrimination), sixth (jury trials, right to confront witnesses, compulsory process to summon defence witnesses, right of defendant to know specific charges, right to counsel), eighth (no excessive bail, no cruel and unusual punishment).

29 *State Trials*, vol. 1, p. 1275 (Udall), vol. 3, p. 1346 (Lilburne).

30 Anthony Milton, "Laud, William (1573–1645)," *Oxford Dictionary of National Biography*.

31 Sir John Fortescue (c 1395–c. 1477), *On the Laws and Governance of England*, pp. 29–44; Blackstone, *Commentaries*, vol. 3, p. 23.

32 Sir Thomas Smith, *De republica Anglorum*, p. 114. Smith's comment takes as given that criminal prosecutions were initiated and run by interested private parties.

BIBLIOGRAPHY

Barnes, Thomas. "Star Chamber Mythology." *American Journal of Legal History* 5, no. 1 (Jan. 1961): 1–11.

Blackstone, William. *Commentaries on the Laws of England*. Oxford: Clarendon Press, 1778; Chicago: U of Chicago P, 1979.

Cosin, Richard. *An Apologie: Of and for Sundrie Proceedings by Iurisdiction Ecclesiasticall.* London: Deputies of C. Barker, 1591.

Fortescue, Sir John (c. 1395–c. 1477). *On the Laws and Governance of England.* Ed. Shelley Lockwood. Cambridge: Cambridge UP, 1997.

Fraher, Richard. "Conviction According to Conscience." *Law and History Review* 7, no. 1 (1989): 34.

Gardiner, S.R., ed. *Reports ofCcases in the Courts of Star Chamber and High Commission.* London: Camden Society, 1886.

Hake, Edward. *Epieikeia: A Dialogue on Equity in Three Parts,* (ca 1585). Ed. D.E.C. Yale. New Haven, CT: Yale University Press for the Yale Law Library, 1953.

Howell, Thomas Bayly, ed. *A Complete Collection of State Trials and Proceedings for High Treason and Other Crimes and Misdeameanors from the Earliest Period to the Year 1793.* 33 vols. London: T.C. Hansard for Longman, Hurst, Rees, Orme and Browne, 1816–26, vols 1–3.

Lambarde, William. *Archeion* (ca 1591; 1st printing 1635). Ed. C.H. McIlwain and Paul Ward. Cambridge, MA: Harvard UP, 1957.

Lamont, William. *Marginal Prynne, 1600–1669.* London: Routledge & Keegan Paul, 1963.

Langbein, John H. *TheOorigins of the Adversary Criminal Trial.* Oxford: Oxford UP, 2003.

– *Prosecuting Crime in the Renaissance: England, Germany, France.* Cambridge, MA: Harvard UP, 1974.

– *Torture and the Law of Proof: Europe and England in the Ancien Régime.* 2nd ed. Chicago: U of Chicago P, 2006.

Laud, William. *The works of the Most Reverend Father in God, William Laud.* 6 vols in 5. 1847–60; rpt, Hildesheim: Georg Olms Verlag, 1977.

Milton, Anthony. "Laud, William (1573–1645)," *Oxford Dictionary of National Biography.* Oxford: Oxford UP, 2004. Web. 18 June 2012.

Smith, Sir Thomas. *De Republica Anglorum.* Ed. Leonard Alston. Pref. Frederic Maitland. Cambridge: Cambridge UP, 1906.

Wigmore, John. "The History of the Hearsay Rule," *Harvard Law Review* 17 (1904): 437–58.

6 Criminal Biography in Early Modern News Pamphlets

DAVID STYMEIST

While interest in crime pamphlets and other forms of popular news reportage in the early modern period has expanded, the body of work by literary critics and social historians is still in its initial stages.[1] Considerable effort has been expended to categorize this material in generic terms; Sandra Clark, for instance, has emphasized the pervasive "adherence to conservative modes of constructing and interpreting human deviance" in early forms of crime reportage.[2] For Clark, the narrative structure of crime reportage "is invariably shaped towards a providential conclusion and the assault on moral and social order contained."[3] Along with this didactic impulse, Peter Lake identifies a second common generic element when he argues that "the relationship of the pamphlets to their subject-matter [was] exploitative, indeed, in some sense, pornographic."[4] The news pamphlet consistently reproduces scenes of "extreme violence, sexual licence, and outlandish and disgusting acts" because of the material's ability to shock and titillate a popular readership.[5] Alongside moral didacticism and exploitative sensationalism, I would argue that news pamphlets include a third, and potentially more culturally subversive, narrative element: that of criminal biography. The inclusion of biographical contexts allowed for the articulation of the offender's voice, point of view, and lived experience; these kinds of life-history materials, in turn, attempted to provide readers with critical insight into the complex preconditions that form criminal subjectivities and motivate criminal acts. While there was considerable variation in how biographical elements were used by pamphlet authors, a significant number of pamphlets interrogated "the overall context of inequalities of power, wealth, and authority," which radical criminologists argue is the basis of social behaviour categorized as criminal by the legal system.[6] In traditional juridical criminology, criminal behaviour was often classified as an aberration tied to the criminal's moral corruption, and as such was seen as a pernicious outgrowth of the *mens rea* or evil-minded nature of that individual.[7] In the emergent alternative narrative of criminality, which I argue is a significant interpretive thread in these news reports, the wider field of social economy becomes formative of criminal subjectivity and the basis for criminal acts.

Biographical contextualization, as an essential part of the crime pamphlet genre, attempts to problematize the criminological narratives of the judiciary and state in a number of ways: not only does it reveal how economic, gender, status, and social disparities are implicated in the production of many types of crime, it also demystifies the process of juridical classification of crime, such as how the charge of petty treason is employed in cases of spousal murder. The biographical element in crime reportage, furthermore, provides a critique of the model of analogical thinking that is fundamental to much early modern judicial practice and legal thought.[8] As a new form of public media, crime pamphlets additionally helped to expose judicial partiality, prejudice, incompetence, and corruption; this exposure, in turn, raised significant questions concerning the model of a fully participatory and equitable justice system. Taken together, all these aspects of crime news reportage provide evidence of Alexandra Halasz's claim that commercial print publishing in the early modern period constituted "a means of producing, disseminating, and mediating discourse independent of the sites and practices associated with and sanctioned by University, Crown and Church."[9] Crime reportage, with its inclusion of biographical material, may help literary critics to redefine the interplay between justice and writing in the period. The generic aesthetic of crime pamphlets – specifically, their ability to uncover traces of the material reality of the relationship of the criminal to the justice system from the perspective of the condemned – can serve to interrogate dominant notions of criminality circulating in forensic rhetoric.

In many ways, the emergence of this alternative criminology can be connected to innovations in print media and marketing in the early modern era. Publishers and authors developed ways to commercially exploit the distinctive publication features of the news pamphlet; as Halasz has observed, the pamphlet form offered a uniquely flexible and efficient use of "the productive capacity of the press."[10] Crime news in particular was written for a wide popular audience of literate, newly literate, and semi-literate readers, and as such was produced with both the budget and thematic tastes of these readerships in mind.[11] The educational revolution in England between 1560 and 1640, as Lawrence Stone describes it, manifested not only an increase in the scale of educational growth but one that precipitated a major shift "in the social distribution of education."[12] With the expansion of rates of basic literacy, new markets for "cheap" print rapidly expanded, and as up to three-quarters of the cost of publishing was due to the cost of paper, short octavo and quarto chapbooks became some of the most profitable and marketable print items. While the "polarization" in printed material into popular and elite audiences has been largely overstated, publishers, as Tessa Watt has shown, produced cheap texts with the market of new reading publics in mind, which may in part explain the extensive inclusion of graphic woodcuts along with ballads and songs in news pamphlets.[13] Moreover, publishers, who often found themselves with problems of cash flow liquidity because of their primary investment in the printing, storage, and distribution of long and labour-intensive texts, were economically interested in a short print form concerning itself with saleable topical subject matter, such as the reportage of recent and often local crimes, which could be rapidly produced with a relatively small demand on print resources.[14] By looking at the publication records of individual printers, we can see that publishers of all kinds were involved in the printing of such material.[15] The typical length of the news pamphlet, six to twenty-four pages of text printed as a short unbound book, ideally suited the ephemeral subject matter of crime news; the size was cost-efficient, yet the format still offered enough space for the inclusion of extended "insider" life histories of criminals that were not available during either the public trial or the scaffold speech. Moreover, unlike a common law court, the news pamphlet did not need to provide a forensic mechanism for determining absolute culpability; thus, it could be much more ambivalent in its representations of criminal motivation and guilt. It is ultimately the flexibility of short, cheap print formats that allowed the crime pamphlet genre to continue to expand even after the innovation of periodical news in the mid-seventeenth century as the truncated reports of periodical news failed to satisfy the reading public's growing demand for more detailed life histories. The sizable volume of crime pamphlets as a commercial product indicates that authors, publishers, and sellers responded to and fed the marketplace demand for these kinds of materials.[16] The recognition by commercial print producers that emergent markets of new readers were interested in criminal life histories resulted in the development of the crime pamphlet as an alternative medium and mode of criminological representation.

In order to provide a clear contrast to news pamphlets that actively interrogate contemporary conceptions of justice through their use of biographical contextualization, I first want to briefly examine a pamphlet explicitly fashioned in defence of the justice system. George Whetstone's *The Censure of a Loyal Subject* (1587) lends support to J.A. Sharpe's argument that early news reportage reveals "the nature of ideological control" in its record of "what people were meant to hear."[17] The execution of Queen Mary's collaborators in their alleged plan to assassinate Elizabeth I was certainly a subject fraught with political danger in Tudor England.[18] Whetstone frames his depiction of the public torture of the fourteen members of the Babington conspiracy as a "matter of necessary instruction and comfort for al dutiful subjects; especially, the multitude of ignorant people."[19] More than simply providing instruction for the masses, this work by extension provides a pointedly informative model to other writers about how they should conceptualize and shape their public reporting of criminal cases and public executions. Whetstone, rather than obscuring the linkage between his news reportage and state power, openly publicizes it in his prefatory address to Sir William Cecil, Queen Elizabeth's chief advisor; not only does he mention that he is in Cecil's debt but claims that he is under Cecil's "sound protection."[20] Francis Walsingham, another member of the Privy Council and Elizabeth's secretary of state, appears as well to have played a role in the production of this pamphlet as he ensured that all printed accounts of these executions were manufactured to show Elizabeth in a positive light.[21]

Whetstone's pamphlet functions as a piece of state propaganda in its attempt to contain potential public unrest surrounding the execution of the Catholic conspirators. Employing the stock scholastic conceit of a dialogic debate between three London citizens, the text describes the reaction of the crowd of thousands to the public torture of seven of the condemned on the first day of the executions. While advertising itself as objective reportage of the relatable facts of the day, the pamphlet attempts to circumscribe the emotional responses of readers: in the words of one of Whetstone's fictionalized commentators, the execution "was a fearful spectacle, yet yee odiousness of their treasons was so settled in every mans heart, as there appeared no sadness or alteration among the people, at the mangling and quartering of their bodies; yea, the whole multitude, without any sign of lamentation greedylye behelde the spectacle."[22] Prior to the executions, the Queen had instructed Sir William Cecil that as this had been an extraordinary crime it required the application of "further extraordinary pain."[23] The extension and intensification of the condemned men's torture, which may have produced a negative public reaction, was mitigated on the second day of the executions through a subsequent royal order: the remaining traitors were "hung until they were … altogether dead" before being dismembered.[24] In order to defuse public sympathy towards the executed men and erase aspersions of excessive cruelty, Whetstone emphasizes the heinousness of the conspirators' betrayal while reaffirming the extraordinary mercy of Queen Elizabeth: "ther treasons were so odious [that] the extremist cruelty that policy may invent would be too mild to punish them," but the state's subsequent reduction of their sentencing was a "token of exceeding mercy in her majesty, and mildness in the justice of England."[25]

Despite the clear didactic intent of pamphlets like Whetstone's *Censure*, the news genre more than simply manufactured public faith in state authority and conventional notions of justice and criminality; as Randall Martin observes in his examination of popular print representations of female violence, news reports were capable of generating "empathy towards the social origins and personal circumstances" of criminals.[26] One instance of this kind of counter-discourse occurs in Henry Goodcole's *Heavens Speedie Hue and Cry sent after Lust and Murder* (1635); while ostensibly a piece of moralistic reportage, this pamphlet typifies the mode of biographical contextualization in that it contains a life history of a thief and murderer named Elizabeth Evans. Instead of producing a stereotypical portrait of the malicious nature of the criminal, the pamphlet narrates the unfortunate sequence of life events that led Evans into an existence of desperate poverty, which in turn fostered her criminal activities. After Evans lured gentlemen into the fields outside London with sexual promises, her consort Thomas Shearwood would bludgeon them, and the couple would steal their victims' possessions. While Evans's parents had provided "carefully for her good education, and future preferment, [and had] sent her up unto London, to [settle] her in a good service … unfortunately … she grew acquainted with a young man in London, who tempted her unto folly, and by that ungodly act her suddain ruine insued."[27] Evans's social network appears to have abandoned her because of her sexual indiscretion: "By reason of such her folly, her Friends failed, and frowned on her: Oh unnaturall blemish! Thus to forsake, cast off, and forget their owne deare flesh, all meanes of livelyhood failing, her left thus destitute, and out of all credit, friends, money, apparrell, and service: A base loose course of life shee resolves on."[28] Instead of simply excoriating Evans, the author constructs a narrative that links a series of causal events: a young woman of good education and parentage is seduced, decried, deserted by friends and family, and eventually turns to crime. In contrast to conventional representations of female murderers, the pamphlet's utilization of significant details from Evans's life serves to emphasize the economic and social determinants of her criminality; in fact, the text concludes by theorizing that youth is easily seduced "in the times of necessitie and extreame want."[29]

Perhaps the most significant biographical detail contained in the pamphlet is that Elizabeth Evans was of "very good parentage descended" and of "honest stock"; this is in contrast to the view articulated by some crime moralists, such as Justice of the Peace Thomas Harman, that criminals for the most part constituted an accursed generation that needed to be physically eliminated.[30] For Harman, female criminals were especially pernicious to civil society due to their ability to reproduce and then indoctrinate their offspring: "wild dells [female rogues], being traded up with their monstrous mothers, must of necessity be as evil, or worse, then their parents, for neither we gather grapes from green briars, neither figs from Thistles. But such buds, such blosoms, such evil seed sown, well worse being growen."[31] Instead of being categorized as an "evil seed," whereby her criminality is naturalized as an inherited biological trait, the pamphlet presents Evans as someone whose economic and social circumstances had more of a causal relationship to their criminal behaviour than their parentage. While the pamphlet in its more moralistic mode unsympathetically identifies her as a "monster of her Sexe," it situates this monstrosity within the frame of the criminal's personal history of poverty and abandonment.[32] While Rosamaria Loretelli contends that crime pamphlets generated consensus about the functioning of justice by "producing a normative discourse," the emergent social reading of crime that appears in this particular pamphlet problematizes the view that pamphlet literature invariably reinforced dominant beliefs and norms surrounding criminality.[33]

Another pamphlet by Goodcole, *The Adultresses Funerall Day* (1635), includes intimate marital details that challenge the equability of the judicial category of petty treason with convincing evidence of significant mitigating circumstances.[34] Petty treason in itself was an indictment instituted to severely punish instances where a fundamental hierarchical relationship was ruptured, such as when servants murdered their masters, a wife her husband, or a prelate his ecclesiastical superior. This indictment was constructed as a "petit" form of insubordination, the example of which implied a meaningful threat to the status and privileges of authority.[35] The judicial deployment of analogy allowed spousal homicide to be read as a replication in miniature of the murder of the King by a subject, and thus the crime required the severest public condemnation and special types of punishment because of the threat it posed to social order. Cementing its linkage with sin, petty treason along with heresy were the only crimes in early modern England where women were punished by being burnt alive at the stake.[36] Significantly, it was also distinguished from homicide in that juries and justices could not employ the categories of self-defence or manslaughter to mitigate sentencing.[37]

The Adultresses Funeral Day reveals a domestic situation of abuse and neglect that creates a degree of sympathy for these women and calls the legal reasoning behind the charge into question. The pamphlet emphasizes the victimization suffered by married women at the hands of their abusive husbands; it is the inclusion of these sorts of biographical details that tends to diminish the culpability of one Alice Clarke in the murder of her husband. Before describing Clarke's marital situation, the text introduces, through a relation of a case of marital abuse, the idea that a history of battery could lead to spousal murder: "Her injuries, and [his] harsh and unmanly usage … almost compeld her to what she did; which, as they would be scarce modest for me to speake, so they were almost beyond the strength of Nature for her to suffer: shee being young and tender, he old and peevish; who notwithstanding his clownish behaviour, and churlish comportment towards her, as seldome or never affording her a smooth brow, or friendly countenance, used not onely to beat her with the next cudgell that came accidently unto his hand, but often tying her to his bed-post to strip her and whippe her, etc."[38] Avoiding a direct confrontation with legal and religious proscriptions against murder and the disorderly conduct of wives, Goodcole does not attempt to justify the wife's killing of her husband, but does contend that domestic abuse "almost compeld" her to commit the crime. The pamphlet, by providing explicit details of spousal battery, attempts to demystify this kind of homicide. Frances Dolan observes that "although these texts present this history as reflecting badly on the husband and setting the limits of his authority, they are reluctant to present it as in any way mitigating a murderous wife's guilt."[39] For Dolan, the narrative of domestic abuse stresses the wife's agency in murder by confirming that her actions were motivated "by revenge not self-defense."[40] While Garthine Walker argues that this line of reasoning contributed to the convictions of wives in legal trials, the news pamphlet form differs significantly from a common law court trial in that it does not need to provide a forensic mechanism that produces absolute levels of guilt or innocence.[41] Simply put, the narrative form allows for more moral ambivalence in constituting motivation for criminal action, and it appears as if this pamphlet attempts to integrate both self-defence and revenge as a plausible motivation for spousal homicide. The extended pattern of abuse portrayed in the text implies a significant threat to Alice Clarke's future well-being and life, and therefore her murderous actions are made, if not excusable, perhaps understandable.

If the demystification of the charge of petty treason requires the weighing of the evidence of marital conditions, this then leads to a substantial but not necessarily complete redirection of blame from the wife onto the husband. Notably, Alice Clarke's marriage was forced on her by a former master: "shee was a yeare since gotten with Child by her Master, [who] matched her unto Fortune Clarke ... whom she could not love, or have any matter of maintenance."[42] Here, Goodcole links the sexual exploitation of Clark to her subsequent violent behaviour. When her husband finds her entertaining a male friend in his house, Fortune Clark is "so with fury enraged, that hee ... freshly fell foule upon her, and so cruelly added blowe upon blow upon her body, that the markes there of were very visible" at her trial.[43] Instead of moralizing about Clark's probable adultery, the text emphasizes the physical abuse she suffers at the hands of her jealous husband and then links this ongoing pattern of abuse to the subsequent poisoning.

The particular stress placed on these marital details within the narrative clearly tends to characterize Alice Clarke as victim rather than victimizer. The title page woodcut portrays the scene of her immolation and shows her stoically embracing her punishment with hands folded in prayer in the manner of a Christian martyr; as the primary marketing tool, especially for the potential semi-literate or newly literate reader, the title page woodcut actively promotes a sympathetic reading of Clark's penitent suffering. The centrality of Clark's suffering body both in the textual and pictorial elements of Goodcole's pamphlet counters Dolan's assertion that textual representations of women's executions "participate in an English, largely Protestant, gendered aesthetic which licenses and records women's speech while downplaying … their bodily sufferings and deaths."[44]

On the whole, this pamphlet offers a striking contrast with the more aggressively stereotypical and demonized representations of husband murderers in court trials, religious sermons, historical accounts, and rogue literature, which by and large tended to reinforce the idea that spousal murder had an especially corrosive effect on familial and political order and thus required the specialized legal category of petty treason. While critics like Susan Staub contend that petty treason texts justify the punishment of women who "transgress … appropriate female behaviour," the emphasis in this report is not on gender transgression but on the cumulative effects of victimization.[45] If crime news biographies tend to portray extensive marital abuse as an intolerable situation for wives, then the charge of petty treason becomes interrogated as a judicial category that is markedly biased and fundamentally persecutory in its reading of husband murder as a form of treason and its concomitant disallowal of manslaughter defences. In this way, crime news casts doubt on the analogical mode of thought that is employed in the prosecution of women under the charge of petty treason. The state's attempt, through the formulation of civil laws and the machinery of the judiciary, to tie spousal murder to sedition is revealed as largely an attempt to police status and gender transgression rather than to provide equitable judgment.

A Horrible Creuel and Bloody Murther (1614) contains a parallel problematization of the judicial thinking behind the charge of petty treason in its representation of the murder of masters by their servants (see fig. 6.1). This pamphlet provides an account of the homicide of the miller Edward Hall that, despite all its ostensible moralism, uncovers how his abuse of authority laid out the groundwork for retributive violence. Ostensibly, this pamphlet exploits public fears of unruly servants and thus reinforces the judicial employment of domestic analogy in the charge of petty treason. For instance, the author, in a conscious echoing of the wording of Tudor homilies on obedience, extols the potential reader to "love, honour, and reverence" their parents and masters.[46] However, the neat opposition between the paternal care of a master and the traitorous infidelity of servants enshrined in the legal fiction of petty treason becomes destabilized in the pamphlet with a contrapuntal investigation of the master's exploitation and abuse of his charges.[47] The miller is characterized as a notorious miser: "notwithstanding his sufficiency of all things needefull … his natural inclination was to bee …

A Horrible Creuel and bloudy Murther,
Committed at Putney in Surrey on the 21. of
Aprill laſt, 1614, being thurſday, vpon the body
of Edward Hall *a Miller of the ſame pariſh,*
Done by the hands of *Iohn Selling, Peeter Pet* and *Edward Streater,*
his ſeruants to the ſaid *Hall,* each of them giuing
him a deadly blow (as he lay ſleeping)
with a Pickax.

Publiſhed by Authority.

Imprinted at London for *Iohn Wright,* and are to be ſold without Newgate at the ſigne of the Bible. 1614.

Figure 6.1 The title page woodcut of I.T.'s *A Horrible Creuel and Bloody Murther* employs a representational strategy common to news pamphlets of actualizing the influence of the devil through the direct portraiture of satanic figures. Reproduced from an original copy at the Bodleian Library.

miserable in his house-keeping, which procured him the hatred of the tenants and familie."[48] The miller's public reputation as a wealthy landowner who had alienated his community, friends, tenants, family, and servants with his parsimony allows the author to engage the persistent negative stereotypes concerning miserly conduct that circulated in the cultural imagination of early modern England. One example of his miserliness occurs when the author relates that Hall sent his pregnant wife back to her family in order to avoid the attendant costs of birth. Hall's excessive thrift is presented not only as a failure of his social responsibilities as a master and husband, but as the very foundation for his murder, for he is described as being "a great moth to his own destruction."[49]

The miller's three servants confess to Surrey JP Sir Thomas Gardener that "they had done this cruell fact to their Master because (as they said) he did not love his wife so well as he ought to doe, and because he did not allow them meat enough."[50] Despite the inclusion of these depositional claims of spousal abuse and deprivation, the authorial commentary attempts to reassert a spiritual rather than a social discourse of criminality: "that which I thinke most is to be believed from them is [that] they did it by the inspiration and instigation of the Divell."[51] Satanic influence is a common narrative element in many early news pamphlets, and the title page woodcut emphasizes this Christian construction of criminality by physicalizing the invisible and inevitable presence of the devil. Nevertheless, the earlier inclusion of the defendants' articulation of their motivation subverts the notion of satanic influence and reveals it as a somewhat hackneyed theological cliché.

Along with critiques of judicial classification and analogical thinking, news pamphlets also show evidence of a much broader criticism concerning the lack of status equity in early modern justice; one of the most searching exposés of the judicial system's partiality towards the gentry is contained in Thomas Brewer's *The Bloudy Mother* (1609). This pamphlet describes how the "most inhumane murthers" of a number of illegitimate children were committed by Jane Hattersley and Adam Adamson, a man of substantial standing in Sussex.[52] Adamson "had a wife, but the ... strength of lust carried his love from her to a servant he kept."[53] He promised to marry his young servant once his wife died, and, along with other assurances, seduced her into carnal relations; when Jane Hattersley subsequently became pregnant, Adamson promptly accused her of being impregnated by another sexual partner and turned her out of house. After she took up lodging in the house of

Goodman King, Hattersley attempted to disguise her pregnancy with "loose lacing, tucking, and other odde tricks."[54] Despite these efforts at deception, her illegitimate pregnancy was discovered by the King family. A few days after the birth, King's wife came home to discover the "babe by his mother breathless with the mouth of it all soyid with fome, that rose by her violent wringing."[55] However, the couple who accuse Jane Hattersley of infanticide before the local constable soon find the tables turned. After the local authorities are convinced to rule the death of the child accidental, Adamson, who had resumed his relationship with Hattersley, launched a counter-complaint against the couple for offering "grievous abuse" to Jane and of stealing a gown of hers. The narrative relates how Adamson had them jointly arrested on charges of assault and theft, "and so wrapped them … in the law, and wrought upon that wrapping [that] he did utterly undoe this poore couple."[56]

The pamphlet employs basic forensic procedures of gathering physical evidence, providing witness depositions, and relating Hattersley's final confession to build a convincing case against Adamson. Brewer describes how over the course of the next ten years a number of suspicious incidents raised communal fears that the couple were murdering their illegitimate offspring. In one instance, a neighbour, Mrs Ford, heard cries and groans coming from behind Jane's locked door, followed by the "weake shrike of a new borne infant" who was never heard from again.[57] As the relationship between the couple began to disintegrate, they were seen exchanging "high words and very bitter reveilings" in public.[58] In this "windie battail" Jane called "her master [a] murderer" and publicly iterated that "there was a tree … which if it could speake, would send him to the gallows."[59] This revelation led to the unearthing of remains of a number of infants near the aforementioned tree. Both Jane and Adamson were subsequently apprehended on charges of murder, but "Adamson on bonds and good security ... was in a little time" released.[60] Against court orders Adamson visited Jane in jail and convinced her to perjure herself in his upcoming trial; he led her to believe that by admitting complete guilt, Adamson would then be able to arrange for her pardon once he was exonerated. After her public confession, Adamson was acquitted and Hattersley was condemned to the gallows.[61] The life-history revelations contained in the pamphlet show how Adamson's social standing and access to power allowed him to manipulate the justice system in order to condemn neighbours and avoid punishment for his own crimes. For the potential popular readership of these kinds of pamphlets, the persistent classist prejudice of the justice system might have been an all too apparent truth, yet one that rarely was publicly formulated and addressed.[62] The mystifying rhetoric of blind justice – a common law that treats all, both king and commoner, equally under its rule, which was one of the fundamental aspects of the evolving early modern civil state and a value that was central to many of the Tudor and Stuart reinterpretations of Magna Carta rights – is revealed by the pamphlet as largely a duplicitous pretence.[63]

Compared to other crime pamphlets, Brewer's crime report is highly unusual in that it depicts a serial child murderer escaping punishment, which radically diminishes its moral and didactic impact.[64] Material evidence of the publisher's discomfort with the implicit conclusions of the Adamson narrative appears in how the text attempts to contain its radicalism with the addition of a moralistic postscript, printed in a large gothic typeset and written with considerable stylistic and tonal differences from the main narrative. The justice system may have failed to punish Adamson, yet perpetrators cannot escape "the just judgement of God."[65] This postscript describes how, after Jane's execution, Adamson fell "into a most miserable, grievous and lamentable consumption" of worms and lice.[66] Over the next year, Adamson expends his entire wealth seeking a cure, but as there can be "no striving against the will of God," he dies "consumed to skinne and bone."[67] This addendum tries to reconstitute the concordance between terrestrial civil justice and divine justice by showing how the failures and oversights of terrestrial justice are corrected and reinforced by providential justice. This reassertion of a homiletic message inculcates the belief that social prestige cannot ultimately protect criminals from justice. The formulation of providential oversight attempts to preserve commoners' faith in the civil legal system despite signal instances of judicial partiality.[68]

Another crime pamphlet that explicitly depicts systemic judicial partiality and corruption is *The Life, Apprehension, Arraignment and Execution of Charles Courtney* (1612). While awaiting the gallows, ex-soldier Courtney apparently had an autobiographical account of his life as a notorious thief and highwayman published by William Hall; this pamphlet, which employs the first-person voice throughout the entire text, constitutes an instance where biographical contextualization and life history supersede other features typical of the news pamphlet genre. Early in the pamphlet, Courtney bemoans the "untimely end of two worthie gentlemen" who "were apprehended, endited, arraignd, condemned, judged and most innocently hanged for a robbery which I did."[69] While it is impossible to verify this claim, Courtney, by making this allegation in print, attempts to discredit the judiciary in a public forum. From Courtney's perspective the justice system shores up its reputation as a defender of public safety through the false accusation and wrongfully execution of two entirely innocent men. Throughout the work, Courtney portrays the legal system as one that can be successfully navigated by those with political access, judicial knowledge, and monetary means. Lodged on "the masters side" of Newgate, Courtney exploits his gentry connections to first get a stay of trial and then a reprieve of execution. According to Courtney, the reprieve is granted through a bribe of one hundred pounds to an intermediary and a further four hundred pounds to the intermediary's "honourable or worshipful friends."[70] This subornment of judicial officials appears to have been effective, as Courtney did receive a reprieve on the day of his scheduled execution.

As Courtney's published confession crystallizes a widespread fear that those with wealth and political access could effectively pervert the course of justice, the publishers of the pamphlet employ a number of techniques to cover the radicalism implicit in this story.[71] During the period of his reprieve, Courtney engineered a daring escape over the walls of Newgate with a fellow prisoner, Clement Sly. Rearrested in London for a subsequent robbery, Courtney was sent to back to Newgate and executed. The fact that he was hanged right in front of the prison gates foregrounds the state's attempt to violently re-establish the sanctity of the prison and the primacy of the law that Courtney flaunted with his actions.

The pamphlet's title page woodcut creates an evocative visual tableau that collapses the moment of Courtney's escape and his execution by showing Courtney climbing down the prison's walls and his body hanging from the scaffold; significantly, the rope used for the escape ends on the ground near the gallows only to reappear and wind around Courtney's neck (see fig. 6.2). The pamphlet also concludes with a didactic poem that stylistically resembles a broadside ballad and operates under the pretence that it was composed by a repentant Courtney in the days leading up to his execution. This supplementary verse composition, which distils the main prose narrative in a more moralistic mode, was designed as an additional saleable feature of the crime pamphlet, one incorporated to widen its appeal to semi-literate and even nonliterate buyers.[72] The didactic emphasis of both the woodcut and the ballad is in tension with the actual content of Courtney's life history

THE LIFE,

APPREHENSIO

Arraignement, and Execution of CHAR

COVRTNEY, alias *Holkice*, alias *Worſley*, and

Clement Slie Fencer: with their Eſcapes and

Breaking of Priſon:

As alſo

the true and hearty Repentance of *Charles Courtney* wi

other paſſages, worthy the note and Reading.

LONDON

Printed for *Edward Marchant*, and are to bee ſold in *Paul*

Churce yard ouer againſt the Croſſe. 1612.

Figure 6.2 The title page woodcut of *The Life, Apprehension, Arraignment and Execution of Charles Courtney* simultaneously depicts Courtney and his accomplice's daring escape from Newgate Prison and their subsequent scaffold executions on either side of the prison gates. Reproduced from the original copy at the British Library.

contained in the body of the pamphlet. While these supplemental publication features show how Courtney's physical body was prey to the dictates and spectacles of justice, the dissemination of his life story in print nevertheless articulates a trenchant critique of status privilege and judicial corruption.

Through the adoption of biographical contextualization, writers and publishers of crime news pamphlets helped to expand the scope of public knowledge about the criminal beyond the moralistic and sensationalistic reporting of crime, trial, and execution. In light of the evidence that this biographical mode provided a radical re-conceptualization of the nature of criminality, the dominant critical view that "these writers [sought] to inculcate proper behaviours and warn of the dreadful consequences of wickedness" needs to be substantively re-evaluated.[73] The inclusion of in-depth life histories within these pamphlets allowed readers to situate the individual criminal in a complex social economy; rather than simply characterizing criminals as naturally malicious, these kinds of sociological representations attempted to illustrate how domestic, gender, and power imbalances inform many types of criminal activity. While many crime pamphlets supported dominant notions of criminality, others presented an alternative picture of criminal life that provided a broader voicing of the point of view of offenders than either the truncated defendant deposition of the public trial or the stage-managed and socially circumscribed scaffold confession. Despite often being embedded within moralistic frameworks, biographical contextualization provided a significantly different criminological narrative, one that questioned judicial categorization of crime and critiqued the dominant use of analogy in forensic rhetoric. While early modern legality attempted to legitimize its practices by claiming to embody impartial and equitable justice, the counter-criminological discourses contained in news pamphlets reveal these judicial claims as ideological distortions. Moreover, news reports that directly depict inequitable and class-biased legal decisions were instrumental in the development of increasingly sceptical and resistant public attitudes towards the judicial status quo. Widespread public scepticism in turn could challenge traditional jurisprudence through the transformation of juristic thought; as the English system of justice "depended ... on the involvement of laymen from a fairly broad social spectrum who acted as local officials and jurors," readers of crime pamphlets directly participated in legal decisions and appear to increasingly mitigate sentencing throughout the seventeenth century.[74] The wider effect of the new criminology found in crime pamphlets may be difficult to evaluate empirically, but biographical contextualization as a method of evaluating crime and assessing levels of guilt clearly influenced early modern habits of forensic evaluation. Although the ethical involvement of individual writers should not be discounted, the producers and publishers of these crime reports were primarily motivated by the commercial interests of the print market. The unique publication features of the pamphlet form, namely, its cost-effective packaging of topical crime content, ultimately proved saleable to both established and emergent early modern readership markets. In sum, the development of the new media form of the crime news pamphlet with its inclusion of biographical contextualization actively generated new ways of conceptualizing and discussing issues surrounding the administering of justice in early modern England.[75]

NOTES

1 Joad Raymond's *Pamphlets and Pamphleteering in Early Modern Britain*, Alexandra Halasz's *The Marketplace of Print*, Margaret Spufford's *Small Books and Pleasant Histories*, and Sandra Clark's *The Elizabethan Pamphleteers: Popular Moralistic Pamphlets 1580–1640* investigate the pamphlet's role in book history. See also Joy Wiltenberg, *Disorderly Women and Female Power in the Street Literature of Early Modern England and Germany*; and Tessa Watt, *Cheap Print and Popular Piety, 1550–1640*. Social historians have utilized pamphlet material as a way to gauge popular responses to criminality: see J.A. Sharpe, *Crime in Early Modern England, 1550–1750*, pp. 225–37, and "'Last Dying Speeches': Religion, Ideology and Public Execution in Seventeenth-Century England"; Garthine Walker, "'Demons in Female Form': Representations of Women and Gender in Murder Pamphlets of the Late Sixteenth and Early Seventeenth Centuries" and *Crime, Gender and Social Order in Early Modern England*; and Vanessa McMahon, *Murder in Shakespeare's England*. Critics who examine the construction of gender have found the pamphlet form especially revealing in its recording of women's lives: Frances Dolan, *Dangerous Familiars: Representations of Domestic Crime in England, 1550–1700*, and *Marriage and Violence: The Early Modern Legacy*; Susan Staub, *Nature's Cruel Stepdames: Murderous Women in the Street Literature of Seventeenth-Century England*; and Linda Woodbridge, *Women and the English Renaissance*.

2 Sandra Clark, *Women and Crime in the Street Literature of Early Modern England*, p. 32.

3 Sandra Clark, *Women and Crime*, p. 30. Joad Raymond, while agreeing that "crime pamphlets were a means of displaying a normative social order," also sees that the form contained enough "heterogeneity" and "malleability" that it did not constitute "an arena of unimpugnable punishment … but a literary genre rooted in commercial exchange, combining entertainment and instruction, and open to divergent uses," *Pamphlets and Pamphleteering*, pp. 119, 121. Clark qualifies her assertion when she notes that the dominant homiletic impulse of pamphlet literature is in constant tension with the narration of "the factual account of the crime, its investigation, the trial and the outcome," for "a claim of veracity of some kind was clearly a selling point," *Women and Crime*, pp. 25, 29. Randall Martin argues that printed murder news had a more radical effect on society as it "nurtured discourses of social and legal equity towards female homicide, while at the same time reproducing traditional negative images of murderous women," *Women, Murder, and Equity in Early Modern England*, p. 5.

4 Peter Lake, "Deeds against Nature: Cheap Print, Protestantism and Murder in Early Seventeenth-Century England," p. 262.

5 Peter Lake, "Deeds against Nature," p. 262.

6 Ian Taylor, Paul Walton, and Jock Young, *The New Criminology: For a Social Theory of Deviance*, pp. 270–1.

7 Richard Singer and John Q. La Fond link moral corruption and notions of criminal culpability: "clearly heavily influenced by religious notions of sin, the criminal law as early as the thirteenth century encapsulated the need for a 'vicious will' in the Latin term *mens rea*," *Criminal Law: Examples and Explications*, p. 55. Preformed malice was especially important for convictions in homicide cases. Edward Coke in his discussion of murder notes how the capacity to act on a predisposed malice constitutes a danger to the community beyond the bounds of any particular case or instance of violence: "This malice is so odious in law, as though it be intended against one, it shall be extended towards another," *The Third Part of the Institutes of the Lawes of England*, p. 51.

8 Susan Dwyer Amussen contends that analogical thinking was pervasive in most formulations of crime and order in the period; Amussen observes, for instance, that "the analogy between the household and the state was available to all those interested in authority and enforcement of order in early modern England," *An Ordered Society: Gender and Class in Early Modern England*, p. 37.

9 Alexandra Halasz, *The Marketplace of Print: Pamphlets and the Public Sphere in Early Modern England*, p. 4.

10 Halasz, *The Marketplace of Print*, p. 14.

11 The price of short pamphlets ranged from under 1p. to 2p. and thus were placed well within the means of even modest households. Raymond, *Pamphlets and Pamphleteering*, p. 5.

12 Lawrence Stone, "The Educational Revolution in England, 1560–1640," p. 41.

13 Tessa Watt, *Cheap Print and Popular Piety, 1550–1640*, p. 8. Watt connects printed ballads with older, "oral and musical traditions" and illustration with the popular practices of "domestic wall painting and painted cloth," p. 8. Watt's reading of what constitutes cheap print counters A.J. Flecher and J. Stevenson's argument in *Order and Disorder in Early Modern England* that specialized publication was an agent of social polarization, pp. 1–15.

14 Raymond describes how printed news could respond quickly to topical events: "a single quarto sheet could be set in type and a few hundred copies printed off in a day or two," *Pamphlets and Pamphleteering*, p. 123.

15 In 1635 Nicolas and John Oakes, as well as publishing two crime pamphlets, *Heavens Speedie Hue and Cry sent after Lust and Murther* and *The Adultresses Funerall Day*, published works such as *Emblema Animae, or Morall Discourses Reflecting upon Humanitie* (270 pages) and *Davids Blessed Man: or, A Short Exposition upon the First Psalme* (301 pages).

16 Popular interest in crime reportage and criminal biography certainly appears to expand throughout the early modern period, and crime pamphlets become a significant area of source material for literature and public drama. Alongside significant growth in crime pamphlet publication throughout the seventeenth century, serial periodicals, such as the *Mercurius Publicus*, begin to include news concerning crime and punishment alongside their reports on parliament, Westminster, and foreign courts.

17 J.A. Sharpe, "'Last Dying Speeches': Religion, Ideology and Public Execution in Seventeenth-Century England," p. 148. Sharpe supports the view of critics such as Sandra Clark and Peter Lake that early modern reportage operated primarily as a form of public homiletics.

18 For instance, Elizabeth publicly called Mary "the worst woman in the world, whose head should have been cut off years ago," *Calendar of State Papers*, Vol. 2: 5 May 1578.

19 George Whetstone, *The Censure of a Loyal Subject upon Certain Noted Speech and Behaviors of those Fourteen Notable Traitors*, title page.

20 Whetstone, *The Censure of a Loyal Subject*, A3v.

21 Robert Hutchinson, *Elizabeth's Spy Master: Francis Walsingham and the Secret War That Saved England*, p. 145.

22 Whetstone, *The Censure of a Loyal Subject*, B1v.

23 *The Bardon Papers: Documents Relating to the Imprisonment & Trial of Mary Queen of Scots*, Vol. XVII, p. 47.
24 Hutchinson, *Elizabeth's Spy Master*, p. 145; Whetstone, *The Censure of a Loyal Subject*, A4v.
25 Whetstone, *The Censure of a Loyal Subject*, A4v.
26 Randall Martin, *Women, Murder, and Equity in Early Modern England*, p. 9.
27 Henry Goodcole, *Heavens Speedie Hue and Cry sent after Lust and Murder*, A4v.
28 Henry Goodcole, *Heavens Speedie Hue and Cry*, A4v.
29 Henry Goodcole, *Heavens Speedie Hue and Cry*, C3v. Susan Staub contends that in depicting female murderers as "matchless monsters," "savages," "unnatural cruel beasts in women's shapes," and "shee wolves," "these writings often view women criminals as aberrations, as deformities of nature," *Nature's Cruel Stepdames*, p. 13.
30 Henry Goodcole, *Heavens Speedie Hue and Cry*, A4v.
31 Thomas Harman, *A Caveat for Common Cursitors*, in *Rogues, Vagabonds, and Sturdy Beggars: A New Gallery of Tudor and Early Stuart Rogue Literature*, p. 144.
32 Goodcole, *Heavens Speedie Hue and Cry*, B2r.
33 Rosamaria Loretelli, "Trial by Cheap Print," p. 45.
34 This pamphlet is more fully discussed in my "Female Criminality in Henry Goodcole's Murder Pamphlets."
35 This law was first formulated in the statute of 1352 (25 Edward III). Michael Dalton emphasizes the idea that as a wife is "in subjection, and oweth faith, duetie, and obedience" to her husband, her act of spousal murder constitutes a fundamental rupture of domestic loyalty, *The Country Justice*, p. 204.
36 Walker, *Crime, Gender and Social Order*, pp. 138–9; Dolan, *Dangerous Familiars*, pp. 21–2.
37 Walker, *Crime, Gender and Social Order*, pp. 141–3.
38 Henry Goodcole, *The Adultresses Funerall Day in flaming, scorching, and consuming fire*, B1v.
39 Dolan, *Marriage and Violence*, p. 83.
40 Dolan, *Marriage and Violence*, p. 89.
41 Walker, *Crime, Gender and Social Order*, p. 143.
42 Goodcole, *The Adultresses Funerall Day*, B3r.
43 Goodcole, *The Adultresses Funerall Day*, B3v.
44 Dolan, "'Gentlemen, I have one more thing to say,'" p. 158.
45 Staub, *Nature's Cruel Stepdames*, p. 37.
46 I.T., *A Horrible Creuel and Bloudy Murther*, A3r. *An Homily against Disobedience and Willful Rebellion*, which was required to be read from the pulpit

in Anglican churches, states "[t]hat in families and households the wife should be obedient unto her husband, the children unto their parents, the servants unto their masters," A3v.

47 Peter Lake contends that the emphasis on the detailed physical actions of the murderers allows "the author to focus on the sight" of the master's mutilated body producing "the literary equivalent of a John Carpenter film," "Deeds against Nature," pp. 259, 261. However, there is at least as much emphasis on the political nature of the murder as on its horror.

48 I.T., *A Horrible Creuel and Bloudy Murther*, B1v.

49 I.T., *A Horrible Creuel and Bloudy Murther*, B1r.

50 I.T., *A Horrible Creuel and Bloudy Murther*, B3v. I.T., who might be the prolific populist author John Taylor, may have included this material to provide a fuller record of the trial. Note that "meat" at this time may be understood in the wider sense of basic comestibles.

51 I.T., *A Horrible Creuel and Bloudy Murther*, B3v.

52 The text indicates that she may have murdered more of her children: "Many great bellies had she, besides three here spoken of, but the unhappie loads of them could never be seene," Thomas Brewer, *The Bloudy Mother, or The Most Inhumane Murthers, Committed by Jane Hattersley upon Divers Infants*, B3r.

53 Thomas Brewer, *The Bloudy Mother*, A4v. Keith Wrightson confirms the commonplace nature of these types of master-servant relationships; up to a quarter of women who bore bastards acknowledged that they had been impregnated by their masters, "The Nadir of English Illegitimacy in the Seventeenth Century," p. 187.

54 Brewer, *The Bloudy Mother*, B1r.

55 Brewer, *The Bloudy Mother*, B2r.

56 Brewer, *The Bloudy Mother*, B2r.

57 Brewer, *The Bloudy Mother*, B3r.

58 Brewer, *The Bloudy Mother*, B4r.

59 Brewer, *The Bloudy Mother*, B4r.

60 Brewer, *The Bloudy Mother*, B4r. As these events occurred before the advent of infanticide legislation in 1624, the normal burden of proof in homicide cases would be employed.

61 The pamphlet reports that she expected to receive her pardon right up to her last minutes on the executioner's scaffold.

62 See Christopher Brooks, *Law, Politics and Society in Early Modern England*.

63 See further, Brooks, *Law, Politics and Society*, pp. 90–1.

64 Susan Staub observes that "the assurance that divine providence will punish the wrongdoer, that 'murder will out,' in the words of one pamphleteer, is crucial to this literature," *Nature's Cruel Stepdames*, p. 76.

65 Brewer, *The Bloudy Mother*, C1v.

66 Brewer, *The Bloudy Mother*, C1v. The author of the addendum appears to borrow the ready-made providential punishments of Foxe's *Acts and Monuments*. In one example, De Roma, who was implicated in the 1540s wave of persecution of Waldensian heretics in France, is reported to have fallen "sycke of a terryble disease, unknowen to any physition," *Acts and Monuments*, p. 650. This providential infection is such that "no man durst come neare unto hym for the great stynche that came out of his body, in so muche that the fleshe fell awaye by great pieces and gobbettes, his body was repleat with sores full of vermine and wormes," *Acts and Monuments*, p. 650. Micheline White was helpful in pointing out the martyrological tradition as a probable source for this pamphlet's description of Adamson's sudden providential demise.

67 Brewer, *The Bloudy Mother*, C2r.

68 The English criminal justice system "depended on unpaid officers of the peace and on the institution of jury trial" and thus was "strongly participatory" in contrast to Continental models. Lorna Hutson, *The Invention of Suspicion*, p. 3; see also pp. 66–7.

69 Charles Courtney, *The Life, Apprehension, Arraignement, and Execution of Charles Courtney*, p. 5.

70 Courtney, *The Life*, p. 15.

71 Sir Christopher Yelverton's speech to grand jurors in Northamptonshire in the 1560s encapsulate the suspicion that corruption and authority go hand in hand: "How swiftlie may the rising authoritie of a great Magistrate decline to oppression" (manuscript quoted in Brooks, *Law, Politics and Society*, p. 283).

72 Watt contends that many printed ballads "satisfied different demands in its functions as reading matter and as song," *Cheap Print*, p. 37. Some buyers, although illiterate, might purchase ballads in order to learn the songs from the oral performance of friends and family.

73 Susan Staub, *Nature's Cruel Stepdames*, p. 12.

74 Brooks, *Law, Politics and Society*, p. 15; Martin, *Women, Murder, and Equity in Early Modern England*, pp. 53, 203.

75 In the longer term, public interest in criminal biography infiltrates penology both in its Continental and English forms. One of the new foci of modern penology that Michel Foucault identifies is the state's intimate knowledge of the criminal. In order to be able to identify and correct criminal behaviour, a variety of disciplinary experts become charged with assessing individuals and identifying the sources of their criminality; for Foucault, this "great transformation" occurs in the

mid-eighteenth century, *Discipline and Punish: The Birth of the Prison*, p. 15. The quantitative shift in penal technology from the punitive style of punishment to the reformative may have had some of its genealogical roots in the emergent alternative criminology pioneered by early modern crime reporters.

BIBLIOGRAPHY

Amussen, Susan Dwyer. *An Ordered Society: Gender and Class in Early Modern England*. Oxford: Blackwell, 1988.

Anon. *A Horrible Creuel and Bloody Murther*. London: G. Eld, 1614. Early English Books Online. Web. 6 November 2011.

The Bardon Papers: Documents Relating to the Imprisonment & Trial of Mary Queen of Scots, Camden 3rd Series, Vol. XVII. Ed. Conyers Read. London, 1909.

Brewer, Thomas. *The Bloudy Mother, or The Most Inhumane Murthers, Committed by Jane Hattersley upon Divers Infants, the Issue of her Owne Body*. London, 1609. Early English Books Online. Web. 6 November 2011.

Brooks, Christopher. *Law, Politics and Society in Early Modern England*. Cambridge: Cambridge UP, 2008.

Calendar of State Papers, Spain (Simancas), Vol. 2, 1568–1579. Ed. Martin A.S. Hume. London: 1894. British History Online. http://www.british-history.ac.uk/source.aspx?pubid=977&strquery=Calendar%20of%20State%20Papers,%20Spain. 6 November 2011.

Clark, Sandra. *The Elizabethan Pamphleteers: Popular Moralistic Pamphlets 1580–1640*. London: Athone, 1983.

– *Women and Crime in the Street Literature of Early Modern England*. Houndmills, Hampshire: Palgrave, 2003.

Cokes, Edward. *The Third Part of the Institutes of the Lawes of England: Concerning High Treason, and Other Pleas of the Crown, and Civil Causes*. 4th ed. London, 1669. Early English Books Online. Web. 6 November 2011.

Courtney, Charles. *The Life, Apprehension, Arraignement, and Execution of Charles Courtney*. London: W. Hall, 1612. Early English Books Online. Web. 6 November 2011.

Dalton, Michael. *The Country Justice*. London, 1618. Early English Books Online. Web. 6 November 2011.

Dionne, Craig. "Playing the 'Cony': Anonymity in Underworld Literature." *Genre: Forms of Discourse and Culture* 30 (1997): 29–50.

Dolan, Frances. *Dangerous Familiars: Representations of Domestic Crime in England, 1550–1700*. Ithaca, NY: Cornell UP, 1994.

– "'Gentlemen, I have one thing more to say': Women on Scaffolds in England, 1563–1680." *Modern Philology* 92, no. 2 (1994): 157–78.

– *Marriage and Violence: The Early Modern Legacy.* Philadelphia: U of Pennsylvania P, 2008.

Flecher, A.J., and J. Stevenson. *Order and Disorder in Early Modern England.* Cambridge: Cambridge UP, 1985.

Foucault, Michel. *Discipline and Punish: The Birth of the Prison*. Trans. Alan Sheridan. New York: Vintage, 1995.

Foxe, John. *Acts and Monuments*. London, John Day, 1563. Early English Books Online. Web. 6 November 2011.

Goodcole, Henry. *The Adultresses Funerall Day in flaming, scorching, and consuming fire: or the burning downe to ashes of Alice Clark*. London: John Oakes, 1635. Early English Books Online. Web. 6 November 2011.

– *Heavens Speedie Hue and Cry sent after Lust and Murder*. 2nd ed. London: John Oakes, 1635. Early English Books Online. Web. 6 November 2011.

Halasz, Alexandra. *The Marketplace of Print: Pamphlets and the Public Sphere in Early Modern England*. Cambridge: Cambridge UP, 1997.

Harman, Thomas. *A Caveat for Common Cursitors*. In *Rogues, Vagabonds, and Sturdy Beggars: A New Gallery of Tudor and Early Stuart Rogue Literature*. Ed. Arthur Kinney. Amherst: Massachusetts UP, 1990. 103–54.

An Homilie Agaynst Disobedience and Wylful Rebellion. London: Richard Jugge, 1570. Early English Books Online. Web. 6 November 2011.

Hutchinson, Robert. *Elizabeth's Spy Master: Francis Walsingham and the Secret War That Saved England*. London: Phoenix, 2007.

Hutson, Lorna. *The Invention of Suspicion*. Oxford: Oxford UP, 2007.

I.T. *A Horrible Creuel and Bloudy Murther, Committed … upon the Body of Edward Hall, a Miller*. London: G. Eld., 1614. Early English Books Online. Web. 6 November 2011.

Lake, Peter. "Deeds against Nature: Cheap Print, Protestantism and Murder in Early Seventeenth-Century England." In *Culture and Politics in Early Stuart England*. Ed. Kevin Sharpe and Peter Lake. Stanford, CA: Stanford UP, 1993. 257–83.

Loretelli, Rosamaria. "Trial by Cheap Print." In *Narrating Transgression: Representations of the Criminal in Early Modern England*. Ed. Roberto De Romanis and Rosamaria Loretelli. Berlin: Peter Lang, 1999. 27–50.

Martin, Randall. *Women, Murder, and Equity in Early Modern England*. New York: Routledge, 2008.

McMahon, Vanessa. *Murder in Shakespeare's England*. London: Hambledon and London, 2006.

Raymond, Joad. *Pamphlets and Pamphleteering in Early Modern Britain*. Cambridge: Cambridge UP, 2003.

Sharpe, J.A. *Crime in Early Modern England, 1550–1750.* 2nd ed. London: Longman, 1999.
– "'Last Dying Speeches': Religion, Ideology and Public Execution in Seventeenth-Century England." *Past and Present* 107 (1985): 144–67.
Singer, Richard, and John Q. La Fond. *Criminal Law: Examples and Explications.* New York: Aspen, 2007.
Spufford, Margaret. *Small Books and Pleasant Histories: Popular Fiction and its Readership in Seventeenth-Century England.* Cambridge: Cambridge UP, 1985.
Staub, Susan. *Nature's Cruel Stepdames: Murderous Women in the Street Literature of Seventeenth Century England.* Pittsburgh, PA: Duquesne UP, 2005.
Stone, Lawrence. "The Educational Revolution in England, 1560–1640." *Past and Present* 28 (1964): 41–80.
Stretton, Tim. "Marriage, Separation and the Common Law in England, 1540–1660." In *The Family in Early Modern England.* Ed. Helen Berry and Elizabeth Foyster. Cambridge: Cambridge UP, 2007. 18–39.
Stymeist, David. "Female Criminality in Henry Goodcole's Murder Pamphlets." *Genre: Forms of Discourse and Culture* 36 (2003): 31–48.
Taylor, Ian, Paul Walton, and Jock Young. *The New Criminology: For a Social Theory of Deviance.* Ed. John Rex. London: Routledge and Kegan Paul, 1973.
Walker, Garthine. *Crime, Gender and Social Order in Early Modern England.* Cambridge: Cambridge UP, 2003.
– "'Demons in Female Form': Representations of Women and Gender in Murder Pamphlets of the Late Sixteenth and Early Seventeenth Centuries." *Writing and the English Renaissance.* Ed. William Zunder and Susanne Trill. London: Longman, 1994. 123–39.
Watt, Tessa. *Cheap Print and Popular Piety, 1550–1640.* Cambridge: Cambridge UP, 1991.
Whetstone, George. *The Censure of a Loyal Subject upon Certain Noted Speech and Behaviors of those Fourteen Notable Traitors.* London: Richard Jones, 1587. Early English Books Online. Web. 6 November 2011.
Wiltenberg, Joy. *Disorderly Women and Female Power in the Street Literature of Early Modern England and Germany.* London: U of Virginia P, 1992.
Woodbridge, Linda. *Women and the English Renaissance: Literature and the Nature of Womankind, 1540–1620.* Urbana: U of Illinois P, 1984.
Wrightson, Keith. "The Nadir of English Illegitimacy in the Seventeenth Century." In *Bastardy and Its Comparative History.* Ed. Peter Laslett, Karla Oosterveen and Richard Smith. Cambridge, MA: Harvard UP, 1980. 176–91.

7 Two-Sided Legal Narratives: Slander, Evidence, Proof, and Turnarounds in *Much Ado About Nothing*

BARBARA KREPS

An important part of grammar school teaching in early modern England was based on the rhetoric of Cicero and Quintilian, from whom students learned (in addition to Latin) that there are at least two sides to almost any question. The merits of being able to argue *in utramque partem*, pounded home early in the schoolchild's development, was a lesson that remained in place for many who (like lawyers and playwrights) continued to study and live by combining word-crafting with mental agility. This ability to argue different sides of a question was certainly in evidence at the Inns of Court, where the students' early training reappeared in the moots – those law debates that span out complicated twists of narrative – as one of the ways to sharpen the young lawyers' logical capabilities.[1] The kind of versatility required by the moots would, at its best, teach the importance of keeping an open mind about information and its credibility. But legal professionals also know that sifting is a crucial element of judicial decision-making, simply because not all information is true – partly because witnesses may entertain mistaken perceptions, partly because the source of information may be unreliable. And this sifting is of course the ostensible purpose of trials. James Boyd White tells us that "While a case can in a technical sense be refuted by disproving one element or another, in practice the lawyer knows that he must do more than that: he must offer the judge or juror an alternative place to stand, another way of making sense of the case as a whole. To do his job, that is, the lawyer must both engage in an accurate retelling of the facts and make his own claim for what they mean."[2] This is no simple achievement: lawyers are well aware that aligning "fact" with "meaning" has become extremely complex in modern courtroom practice, partly because the law of evidence has burgeoned in ways that once would have been unthinkable. In our own time, the law concerning evidence has become highly technical, largely because one aspect of developments in the jury's role in evaluating fact is that the norms governing admissibility have become far more protective of defendants' positions than they were four centuries ago.[3] The necessity of finding and arguing from "an alternative place" is nonetheless an important directive, particularly since – as White points out – where you are (emotionally and intellectually as well as physically) determines what you see.

This is an elemental truth about appearance and reality that Shakespeare put to use in almost all of his plays. But the problems of judging fact when there are two competing narratives are very specifically foregrounded in four of them (*Much Ado About Nothing*, *Othello*, *Cymbeline*, and *The Winter's Tale*), where the plots – all of which involve cases of sexual slander – grow specifically from the issue of false or erroneous witness. My essay focuses on *Much Ado*, but this play shares several situations found in the other three, not least of which is the limited recourse the victim of such slander was likely to find in the legal machinery of the period.

From the first scene the dialogue insists on the importance of the language game. (Comically represented in act 1, scene 1 by Benedick's verbal sparring with Beatrice and with his male friends, the language game bears a weighty role in a play whose primary plot will be shaped later by the particular linguistic abuse of defamation.) Family and gender roles are quickly made explicit through conversations underscoring a double standard of sexual behaviour that, for lusty young males like Benedick ("loved of all ladies" [1.1.126]), noticeably contrasts with the norms by which Hero will later be judged and condemned.[4] Shakespeare also inserts the puzzling business of the Prince (Don Pedro), who outlines for Claudio his plan to "assume thy part in some disguise" (1.1.323) in order to woo Hero for his friend at the masked revels that evening. The subterfuge does not advance the plot in any way, but it does set the stage for the display of contrasting attitudes towards the issues, fundamental to the play, of reliable evidence and what constitutes proof. On the most immediate level the apparently pointless plan helps to distinguish appropriate and inappropriate reactions to hearsay evidence. In the scene that follows, Leonato sets the gold standard: in act 1, scene 2 his brother Antonio comes to him with a tale, recounted in turn by a servant who has overheard the prince's wooing plan, but (as the audience knows) the servant has completely misunderstood its meaning ("the prince discovered to Claudio that he loved my niece your daughter and meant to acknowledge it this night in a dance" [1.2.11–13]). This is hearsay at several removes, and though Leonato verifies the tale-bearer's good character and intelligence, he still quite rightly concludes that only further evidence will determine the tale's veracity: "No, no; we will hold it as a dream till it appear itself" (1.2.21–2). Leonato's correct reaction to hearsay is counterbalanced by Claudio, who noticeably lacks Leonato's acumen. Upon hearing Don John's repetition of the same tale of Don Pedro's love for Hero that Leonato has rejected, Claudio takes the story at face value, even though he has two strong personal reasons to question it: (1) the prince has already cleared this script with Claudio, and (2) the masked Claudio himself has just – falsely – told John that he is Benedick. Claudio is incapable of reflecting that, just as he is not telling the truth, Don John might also be lying. Instead, he precipitously concludes from "hourly proof" of others' infidelities that he has been a fool to trust his friend to speak on his behalf (2.1.187). Thus, his conviction of the prince's perfidy is already proved to his own satisfaction when Benedick arrives to corroborate Claudio's suspicions. Benedick is of course mistaken, though his purpose has simply been to tell the truth ("I told him, and I think I told him true" [2.1.222]).

For all his vivacious love of talk, Benedick always aims for truth when he speaks. Although at first he identifies Beatrice as his antagonist ("she speaks poniards, and every word stabs," she is "a dish I love not: I cannot endure my Lady Tongue" [2.1.254, 2.1.281–2]), it is clear to all that they are a good match, not only for their wit but also for their adherence to the values of honesty and loyalty. For her part, Beatrice locates Benedick's true opposite in Don John: "the one is too like an image and says nothing, and the other too like my lady's eldest son, evermore tattling" (2.1.9–11). Beatrice has hit the mark. Don John's very first words in the play publicize that "I am not of many words" (1.1.158). The audience, however, gets another of its privileged glimpses two scenes later, when Don John opens up to his cronies: "though I cannot be said to be a flattering honest man, it must not be denied that I am a plain-dealing villain. I am trusted with a muzzle … If I had my mouth, I would bite" (1.3.31–6). His dangerous mouth is of course not muzzled, and the inventive liberty he takes with it is what fires the Hero-Claudio plot. Significant to *Much Ado*'s action is how one meaning can be paradoxically inverted to become its opposite, briefly instanced here as Don John boasts that he will "cross him [Claudio]" to "bless myself" [1.3.70–1].

His pun not only abruptly inverts the semantic direction of "cross"; it also points ahead towards the major distortions about to unfold, as his defamation successfully transforms an innocent woman into one who appears guilty. This, the central inversion in *Much Ado*'s recurring play with the reversal of expectations, has no direct cause-effect motive. Don John has no personal reason to take Hero as his adversary: his determination to slander her is – like the pun – itself born of a deflected logic. She is for him simply a way of getting at his brother's friend Claudio – a manoeuvre that a much later audience would understand to be a classic case of Freudian displacement.

Historical studies of defamation in early modern England have shown that in cases of sexual slander this was frequently the case: women's sexuality provided an easily accessible target for wounding both sexes. An accusation of whoredom damaged the status of both husbands and wives within their community's notions of honour. For men, being identified as an adulterous husband did not have anything like the insult value attached to being known as a cuckold. Though a man might be called a "whoremaster" or a "whoremonger," the damage attaching to a man's reputation from sexual activity was more likely to concern his wife's doings than his own. When men went to court to challenge defamatory statements, the slanders were more likely to concern attacks on their status (such as being called a villain) or other areas more traditionally concerned with masculine probity, which as Susan Amussen points out involved "a much broader range of activities than those complained of by women."[5] For women, the damage that sexual slurs caused within their marriages or to their prospective value in the marriage market explains why women, far more than men, were willing to spend the money to go to law. And go to law they did. For though English women (particularly married women, who were subordinated to their husbands through coverture) were yoked with some serious legal restrictions, they were never completely legally disabled. As Tim Stretton points out, while "the equity courts recognised exceptions to the doctrine of coverture," the "outstanding example" in which women brought their own suits were the cases of defamation argued largely through the church courts where women, allowed "to sue in their own names ... came to outnumber men as plaintiffs."[6]

The falsehoods in both of *Much Ado*'s love plots uncover how linguistic uncertainty is always necessarily joined with epistemological problems of interpretation. Lying and hearsay generate common problems, separated at the source only by either good intentions or *mens rea.* If we can't take what people say at face value, then who people are (and the meaning of their actions) is no longer certain, a point several times made physically clear from the stage, not only through those rehearsed, metatheatrical conversations purposely set up to be overheard and intending to deceive, but also through the recurring conversations conducted from behind masks and veils – a device that at least temporarily permits characters to claim different identities. Having listened in on the trumped-up story about Beatrice, Benedick must now reason about the validity of what he has heard, and understanding (as Claudio earlier failed to do) that he needs to evaluate the reliability of the evidence before him, he does what some trial procedures do, and makes use of character evaluation: "I should think this a gull, but that the white-bearded fellow speaks it: knavery cannot, sure, hide himself in such reverence" (2.3.123–5). Leonato's known character is presumably a guarantee, and his solid reputation is sufficient here to convince Benedick that the story he has overheard is factual; but – as several Ponzi schemes have recently shown – the problem with trying to judge truth on the basis of character history is that we never really know for sure what knavery will look like. In his subsequent meeting with Beatrice, he finds himself therefore suddenly faced with the problem of how to interpret what she says. She speaks to him with as much hostility as ever, but Benedick's mind now fiddles with her words, and, already in the throes of nascent love, he turns their meaning quite around:

> BENE. "Ha! 'Against my will I am sent to bid you come in to dinner'; there's a double meaning in that. 'I took no more pains for those thanks than you took pains to thank me'; that's as much as to say, 'Any pains that I take for you is as easy as thanks.'" (2.3.267–70)

The sudden need to translate, to find the right language, is a new situation for Benedick, who has never before been at a loss for words. But the discovery of double meanings is only a symptom of the difficulties besetting language from here on. The hearsay lesson is part of this, and is writ increasingly larger, as the double plots become thematically and structurally entwined.[7] The scenes showing the untruths being successfully foisted off on Beatrice and Benedick occur back to back (2.3 and 3.1), but these scenes of mirth are not only paired to go with each other but give quite another insight into the deforming power of lies by being sandwiched between the scenes (2.2, 3.2) in which Don John first plots and then carries out his defamation of Hero. Well aware that words alone will not suffice to convince the company that Hero is "a contaminated stale" (2.2.25), Don John knows that he needs "proof" (2.2.27 and 2.2.28), "trial" (2.2.41), and "instances" (2.2.41). He finds what will pass for proof in the plan to have Margaret appear at Hero's window, speaking lovingly to Borachio. The epistemological problem that attends Don John's disruptive announcement in act 3, scene 2 is linguistically re-enforced, from line 92 on, by the ironic repetitions of "know" and "think," invitations to know and think that culminate in "If you dare not trust that you see, confess not that you know: if you will follow me, I will show you enough; and when you have heard more and seen more, proceed accordingly" (3.2.122–5). Just as the friends of Beatrice and Benedick know how to put on a convincing show, Don John is also aware that, if words are to take on an aspect that looks like ocular proof, staging is all-important.

The Dogberry and Verges plot adds another dimension to *Much Ado*'s language games and, from within the stylized humour that parodies the constable's difficulty in dealing with legal or Latinate English terms, one of Dogberry's substitutions bumbles the villains' "flat perjury" (4.2.44) into an accusation of "flat burglary" (4.2.52). Dogberry's lexical mistake inadvertently lands on a real core of truth. For the slander of Hero is a purposeful act of identity theft (which, by the way, is why early modern women were willing to venture court actions in defamation suits, in an attempt to publicly redeem their characters and, in authoritative forums, regain their true identities). The audience is perfectly aware from the first scene that a large part of the comedy derives from the surprising potential for ambiguity in signs, as words (which are, of course, signs) are bantered self-reflexively, pointing to the coexistence of surfaces and undercurrents by redirecting or deflecting meaning through witty word exchanges. The discrepancy between a sign and its unstable meaning is also inherent in the masks and disguises. But from the moment the defamation is made public at church in act 4, scene 1, the visual strategies of *Much Ado* are also permeated by indices of legal and cultural values that are deeply inscribed. Claudio depends on such shared cultural significance when he determines to stage his own show for Hero, selecting the church as his dramatic backdrop and the celebration of the nuptials as the time for his repudiation.

Compressing arraignment and conviction into one scene, the ceremony is rapidly transformed into a brusque parody of the (civil) law's inquisitorial trial formulae, with the relevant linguistic paraphernalia of "evidence," "witness," "guiltiness," and "proof." Once again Claudio's tendency to rush to judgment shows up: here, as earlier, he has already determined what Hero's behaviour has been, and hence what the outcome of her examination must be. Aware of discrepant signs that make his accusation problematic, he brushes away all the evidence that puts his foregone conclusion in doubt, arguing that the meaning of signs resides in the interpreter, not in the sign itself:

> She's but the sign and semblance of her honour.
> Behold how like a maid she blushes here!
> ...
> Comes not that blood as modest evidence
> To witness simple virtue? Would you not swear,
> All you that see her, that she were a maid,
> By these exterior shows? But she is none:
> She knows the heat of a luxurious bed;
> Her blush is guiltiness, not modesty. (4.1.34–41)

As the scene of marriage at the church is joylessly transformed to a "kind of catechising" (4.1.79), Claudio briefly convinces even Leonato to read the few facts available to him as proof of his daughter's guilt. In a play that turns so centrally on the quality of evidence, the word "noting" (and its variant forms) is iterated over and over throughout *Much Ado About Nothing* (including the noting/nothing assonance many have remarked in the play's title), and it is the friar's "noting" here that reclaims Hero's father. Hero's blushes provide Claudio with evidence of her guilt. "Noting ... a thousand blushing apparitions" (4.1.160–1), the friar adduces that same blushing as proof that "this sweet lady ... [is] guiltless" (4.1.171). This is only one of this scene's reversals. Another is that the symbols of death henceforth replace those of marriage as bringers of hope. The friar is certain that the family's "mourning ostentation ... on your family's old monument," with "all rites / That appertain unto a burial" will restore Hero's esteem: "strange sores strangely they strain the cure. / Come, lady, die to live: this wedding- day/ Perhaps is but prolong'd" (4.1.254–6). For the moment I am simply concerned with the alternate readings of signs made available in this scene and the inversions of plot direction these readings help to produce, but later I shall be returning to consider the metaphoric as well as the legal significance of death as it is propounded here by the friar.

Left alone with Benedick in the church, Beatrice is horrified when she calls to mind Claudio's calculated hardness in his choice of place and occasion:

BENE. Is Claudio thine enemy?

BEAT. Is 'a not approved in the height a villain, that hath slandered, scorned, dishonoured my kinswoman? O that I were a man! What, bear her in hand until they come to take hands; and then with public accusation, uncovered slander, unmitigated rancour, – O God that I were a man! I would eat his heart in the market-place. (4.1.302–9)

This passage is remarkably mimetic in its reproduction of Beatrice's mental processes as she outlines how Claudio has "approved" (proved) his villainy. The past and the future melt together in the heat of her anger, and syntactic boundaries blur in consequence, as memory of the affront shifts to desire for revenge, and a well-known metaphor for glozing deceit (bear in hand) slides into what was the early modern period's key symbol of the mutual consent deemed necessary to the making of a legal marriage contract (to take hands). Beatrice's repetitions, "O that I were a man," and her ensuing demand that Benedick "Kill Claudio" reflect her perception that for women the official paths of justice provide remedies altogether too pale to make up for a broken heart or a tattered reputation. But for all the cruelty Beatrice finds accentuated by Claudio's waiting until he can accuse Hero "in the congregation, where I should wed" (3.2.127–8) if Hero had been guilty of the incontinence she is charged with, his choice of the church and his tactics within its confines represent a move that in the community life outside the theatre would have been recognized as one of the most obvious choices open to him.

The scene in the congregation is a synecdoche, the single parish church and the handful of people in it standing in for the larger forums of ecclesiastical power exercised either in the diocesan or in the consistory courts where spiritual matters of all sorts (from Sabbath-breaking to heresy) were most usually heard. The ceremonies attending birth, marriage, and death were all officially administered by the church, since it was the church's role to consecrate and superintend the spiritual realities these events represented for individuals and for the Christian community of which they were a part.[8] As for punishment, there are several instances of whipping being inflicted, but officially – particularly after the break from Rome – canon law in England had no authority over the body. Its dominion was the soul, and its punishments were to be the spiritual punishments of humiliating public penance (usually in the parish church) and, in extreme cases, excommunication.[9] The jurisdiction of canon law underwent some important changes in the first part of the sixteenth century, partly as a result of Henry VIII's break with Rome, but more so as a result of changes in the period, particularly with regard to debt and contract, which were increasingly being litigated in common law courts as "actions on the case." The broadening of venue away from the church courts is noticeable in certain kinds of defamation cases. The defence of reputation within the community was, in an earlier period, a matter to be handled under canon law, but as economic consequences increasingly attended certain kinds of defamation (such as dishonesty in trade), an assessment of monetary damages in the plaintiff's favour – a penalty consistory courts could not usually make available[10] – was understood to provide more appropriate satisfaction than simply the vindication of seeing public humiliation visited on one's accuser. Undermining the reputation of a tradesperson could severely damage the victim's economic relations within his or her business community. The sexual defamation of women did not ordinarily have similar commercial consequences, which partly explains why most of these cases continued to be litigated through the church courts.[11]

The publication of archival research has made available a number of early modern defamation cases. Each of these gives small insights into moments of what must have been high drama in the personal lives of plaintiffs and defendants, and provides valuable information about the kinds of difficulties that could arise in keeping community peace. Some colourful variations can be found among them, but there are also important lines of similarity, a point R.H. Helmholz makes by stressing the "repetitiveness and purely formal character of most of the documents" that necessitated his "selective approach" in presenting them.[12] Aside from the high number of women involved in these suits, one of the common features to be noted in many of them included the ongoing attempts to "bring the parties to agreement." As Martin Ingram points out, the success of third-party arbitration (or simply second thoughts about proceeding) meant that "only a minority of cases passed through all procedural stages and were prosecuted to a finish."[13]

As I have indicated, the church's principal punishment for sexual misconduct was public shaming, so Claudio's choice of revenge was – though not imposed here by the church – aligned with the church's method: his determination to transform the nuptials into a parish church shaming ritual – "there will I shame her" (3.2.128), seconded by Pedro's "I will join with thee to disgrace her" (3.2.130) – shows no tendencies towards cruelty not already sponsored by community practice.[14] The sheet and the candle prescribed by penitential ritual are missing, but the essence is the public shaming of Hero that enacts a type of church discipline known to really happen.

But when accusations are false, when the punishment meted has been unjust, what recourse do victims have? Hero knows, and her friends are convinced, that she is a victim of slander, but the plot makes no move towards a defamation suit. Instead the friar proposes to restore peace among the disputants through the fiction of her death. But his plan that her family should assume the identities of mourners has no meaningful impact on the direction taken by events. The plot appears to set him up for success, but in reality his assertion that "supposition of the lady's death / Will quench the wonder of her infamy" (4.1.240–1), that she "Shall be lamented, pitied, and excus'd" (4.1.218), turns out to be all too optimistic. When the friar's plan is put to the test in act 5, scene 1, humour combines with pathos as Hero's elderly father and uncle try to challenge the much younger Claudio and Don Pedro to physical combat, but when the young men are accosted by their elders, remorse is nowhere in sight. On the contrary: after the failure of their initial attempts to dismiss Hero's relatives with a curt greeting ("We have some haste, Leonato" [5.1.47]), the ensuing conversation contains an implicit stage direction for an irritated Claudio to make a gesture towards his sword (5.1.54–7). Leonato's accusation that Claudio's slander has killed his daughter and lain her in a tomb "fram'd by thy villainy" (5.1.71) elicits from Claudio yet another attempt to get rid of the old man, but words of regret for Hero are still not forthcoming: "Away! I will not have to do with you" (5.1.77). Don Pedro concedes a small sign of commiseration for the father, but he too persists in justification of Claudio's rejection of Hero, repeating that the accusation against her "was true and very full of proof" (5.1.105). The friar's attempt to find a ground of conciliation on all sides here simply comes to nought. Had it not been for the representatives of the common law stumbling onto the facts of the case and – after some dithering – managing to expose them, Hero would simply have been left with the friar's alternative church solution:

> If it sort not well, you may conceal her,
> As best befits her wounded reputation,
> In some reclusive and religious life,
> Out of all eyes, tongues, minds and injuries. (4.1.242–5)

What the friar is proposing here is the legal fiction of death that attended those religious persons who lived out their lives in convents and monasteries (a fiction devised to enable property dispositions) – before, that is, the 1539 dissolution of the monasteries by means of which, as J.H. Baker so charmingly puts it, "parliament brought all the monks back from the dead."[15]

Some comment needs to be made about the coalition of parish officials that makes a happy ending possible. Don John infects Claudio's mind with his slander in act 3, scene 2, and in the following scene Dogberry and Verges make their first appearance. It is only clear in retrospect that this structure is not fortuitous. Though it is far from obvious when they appear, these are the men who will right the wrongs that have just taken shape in the preceding scene. The constables who initially show so little promise of being able to clear up any kind of disorder turn out to be the ones who uncover the slander plot, thereby holding the key to the evidence that frees Hero from the prospects of living out her life in a convent. The audience is well aware, though, how much of an accident this lucky turn is. Shakespeare also makes clear that the constables were successful in large part because of the competent help they got from the character usually known as the sexton, the title and job description consistently assigned to him in the dialogue. I would like to point out, though, that a different title is attributed to the sexton when he puts in his very first *textual* appearance in the stage directions, where he is called the Town Clerk (the title accorded him in both Q1 and F1). If Shakespeare wrote these stage directions, the discrepancy points to a split in his conception of this character's social role. If the paratext was added by another hand, "Town Clerk" would then seem to indicate how the character was perceived by those who knew the play and were preparing the text for print. (And of course "town clerk" is only available to those approaching the play through the printed text, rather than in the theatre.) In the crucial interrogation of Borachio and Conrade, the sexton's command of both English and legal procedure obviously contrasts to that of Dogberry, and his skills in both fields give him the authority to take charge, giving orders to Dogberry at two different points about how to do his job (4.2.34–6 and 4.2.66–8). It is the sexton's assumption of control that puts a stop to the incompetence and permits the information just gathered to arrive at an appropriate destination: "Master constable, let these men be bound, and brought to Leonato's: I will go before and show him their examination" (4.2.66–8). The sexton's is a relatively minor role, but, as this last interchange shows, his decisiveness is responsible for the correct presentation of facts, facing Don John's slander with the alternative narrative necessary to shape the play's outcome. In order for this to happen, it is clear that somebody had to take over from Dogberry and his crew. But textual critics at least might find that the question remains: why a sexton? (A sexton's job as church caretaker might also involve digging graves, but there was no requirement that he have the educational skills that could make him interchangeable with the town clerk; and though his job makes him a fairly humble representative of the church, in no way does a sexton represent the force of ecclesiastical law. His presence at the interrogation of Borachio and Conrade can hardly be justified then by his job description.) The early texts leave us with the puzzle of the discrepancy; but this is something that, in the theatre, passes from the stage without notice, particularly since both church and crown had some claims for jurisdiction in deciding the issues *Much Ado* has raised. And costume here is a visual factor that unites them. The "gowns" specified in the stage directions of both Q1 and F1 would confer on all these minor officials the appearance of authority sufficient to represent the local forces of order, without anyone in the audience questioning overmuch whether they involved lay or religious jurisdictions.

Defamation can permanently alter identity: when a reputation is ruined, the community no longer recognizes the person as he or she existed for them before the mud got flung. In counselling Hero's family and friends to avail themselves of the metonymic trappings of death, the friar correctly locates the ruptured relationship between the individual and the community, even though he puts altogether too much faith in the paradoxical reversal he is looking to achieve through what he believes will be death's healing powers. So while Hero does not literally die, death provides her and her family with a singularly apt metaphor for slander. For Hero's resuscitation within the community is possible only when her name is fully cleared: "She died, my lord, but whiles her slander liv'd" (5.3.66). Given the possibility that her future might have been life in a convent, her father's paradox rings uncomfortably closer to truth than metaphor.

This paradox is but one of several inversions in *Much Ado*. Dogberry's interrogation of Borachio and Conrade provides a clear example of what rhetoricians recognize as hysteron proteron: "Masters, it is proved already that you are little better than false knaves; and it will go near to be thought so shortly." The inversion of the correct order, which makes the certainty of proof precede the stirrings of suspicion, provokes laughter here, but (as we have already seen) this is very similar indeed to the error in logic that Claudio has committed earlier when he undertook his public "proof" of Hero's unchastity. His was no trial at all. He had already determined the outcome the night before.

In slander cases, community reaction tends to be inverted vis-à-vis the relationship between victim and perpetrator. In all other circumstances, when one is the victim of a crime, the community may not be able to offer any satisfactory restitution, but it does usually offer at least its compassion. In slander, the whole point is to make the community turn on the victim: the paradox of slander is that the instigator would have no power were it not for the power of community collusion. As I have briefly indicated, both common and canon law made remedies for defamation available, enabling a measure of social rehabilitation if one was willing to spend the time and money to seek reparations.

The mooting exercises at the Inns of Court trained young lawyers for their work in the common law courts, where they would have to be prepared to deal with two versions of events – because of course a court's raison d'être is to hear both sides of a story, through a trial process meant to determine which of the two narratives is able to present the most reliable evidence. The situation thus hinges – at least in theory – on evidence, recognized today to be one of the most difficult areas of modern law. At least with regard to the auricular sin of slander, Shakespeare made a similar point over four centuries ago in *Much Ado About Nothing*. Hearsay and even what appears to be ocular proof – the central noting of the play – are shown (in both plots) to be not particularly reliable. For much of the play, neither are the law's representatives. That they finally ended up being of help to the right side was simply because as they bumbled, they happened at last to bumble in the right direction. If one does not look too deeply and accepts as felicitous the solution that unites Hero to the undeserving Claudio, a happy ending of sorts ostensibly gets patched together. But the legal process that leads to it is far from reassuring.

NOTES

1 Wilfrid R. Prest, *The Inns of Court Under Elizabeth I and the Early Stuarts 1590–1640*, pp. 115–36. Lorna Hutson, in *The Invention of Suspicion*, emphasizes the importance of rhetorical studies in the social construction of fact; Karen Cunningham studies the practice of mooting in the inns in her chapter "So Many Books, So Many Rolls of Ancient Time …". Joel Altman's study of rhetoric and theatrical practice in *The Tudor Play of Mind*

emphasizes that early modern writers were "accustomed to examine the many sides of a given theme, to entertain opposing ideals," p. 6. See also R.J. Schoeck, "Rhetoric and Law in Sixteenth-Century England," and Alessandro Giuliani, "The Influence of Rhetoric on the Law of Evidence and Pleading."

2 James Boyd White, *Heracles' Bow: Essays on the Rhetoric and Poetics of Law*, p. 160.

3 James B. Thayer, *Preliminary Treatise on the Law of Evidence at the Common Law*; F.C.Milsom, "Law and Fact in Legal Development"; Barbara J. Shapiro, *Beyond Reasonable Doubt* and *A Culture of Fact*; Roderick Bagshaw, *Cross and Wilkins Outline of the Law of Evidence*; Raymond Emson, *Evidence*; William Twining, *Rethinking Evidence: Exploratory Essays*; and Roderick Munday, *Evidence*.

4 Even the venerable Leonato is willing to joke about his wife's fidelity in order to get a laugh. When Pedro asks if the old man is Hero's father, Leonato banters: "Her mother hath many times told me so." Benedick immediately jumps in ("were you in doubt, sir ...?"), thus eliciting a testimonial of Benedick's lusty reputation ("Signior Benedick, no; for then you were a child" 1.1.104–9). Citations are from *The Complete Works of Shakespeare*, edited by Hardin Craig.

5 Susan D. Amussen, *An Ordered Society*, p. 102. After the 1500s, men who had been defamed increasingly availed themselves of developments that permitted them access to the common law courts. Well documented studies of sexual litigation, including defamation, are Martin Ingram, *Church Courts, Sex and Marriage in England, 1570–1640*; L. Gowing "Language, Power and the Law: Women's Slander Litigation in Early Modern London," pp. 26–47; L. Gowing, chapters 3 and 4, in *Domestic Dangers: Women, Words, and Sex in Early Modern London*; and Tim Stretton, *Women Waging Law in Elizabethan England*.

6 Tim Stretton, *Women Waging Law in Elizabethan England*, pp. 29, 30.

7 Hero's comment about hearsay is doubly ironic, given the storm about to open over her: "Of this matter is little Cupid's crafty arrow made, / That only wounds by hearsay" (3.1.22–3).

8 This description is necessarily telegraphic, since even an issue such as marriage formation – which both did and did not require church sanction – was more complicated than can be briefly covered. For the jurisdictions and administration of canon law in England, see Martin Ingram, *Church Courts, Sex and Marriage in England, 1570–1640*, and Ronald Marchant, *The Church Under the Law: Justice, Administration and Discipline in the Diocese of York 1560–1640*. Aberrations at any point along the cradle-to-grave scale

of life events were, upon presentation, subject to the corrections of the canon law, although the fouler infractions were passed on to local justices of the peace, who possessed and exercised common law commissions. The official obligation of "presenting" (passing on information about sinners at the bishop's visitation) lay with the parish's church wardens, although there are also numerous instances of parishioners taking the initiative of "presenting."

9 The shaming ritual of penance was prescribed for irregular sexual activity, as it was for other areas requiring spiritual correction, but though this ritual could also be imposed on slanderers, these occasions should not be confused with the more diffuse community issues and legal remedies involved in defamation suits.

10 The Courts of High Commission sitting at London and York could, however, inflict penalties not available to the ordinary church courts. Those found guilty could suffer both heavy fines and imprisonment. See James S. Hart Jr, *The Rule of Law 1603–1660*, p. 35.

11 Tim Stretton has ably demonstrated that an increasing number of women also sought justice through the equity courts, particularly the Court of Requests.

12 *Select Cases on Defamation to 1600*, p. 1.

13 Ingram, *Church Courts*, p. 50. Several cases transcribed in Helmholz demonstrate these repeated attempts to achieve concord between the parties. One example, *Herbert v. Garrett*, is given here: "*Elizabeth Herbert against Agnes Garrett of the parish of St Andrew*. Herbert has this day for libelling in the event that peace should not be made. On which day the aforesaid Elizabeth appeared and alleged during proceedings that the aforesaid Agnes Garrett publicly defamed her, Elizabeth, in the parish church of St Andrew by calling her, Elizabeth, the following in English, namely, 'Thou art a filthy and a naughty drab,' and ... his lordship ... ordered that Thomas Kingsbury and John Cleydall should bring the aforesaid parties to agreement before the next court" (Helmholz, p. 25).

14 The force of the shaming procedure in parish life lies in its success in saturating an entire community. For different reasons that is what happens here: repeated by Borachio, then later recounted by the first watchman to the sexton, the repetitions show how it was not necessary to be physically present at the scene(s) of defamation. By act 5, no one at any level in the play remains unaware of Hero's disgrace.

15 J.H. Baker, *An Introduction to English Legal History*, p. 531. The legal fiction was still being mentioned in Common Pleas decisions about the time *Much Ado* was written. *Corbett v. Corbett* (1600), a suit between two brothers over

their father's estate, makes the point that "death, either civil (such as entering religion) or natural (that is, dissolution of the soul from the body) is requisite to every descent, remainder or reversion upon the determination of an estate tail" (J.H. Baker and S.F.C. Milsom, *Sources of English Legal History*, p. 159).

BIBLIOGRAPHY

Altman, Joel. *The Tudor Play of Mind: Rhetorical Inquiry and the Development of Elizabethan Drama*. Berkeley and Los Angeles: University of California Press, 1978.

Amussen, Susan D. *An Ordered Society*. New York: Columbia UP, 1988.

Bagshaw, Roderick. *Cross and Wilkins Outline of the Law of Evidence*. 7th ed. London: Butterworths, 1996.

Baker, J.H. *An Introduction to English Legal History*. 3rd ed. London: Butterworths, 1990.

Baker, J.H., and S.F.C. Milsom. *Sources of English Legal History*. London: Butterworths, 1986.

Cunningham, Karen. "So Many Books, So Many Rolls of Ancient Time …" In *Solon and Thespis: Law and Theater in the English Renaissance*. Ed. Dennis Kezar. Notre Dame, IN: U of Notre Dame P, 2007. 197–217.

Emson, Raymond. *Evidence*. 3rd ed. Basingstoke: Palgrave Macmillan, 2006.

Giuliani, Alessandro. "The Influence of Rhetoric on the Law of Evidence and Pleading," *Juridical Review* 62 (1969): 215–61.

Gowing, L. *Domestic Dangers: Women, Words, and Sex in Early Modern London*. Oxford: Clarendon, 1996.

– "Language, Power and the Law: Women's Slander Litigation in Early Modern London." In *Women, Crime and the courts in Early Modern England*. Ed. Jennifer Kermode and Garthine Walker. Chapel Hill and London: U of North Carolina P, 1994. 26–47.

Hart, James S., Jr. *The Rule of Law 1603–1660*. Edinburgh: Pearson/Longman, 2003.

Helmholz, R.H., ed. *Select Cases on Defamation to 1600*. London: Selden Society, 1985.

Hutson, Lorna. *The Invention of Suspicion: Law and Mimesis in Shakespeare and Renaissance Drama*. Oxford; New York: Oxford UP, 2007.

Ingram, Martin. *Church Courts, Sex and Marriage in England, 1570–1640*. Cambridge: Cambridge UP, 1987.

Marchant, Ronald. *The Church Under the Law: Justice, Administration and Discipline in the Diocese of York 1560–1640*. Cambridge: Cambridge UP, 1969.

Milsom, F.C. "Law and Fact in Legal Development." *Univ. of Toronto Law Review* 17 (1969): 1–19.

Munday, Roderick. *Evidence*. 4th ed. Oxford: Oxford UP, 2007.

Prest, Wilfred R. *The Inns of Court Under Elizabeth I and the Early Stuarts 1590–1640*. London: Longman, 1972.

Schoeck, R.J. "Rhetoric and Law in Sixteenth-Century England." *Studies in Philology* 50 (1953): 110–27.

Shakespeare, William. *The Complete Works of Shakespeare*. Ed. Hardin Craig. Rev. David Bevington. Glenview, IL: Scott Foresman, 1973.

Shapiro, Barbara J. *Beyond Reasonable Doubt*. Berkeley: U of California P, 1991.

– *A Culture of Fact*. Ithaca, NY: Cornell UP, 2000.

Thayer, James B. *Preliminary Treatise on the Law of Evidence at the Common Law*. 1898; reprint New York: Rothman Reprints, 1969.

Stretton, Tim. *Women Waging Law in Elizabethan England*. Cambridge: Cambridge UP, 1998.

Twining, William. *Rethinking Evidence: Exploratory Essays*. 2nd ed. Cambridge: Cambridge UP, 2006.

White, James Boyd. *Heracles' Bow: Essays on the Rhetoric and Poetics of Law*. Madison: U of Wisconsin P, 1989.

8 No Boy Left Behind: Education and Distributive Justice in Early Modern England

ELIZABETH HANSON

When the U.S. Elementary and Secondary School Act of 1965 was revised and reauthorized in 2002 it was also renamed. The new title, "No Child Left Behind," proclaimed that the bill's allocation of funds and notorious accountability measures were actions for social justice. Although the legislation was one of the first measures proposed by the administration of George W. Bush, it was co-authored by the late Senator Ted Kennedy, who also supervised its passage in the Senate. We can, of course, detect in the bill's name that Orwellian tang that characterized so many Bush-era initiatives, but Kennedy's involvement suggests that the ideological foundations on which the bill rests are wider than those of the Bush presidency. Chief among the ideas asserted by the bill's name is that *all* children are entitled to good, sustained schooling leading to a reasonably high level of literacy and numeracy and, in fact, that neglecting the provision of such schooling is tantamount to child abandonment. This extraordinary proposition is subtended by the modern social practice of mandatory universal schooling, which naturalizes school participation, making plausible the bill's implied equivalence between good schooling and the necessities of human life. The bill's accountability mechanisms derive from another social form that the school itself has in turn naturalized – the test – which renders diverse individuals comparable by gauging their command of skills and knowledge abstracted from situated use, only now the form is to be applied not to pupils but to schools themselves.

"No Child Left Behind" is arguably responsible for the impoverishment of curricula, the fetishizing of the test, and the undermining of public school systems.[1] Nevertheless, in its assertion that every child can and must succeed in school, it offers a relatively generous expression of the modern universalization of the school form compared to the view promulgated eight years earlier by Richard J. Herrnstein and Charles Murray in *The Bell Curve*. Published over a decade into the neoliberal ascendancy that began with the elections of Ronald Reagan in the United States, Margaret Thatcher in Britain, and Brian Mulroney in Canada, and that has brought increasing economic inequality, *The Bell Curve* asked its readers to imagine a society with two small groups "at the opposite ends"; the people in one group

> are welcomed at the best colleges, then at the best graduate and professional schools, regardless of their parents' wealth. After they complete their education, they enter fulfilling and prestigious careers. Their incomes continue to rise, even when income growth stagnates for everyone else ... In the other group life gets worse and its members collect at the bottom of society. Poverty is severe, drugs and crime are rampant, and the traditional family all but disappears. Economic growth passes them by. (xxii)[2]

The "underlying element" that explains both these trends turns out to be not the fictitious premises of the scenario but "cognitive ability," also called "human intelligence" (xxii). Although the hypothetical scenario Herrnstein and Murray advance stresses the education of the first group, as we learn later, education level needs to be understood "primarily as a proxy for cognitive ability" (253). And because superior wealth was a direct outcome of attendance at the "best graduate and professional schools," wealth too turns out to be an index for cognitive ability (428). It will be recalled that *The Bell Curve* provoked a storm of controversy primarily because of the further connection it made between cognitive ability and race, arguing that inequality in income levels between blacks and other racial groups could be explained via IQ scores, in terms of differences in cognitive ability. So what were the implications of this relentless demonstration that difference in cognitive ability is the universal key to all social difference? Lamenting that "the phrase *social justice* has become virtually a synonym for economic and social equality," Herrnstein and Murray offer a prescription actually more paternalistic than neoliberal in flavour: that Americans revalue the simple places of simple folk, make sure that their income is adequate, and desist with futile equalizing measures like affirmative action and, proleptically, "No Child Left Behind" (527).

In fact, Herrnstein and Murray have very little to say directly about schools (as opposed to SAT scores), probably because of the challenge the varying quality of schools would pose to their naturalization of difference in cognitive ability. At the same time, however, it is the universal operation of the school that produces the categories of their analysis. Their subject, general cognitive ability, is conceivable only because of the sustained comparison of individuals' abstract intellectual proficiency that schooling promotes while their tool, the IQ test, simply marries the form of academic assessment to the stance of natural historical observation. For Herrnstein and Murray the practices and habits of thought associated with schooling are so reflexive that the role schools actually play in producing the phenomena they set out to analyse disappears from view.

These examples from recent American experience – experience that resonated in Canada and the United Kingdom – reveal the imbrication of schooling and distributive justice in modern social thought even where apparently quite different points of view are being expressed. The reason for this reflexive connection between schooling and distributive justice, of course, is that schooling is universal and education (or its naturalized form, "cognitive ability") has for us become "cultural capital," to adopt Pierre Bourdieu's famous term, a resource we take to market and for most of us the principal determinant of our share in society's goods. Clearly, in early modern England where school participation was restricted and birth functioned as the chief determinant of social place, education could not so readily be thought of in this way. As for distributive justice itself, although the Aristotelian idea that one of justice's two aspects pertains to the fair allocation of a community's wealth, offices, and honours was certainly available in this period, there is considerable question about what the applicable principle of fairness might have been. Samuel Fleischacker has recently made a widely accepted argument that distributive justice, as an *economic* principle, doesn't appear until the eighteenth century.[3] Certainly, Sir Thomas Elyot's famous statement in book 4 of *The Book Named the Governor* (1531) that "the first and principal part of justice distributive is, and ever was, to do to God that Honour which is due to his Divine Majesty; which honour consisteth in love, fear and reverence," would appear to support this claim, assimilating the idea of distributive justice to the hierarchically differentiating principal of decorum.[4] Nevertheless, as Kenneth Graham and others have demonstrated, the word "distribution" was regularly used in the sixteenth century to denote almsgiving and shaking the superflux to the poor.[5] Moreover, Siegfried van Duffel and Dennis Yap have recently challenged Fleischacker's claim, by tracing the development of the right of necessity from its emergence in canon law in the twelfth century through evidence of its acceptance in common law in the sixteenth and seventeenth centuries.[6] Necessity existed, according to a fifteenth-century commentator, whenever a man lacked the means of subsistence. For this reason a poor man who stole food worth 12d or less could not be convicted of theft because, as one sixteenth-century jurist put it, "it could be presumed from the smallness of his theft that he was taking only what he needed to stay alive."[7] Van Duffel and Yap cite Matthew Hale's approving comment that such laws from the reign of Edward I were responsible for the "settling and establishing of the *distributive justice* of the Kingdom."[8] But what is at issue here is food (and just a bit at that) and the right to stay alive, not access to good schools and what we might call a right to flourish.

Nevertheless, as I hope to demonstrate in this essay, there is a relation between sixteenth-century pedagogical discourse and the modern conviction that access to formal education is, one way or another, a matter of distributive justice. My focus will be on humanist educational ideas and on the grammar school rather than the petty school, a choice that may seem surprising in view of the narrow segment of the population that participated in humanist schooling. My reasons are partly opportunistic; the archive with respect to both the theory and practice of humanist education is more extensive than for petty schooling. More importantly, though, the sustained teaching the humanist curriculum demanded, and the increasing institutionalization of that commitment in the endowed grammar school meant that the idea of the school, as a place to spend all of childhood, which could transform a life, and to which access could be contested, emerged more clearly in this period in relation to humanist education than in relation to more widespread but briefer schooling in the vernacular.

In pursuing a genealogical relation between humanist educational ideology and modern ideas of distributive justice, I am preceded most notably by Richard Halpern, who in his 1991 book, *The Poetics of Primitive Accumulation,* argued that humanist pedagogy provided an ideological framework for economic developments that Marx posited as preliminary to capitalism's emergence. In particular, Halpern credited both Erasmus and Richard Mulcaster, the two writers on whom I will also focus, with articulating a "discourse of capacities" that divides the world into two sorts of people, those with "intelligence, talent, creativity, or cleverness [and] the abilities to impose and endure various kinds of self-discipline" and those without these qualities.[9] This division in turn explained and implicitly justified different fates as some people prospered in the period while others were forcibly separated from the means of subsistence by practices such as enclosure, thus creating a necessary precondition for capitalism: a "free" labour force. Once capital could use this freed labour as an industrial proletariat, Halpern argues, then the division of the world into two sorts of people no longer required explanation and the socially heterogeneous grammar school disappeared (98).

This argument has the virtue of acknowledging some key features of humanist education. One is that humanist pedagogical theory made salient in European discourse for the first time since classical antiquity the question of what Mulcaster calls "ingenerate abilities," the difference in intellectual capacities among human beings. Another is the fact that the admission practices of Tudor grammar schools made them more heterogeneous demographically, except with respect to sex, than schools would be again for several centuries. At the same time, however, the argument depends on a significant distortion of both Erasmus's and Mulcaster's ideas, construing their comments on "ingenerate abilities" as a sixteenth-century version of *The Bell Curve.* Against this reading I want to argue that while humanist pedagogy produced ideas and information about the "human" that had implications for distributive justice, it did not do anything so conclusive as dividing the world into those who deserve more and those who deserve less. Instead it disclosed the limited and uncertain social impact that the abilities schooling made salient actually could have. Schooling could reveal that some boys were quicker to learn than others, and that some had a bent for one kind of knowledge and others for other kinds, and that these differences were one way that the "human" could be parsed. But humanist educators also had a strong sense that what these different abilities and inclinations might mean was not easy to predict either with respect to the individual's ultimate capacities or to their future use in the commonwealth.[10] This uncertainty was compounded by the fact that, for the most part, social fates were determined by forces other than men's educational attainments. All of which might be to say simply that the "discourse of capacities" is nascent and thus more tentative in its operation than Halpern allows for. However, to fasten on the emergence of a "discourse" is to miss the genealogical significance of this moment. The social heterogeneity of the grammar school, which is a necessary precondition for academic ability to emerge as a basis for sorting human beings, arose not from an ideology of ability proleptically functioning as a principle of distributive justice, but from older ideas of social order and obligation operating under new conditions. The humanist contribution to the modern link between schooling and distributive justice must be understood in terms of residual as well as emergent social forms.

In this respect Pierre Bourdieu offers a useful supplement to Halpern's Marxian narrative when he asserts in *The State Nobility* that Europe in the early modern period saw "a completely new combination [in the] principles of domination and the legitimation of domination: cultural capital as with the clergy; heredity and the transferability of wealth, as well as devotion to public service as with the nobility."[11] Bourdieu offers this statement in the course of an analysis of how hereditary privilege persists, via the logic of cultural capital, in the production of the modern university-credentialed ruling class, despite the powerful role of apparently meritocratic schooling in the process. There are some problems with Bourdieu's historical gesture, most notably the fact that it conflates the *outcome* (the modern social form) with the historical process that is meant to have produced it; both are described according to the same formula, as the "combination" of hereditary and meritocratic modes of reproduction.[12] Thus "cultural capital" is adduced both as a pre-existing ingredient that goes into the historical combination and as the mechanism of the combination itself in the modern form. I return below to the problem of historicizing cultural capital. More generally though, in the remainder of the paper I will explore the proposition suggested by Bourdieu's formulation that in England the humanist educational program can be understood in terms of an expansion in specifically *clerical* jurisdiction, a redistribution across the polity of the distinctive burden of one estate. I also want to suggest, however, that the unmooring of learning in letters from a more narrowly defined function made the question of who should be learned a matter of ideological and material struggle. My focus now turns to two texts that engage with this problem, Erasmus's *De Pueris Instituendis* and Richard Mulcaster's *Positions Concerning the Training Up of Children*. The first of these is blithely theoretical; the second presents itself as the distillation of a long encounter with biting reality. Together they indicate the way that humanist pedagogical thought was haunted by a question of justice that it could not fully articulate, let alone resolve.

Erasmus

De Pueris Instituendis was published in 1529 with a dedication to the thirteen-year-old Prince William, Duke of Cleves, claiming the intent "to induce other young men distinguished by noble lineage to model themselves after your splendid example."[13] It had, however, been written in 1509 in order to illustrate the principles set out in *De Copia*. The text is also an imitation of Quintilian's *Institutio Oratoria*, so deeply indebted to its original that it makes reference to "the lyre" when it means "music" (302) and to "Alexandrian pleasure-boys" (308) when it speaks of corruption. Nevertheless, despite this double subservience, *De Pueris* reads as a passionate revolutionary manifesto proclaiming the plasticity of human nature and the universal value of learning that could be entitled "No Boy Left Behind." That is to say, the text speaks within multiple situations including those of a cleric admonishing a young nobleman, of a clerk virtuosically imitating an "auctor," and of a teacher who has assumed the self-generated authority of a philosopher pontificating to the world at large. The result is an ongoing strain between multiple and contradictory social specifications and an expansive universalism; a set of prescriptions that for the most part could only be followed by a nobleman – except when they seem inappropriately clerical – are set forth in a manner that applies them to humanity at large. This contradiction is the sign of what Hanan Yoran has identified as Erasmus's utopianism, his "'abstract[ion] from a concrete social and political context" that bespeaks his desire "to educate the citizens of a fully civilized society that does not yet exist."[14] But in *De Pueris* Erasmus doesn't imagine a new social identity so much as resist performatively the idea of identity itself. His purpose is precisely to demonstrate that one kind of being can become another, and his emphasis is at least as much on the power and freedom manifest in transformation as on the moral superiority of the destination.

This enthusiasm for metamorphosis manifests itself in his discourse in the constant assertion of categorical distinctions, most notably between humans and animals, only to immediately dissolve them in the onrush of his argument. "Your primary concern," Erasmus tells his addressee (who can be assumed to be a patrician father), "must be for that part of [your son's] character which distinguishes him from the animals and comes closest to the divine" (300). This initial invocation of the human/animal boundary establishes the province of education:

> Education is that special task that has been entrusted to us. This is why to other creatures nature has given swiftness of foot or wing, keenness of sight, strength or massiveness of body, coverings of wool or fur … Man alone she has created weak, naked and defenceless. But as compensation, she has given him a mind equipped for knowledge, for this one capacity,

> if properly exploited, embraces all others. Animals are less easily taught than humans, but their instincts are more highly developed. Bees, for example, do not have to be taught how to construct cells, gather nectar or make honey ... But man cannot even eat, walk or speak without instruction. (301)[15]

The alignment of the "human" with education, understood as intellectual cultivation, has some important implications for the relationship between education and distributive justice. For one thing, it conspicuously displaces the connection one might expect, and which Sir Thomas Elyot makes at length in *The Governor*, between learning and social status, with one between learning and the quasi-religious, quasi-natural category of "man." The point here is not exactly that Erasmus is suggesting a general human entitlement to a classical education, but more precisely, that his invocation of the human has the effect of suspending the operation of social categories such as "birth" even as he discourses on a resource-intensive pursuit that can only be engaged in by a few. Of course, this tactic also has the potential to recategorize those people who don't show a disposition for learning as less than human and therefore entitled to nothing. This is the point that Halpern makes, and one to which I will return.

Whatever the implications of Erasmus's deployment of the human/animal boundary, they are complicated by the fact that the boundary erodes under the force of the analogy that constitutes it in the first place. Thus he continues: "A hound is not prepared by nature for the hunt, nor a horse for the saddle, nor an ox for the plough, unless we apply our efforts to their training," and proceeds to the tell the story of Lycurgus's two hounds, the one purebred but untrained and the other a trained mongrel whose superior behaviour demonstrates that while "nature is strong, education is more powerful still" (301). Having adduced dogs to exemplify human capacities, he pauses to acknowledge another kind of difference: "There is also, however, a nature unique to each individual being. Thus one child may have an aptitude for mathematics, another for theology, a third for poetry and rhetoric, and again another for military life," and he proceeds to tell the story of a friend who was a "distinguished Greek and Latin scholar" but intractably hated the law, for which his patrons had chosen him, and concedes, "as the common saying has it, one should not draw an ox to the wrestling pit or an ass to the lyre" (316). The difference among human abilities is as firm as that between animal and human ones, a comparison interestingly that elides a hierarchical distinction (between humans and animals) with a merely horizontal one (between mathematicians and theologians). But either way, the difference doesn't amount to much because he immediately announces: "I still hold that human nature is amenable to almost any form of learning provided we subject it to instruction and practice. We can teach elephants to walk a rope, bears to dance, and donkeys to perform amusing tricks. So is there anything we could not teach a human being?" (317).

This slipperiness in the tropes of distinction, which characterizes the entire treatise, should serve as context for the declaration that is Halpern's prime evidence for the invidious effect of the discourse of capacities.[16] Responding to a hypothetical schoolmaster's exasperated exclamation, "What then should be done with boys who can be driven to their studies only by flogging?" Erasmus replies, "What would you do if an ox or donkey wandered into your classroom? Would you not drive them back to the country? Well there are boys, too, who are good only for the plough or the mill" (333). If it seems that Erasmus's universalism has at last hit a limit case, we should notice that what is at stake here is not really the *boy's* abilities so much as those of the teacher who cannot make the boy learn. The passage is in fact an adaptation of one in which Quintilian makes a point, not about flogging, but about the fact that different people have different talents and inclinations – the same point that Erasmus makes in the passage above. But Quintilian concludes the horizontal survey of talents with a shrug, opining that "some perhaps will have to be sent home to the farm." (319) Thus where Quintilian links the fact that people have different talents to the question of who should be schooled, Erasmus separates these matters, making the differing talents among students a minor problem that a good teacher can manage by thinking like an animal trainer, while the exclusion of a boy from school is the absolute last resort, to be preferred to flogging when the *teacher* is incompetent. As I have tried to suggest, for Erasmus the ox and the ass are not figures for a dumb animality that could have no claims on education but rather, in their continuous slippage from brute to trainee, a reminder of the plasticity of capacities and of the teacher's powerful role in educing the human from the animal.

Developing this vision of a teacher responsible for producing the humanity of both noblemen's sons and boys otherwise bound for "the mill," I would argue, is Erasmus's real aim in *De Pueris*. If Erasmus's program can be appropriated as a new elite style, it is nevertheless propounded in the service of a remarkably expanded sense of the power of the *teacher*. The point here though is not exactly about an emerging sense of professionalism – Erasmus himself taught little and hated teaching when he did it – but about a re-imagining of clerical agency generally, a recalibration of the clergy's traditional sacerdotal and pedagogical functions.[17] Thus, while Erasmus concedes at one point that the human is itself a degraded condition, that "since Adam, the first man of the human race, a disposition to evil has been deeply engrained in us," this observation, which might make us want to take the sacrament, is followed almost bathetically by the reassurance that, "While this is indisputably man's condition ... we cannot deny that the greater portion of this evil stems from corrupting relationships and a misguided education, especially as they affect our early and most impressionable years" (321). Such dismissal of medieval preoccupations with human sinfulness in favour of the celebration of human potential is, of course, the whole point of the Renaissance. But it is worth pausing here over the implications of this gesture for the relationship between the clerical part and the social whole. The pre-Reformation clergy functioned synecdochically in relation to the Christian community, singing mass, studying scripture, theology, and sacred tongues on behalf of the other estates, who themselves had different work to pursue. In shifting the bulk of "this evil" from a metaphysical domain to an educational one, however, Erasmus troubles this synecdochic economy, suggesting that anyone who would repair "this evil" – presumably every Christian – needs *himself* to acquire the literacy that is the distinctive possession of the clerk.[18] With respect to the representational economy of spiritual practice, then, Erasmus's argument parallels the Reformation emphasis on individual literacy and the personal relation to scripture it enables, but with one key difference. Where Protestants sought a widespread but merely vernacular literacy to support the reading of the Bible, Erasmus plotted the route to spiritual repair, if not redemption, through the full program of humanist education, including the acquisition of several dead tongues and knowledge of the classical canon: in other words, through prolonged impractical schooling.

In light of the extravagance of this idea, the question ineluctably arises: "What about those of slender means, who can scarcely feed their children, let alone hire a tutor for them?" "To this," Erasmus announces,

> I can only reply with the comic poet, we must do as we may since we cannot do as we would. I offer only a superior theory of education, not the means to put it into practice. Nevertheless, the rich ought to be generous

> and come to the aid of gifted children who, because of their family's poverty, are unable to develop their talents ... The more humble his position is, the more a person needs the mainstay of a liberal education in order to raise himself from his lowly station ... Not all men rise to ... distinction but all should be educated towards that end. (333–4)

What is interesting here about this generally lame response to the impossible claim on distributive justice that his "superior theory" generates is the elision Erasmus attempts of the exceptional – the gifted poor child – with the general – "all men." Gifted poor children, as we shall see, figure conspicuously in sixteenth-century discourse around the place of the grammar school. But Erasmus's argument carries him beyond exceptionalism: "all men," he insists, "should be educated towards that end." The confusion here between the exceptional and the universal is also complicated, however, by a third implication: that education should *especially* be provided where a person lacks any other resources. In other words, the claims of the gifted poor child arise as much from his poverty as from his gifts, an idea that, as we shall see, was embedded in the charitable practice of early modern England. In fact, this proposition presents learning as cultural capital, but of a particularly clerical kind: a resource at once analogous to economic wealth but also specifically alternative to it. This jumble of claims on schooling bespeaks the way in which Erasmus's thinking is subtended by very old ideas about the place of learning that associates it with the poor and opposes it to worldly wealth. But, as he relentlessly frees these ideas from their particularizing import through the logic of Christian universalism and the slipperiness of his own analogies, he also exposes a widening gulf between the pedagogical imaginary and actual social structure. As a result, the refashioned clerical agency that *De Pueris* promulgates is not described so much as performed for the reader. It manifests as the vatic enunciating subject of the oration, enthusiastically proclaiming that elephants can learn to dance and poor boys and noblemen's sons alike – indeed, "all" – can become human, which is to say, learned in classical literature. As actual objects of representation, however, clerks are present in the text mostly negatively, as the spirit-breaking, marginally literate schoolmasters who have made schools "torture-chambers [where] you hear nothing but the thudding of the stick, the swishing of the rod, howling and moaning and the shouts of brutal abuse," the would-be humanist scholar forced to study the hated law by his patrons, and the poor boy who needs learning because he has nothing else to set him up in the world (325). Even as teaching serves in *De Pueris* as the vehicle for a clerical hegemony, the remaking of "all" in this one estate's learned image, it emerges in anecdote and example as the site of poverty, restriction, and frustration. In this manner the text may reveal itself as a compensatory fantasy for the real conditions of clerical life; the dream of a teacher whose art produces the very humanity of humans bespeaks the low status of the learned. In any case, the contradiction between infinite possibility and restricted reality endures as a structuring principle in writing about educational experience throughout the sixteenth century. Nevertheless, what is also remarkable about Erasmus's educational *fiat* is that to some extent it worked. In the century that followed the composition of *De Pueris*, the number of English boys who participated in the learning he celebrates did indeed expand considerably. In the next section, we will consider how an agent and custodian of that expansion understood the intersection of schooling and distributive justice.

Richard Mulcaster

Richard Mulcaster had served as headmaster of the Merchant Taylor's School for twenty years when he published *Positions on the Training Up of Children* in 1581, seven decades after Erasmus's *De Pueris*. In that interval, England saw what historians refer to as the "education revolution," a rapid expansion of participation in formal education, one aspect of which entailed the foundation or refoundation of numerous grammar schools in English towns.[19] In the process many schoolboys came under Erasmus's influence insofar as the curricula of St Paul's School and the Magdalen College School, which he had shaped, became templates for schools across England.[20] With respect to the claims of "those of slender means," which Erasmus endorses hypothetically, what is perhaps more significant about these schools was the near-universal insistence of their founders that they were to accommodate the "poor." The Company of Merchant Taylors' proclamation that it had founded "a schoole for liberty most free, being open expressly for poore men's children, as well of all nations as for the merchaunt tailors themselves," is typical.[21] What "poor" meant and the degree to which the poor by any definition were actually accommodated probably varied considerably from school to school and appears to have shifted over the course of the sixteenth century. In general, though, evidence seems to support the generalization that schoolboy backgrounds could extend quite far down the social hierarchy so that the grammar school bore a complex and challenging relation to the status system of the larger society.[22] Setting aside for the moment actual school demographics, however, there are two points that should be made about these repeated references to the "poor" in statutes, wills, and other founding documents. The first is that the claims of those of slender means to a presence in the humanist grammar school were widely endorsed. The second is that while the sixteenth-century wave of school foundations may have added up to a "revolution" – the emergence of schooling as a prominent if not yet dominant social practice – the discursive association of schools with the poor in founding documents bespeaks a long-established link between learning and Christian charity that was attenuated as the school form became more widely established.

With respect to the first point, it is instructive to consider Ralph Morice's account of the debate among the commissioners charged with the refoundation of the Canterbury school in the wake of the Chantries Act of 1547. According to Morice,

> it came to passe that when thei sholde electe the children of the grammer scole, there were of the commissioners mo than one or two which wolde have none admitted but younger brethren and gentilmenys sonnes; as for other husbende mennys children, thei were more mete (thei saied) for the plough and to be artificers than to occupie the place of the lernyd sorte … Whereunto that moste reverend father Thomas Cranmer archebisshopp of Canterbury being of a contrary mynde, saied that he thought it not indifferent so to order the matter, for (saied he) pore mennys children arr many tymes enduyd with more synguler giftes of nature, which are also the giftes of God, as with eloquence, memorie, apte pronunciacion, sobrietie, with such like, and also commonly more given to applie thair studie, than ys the gentilmannys sonne delicatelie educated.[23]

There ensued a nuanced exchange about the relationship between fitness to learn and status in which Cranmer would appear to have prevailed inasmuch as the proposed restriction was never put in place. Maria Dowling has styled Cranmer's position here "radical," by which she seems to mean daringly progressive.[24] But what is remarkable about this exchange is that while it may signal that there was a more widespread debate at mid-century about the relationship between social status and learning, in fact, it is the articulation of the *opposing* position, that learning should be limited to the gentlemen's sons, that is startlingly unusual. Even Sir Thomas Elyot, who seeks in *The Book Named the Governor* to align governance, birth, and learning, only makes the familiar humanist argument that the high-born should *join* the learned because they are natural governors, not that they alone should constitute that group. Moreover, Cranmer himself argues that to implement such a restriction would be to attempt a dangerous innovation comparable to the Tower of Babel – to "shitt up into a straite corner the bountifull grace of the holie Goste, and therapon attempt to buylde our fanseis" – albeit an innovation that supplants the unpredictable divine order rather than social custom (274). Morice does not disclose the identities of the commissioners who advance the opposing position, but it is perhaps significant that Cranmer is the only cleric among the commissioners he names. (Sir Richard Rich, Sir Christopher Hallis, and Sir Anthony St Leger are the others.) When Cranmer advances the argument that "none of us all here being gentilmen borne (as I thincke) but hadd our beginning that wey from a lowe and base parentage; and thorough the benefite of lernyng and other civile knowledge for the most parte all gentil ascende to thair estate," he is shot down with the riposte that "the moste parte of nobilitie came up by feate of armes and martiall actes." This exchange suggests that Cranmer's advocacy for the claims of the poor to schooling evinces not so much radicalism as a clerical sensibility that is as yet "uncombined" (to return to Bourdieu's recipe for the modern ruling class) with the ideology of nobility (*The State Nobility*, 274–5).

This struggle occurs at the juncture produced by the Chantries Act, which required the dissolution of chantry and cathedral schools and initiated their refoundation in many cases as town schools. In the long run, this break may have been important for the secularization of schools, but it is doubtful that it signified an immediate ideological rupture with respect to what a school was understood to be. Rather it can serve as a useful reminder of what the grammar school *had been*, and would in some ways continue to be: one face of usually multifaceted institutional expressions of piety that linked poor relief, worship, and schooling. Consider, for instance, the 1440 Eton Statutes, which specify: "the College shall consist of a Provost, 70 poor Scholars, 10 Priest-Fellows, 10 Chaplans, 10 Clerks, 16 Choristers, a Head-Master, an Usher, and 13 poor infirm men."[25] Though the almshouse was soon suppressed, the link between the care of the poor and infirm and the education in Latin grammar of deserving boys persisted. Hence we find arrangements like that in Leicester where the merchant William

Wigston founded the Hospital of St Ursula, an almshouse, in 1513 and made provision in his will for further "works of Mercy and Piety" that were construed by his brother and widow as including a grammar school that shared an endowment with the hospital through the sixteenth century. Or we find the simultaneous foundation in 1587 of twinned hospitals (almshouses) and grammar schools in Oakham and Uppingham.[26] Thus, while Erasmus is conscious that the education he promotes for "all" is a restricted good, fit for the young Duke of Cleves and more likely to fall to rich men's sons than to those of slender means, the English institution whereby his program was to be disseminated, the grammar school, was firmly linked, as an expression of piety, to provision for the poor. This is not to say that the grammar schools catered exclusively or even especially to the genuinely poor, even in the fifteenth century. The Eton statutes also make provision for up to twenty sons of noblemen to board in the college as long as the only cost they incur is that of grammar instruction. Grammar schools like the one in Leicester, or more famously St Paul's and later Merchant Taylors' in London, were well stocked with the sons of well-to-do merchants as well as the sons of shoemakers, husbandmen, and water-bearers who the records tell us were admitted to the schools.[27] But the point remains that Erasmus's lightly defended, idealistic "all" was subtended in England by a piously asserted and materially supported "poor" that meant that the grammar school population could neither be imagined nor determined according to the logic of status that underpinned the allocation of other kinds of goods. Moreover, this condition persisted at the same time that the humanist curriculum had loosened the connection between the study of Latin grammar and the clerical estate.

This is the complex situation that Richard Mulcaster confronted during his career at Merchant Taylors'. Not surprisingly, he defines his expertise in terms of his capacity to manage the shortfall between idealistic prescription and messy material reality, differentiating his book from those of writers such as Erasmus who offer only "superior theories": because their "wishe wandereth still, not like to win the rode," he says of his predecessors, "[matters] they handle formally as in an absolute picture, I tuche but by the waye, as being quite of an other perswasion, nothing given to the unpossible, where possibilitie must take place, though the unpossible *Idaea* offer great force to fansie."[28] A range of factors counter the "unpossible *Idaeas*" of educational theorists, but the one Mulcaster chooses to signify the general lack of realism in his predecessors' work is the way in which they try to harness universal values to the restricted good of classical education. Chief among the former is parental love; the impulse that Erasmus worked so hard to recruit for his educational project is to Mulcaster a source of insatiable consumer demand for schooling. Thus he comments sarcastically:

> But to returne from this so exquisite, to our ordinarie traine, I perswade my selfe, that all my countreymen wishe themselves as wise and as well learned, as those absolute parentes are surmised to be, though they be content with so much of both, or rather with so little as God doth allot them: ... For [their son's] well schooling, they that cannot, will wish it, they that can, will have it, with small charge if they may, if they may not with some coste. (29)

To this commendable impulse he sternly replies: "sure all children may not be set to schole" (143). The point here is not just that Mulcaster counters both Erasmus's idealism and the pious charity expressed in his school's statutes with an impulse towards restriction, but more precisely, that he thinks about school access in terms of economic actors and economic principles. These last are famously inelastic; "the rowmes which are to be supplied by learning being within number," observes Mulcaster, "if they that are to supply them, grow on beyond number, how can yt be but too great a burden for any state to beare" (139)? Mulcaster links this need for limitation to the Reformation: "the expelled religion was supported by multitude ... the retained must pitch the defence of her truth in paucity of choice," a reference, it would appear, to the loss of the monasteries and mendicant orders (152). Now the purpose of the grammar school is to train enough men to serve the commonwealth, presumably as clergymen and secretaries, and no more.

But if Mulcaster imagines this post-Reformation world in terms of a static economy within which learning has a fixed function and a limited number of "rowmes," the economic actors he populates it with nevertheless possess an unruly vitality.[29] This quality shows up in the wonderful verbs – "gaping," "fleeting" [i.e., "flitting"] (139), "flocking" (148, 153), "snuffing," and "repining" (143) – that Mulcaster assigns to these actors, their attributes, and their effects. The lexis of school admissions and its attendant concerns, which are matters of "fantsie and desire" (140) "overflow" and "restraint" (146), seems to belong to *A Midsummer's Night's Dream*, except that here not sex but humanist education is the goal of all. To put the point less fancifully, whatever

Mulcaster may say about subordinating the desire for learning to the needs of the commonwealth, he aligns this desire with the irresistible force of nature. Regarding the poor but talented he observes that

> Againe wittes misplaced most unquiet and seditious: as any thinge else strayned against nature: light thinges prease upward, and will ye force *Fire* downe? Heavie thinges beare downeward: and will ye have *Leade* to leape up? An imperiall witte for want of education and abilitie, being placed in a meane calling will trouble the whole companie, if he have not his will, as winde in the stomacke: and if he have his will, then shall ye see what his naturall did shoote at. He that beareth a tankarde by meanesse of degree, and was borne for a cokhorse by sharpenes of witte, will keepe a canvase at the Conduites, tyll he be Maister of his companie. Such a sturring thing it is to have wittes misplaced and their degrees mislotted by iniquitie of *Fortune,* which the equitie of nature did seem to meane unto them. (142–3)

This observation is made in the service of an argument for "choice in restraint." Places are restricted but this means that judgment must be used so that places are awarded "where *nature* deserveth by *abilitie* and *worth,* not where *fortune* friendeth by *byrth* and *boldnes*" (143). If the logic of Mulcaster's observations is that the equity of nature must be respected, however, this principle can only be applied in a limited way insofar as "nature" is, of course, also the force that has produced the flocking to school that Mulcaster is trying to beat off. For, as Mulcaster argues, "everie parent [is] thus affected toward [i.e., desirous of humanist education for] his owne child, as nature leades him to wish his owne best" (146). The reason nature bends this way is not only that learning leads to advancement but that unlike other endowments, it is in Mulcaster's view essentially a *spiritual* good, "incorporate in the person, till the soule dislodge," as Erasmus would also have insisted (146). What virtuous parent would *not* wish it for his or her child? Nevertheless, in the face of this natural impulse towards the good, Mulcaster can only counsel "patience" because it must either "forcibly bend or voluntarily breake" before the brute fact that not all children can go to school. Those who cannot get places may "passe on and bewtifie some other trade: that also is very good, seeing they serve their country" (149). It is not clear, however, given the observation about the danger of thwarting nature in the passage cited above, why unquiet and even a shaking of the state are not likely to ensue from this course.

This inability to embrace the conclusion to which his own observations compel him is typical of Mulcaster's argumentation and derives from the fundamental contradiction between his drive to think economically and the conviction, which he shares with Erasmus, that humanist learning not only is, but ought to be, universally desired. However, where for Erasmus the desire for learning had belonged to the orator/teacher – the humanist pedagogue extending his dominion while repairing fallen nature – for Mulcaster that desire has become part of nature itself. As such it occupies a double position, at once the spirit the schoolmaster must lovingly cultivate and the ravening appetite that the state must restrain. Thus, where Erasmus's imagined teacher is endowed with the nearly magical ability to transform the brute into the human, the professional virtue Mulcaster claims is "discretion," the ability to make narrow judgment calls (145). But given his appreciation for the different claims he must adjudicate, it is hard to believe any of these judgments will really be satisfactory.

As a result, the form this discretion takes in Mulcaster's text is oddly formal, an attempt to achieve equity through balanced periods, as in this reflection on admission criteria:

> Some doubt may rise here betwene the *riche* and *poore,* whether all *riche* and none *poore,* or but some in both maye and ought to be set to learning. For all in both that is decided alreadie, No: bycause the whole question concerneth these two kindes, as the whole common weale standeth upon these two kindes. If all *riche* be excluded, *abilitie* will snuffe, if all *poore* be restrained then will *towardnesse* repine. If *abilitie* set out some *riche* by private purses for private preferment: *towardnesse* will commende some *poore* to publike provision for publike service. (143)

What he proposes here in place of universal access is a balanced classroom. But from the strictly structural and utilitarian perspectives that he rigorously advances, there is no good reason why the poor need to be there at all. To the widely acknowledged claims of the gifted poor boy, he provocatively responds: "Be great giftes tied to the meane, or banished from the mighty? Be there not as good wittes in wealth, though oftentimes choked with *dissoluteness* and *negligence,* as there be in *povertie* appearing through *paines* and *diligence*? Nay be there not as untoward *poorelinges,* as there be wanton *wealthlinges?*" (151). And given that there is no necessary correlation between poverty and intellectual ability, the commonwealth in fact has no need of the gifted poor, because "he which defendes states [i.e., God] will provide sufficient persons by whom they shall be served" (149). And yet, Mulcaster makes provision for the poor, their "repining" receiving as much concern, at least rhetorically, as the snuffing of the wealthy.

In part, Mulcaster's lingering commitment to the poor bespeaks the deep residual association of schooling with charity in Elizabethan England. A school *without* poor boys would be simply inconceivable. More generally, though, the contradiction in his thinking that forces him to balance the claims of two competing absolutes – nature, understood both as intellectual ability and parental love, and restriction in the places for the learned – suggests the way in which the complex relation between education and distributive justice shifts over the sixteenth century. Distributive justice is fundamentally an economic principle, pertaining to the means of life. Goods come within its imagined jurisdiction to the extent that they support life. Throughout this period learning bears an ambivalent relation to other more material goods. Before the "education revolution," as a vehicle for charity, it was proffered in the absence of – and thus on analogy with – patrimony, an idea that both Erasmus and Mulcaster reiterate. Intriguingly then, cultural capital (knowledge that can function on analogy with monetary capital) enters the world as an expression of Christian love. At the same time, the specifically ecclesiastical "market" for that learned "capital" meant that whatever the myriad practical clerical uses it was put to, it remained first and foremost the means of worship. One effect of this dispensation was a specific but limited relation between education and distributive justice. Education could serve the purposes of distributive justice where other means of subsistence were lacking, but no one was entitled to learning as such precisely because the more general good it provided, the repair of man's fallen nature, was provided to all by a synecdochically functioning clergy.

The advent, first of the humanist program and then of the Reformation, undermined this dispensation. But the effect of these seismic shifts was not a simple strengthening of the connection between education and distributive justice. To be sure, Erasmus's exuberant "all should be educated," as we have seen, is connected to his implicit shifting of the burden of repairing fallen nature from collective worship to individual learning. But Mulcaster's canny account of the Reformation's impact makes it responsible for a general loss of elasticity in the domain of learning that subtends the economic turn evident in his thinking, and its concomitant insistence on restriction. Mulcaster has no doubt that everyone is entitled to vernacular literacy "for *religion* sake, and their necessarie *affaires*" (143) and he has a typically Elizabethan sense that the poor have a place in the grammar school. But he also suggests that from a pragmatic point of view the Reformation made it more dangerous to use learning for purposes of distributive justice because to do so could actually *create* need – specifically the need for a job – and need, he observes, "is an imperious mistres to force conclusions" (139). At the same time, however, the Tudor expansion of the free grammar schools meant a greater saturation of the culture with a good that was designed to be distributed across the status hierarchy, at least to some degree, even as it afforded a new vehicle of distinction. What Mulcaster grasps (or perhaps only imagines) is that this cultural development has remade need itself, creating the curious state of affairs whereby the desire for Latin learning could be as urgent as a hunger pang. Mulcaster strives to disallow the validity of this need; it is a "*maniheaded neede*, even before *neede*, and mostwhat without *neede*" (140). But in so doing he only underscores what he concedes at every turn, that the plangent desire for learning is indeed need and cries out for justice before the economic structure that he insists cannot accommodate it. Mulcaster's solution, inevitably, is not structural but symbolic: not a universally accessible school but a heterogeneous school population.

In fashioning a student body for his prestigious school that bears a (somewhat) representative relation to the broader population, even as he acknowledges and justifies the structural exclusion and frustration of the majority of people, Mulcaster adopts something that resembles the modern educational concern with diversity.[30] I have sought in this essay to identify the specific ideological and structural forces that obtained in the sixteenth century and thus inflected the relationship between humanism and distributive justice in that place and time. And so, I would underscore in conclusion that the impasse which Mulcaster's merely symbolic solution addresses is modern more in form than in essence, arising as it does from an ability to think in terms of *something like* cultural capital but not of capitalism. I prevaricate because while both Erasmus and Mulcaster imagine learning as an endowment that can get a poor boy a living, what they mean is that it can get him a "rowme," one of a fixed number of places, mostly in the church. Neither entertains the possibility that the "maniheaded neede" of learned men for work might generate new work and new wealth, and Mulcaster's sense that this "neede" would just lead to suffering was in fact well founded. Moreover, the restriction that makes the presence of the "poor" in the humanist classroom the effect of symbolic action rather than real structural accessibility is neither industrial capitalism's need for a proletariat, nor the collusion between the upper-middle-class strategies of reproduction and late capitalism's meritocratic ideologies of which Bourdieu writes, nor neoliberalism's relentless impoverishment of the commonweal. In fact, as the seventeenth century progressed, any widely acknowledged ideological claim of the "poor" on learning withered away. For all these reasons, I do not want to argue that the presence of poor boys in the humanist classroom represented the emergence of a modern social form. However, in grafting a residual sense that schooling served the ends of charity to a new belief that humanist learning could unleash untold human potential, these sixteenth-century educational theorists brought education within the jurisdiction of distributive justice and in so doing opened for the future a rich vein of social unease.

NOTES

1 See Diane Ravitch, *The Death and Life of the Great American School System*.

2 Richard J. Herrnstein and Charles Murray, *The Bell Curve: Intelligence and Class Structure in American Life*.

3 Samuel Fleischacker, *A Short History of Distributive Justice*.

4 Sir Thomas Elyot, *The Book Named the Governor*, p. 160.

5 Kenneth Graham, "Distributive Measures: Theology and Economics in the Writings of Robert Crowley."

6 Siegfried Van Duffel and Dennis Yap, "Distributive Justice before the Eighteenth Century: The Right of Necessity."

7 Edmund Plowden, *An Exact Abridgement of the Commentaries*, p. 9.

8 Matthew Hale, *The History of the Common Law of England*, p. 159, cited in Van Duffel and Yap, p. 9.

9 Richard Halpern, *The Poetics of Primitive Accumulation*, p. 88.

10 Rebecca Bushnell, *A Culture of Teaching*, pp. 73–116, offers a more nuanced and accurate account of the place of "ingenerate abilities" in humanist pedagogical theory.

11 Pierre Bourdieu with the collaboration of Monique de Saint Martin, *The State Nobility*, p. 378.

12 The word in both cases is *combinaison*. Pierre Bourdieu, *La Noblesse d'Etat*, p. 542.

13 All quotations are from "A Declamation on the Subject of Early Liberal Education for Children" and are cited parenthetically in the text.

14 Hanan Yoran, *Between Utopia and Dystopia: Erasmus, Thomas More and the Republic of Humanist Letters*, p. 75.
15 Cf. Quintilian, *The Orator's Education*, pp. 64–5.
16 Halpern, *Poetics of Primitive Accumulation*, p. 92.
17 See Yoran, *Between Utopia and Dystopia*, p. 54, for Erasmus's dislike of his stints both as tutor and as university lecturer.
18 For Erasmus's contempt for actual clerical literacy, see *The Antibarbarians*.
19 On the "educational revolution," see Lawrence Stone, "The Educational Revolution in England, 1560–1640"; Joan Simon, *Education and Society in Tudor England*; and Rosemary O'Day, *Education and Society in Early Modern England*.
20 The statutes of the King's School, Bruton, for example, specify that the school be taught "after the gode newe Fourme used in Madgdalene College in Oxford or in the Scoole of Powles in London." *Calendar of the MSS Belonging to the King's School*, p. 6.
21 Merchant Taylors' court books cited in Howard Staunton, *The Great Schools of England*, p. 177.
22 Historians have adduced various kinds of evidence for the degree to which the poor were represented in school populations. For instance, Sir Michael McDonnell argues that the fact that an entry fee of four pence was charged at St Paul's School to be given to "the poor scholar to sweep out the school," and boys were responsible for the supply of their own candles indicated that it was intended for gentlemen. *A History of St. Paul's School*, pp. 40–1. Maria Dowling follows this argument unquestioningly in *Humanism in the Age of Henry VIII*, p. 115. However, an entry fee of twelve pence was stipulated by the Merchant Taylors' statutes, which nevertheless also made provision for the supply of candles "for the poor children to reason of their bookes," suggesting that a modest entry fee does not preclude the presence of boys poor enough to require other forms of assistance. F.W.M. Draper, *Four Centuries of Merchant Taylors' School*, p. 246, pp. 249–50. School registers that supply the status of boys' fathers furnish better, though still inferential evidence. See Charles Robinson, *A Register of the Scholars Admitted to the Merchant Taylors' School*; and E. Calvert, *Shrewsbury School Regestum Scholarium*. Both registers suggest that the respective school populations grew more genteel around the beginning of the seventeenth century.
23 J.G. Nichols, *Narratives of Days of the Reformation*, pp. 273–4.
24 Dowling, *Humanism in the Age of Henry VIII*, p. 125.
25 H.C. Lyte, *A History of Eton College*, p. 489. Henry VI's original plan had called for an equal number of poor scholars and poor and infirm men

(p. 7). "Poverty" for scholars is defined in the statutes as not having an annual income worth more than five marks a year. The statutes also specify that the election of scholars shall be made "disregarding the instances, prayers or requests of kings or queens, princes or prelates, nobles or gentlemen, and looking rather to the proficiency of the boys in grammar and to their moral character" (pp. 494–5).

26 Claire M. Cross, *The Free Grammar School at Leicester*, pp. 7–9. Initially the school and hospital were administered together. In 1557 the school's lands were formally conveyed to the hospital but the income was earmarked for the headmaster's support. See also *A Translation of a graunte from hir Mtie to Robert Johnson, Clarke, to erecte twoe grammer schooles and twoe Hospitalls in Okeham and Uppingham for a similar link between grammar schools and almshouses*. However, in the 1651 will of Humphrey Chetham of Clayton in Lancashire, we can discern a new pattern whereby provision is made for simultaneous founding of a grammar school and a Bluecoat Hospital for poor boys "to be brought up to learning, or labour" suggesting the emergence of a harder, but still not impenetrable, distinction between elite education and poor relief. See *The Charters of the Collegiate Church, the Free Grammar School, the Blue Coat Hospital, and the Last Will and Testament of the Late Catharine Richards with other Ancient Curiosities*, p. 90.

27 Ambrose Mollyneux, son of Lawrence, water-bearer, was admitted to Merchant Taylors' on 28 April 1595. There are a number of shoemakers and husbandmen throughout the register including John Britten, son of John, shoemaker, admitted 22 April 1594. The 30th of April 1582 saw the admission of Ellis Davis, son of Robert, husbandman, while the 25th of February 1585–6 saw the admission of Christopher Andrew, son of Godfrey, husbandman. A majority of boys came from the Merchant Taylors' or equally wealthy guilds, but the school was by no means limited to them.

28 Richard Mulcaster, *Positions Concerning the Training Up of Children*, p. 29. Subsequent references are to this edition and appear parenthetically in the text.

29 "Rowme" or "room" means "place" in the sense of the number of places fixed by statute or endowment in a school or college and occurs frequently in university documents from the period. When a scholar acquires a university fellowship vacated by a man who has received a church living, he takes the latter's "room."

30 For an account of the way in which the concern with "diversity" functions to divert attention from the structural inequities of modern education, particularly in the United States, see Walter Benn Michaels, *The Trouble with Diversity: How We Learned to Love Identity and Ignore Inequality*.

BIBLIOGRAPHY

Bourdieu, Pierre. *La Noblesse d'Etat*. Paris: Editions de Minuit, 1989.

Bourdieu, Pierre, with Monique de Saint Martin. *The State Nobility.* Trans. Lauretta C. Clough. Stanford, CA: Stanford UP, 1996.

Bushnell, Rebecca. *A Culture of Teaching*. Ithaca, NY: Cornell UP, 1996.

Calendar of the MSS Belonging to the King's School, Bruton. Ed. T.D. Tremlett. Bruton, 1939.

Calvert, E. *Shrewsbury School Regestum Scholarium*. Shrewsbury: Adnitt and Naunton, 1892.

The Charters of the Collegiate Church, the Free Grammar School, the Blue Coat Hospital, and the Last Will and Testament of the Late Catharine Richards with other Ancient Curiosities. Manchester: T. Harper, 1791.

Cross, Claire M. *The Free Grammar School at Leicester*. Leicester: University College of Leicester, 1953.

Dowling, Maria. *Humanism in the Age of Henry VIII*. Dover, NH: Croom Helm, 1986.

Draper, F.W.M. *Four Centuries of Merchant Taylor's School*. London: Oxford UP, 1962.

Elyot, Sir Thomas. *The Book Named the Governor*. London and New York: Everyman, 1962.

Erasmus. *The Antibarbarians / Antibarbarorum liber.* Trans. Margaret Mann Phillips. Ed. Craig R. Thompson. *Collected Works of Erasmus*, vol. 23. Toronto: U of Toronto P, 1978. 1–122.

– "A Declamation on the Subject of Early Liberal Education for Children" / *De pueris statim ac liberaliter instituendis declamation.* Trans. Beert V. Verstraete. Ed. J.K. Sowards. *Collected Works of Erasmus*, vol. 26. Toronto: U of Toronto P, 1985. 291–346.

Fleischacker, Samuel. *A Short History of Distributive Justice*. Cambridge, MA: Harvard UP, 2004.

Graham, Kenneth. "Distributive Measures: Theology and Economics in the Writings of Robert Crowley." *Criticism* 47, no. 2 (2005): 137–58.

Hale, Matthew. *The History of the Common Law of England*. London: J. Walthoe, 1713.

Halpern, Richard. *The Poetics of Primitive Accumulation*. Ithaca, NY: Cornell UP, 1991.

Herrnstein, Richard J., and Charles Murray. *The Bell Curve: Intelligence and Class Structure in American Life*. New York and London: The Free Press, 1994.

Lyte, H.C. Maxwell. *A History of Eton College*. London: MacMillan, 1877.

McDonnell, Sir Michael. *A History of St. Paul's School*. London: Chapman and Hall, 1909.

Michaels, Walter Benn. *The Trouble with Diversity: How We Learned to Love Identity and Ignore Inequality.* New York: Metropolitan Books, 2006.

Mulcaster, Richard. *Positions Concerning the Training Up of Children.* Ed. William Barker. Toronto: U of Toronto P, 1994.

Nichols, J.G. *Narratives of Days of the Reformation.* London: Longmans, Camden Society, 1859.

O'Day, Rosemary. *Education and Society in Early Modern England.* London and New York: Longman's, 1982.

Plowden, Edmund. *An Exact Abridgement of the Commentaries.* Trans. Fabian Hicks. London, 1659.

Quintilian. *The Orator's Education, Books 1 and 2.* Ed. and trans. Donald A. Russell. Cambridge, MA, and London: Harvard UP, 2001.

Ravitch, Diane. *The Death and Life of the Great American School System.* New York: Basic Books, 2010.

Robinson, Charles. *A Register of the Scholars Admitted to the Merchant Taylors' School.* Lewes: Farncombe, 1882.

Simon, Joan. *Education and Society in Tudor England.* Cambridge: Cambridge UP, 1966.

Staunton, Howard. *The Great Schools of England.* London: Strahan, 1869.

Stone, Lawrence. "The Educational Revolution in England, 1560–1640." *Past and Present* 28 (1963): 41–80.

A Translation of a graunte from hir Mtie to Robert Johnson, Clarke, to erecte twoe grammer schooles and twoe Hospitalls in Okeham and Uppingham. London: Constable and Co., 1929.

Van Duffel, Siegfried and Dennis Yap. "Distributive Justice before the Eighteenth Century: The Right of Necessity," 8 October 2009. http://www.academia.edu/192328/Distributive_Justice_before_the_Eighteenth_Century_The_Right_of_Necessity. 18 June 2012.

Yoran, Hanan. *Between Utopia and Dystopia: Erasmus, Thomas More and the Republic of Humanist Letters.* Lanham, MD: Lexington Books, 2010.

9 Warding off Injustice in Book Five of *The Faerie Queene*

JUDITH OWENS

It is a notable feature of Spenser's Legend of Justice that its hero is educated, in effect, as a ward of Astraea. While this fact has gone unremarked, it figures significantly in Spenser's conception of a just commonwealth. Developed in the Middle Ages as a means to ensure seamless military service from knights, wardship had become a magnet for criticism by the middle of the sixteenth century, with the Court of Wards and its officers widely assumed to be corrupt.[1] Writers such as Thomas Smith condemned the court for profiteering in the arranging of marriages, but lamented as well, among other ill effects on the commonwealth, the grievous neglect of the education of wards. In Book V, Spenser imagines a version of wardship that both corrects contemporary abuses regarding its mandate to furnish education *and* recreates ancient military wardship by joining "right" to "might." Thus envisioned, wardship serves, rather than subverts, the interests of a just commonwealth. Educated under this brand of wardship, Artegall undertakes his heroic quest to help right a world that has "runne quite out of square," even if all the needed adjustments remain, finally, beyond his skill (V.proem.1.7).[2] His education under wardship helps us also to assess his limitations, particularly his heavy reliance on violence. Astraea's tutelage, while clearly principled, proves surprisingly cold, a fact suggesting that Artegall's heavy-handedness can be understood as a difference between morality and ethics.[3]

When at the start of Book V Spenser surveys the many ways in which his world "growes daily wourse and wourse," falling further and further away from the "[m]ost sacred vertue" of Justice, he casts the problem at least partly as a failure in education (V.proem.1.9, V.proem.10.1). Far from being a "golden" age in which "Justice" sits "high ador'd," the present day is a "stonie one" in which men are "backward bred," like the children of Pyrrha and Deucalione, with "bred" here carrying also its sense of education or upbringing (V.proem.9.8, V.proem.2.2–6). Instead of breeding into their children the "vertue" and "civill uses" that Spenser identifies as the *sine qua non* of the "discipline" that aims to form civil subjects and commonwealths, these backward parents produce men of "hardest stone," men incapable of being animated by heroic spirit or even private virtue (V.proem.3.1–2, V.proem.2.5). Yoked to this mythical instance of what my own daughters might call a "parent-fail" are the proem's stories, written in the heavens, of fractured or unsettled families, and of youth who "all range, and doe at randon rove / Out of their proper places farre away" (V.proem.6.5–6). Fleeing or forced from their familiar homes, Phrixes, Castor, and Pollux will all become linked in myth to the Argonauts. But Spenser stops short of placing these figures into their future heroic roles. Castor and Pollux are shouldered into the Nemean lion's grove at some moment before the heroic Hercules's labours begin (V.proem.5, V.proem.6). The night skies of the proem have as their stars heroes who are caught between the moment of familial fracture and the promise of heroic destinies.[4] In the antique times of Spenser's own historical England, military wardship interceded in such a precarious moment, serving as a means both to repair a family fractured by a father's death and to ensure uninterrupted knight-service.

Against this backdrop of backward education and precariously poised heroes, Spenser introduces Artegall as fit for the task of restoring justice by virtue of his having been raised under the guardianship of Astraea. It is not surprising that Spenser turns to wardship when thinking about the commonwealth. Several of the individuals in his literary network, eminent "statesmen" all, were involved with the institution: Lord Burghley, the earls of Oxford, Essex, and Leicester, and Sir Walter Ralegh all participated, as guardians or as wards; Burghley served as Master of the Court of Wards for an astonishing thirty-seven years, and was succeeded in that post by his son. Even without these quasi-personal connections, Spenser could hardly have escaped knowing something about the business of wardship. According to Joel Hurstfield, the foremost historian of the subject, the mastership of the Court of Wards was well on its way by 1540 to becoming "one of the most influential offices of Tudor England," while the "fiscal feudalism" of the Court became a significant source of revenue as the sixteenth century unfolded.[5]

In considering what it is about wardship, as Spenser conceives it, that makes it useful to the forming of a just commonwealth, I am bracketing off the kinds of questions critics often pose when evaluating Artegall's relationship to Astraea. While it makes immediate, broad, allegorical sense that the knight of justice should be raised by the goddess of justice, the finer points of the allegory remain debatable, and critics have turned to the narrative details to augment interpretation, particularly to Astraea's alluring of the child Artegall with "gifts and speaches mild" (V.i.6.5). A.C. Hamilton noted some time ago that "the education of worldly justice begins with bribery," while David Lee Miller has recently remarked on the "fraudulent" means used by Astraea and added kidnapping to her crimes.[6] Hamilton and others relate Astraea's actions (here and in her "pilfering" from Jove the sword she gives to Artegall) to the imperfectness with which the ideal of justice must be instrumentalized in the world. Miller builds a different case from the same narrative evidence, his allegations of fraud and kidnapping serving his larger argument that Book V calls into question divine sanction of many kinds.[7] The context that I adduce directs us away from Astraea's questionable tactics to consider instead how the social institution of wardship might advance the ideals of a commonwealth.

Astraea's Guardianship

Like the orphaned Ruddymane of Book II, Artegall grows up as the ward of a female figure who represents or advances the ideals specific to her book of the poem. Unlike Ruddymane, however, whose very name registers trauma, Artegall is unmarked. He is "with no crime defilde," sullied with no sin of his own or of his parents (V.i.6.4). It is this spotlessness that recommends him to Astraea as a fit pupil. Nor are her methods of gaining control over him especially traumatizing. While her enticing of Artegall "with gifts and speaches milde" (V.i.6.5) might alarm readers in the twenty-first century (especially parents), by the standards of sixteenth-century practices of wardship these methods of gaining possession of the child represent a corrective to the notorious abuses of that system. In his scathing indictment of "the court of wards and liveries," Thomas Smith rails against guardians who "seaseth" upon the "body of the [ward] and his landes," "taketh the profite without accounts," and subject the ward to tyrannous control in the matter of marriage.[8] By comparison, Astraea's mildness and generosity towards Artegall are praiseworthy. Indeed, unlike Smith's unscrupulous guardians who squeeze or extort all they can from their wards, Astraea leaves to her ward a legacy, Talus, having "willed" Talus to remain with Artegall (V.i.12.4). We should note as well that, because she is not Artegall's mother, Astraea can only gain by artificial means, by "gifts and speaches milde," the respect and obedience that children were supposed by nature and by exhortation to offer to their parents.[9] Her allurements, then, should not necessarily be chalked up as particularly fraudulent or coercive measures.

Astraea's guardianship can be differentiated even more sharply from the corrupt practices of Spenser's day, when the aim of marrying off the ward profitably, willy-nilly, to a bride of the guardian's choosing occasioned other vices. Smith waxes especially indignant on this score, siding with those who "esteeme this wardship ... very unreasonable and unjust, and contrarie to nature, that a Freeman and Gentleman" should be made "to marie at the will of him ... who hath bought him, to such as he like not peradventure, or else to pay so great a ransome."[10] This Tudor "racket," to adopt a term from Hurstfield, is a slick one: if the ward marries, profit falls to the guardian; if the ward refuses to marry, profit falls to the guardian, in the form of a fine. Just as bad, in Smith's estimation, is the fact that the guardian's designs for the ward's marriage, and on the ward's lands, lead him to neglect the ward's education. Wardship, Smith writes, "is the occasion they say, why many gentlemen be so evil brought up touching vertue and learning." The "buyer" of a ward "will not suffer his warde to take any great paines, either in studie or any other hardeness, least he should be sicke and die" before he can be married to the guardian's "daughter, sister, or cousin, for whose sake he bought him."[11]

Smith is not alone in lamenting the neglect of the ward's education. In 1548, eight years after the establishment of the Court of Wards, Hugh Latimer asks in a sermon, "why is there not a school for the wards as well as there is a Court for their lands?" Nicholas Bacon, who was Attorney of the Wards for fourteen years, petitions for a school of wards, observing that "the chief thing and most in price in wardship is the ward's mind," yet "the chief care of governance hath been to the land … and … body" while "to the mind being the best [thing]" there been no care at all.[12] As does Smith, Bacon believes one of the purposes of wardship should be to furnish a ward with the opportunity to be raised according to high standards. But nowadays, Bacon complains, "the greater the personage is to whom the ward appertains, the less courtesy for the most part is had of the ward's bringing up." The whole of Astraea's intention, in contrast to the emphases of the Court of Wards, is the education of Artegall. She chooses him, we recall, because she knows he will make a "fit pupil."[13]

In decrying the contemporary neglect of a ward's education, Smith, Latimer, and Bacon are not only assessing the price paid by the individual ward. They are also identifying a cost to the commonwealth. Treating in one chapter wardship and other matters pertaining to the state of the nation, including matters of "supreme justice," Smith acknowledges that "some inconvenience has been thought to grow" from Parliament's long-ago granting of the royal prerogative of wardship to the King. He admits that it would be very difficult to wrest back that power from the King: "once annexed to the crowne," he asks, "who canne go about to take the clubbe out of Hercules hand," the wryness of his question raising the possibility that as currently practised wardship does not accord with "supreme justice."[14]

It is surely with Smith's critique in the back of his mind at least that Spenser imagines a version of wardship that can help to generate a just commonwealth. With its emphasis on education, his version corrects for the bias against education in contemporary practices of wardship. What is more, Artegall's education under guardianship recreates ancient military wardship in a form that joins "right" to "might" in a way the *ancient* chivalric tradition did not aim to do. In tracking wardship back from its current state of corruption to the conditions that necessitated its invention, Smith describes its origins as a presumably temporary measure, reporting that "it was first graunted upon a great extremitie to King Henrie the 3. for a time upon the warre which he had with his Barons."[15] Given its creation as a military expedient, it followed that the ward's "education was at the first militarie." Smith continues: "It was thought that most like, that noble men, good knights, and great captaines would bring up their wards in their owne feates and vertues."[16] As the latter expectation makes clear, the ancient institution of wardship not only furnished an education that was primarily military, but it also promoted mimetic bonds between ward and guardian. This latter condition of instruction is one that Spenser, rather surprisingly, is careful *not* to reproduce in Artegall's education, as we shall see.

Artegall's Education under Wardship

Artegall's education under Astraea includes much training in arms, in keeping with the ancient form. Before he undertakes that training, however, he is "noursled" by Astraea in the "discipline of Justice" "till yeares he raught" (V.i.6.8–9). Spenser uses the term "nourseled" only three times in the whole of *The Faerie Queene,* always in the context of instruction from a parent or surrogate parent. Here, the instruction is clearly in moral virtue.[17] In thus joining "right" to "might," Artegall's instructional regimen distinguishes him from Bacchus and Hercules, who are like Artegall part of the "vertuous race" who "rose up" to defeat the ranks of the wicked, base, and lawless. Bacchus "ouerronne[s]" with "furious might" the "East before untam'd" (V.i.2.1–2), while in the West Hercules, using his "club of Justice dread," subdues "monstrous tyrants" with "equall conquest," a modifier that equates Hercules's strength with that of the monstrous tyrants whom he conquers (V.i.2.7–9). The campaigns of both Bacchus and Hercules are swiftly successful. Artegall's quest, by contrast, is "an hard adventure" that calls him forth "into redoubted perill" (V.i.3.4–5). Most tellingly, while Artegall's tyrannical foe is twice in the space of three lines described as "strong," Artegall's own strength is quite pointedly not set up as a countering force: although Grantorto withholds a distressed dame's heritage with "strong hand," Artegall is chosen by the Faerie Queene "For that to her he seem'd best skild in righteous lore" (V.i.3.7, V.i.3.9, V.i.4.9).

Later, Spenser suggests that Artegall surpasses both Bacchus and Hercules in sheer strength. But throughout his description of Artegall's tutelage, Spenser insists that Artegall can wield both judgment and force, unlike Hercules, who, in Spenser's brief canvassing of how the West was subdued to Justice, wields only his club. So effectively can Artegall employ both instruments that he elicits at once "feare" of his "awfull sight" (with "sight" including the idea of discernment) and admiration for his "overruling might" (V.i.8.4–5). Spenser's characteristically flexible syntax allows us to understand that what men admire is Artegall's overruling *of* might, that is, his practising judgment that supersedes and renders unnecessary the exercise of might.[18] It is just this privileging of judgment over force that marks the Faerie Queen's assigning of this quest to Artegall. With its emphasis on virtuous lore, Astraea's guardianship likewise distinguishes Artegall from Smith's hapless wards who are "so evil brought up touching vertue and learning." Artegall is brought up "in discipline / Of vertue and of civill uses lore," taught "to weigh both right and wrong" and "equity to measure out along / According to the line of conscience" (V.proem.3.1–2; V.i.7.1–4).

Artegall's mixed education in righteous lore and arms suggests that, however much Spenser endorses sheer "might" subsequently in Book

V (and elsewhere in his writing), he does not accept uncritically the need for occasional or systematic force. Nor does Spenser accept uncritically the primacy of martial prowess, long established in chivalric romance, in Tudor myth-making, and in the ancient institution of wardship.[19] Artegall's very first adventure, his adjudication of the case of the Squire and Sir Sanglier, advances a significant critique of the chivalric order. The episode, in which one lady has been slain and another is offered up for division, is typically singled out by critics for Artegall's adaptation of a Solomonic solution.[20] Since both Sir Sanglier and the Squire disclaim responsibility for killing the lady and since each claims as his the living lady, and since the matter cannot be resolved with trial by combat (a point to which I shall return), Artegall proposes that the lady fortunate enough to be still alive be cut in two, and half of her given to each claimant. Sir Sanglier is delighted with the proposed solution; the Squire is not. He loves the lady and, accordingly, offers to be considered the guilty party so that she may live. Artegall declares the case settled and imposes upon the murderer, Sir Sanglier, the penalty of carrying before his breast for the space of a year the severed head of his own former lady.

Spenser does not let us forget the chivalric cast of this Solomonic episode, however. Throughout Artegall's adjudication, the fact that Sanglier is a knight is stressed repeatedly: Artegall interrogates the Squire abruptly, as befits his inferior status, but questions the knight "gently" (V.i.23.3), in deference to his status, and perhaps in recollection of his previous encounter with Sir Sanglier in Book IV at Satyrane's tournament for Florimell where Sanglier is "well known to be a valiant Knight" (IV.iv.40.4). Throughout the present episode, Sir Sanglier presumes upon his status as knight, answering Artegall with "sterne countenance and indignant pride," challenging the Squire to trial by combat, and readily agreeing to abide by Artegall's judgment (before he hears it, that is) – no doubt on the assumption that a fellow knight would stand by him (V.i.23.5).

Chivalric values are deployed in this episode in ways that frame larger questions of justice by highlighting the benefits of Artegall's education. In a recent essay on *Titus Andronicus*, Dympna Callaghan and Chris Kyle locate at the heart of revenge what they call "mimetic violence."[21] One of the benefits to Artegall of his education in wardship, with its instruction in virtuous lore, is his ability to restrain his own impulses to avenge, to refrain from replicating the violence he confronts. When Spenser says at the outset of Book V that Artegall is trained up by Astraea in "civill uses," he surely has in mind the tempering of violent reactions. Seeing the headless lady, Artegall responds feelingly: "Much was he moved at that ruefull sight / And flam'd with zeale of vengeance inwardly" (V.i.14.6–7). However inflamed he is, though, he does not raise his sword – despite our being led grammatically to expect that he would since the adjectival phrase "flam'd with zeale of vengeance inwardly" modifies the line to come. Instead, all aflame, Artegall "askt, who had that Dame so foully dight? / Or whether his own hand, or whether other wight?" (V.i.14.8–9). Hearing the Squire accuse the now-fled knight, Artegall seeks the truth. Sir Sanglier's guilt makes this truth an inconvenient one for a chivalric romance; Artegall's inquest into the matter will call into question assumptions at the core of the chivalric order.

Emphasis on the Solomonic solution can obscure surprising features of Artegall's handling of the case: the fact that Artegall determines the truth before asking the litigants whether they will accept his decision and before proceeding to his Solomon's device; and the precise means by which he ascertains the truth. "Artegall, by signes perceiving plaine" that it was not the Squire who killed the lady "but that strange Knight," did "cast about by sleight the truth thereout to straine" (V.i.24.6–9). Exactly what these "signs plaine" are we are not told, but the narrative and imagistic logic of the passage suggest that they are the Squire's tears. Asked by Artegall – who is, we recall, all aflame with zeal of vengeance – whether or not he is guilty, the Squire cries "woe is me," "Bursting forth tears, *like springs out of a bank*" (V.i.15.1–2; my emphasis). By conveying a sense of renewal incongruous with his desolate circumstances, the simile confirms that the Squire's sorrow is truly felt, not feigned in an attempt to mislead (as is often enough the case with weeping figures in *The Faerie Queene*). It is from this moment that Artegall eliminates the Squire as a suspect: "Who was it then (sayd *Artegall*) that wrought" the deed, "[a]nd why?" (V.i.16.1–2).

I will return to Artegall's newly formed interest in motive, but first I would like to suggest that the Squire's tears register a truly momentous shift in paradigms. The Squire's tears signal his innocence, as I have indicated. They also render him physically unfit to match Sir Sanglier in battle; as he recognizes himself, he is "too weake / To aunswere [Sanglier's] defiaunce in the field" (V.i.24.1–2). Gail Paster, Michael Schoenfeldt, and others have taught us to understand early modern bodies as humoral. What humoral psychology and physiology encourage us to surmise is that it is the Squire's tearful sorrow that has weakened him in body.[22] The very thing that proves his innocence to Artegall is the thing that would prove him guilty under the chivalric terms of trial by combat were the physically stronger Sanglier to defeat him. In this case, the justice practised by Artegall privileges moral over physical strength and recognizes that right and might are not always commensurate, as they are at least theoretically assumed to be in chivalric contexts.

It is not only that the same evidence, the Squire's weeping, supports diametrically opposed conclusions about his innocence. The initial juxtaposition of Artegall's "flaming zeal" and the Squire's "springing tears" – fire and water – highlights an elemental logic, according to which the Squire's ethical framework supplants chivalric, martial ethics. An economical way to make this point is to say that the Squire's tears quench the flames of Artegall's fiery zeal for vengeance, his instinct to raise his sword. Spenser's Knight of Justice is prepared by his training to proceed in calculated steps, to weigh and sift evidence – a predilection registered in the first conclusion he draws when he comes upon the scene and wants to know if the lady died by the Squire's hand *or* that of "other wight" (V.i.14.9). Thus prepared to proceed in measured ways, Artegall is open to the tempering influence of the Squire's tears.

Even more significant is the fact that, squared against Sir Sanglier's conduct, the Squire's ethical framework exposes sham at the core of the chivalric, martial order. The Squire's is a compellingly ethical position, grounded in a love for the lady that is self-sacrificing (always an important moral measure in Spenser): he values her life more than he fears public shame. His is also, as we have seen, an ethical position reinforced by physical inaction. Sanglier's position is compellingly unethical, a series of rearguard actions in self-defence. He is self-interested rather than self-abnegating, and careless of the life of his lady rather than solicitous. This latter fact is bluntly recorded in his killing of her. It is also subtly registered in his being sentenced to carry her severed head in front of his breast. Much of the *theoretical* ethical value of chivalry lies in the relationship of knight and lady, in the love that is ennobling. In the Neoplatonic terms that characterized Renaissance thinking about the ennobling effects of love, the knight carries an image of the beloved in his heart. Sir Sanglier's being forced to "bear" his beloved's actual head, outside his body, "before his breast," emblematizes justly and for all to see his ignobleness and his failure to esteem his lady (V.i.29.4–8).

Sir Sanglier's failure in this regard comes to light because Artegall's inquest takes a crucial turn in response to the Squire's initial testimony.

When Artegall asks whose "hand" had "that Dame so fouly dight," the Squire does not talk about action at all: "Fulle farre was I from thinking such a pranke," he insists, introducing a new line of enquiry for Artegall who commands again that the Squire declare "who wrought" this foul deed, but asks, in addition, "why?" (V.i.14.8, V.i.15.4, V.i.16.1–2). The answer to the "why" does not have any real bearing in the determination of who committed the deed; Artegall knows the knight is guilty before he proceeds to formal adjudication of the case. The answer to the "why" does shape the punishment in instructive ways, however. In pronouncing the sentence, Artegall links it to what motivated Sanglier to "so fouly dight" the Lady, saying "you, sir knight, that love so light esteeme / Take here ... / Your own dead Ladies head" (V.i.28.5–9). Spenser's word "dight," typically glossed as "treat," includes the ideas of physical and conceptual treatment. It therefore gauges perfectly the full extent, or trajectory, of Sanglier's crime: his conceiving of his own Lady as "foul" in comparison to the Squire's lady leads to his foul act of murdering her. Spenser's language also holds the promise that Sir Sanglier's punishment will prove reformative: in "bearing" his Lady's head *before* his breast, Sir Sanglier might learn that regard for his Lady should have come before self-regard.

In probing motives and in establishing a causal link between attitude and action, Artegall is practising principles of adjudication that subordinate force to discernment – "civill uses" that he learned under Astraea's tutelage. As many critics have observed, Artegall frequently acts in ways far less balanced. But my purpose is not to rehearse his failings or to trace his progress, but rather to explore what Spenser imagines would be a pedagogical program commensurate with the forming of a just commonwealth.[23]

Other key aspects of such a program emerge from Artegall's closing exchange with the Squire. Exonerated by Artegall, filled with admiration for him, and believing himself indebted, the Squire offers his allegiance and service. Artegall declines firmly: "by no meanes" will he accept the Squire's offer to follow him. The Squire's admiration for Artegall – "Much did that Squire Sir Artegall adore / For his great justice" – is no doubt meant to prompt in the reader a similarly expansive estimation of the Knight of Justice here at the conclusion of his first case (V.i.30.1–6). But this small exchange also cues us once again to Book V's concern with instructional regimens. The relationship of knight and squire is a fundamentally pedagogical one characterized by close mimetic bonds between teacher and pupil.[24] In this feature, it resembles the instructional milieu described by Smith as characteristic of the ancient institution of wardship, education in which noble knights and brave captains brought up wards in their own feats and virtues. We have seen already that Spenser revises significantly the ancient institution of wardship by linking right to might. In declining to have Artegall enter into a pedagogical relationship with the Squire, Spenser signals his concern to revise also the structural principles governing education in the ancient institution of wardship. Learning by imitation has little or no place in Artegall's education under wardship as Spenser conceives it. Astraea does not model for her ward, Artegall, her "own feats and vertues." Instead, she instructs him in principles – "all the discipline of justice there him taught," "she him taught," "Thus she him trayned and thus she him taught" (V.i.6.9, V.i.7.1, V.i.8.1) – and furnishes opportunities for him to practice – "She caused him to make experience / Upon wyld beasts" (V.i.7.7–8).

The closing exchange between the Squire and Sir Artegall brings into high relief one further factor that distinguishes Artegall's education, one that might be understood, finally, to set the limit to what the Knight of Justice can hope to accomplish. In declaring that iron-man Talus, whose loyalty to Artegall is robotic and instrumental, is all the help that Artegall needs, Spenser signals the need for Artegall to remain detached from affective bonds of the kind that would characterize the Squire's service and pupillage. Adoring loyalty is certainly a desideratum of chivalric ideals. A slightly paler version of the same affective response, directed by pupils towards teachers, is supposed by many humanists to be necessary to the chemistry of the schoolroom.[25] For Spenser, in contrast, a measure of detachment from strong affective bonds seems essential to the education of the Knight of Justice.

The absence of affect is initially registered at the scene of Artegall's instruction. Astraea, we are told, "noursled him, till years he raught" (V.i.6.8). But any tenderness suggested by "noursled" remains completely inert. Tender feeling or sentiment on the part of either teacher or pupil does not inflect Artegall's education. The very grammar of the stanzas describing Astraea's tutelage rules out the possibility of mutual regard or affective interdependence: "she him taught" remains the underlying syntax of their relationship. The distance that is structured into their relationship can be gauged as well in Astraea's leaving of the world, an event in the poem that, given the contemporary popularity of deathbed scenes in treatises, literature, and art, would lead Spenser's readers to expect certain conventions and rites, such as the blessing or admonishment, heartfelt, of even adult children (or wards). When loathing for sinful humankind compels Astraea's departure from the world (V.i.11,12), however, her leave-taking includes no moment of farewell or benediction for Artegall, just the due provision, in her will, as it were, of Talus as a bequest to Artegall.[26]

Just how central it is to Spenser's conception of the Knight of Justice that in his upbringing he be disengaged from affective ties, including any to family, home, or place, is evidenced by the small but telling narrative facts that Artegall is not once, but twice, removed from familiar surroundings while still in infancy. According to Merlin in Book III, Artegall – "no sib at all / To Elfes" – was by "false *Faries* stolne away / Whiles yet in infant cradle he did crall" (III.iii.26.6–7). Where Merlin's history of Artegall leaves off, that of Book V begins. There we learn that, finding "this gentle childe, / Amongst his peres playing his childish sport," Astraea lures him away to "wend" with her (V.i.6.2–3, V.i.6.6). Her removal of Artegall from the familiar is especially thoroughgoing; while the faeries who abduct Artegall still permit him the proximity of elfin siblings, Astraea takes him far away "into a cave from companie exiled" (V.i.6.7).

For the Knight of Justice, it seems, there cannot be too much detachment from affective ties. But the troubling figure of Talus suggests that there is no easy way to calculate how much would be too much. In her insightful study of the links between humanism and machinery, Jessica Wolfe argues compellingly that through Talus Spenser registers the cost of Stoic apathy: military humanism inured men to violence that could all too readily degenerate into the fury of the Stoic madman and relied on developments in "military technologies and tactics that preserve and enhance the distance between adversaries." Talus, she observes, "exposes the ethical hazards of the ideologies and tactics that inure the soldier to his own violent acts." More than that, Talus, who figures also "the instrumentality of the law," becomes a metaphor for the "potentially dehumanizing effect [of the law] upon its executor."[27] Ultimately, Wolfe concludes, Spenser doubts that chivalric heroic virtues can be exercised in the absence of human affection and capacity to feel. Figuring the damaging costs of detachment from emotional bonds, Talus is a leaden counterweight to the "civill uses" in which Artegall is schooled, those practices that subordinate force to judgment and that modify violent impulses.

Given that the mechanical Talus racks up such high costs, we might suppose Spenser to have nodded in proposing that the Knight of Justice be disengaged from affective ties. But comparing Artegall's upbringing to that of his half-brother, Arthur, confirms that Spenser deliberately detaches Artegall from such bonds, allowing us at the same time to contemplate the respective roles of the Knight of Justice and Prince Arthur in fashioning a just commonwealth. Arthur's experience of wardship is infused with sentiment. Like Artegall, Arthur is brought up in a version of wardship, "delivered to a Faery knight, / To be upbrought in gentle thewes and martiall might," but the prince underscores the emotional cost when he says that he was "unfit" to be so taken from his "mother's pap" (I.ix.3.7–8). Unlike Artegall, whose sole tutor is the distant Astraea, Arthur receives instruction from "old Timon" under the direction of Merlin. He recalls both of his mentors in respectful terms that suggest abiding affection between pupil and teacher (I.ix.4, I.ix.5). Arthur's affection for old Timon, with whom he dwelt, seems especially deep, and deeply entwined with an almost Wordsworthian attachment to place:

His dwelling is low in a valley greene,
Under the foot of *Rauran* mossy hore,
From whence the river *Dee* as silver cleene
His tombling billowes rolls with gentle rore:
There all my daies he trained me up in vertuous lore. (I.ix.4.5–9)

The specificity of place – so different from the generic cave and forest of Artegall's upbringing – is only partly a function of Arthur's greater historical role and well-known connection to Wales. Like the personalized landscape of "December," the eclogue in which Spenser recalls his tutor, Wrenock, Arthur's green valley registers depth of feeling. That Arthur himself recounts the story of his upbringing, while Artegall's is narrated to us, provides another measure of the very different emotional charges of their respective scenes of instruction. The differences in strength of feeling extend as well to each knight's relationship to his "national destiny." Arthur's recollection is filled with longing to know "of what loynes and lignage [he] did spring" (I.ix.4–6). In contrast, according to Merlin's prophecy in Book III, Artegall will need to be brought back by Britomart to any sense of home and lineage sufficient to the national causes he will champion (III.iii.27).

This difference between their respective ties to nation and commonwealth – and, accordingly, between their respective virtues –

can be illuminated by the terms developed by Avishai Margalit to distinguish morality from ethics. For Margalit, the "thick relations" of ethics are "grounded" in deeply personal connections with individuals such as "a parent, friend, lover, fellow-countryman," and are "anchored in a shared past or moored in shared memory"; while the "thin relations" of morality involve connections to "the stranger and the remote" and are a function of our simply being human.[28] Extending this distinction to describe the depths and textures of emotion characterizing ethics and morality respectively, we can note that Arthur's particular cluster of virtues – honour, grace, and magnificence – demand considerable emotional investment, whether they are privately or publicly exercised, whereas Artegall's virtue of justice, even when it includes equity, must remain emotionally indifferent.[29] Artegall's connection to nation is fundamentally more abstract, more likely to trade in "respect" and "humiliation," the "attitudes" that Margalit defines as central to morality.[30] In contrast, and in keeping with the attitudes and responses that Margalit associates with ethics, Arthur's links with and service to the commonwealth are secured above all in fervent "loyalty" to the Faerie Queen. Spenser's term for the "thick relations" and the more complex, internalized attitudes or emotions that define those relations is "love," as Arthur's quest-initiating dream of the Faerie Queen makes clear: it is a dream that "ravishes" the Briton in body, mind, and spirit (I.ix.13–15). While Artegall's virtue is essential for just commonwealths in general, it is insufficient for the British commonwealth whose destined contours glimmer in *The Faerie Queene* and whose full realization, outside of time, awaits Arthur's loving union with Gloriana.

NOTES

1 Guardianship was so much a byword for profiting that even in so otherwise unrelated an occasion as the dedicatory epistle in the 1623 First Folio, Heminge and Condell can distinguish the noblemen whose countenancing of Shakespeare's work they seek from profit-mongers in terms drawn right from wardship: the compilers of the Folio declare that in publishing Shakespeare's plays they have "done an office to the dead, to procure his Orphanes, Guardians; without ambition either of self-profit, or fame." John Heminge and Henry Condell, "The Epistle Dedicatorie," p. 6. Concerning the Court of Wards and the abuses of wardship in relation to existing English law devised expressly to protect young women from fraudulent

conveyance through allurements into marriage for their property, see Charles Ross, "Avoiding the Issue of Fraud: 4, 5, Phillip & Mary c.8 (The Heiress Protection Statute), Portia, and Desdemona," pp. 91–108. In part due to the inadequacy of this legislation, and the exemptions that included the Court of Wards that "controlled most of the great heiresses of the realm" (94), inverse situations arose in which heiresses became imprisoned by the financial ambitions of their wardens, leading to January-May marriages and other unhappily enforced arrangements.

2 *The Faerie Queene* (2001), V.proem.1.1–5. All citations are to this edition and will appear parenthetically in the text.

3 I am indebted to an anonymous reader for the press for the formulation of this point.

4 In a stimulating recent essay, David Lee Miller has described the skies of the proem as enacting a "cosmic Keystone Cops routine" ("Gender, Justice and the Gods in *The Faerie Queene*, Book 5," p. 21). Miller's emphasis on the humour aligns with that of Alfred B. Gough, who comments on the "quaint and even playful language with which Spenser illustrates the supposed physical deterioration of the universe, especially in the passage describing the displacement of the zodiac" (*The Works of Edmund Spenser*, vol. 5, p. 156.) For both Miller and Gough, the humour underscores serious matters: Spenser's pessimism about the degenerate age in which he lives, in the case of Gough; Spenser's scepticism about the analogy between god and monarch that secures Elizabeth's authority, in the case of Miller.

5 *The Queen's Wards: Wardship and Marriage under Elizabeth I*, p. 243. For a discussion of wardship in the context of an emergent sixteenth-century bureaucratic culture, see Bradin Cormack, *A Power to Do Justice: Jurisdiction, English Literature, and the Rise of Common Law*, pp. 60–2.

6 Gifts to the Master of the Courts of Wards or to his agents (as well as to members of his family), which were expected, were also the basis for the charges of corruption that dogged the Court. Hurstfield estimates that in one span of two and a half years Burghley received about 3,000 pounds sterling from petitioners while his official salary for that same period amounted to less than 400 pounds sterling and that Burghley's share of fees and gifts paid by petitioners was about triple the Queen's share (*Queen's Wards*, p. 268). Spenser is vague about who receives Astraea's gifts, but the implication is that they go to the ward himself, Artegall. Hamilton's comment is in his note to V.i.6.5 in his first Longman edition of *The Faerie Queene*. Miller's charges against Astraea are in his "Gender, Justice, and the Gods," p. 21.

7 Jane Aptekar, *Icons of Justice: Iconography and Thematic Imagery in Book V of "The Faerie Queene,"* p. 122, contends that Astraea's "slight [sleight]" gives "more or less divine sanction" to Artegall's own use of guile in his adventures, concluding further that "Spenser recognized the ironical truth that in the actual world of practical men, force and fraud, though they are less than honorable, less than good, are the very means which the governor must use in order to maintain God's justice" (p. 7). Not every commentator on Astraea's education of Artegall even notes the niggling details. In *Spenser's "Fierce Warres and Faithfull Loves,"* for example, Michael Leslie overlooks Astraea's tactics even while acknowledging that any expectations, established iconographically, that Artegall will prove a messianic figure who will restore the Golden Age are "mercilessly dashed." For Leslie, the flaw is entirely in Artegall because "Spenser's subject is as much the limitations of human virtue as it is its power for good" (pp. 61–2). More recent critics are not as sanguine as this in noting Artegall's reliance on, and by extension Elizabeth's condoning of, force and fraud. But, as Miller remarks, however critical of Elizabeth current readings might be, they tend not to criticize "sovereign power as such" (p. 34 n.1). Miller, in contrast, finds that, by "push[ing] the laws of grammar too far," Spenser calls into question the very hermeneutical practices and the "metaphysical basis" that grant "the prince's divine warrant" (pp. 34, 19).

8 *De Republica Anglorum,* ed. Mary Dewar, p. 127.

9 See, for example, Gouge on the "Duties of Children," pp. 304–56, for a compendious survey of the "inward" and "outward" disposition of the child toward the parent.

10 Smith, *De Republica,* pp. 128–9. As does Smith, I use only the masculine pronoun in referring to a guardian. Mothers were among the petitioners to the Court of Wards, but did not always gain custody; wardships tended to go to the highest bidder and the motives for the majority of petitions to the Court were strictly "pecuniary" and not brought on "behalf of a ward's relative" (Hurstfield, *The Queen's Wards,* p. 60). Throughout this paper, I refer only to the practices of the Court of Wards, a crown corporation, not to the very different practices and purposes of the Courts of Orphans established in several cities to safeguard the person and inheritance of orphans; the usual practice in those courts was to award guardianship to a close friend or a relative, very often the remarried widow. See Carlton, *The Court of Orphans.*

11 Smith, *De Republica,* p. 129.

12 Latimer and Bacon are quoted in Hurstfield, *Queen's Wards,* pp. 25, 26.

13 For a discussion of humanist pedagogy as producing ideas about the "human" that have implications for distributive justice, see the essay by Elizabeth Hanson in this volume (pp. 179–203).
14 Smith, *De Republica*, p. 87.
15 Smith, *De Republica*, p. 129.
16 Smith, *De Republica*, p. 130.
17 In I.vi.23.8 we read that Sir Satyrane is "noursled up in life and manners wilde / Emongst wild beasts and woods, from lawes of men exildle" by his "salvage sire" (I.vi.23.4), "taught" only "To banish cowardize and bastard feare" (I.vi.24.1–2). The parallel in setting – wild woods, far from men – heightens the contrast in the content of the instruction given to Sir Satyrane and Artegall, respectively. In VI.iv.35.8–9, we read that the child rescued from a bear by Calepine will be given to the wife of Sir Bruin, who can choose "him to train in chevalry, / Or noursle up in lore of learn'd Philosophy." Here, "nourseled" stands in clear contrast to training in arms; in addition, the parallel between Artegall and the bear-child – both raised by women who are not their mothers – strengthens the parallel in the content of the instruction each receives.
18 Miller, "Gender, Justice," p. 34, describes a key moment in Spenser's discussion of Artegall's education in equity when "Subject and predicate ... change places undecidably" in the course of demonstrating that it is characteristic of Spenser to "[push] the laws of grammar too far," and so to permit readings that can undermine his own categories.
19 In *"The Faerie Queene" and Middle English Romance*, p. 197, Andrew King describes Artegall's "own sense of … chivalric authority" as being "continuously undermined by a landscape which denies idealized romance fictions," making this observation in the course of arguing persuasively that Book V is concerned "with the attempt to derive national identity through the perception or recollection of history according to a romance, providential narrative" (p. 189). Although I am covering very different ground, I share with King an interest in Spenser's critical reception of historical traditions.
20 Jeff Dolven, in *Scenes of Instruction in Renaissance Romance*, offers a brilliant reading of Artegall's Solomonic solution in the course of arguing that "punishment is itself a mode of instruction" (p. 207). "What Arthegal has done in meting out his punishment [to Sanglier] is to produce an emblem legible … inside and outside the poem" (p. 210). Dolven is not interested in the processes of enquiry leading up to the Solomonic solution or concerned to tease out the chivalric assumptions.

21 "The Wilde Side of Justice in Early Modern England and *Titus Andronicus*," pp. 38–57.

22 See Gail Kern Paster, *The Body Embarrassed: Drama and the Disciplines of Shame in Early Modern England*, and Michael Schoenfeldt, *Bodies and Selves in Early Modern England*. In *Castel of Helth* (1541), Thomas Elyot observes that sorrow, or "hevynesse," "hydeth vertue of strengthe" (fol. 66v); Timothy Bright observes that, among other physiological effects of tears, "the muscles receive a weakenes, by reason of retraction of spirites" (*A Treatise of Melancholie*, p. 157).

23 For an analysis of Book V that understands Artegall as a hero who "undergoes a series of adventures which reveal his weaknesses and ultimately perfect him in his virtue," see, for example, Dunseath, *Spenser's Allegory of Justice in Book Five of "The Faerie Queene,"* p. 16. See also Evans, *Spenser's Anatomy of Heroism: A Commentary on "The Faerie Queene,"* who stresses the role that "personal failure" plays in Artegall's quest to "establish the proper hierarchy of reason and passion within [himself]" (p. 199).

24 At about age fourteen, after having served as a page and valet for several years, the aspiring knight was typically assigned to a castle and apprenticed to a knight, tending to the knight's horses and armour, accompanying the knight on hunts, tournaments, and to battles, where the squire would learn the arts of chivalry by watching. See, for example, Raymond Rudorff, *The Knights and Their World*, and, for an illustrated history, Christopher Gravett, *Knight: Noble Warrior of England 1200–1600*.

25 See, for example, Erasmus, who contends that the "first duty of the teacher is to inspire affection in his pupils" (*On Education for Children*, p. 90). For an illuminating discussion of how fraught could be the humanist endeavour to "[structure] the relationship of student and teacher as one of love," see Rebecca Bushnell, *A Culture of Teaching: Early Modern Humanism in Theory and Practice*, p. 30.

26 Part of the art of dying well in early modern England was the careful staging of a deathbed scene, very often the occasion for the dictating of the dying man's will, at which the testator, surrounded by family and friends, not only disposed of his worldly possessions, but dispensed moral and spiritual advice as well. For a representative treatise on the art of dying well and the importance of leaving a legacy of moral and spiritual well-being, see the enormously popular *The sycke mans salve* by Thomas Becon. Written in the late 1550s, it was reprinted twenty-eight times over the next few decades.

27 *Humanism, Machinery, and Renaissance Literature*, pp. 213, 235, 204, 210.

28 *The Ethics of Memory*, p. 7. For a seminal discussion of the conflict in the second half of *The Faerie Queene* between moral philosophy and emerging political theory in relation to questions about dominion, see Elizabeth Fowler, "The Failure of Moral Philosophy in the Work of Edmund Spenser."

29 The relations among clemency, mercy, pity, and equity are intricate ones in Book V and in early modern English society. For a discussion of Seneca's belief that mercy and pity are unrelated to clemency, see John Staines, "Compassion in the Public Sphere of Milton and Charles," pp. 98–9. For a detailed discussion of the influences of Aristotle and Plato on Spenser's notion of equity, see Andrew J. Majeske, *Equity in English Renaissance Literature: Thomas More and Edmund Spenser*, chapter 4 and passim. Notably, at the trial of Duessa in Book V, it is Arthur who is "sore empassionate" in "tender heart" (ix.46.1–2), although his "former fancies ruth he [does] repent" (ix.49.2), while Artegall remains "with constant firm intent / ... against her bent" (ix.49.4–5).

30 Shame, humiliation, respect, and reputation are central to most, if not all, of Artegall's encounters. Sanglier is shamed by his punishment, as is Braggadochio in canto iii; Bourbon's shameful renouncing of his faith necessitates Artegall's armed intervention in canto xi; Artegall himself is dogged by the Blatant Beast, whose hundred tongues "bray" words "Most shameful" against him (xii.41.1–2).

BIBLIOGRAPHY

Aptekar, Jane. *Icons of Justice: Iconography and Thematic Imagery in Book V of "The Faerie Queene."* New York: Columbia UP, 1969.

Bright, Timothy. *A Treatise of Melancholie* (1586). Ed. Hardin Craig. New York: Columbia UP, 1940.

Bushnell, Rebecca. *A Culture of Teaching: Early Modern Humanism in Theory and Practice.* Ithaca, NY: Cornell UP, 1996.

Callaghan, Dympna, and Chris Kyle. "The Wilde Side of Justice in Early Modern England and *Titus Andronicus*." In *The Law in Shakespeare*. Ed. Constance Jordan and Karen Cunningham. New York: Palgrave MacMillan, 2007. 38–57.

Carlton, Charles. *The Court of Orphans*. London: Leicester UP, 1974.

Cormack, Bradin. *A Power to Do Justice: Jurisdiction, English Literature, and the Rise of Common Law.* Chicago: U of Chicago P, 2007.

Dolven, Jeff. *Scenes of Instruction in Renaissance Romance.* Chicago: U of Chicago P, 2007.

Dunseath, T.K. *Spenser's Allegory of Justice in Book Five of "The Faerie Queene."* Princeton, NJ: Princeton UP, 1968.

Elyot, Thomas. *Castel of Helth*. 1541.

Erasmus. *On Education for Children*. In *The Erasmus Reader*. Ed. Erika Rummel. Toronto: U of Toronto P, 1990. 65–100.

Evans, Maurice. *Spenser's Anatomy of Heroism: A Commentary on "The Faerie Queene."* Cambridge: Cambridge UP, 1970.

Fowler, Elizabeth. "The Failure of Moral Philosophy in the Work of Edmund Spenser." *Representations* 51 (1995): 47–76.

Gouge, William. "Duties of Children." In *Of Domestical Duties*. Ed. Greg Fox. Pensacola, FL: Chapel Library, 2006. 304–56.

Gravett, Christopher. *Knight: Noble Warrior of England 1200–1600*. Oxford: Osprey Publishing, 2008.

Heminge, John, and Henry Condell. "The Epistle Dedicatorie." In *The First Folio of Shakespeare: The Norton Facsimile*. Ed. Charlton Hinman. New York: Norton, 1968. 5–6.

Hurstfield, Joel. *The Queen's Wards: Wardship and Marriage under Elizabeth I*. London: Frank Cass, 1973.

King, Andrew. *"The Faerie Queene" and Middle English Romance: The Matter of Just Memory*. Oxford: Clarendon Press, 2000.

Leslie, Michael. *Spenser's "Fierce Warres and Faithfull Loves": Martial and Chivalric Symbolism in "The Faerie Queene."* London: Boydell & Brewer, 1983.

Majeske, Andrew J. *Equity in English Renaissance Literature: Thomas More and Edmund Spenser*. New York: Routledge, 2006.

Margalit, Avishai. *The Ethics of Memory*. Cambridge, MA: Harvard UP, 2002.

Miller, David Lee. "Gender, Justice and the Gods in *The Faerie Queene*, Book 5." In *Reading Renaissance Ethics*. Ed. Marshall Grossman. London: Routledge, 2007. 19–37.

Paster, Gail Kern, *The Body Embarrassed: Drama and the Disciplines of Shame in Early Modern England*. Ithaca, NY: Cornell UP, 1993.

Ross, Charles. "Avoiding the Issue of Fraud: 4, 5, Phillip & Mary c.8 (The Heiress Protection Statute), Portia, and Desdemona." In *The Law in Shakespeare*. Ed. Constance Jordan and Karen Cunningham. Basingstoke; New York: Palgrave Macmillan, 2007. 91–108.

Rudorff, Raymond. *The Knights and Their World*. London: Cassell, 1974.

Schoenfeldt, Michael. *Bodies and Selves in Early Modern England*. Cambridge: Cambridge UP, 1999.

Smith, Thomas. *De Republica Anglorum*. Ed. Mary Dewar. London: Cambridge UP, 1982.

Spenser, Edmund. *The Faerie Queene*. Ed. A.C. Hamilton, text ed. Hiroshi Yamashita and Toshiyuki Suzuki. New York: Longman, 2001.

– *The Faerie Queene*. Ed. A.C. Hamilton. New York: Longman, 1977.
– *The Works of Edmund Spenser: A Variorum Edition*. Ed. Edwin Greenlaw et al. Baltimore: Johns Hopkins UP, 1936.
Staines, John. "Compassion in the Public Sphere of Milton and Charles." In *Reading the Early Modern Passions*. Ed. Gail Kern Paster, Katherine Rowe, and Mary Floyd-Wilson. Philadelphia: U of Pennsylvania P, 2004. 89–110.
Wolfe, Jessica. *Humanism, Machinery, and Renaissance Literature*. Cambridge: Cambridge UP, 2004.

10 Torture and the Tyrant's Injustice from Foxe to *King Lear*

JOHN D. STAINES

England famously departed from most European nations in failing to embrace judicial torture. As John Langbein has shown, while the Roman-canon law of proof established in Continental Europe demanded a confession for a person to be convicted of a capital felony, English common law granted juries the power to convict on the basis of their members' judgment of the facts. Since English law did not require a confession, it did not need to resort to torture for convictions, whereas the Continental courts depended on torture to bring the judicial process to a successful close with the confession of the accused. That history is complicated, of course, by what Langbein has called the "century of torture," a period during which the Privy Council regularly issued warrants to torture prisoners usually, though not always, suspected of political or religious crimes.[1] Thus, although Thomas Smith's boast in *De republica Anglorum* that torture was unknown in England has long since been disproved, its appearance and ultimate disappearance by the 1630s remains something of a puzzle.[2] With the Council acting under royal warrants, the English torture regime faced no judicial restraints, unlike the European system, which functioned under clear, if frequently ignored, rules and regulations. If, as Michel Foucault, Paige duBois, and others have suggested, torture somehow expresses the heart of Western thought and epistemology, the way to unveil the hidden essential truth, torture presumably should have flourished once it was introduced into England.[3] Yet the one restraint upon the government's actions, what the English public itself would accept as legitimate and just, seems to have checked the development of legal torture. Indeed, we have a situation where torture was embraced by the Tudors when their power and legitimacy were under grave threat, but then was gradually abandoned by James and Charles when their claims to the throne were secure. As Langbein has pointed out, by 1628, torture under royal warrant had become a non-issue, not worth even a mention in the Petition of Right.[4]

I want to suggest that one element in torture's disappearance from England was its place in narratives of tyranny. Foxe's *Actes and Monuments* is the exemplary text, story after story unmasking judicial torture as being not about the search for truth but about a tyrant's cruel and illegitimate expression of power.[5] The torturer's uncontrollable urge to inflict pain becomes a way to identify a ruler as a tyrant and to undermine his or her claim to authority. For instance, Foxe centres his devastating attack upon Bishop Bonner around dramatic scenes involving the enraged torturer, a stoic victim, and an audience asked to respond and resist. When Elizabeth's government pursued torture as a preferred tactic against subversion, her enemies responded by framing new martyrologies around this equation of torture with an illegitimate tyranny that must be resisted. Richard Verstegan, for instance, models the scenes of torture in *Theatrum Crudelitatem Haereticorum Nostri Temporis* on Foxe's stories and illustrations. Shakespeare finally uses the dramatization of the tyranny of torture to create the character of Cornwall in *King Lear*. Cornwall's unjust torture of Gloucester draws on the equation of torture with tyranny, showing how entrenched the connection had become to an English audience. Although Foxe's narratives did not cause the failure of torture in England – Langbein's arguments adequately explain why it was institutionally unnecessary for the workings of English justice – they did help shape a world view in which torture became an unacceptable option, the mark of the foreign tyrant.[6] Moreover, as men and women claim the right to name the torturer a tyrant for committing violence against their bodies and consciences, they take crucial steps towards revolutionary thought.

Tyrants and Torture in Theories and Narratives of Justice

In his "Epistle Dedicatorie" to Elizabeth, Foxe praises "Gods great mercies and iudgmentes in preseruing his Church, in ouerthrowing tyrauntes, in confounding pride, in altering states & kingdomes" (fol. *ir).[7] Thanking God for overthrowing tyrants is not, of course, quite the same as justifying the people who actually bring about the revolution, but naming the tyrant is an important step in that direction. As Rebecca Bushnell has shown, sixteenth-century writers inherited the opposition between a rational king and an irrational tyrant that was first developed by Plato and circulated throughout Greek and Roman accounts of tyranny; the tyrants of Plato and much of the Greek and Roman stage are bestial, inhuman, effeminate, violent, and controlled by desire.[8] In the religious wars of the sixteenth century, however, political events rather than philosophical considerations drove the discussion, giving a new urgency to the term *tyrant* and the ancient debate over whether it was better to resist him or accept his rule as a bulwark against political chaos. As the conflicts intensified between Catholics and Protestants and, ultimately, within the Catholic and Protestant camps, the traditional Pauline and Augustinian injunction to accept the tyrant as the will of God or even the punishment of God fell away. The people who could interpret their scriptural texts themselves would claim the right to interpret their political texts, too.

To confront the traditional Christian teaching to obey the magistrate, which would not provide much protection against a repetition of the Massacre of St Bartholomew's Day, the *Vindiciae contra Tyrannos* of 1579 begins by identifying tyrants as these princes: "being not content to command the bodys, and goods of their Subjects at their pleasure, but they assume licence to themselves to inforce the Consciences, which appertaines cheifly to Jesus Christ, holding the earth not great enough for their ambition, they will climbe and conquor heaven it selfe" (2).[9] By defining tyranny as the ambition to claim sovereignty over the consciences of subjects, Philippe du Plessis Mornay carves out an independent space for the individual soul not just in matters of religious faith but in political allegiance.[10] The tyrant is the giant who challenges heaven's authority by forcing the consciences of the people. It is this founding observation that eventually leads to the constitutional principle that "Kings receive Lawes from the people" (sig. K2r). As Quentin Skinner notes, such constitutional arguments allowed Huguenot theorists to circumvent Pauline injunctions to obedience.[11] Given the extreme violence of the Wars of Religion, it is not surprising that much of the ensuing discussion concerns the power to inflict violence upon the people and their individual consciences. The claim that the laws come from the people implicitly restricts the King's power to use violence against them: "the Prince is but as the Minister and Executor of the Law, and may only unsheath the Sword against those whom the Law hath condemned; and if he do otherwise, he is no more a King, but a Tyrant; no longer a Judge but a Malefactor, and instead of that honourable Title of Conservatour, he shall be justly branded with the foule terme of Violator of the Law and Equity" (sig. K4r). Mornay takes the standard distinction between the usurping tyrant and the "tyrant by practise" and argues that the ruler who earns the name *tyrant* by his deeds in office is to be considered the greater danger: "he seemes rather worthy the name of a tyrant, which unworthily acquits himselfe of his charge, than he which entered into his place by a wronged dore" (sig. O2r). Therefore, in the radical conclusion to the argument, just as the people are justified under natural law in resisting a usurping tyrant, so the people are bound to resist, depose, and punish the "tyrant by practise" (sigs P4v–Q2v). Making a bold challenge to the growing absolutist claims of monarchy, Mornay declares, "The whole people considered in one body, is above and greater than the King," and they and their consciences have the power to judge whether or not the King is an unjust tyrant whose actions nullify their allegiance to him (sig. Q2r).[12]

The definition of a tyrant was thus coming to encompass the magistrate who employs violence when persuasion has failed. In George Buchanan's tragedy *Baptistes*, Malchus, the villainous chief rabbi who conspires for John the Baptist's death, is warned, "What you will achieve is to be thought an aggressor, using all the violence of tyranny until you could bring down the holy man whom you could not refute by reason" (138, ll. 208–11).[13] In Buchanan's stoic account, anger is the mark of the tyrant: Malchus, representing a clerical establishment affronted by John's challenge to its authority, is "fired with anger and swollen with pride" (138, l. 221). This anger in turn inflames Herod's tyranny: "Is the monstrous behaviour of Herod not sufficient, without the uncontrolled cruelty of his savage mind blazing higher through anger's torches being thrust beneath it?" (140, ll. 278–80). Anger, pride, and cruelty thus become the marks of a tyrant.

In his political tracts, Buchanan goes further by granting the people the right to determine whether the ruler's actions and character meet the definition of tyranny. Indeed, for Buchanan resistance is not a corporate right or responsibility to be lodged in an institution like a parliament but one belonging to every single member of the civic polity. He asks in *De Iure Regni Apud Scotos*, "What about the tyrant, the public enemy, with whom all good men are constantly at war? Cannot any individual from the whole mass of the human race lawfully exact from him all the penalties of war?" His interlocutor Maitland agrees, though he worries about the potential for chaos if every person has this right, a fear that Buchanan simply dismisses.[14] Holding a king up to judgment is thus a right and responsibility of every citizen. Therefore, to call a monarch by the name of *tyrant* is a speech act that undoes his or her legitimacy and makes resistance lawful. As Bushnell puts it, "The naming itself is thus marked as a political act."[15] Indeed, in his tragedies and histories, Buchanan uses historical narrative to defend his theories of resistance and to defend the Scottish revolution in which he participated, recognizing the power of stories to give life to the name of tyrant and to make heroes of those who resist.[16] He even ends his one theoretical defence of resistance, *De Iure Regni*, with a passage from Seneca's *Thyestes* that defines the true king as a man of stoic self-possession against the implied example of the irrational, violent, lustful tyrant. That tyrant, as Gordon Braden explains, is the embodiment of a stoic mentality gone to such an extreme that it becomes essentially its insane opposite, conquering self and world but forever obsessively needing more to conquer: "A ruler whose power goes beyond all opposition and faction has to create opponents and factions in order to experience that power."[17]

For the tyrant, torture is thus less a tool to ascertain and justify the truth than one to assert and maintain political power. As Elaine Scarry notes in her study of twentieth-century torture, the interrogator aims not to uncover knowledge but to bring about "the disintegration of the [prisoner's] world, the obliteration of consciousness."[18] That is, torture inflicts pain with the aim of unmaking the victim's consciousness by breaking his or her body and thus spirit. That the Continental interrogators were officially only permitted to torture those prisoners whose guilt had been established circumstantially but who had not submitted their confession conforms to Scarry's account, as does the inquisitor's desire to use pain to force the heretic to abandon his or her conscience. Although England used torture less often, its torture regime was arguably even more prone to such tyrannical abuse. Since English torture was not regulated by the law of proof, it was by definition an arbitrary power that usurped the legal trial of a suspect in favour of breaking his world. Nonetheless, the ability to issue the warrant did not necessarily give the torture regime absolute power to obliterate any given subject's consciousness; particularly among men and women animated by zealous beliefs and bolstered by their faith in the power of martyrdom, it was possible to frustrate what Scarry has described as the inquisitor's aims. Foxe's stories of martyrs under torture repeatedly show that the tyrant's infliction of pain often could not touch the conscience of the faithful, could not destroy their worlds. One martyr would later claim that, as his hand was burned by Bishop Bonner, "hys spirite was so rapte vp, that he fealt no paine" (1534). The martyr's faith could rise above physical pain and torture, and each martyr's story thus confirms the endurance of his or her world despite the violent efforts of tyrants to destroy it.[19]

The nineteenth-century historian David Jardine was the first to prove that, despite claims that there was no law of torture in England, torture was a native English practice; after demonstrating that the issuance of English torture warrants was even governed by fewer restrictions than in Continental Europe, he concluded damningly, "in England the only limitation was the will of the sovereign."[20] While under Mary, the Catholic clergy interrogated heretics independently, without warrants from the government, under Elizabeth, torture was the sole prerogative of the Queen. Elizabeth and her council jealously protected that prerogative, even though an institutional structure of judicial warrants might have isolated her from direct implication in tyrannical cruelty. Since the Queen's personal involvement in the torture regime made her subject to the charge of ruling as a tyrant, her sovereign will could not act with complete freedom but was under constant pressure to justify itself. As Lorna Hutson has persuasively argued, we misapply Foucault if we look at representations of torture in England as pure expressions of the sovereign will; the English jury system made popular judgment central to the legal process.[21] The torture regime's cruel circumventing of that proud tradition threatened to become the public sign of the state's tyranny, rather than of its truth and justice. We should thus take seriously Smith's stated reasons for the rejection of torture: "it is taken for seruile. For what can he serue the common wealth after as a free man, who hath his bodie so haled and tormented, if he be not found guiltie, and what amends can be made him? And if he must die, what crueltie is it so to torment him before?"[22]

Although there were no institutional limits on torture, such sentiments about the tyranny of torture did put limitations on the sovereign's will to act since to become a torturer was to become a tyrant. Indeed, this is a tradition at least as old as Seneca, who complains in *De ira*, "If only the examples of such cruelty had been confined to foreigners, and that along with other foreign vices the barbarity of torture and rages had not been imported into the morals of Romans!" He describes the cruel anger of tyrants like Caligula, who tortured men "not to extract information but for his amusement."[23] Torture, unleashed by uncontrolled anger, is the mark of foreign tyrants and the sort of vice that destroyed the republican virtues of Rome. Thus the tyrannical Alexander kills his friend Clitus for being "reluctant to transform himself from a Macedonian and a free man [*libero*] into a Persian slave."[24] Anger, torture, tyranny, and slavery are opposed to *libertas*, which was indeed the practice in ancient Athens, where only slaves, not free citizens, could be put to torture.[25]

Torture is unworthy of the free man and the free commonwealth, and to force the conscience of the believer is likewise an act of tyranny. Ironically, though, England's Protestant regime turned to torture primarily in cases of religiously motivated treason, trying to save itself by investigating and forcing the consciences of its subjects.[26] In doing so, it found itself entering into the narrative of tyranny established a generation earlier. Anne Askew's interrogation and torture is the most famous of those early narratives, made all the more powerful by being presented in Foxe as a direct first-person narrative: "Then they did put me on the racke, because I confessed no Ladies or Gentlewomen to be of my opinion, and thereon they kept me a long tyme. And because I lay still and did not cry, my Lord Chancellour and M. Rich, tooke paynes to racke me with theyr owne handes, tyll I was nigh dead" (1239). Askew was perhaps the only woman ever put to the rack in England, and her plain, sparse account of her torment contrasts her simple, steadfast courage with the eagerness of the Lord Chancellor and Rich to participate in the torments "with theyr own handes." She is the model of a Christian martyr: "But my Lord God (I thanke his euerlasting goodness) gaue me grace to perseuer, and wil do (I hope) to the very end" (1239). The others earn the name of tyrants, as John Bale ceaselessly reminds his readers in his version of 1547: "Where was the feare of God ye tyrauntes?"[27]

In Bale and then Foxe, torturing a woman represents the violation of not only the common law but the laws of nature, the magistrate slipping out of the bonds of law and custom into tyranny.[28] Foxe describes her rejection of an offer of clemency for her if she were to say she were with child, "ye shall not neede to spare for that, do you willes vpon me: and so quietly and patiently praying vnto the Lord: she aboade their tiranny, till her bones and ioints almost were pluckt a sunder, in such sort, as she was carried away in a chaire" (1239).[29] The tyrant only violates the body and fails to get the victim to violate her conscience.[30] Indeed, there is a typological connection to be drawn here in the torture of a woman. According to Tacitus, as Nero started to plunge into mad paranoia, he tortured a brave woman, the former slave Epicharis: "But neither the scourge nor fire, nor the fury of the men as they increased the torture that they might not be a woman's scorn, overcame her positive denial of the charge. Thus the first day's inquiry was futile." The next day, as her broken body was carried back for more of the rack, she managed to hang herself and become a model of Roman courage. "All the nobler was the example set by a freedwoman at such a crisis in screening strangers and those whom she hardly knew, when freeborn men, Roman knights, and senators, yet unscathed by torture, betrayed, every one, his dearest kinsfolk."[31] A torture warrant might give the form of law to what Bale and Foxe define as the actions of a tyrant, but the torturing of a woman without a warrant reflects the frustration of a tyrannical power losing its control over the hierarchical system. The woman, who withstands torture despite her lower position in the social order, becomes the prime model for heroic resistance.

The Injustice of Foxe's Bonner: Torture as the Sign of the Archetypal Tyrant

In Foxe's great compendium of Catholic tyranny, the sequence of stories that centre on Edmund Bonner, Bishop of London, serve not only to discredit the bishop and his authority but to develop a character sketch of the archetypal tyrant: a proud sadist, arrogant in his ignorance, quick to anger when his personal authority is challenged. The stories are joined together by the woodcuts, which not only turn the written text into a visible image but go beyond the historical narratives and comment upon them.[32] The woodcuts themselves grotesquely mix horror with scatological satire to create a portrait of the tyrannical bishop that endures to this day.[33]

Foxe's martyrs create a godly community that stands in opposition to the political and social establishment, and the book demands its readers to oppose that system. The torture regime becomes the most visible and cruellest representation of this unjust system, and defences of active resistance, which would burst out more publicly in response to the revolutions and massacres in Scotland and France, form an undercurrent. Indeed, these texts make a point of taking torture, which usually occurs in hidden spaces away from public eyes, and putting it out in public for all to see and witness. It is torture's secrecy that distinguishes it from the penal violence of the scaffold, and by publicizing this hidden cruelty, Foxe's stories and images actively destroy the authority of the putative leaders of the political, religious, and social hierarchy.

The stories about Bonner's tortures frequently expose conflicts between social orders. Foxe sets up the martyrdom of the weaver Thomas Tomkins as a battle with the bishop that extends from religion to

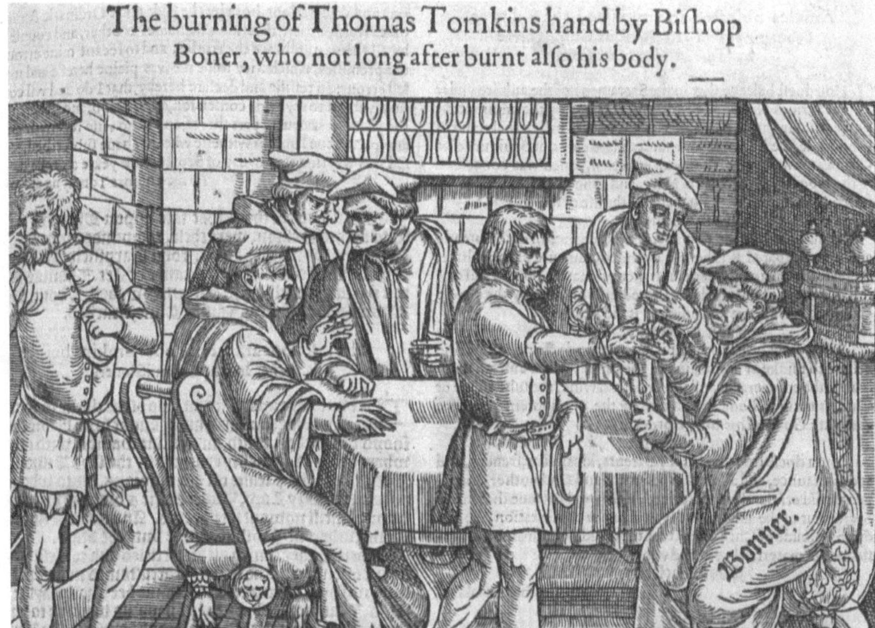

Figure 10.1 "The burning of Thomas Tomkins hand by Bishop Boner, who not long after burnt also his body." In John Foxe, *Actes and Monuments of matters most speciall and memorable ...*, 4th ed. (London, 1583), 1534. Beinecke Rare Book and Manuscript Library, Yale University.

politics and social class. We can see it in the contrast between the well-fed bishop, surrounded by other clergy in fine vestments and square caps, with the stern face, and strong body of the weaver (see fig. 10.1).

The weaver, who (we are told) prays with any woman or man who comes to him with work and lends out money for charity, not usury, understands scripture better than the Catholic clergy in their rich garments, although, it is safe to say, he probably can't read it (1533). Foxe makes no mention of him reading the Bible, and we can assume that a weaver had limited literacy, if any; nonetheless, through conversations and discussions about scripture, he participates in what Cynthia Zollinger calls "a textual community, an interaction between speakers and listeners situated around the knowledge and interpretation of a text."[34] As Tomkins persists in his allegiance to the interpretations created by his textual community, the bishop becomes enraged by his loss of authority over the text and thereby the entire hierarchical order: "That Doct. Boner B. of London kept the sayd Tomkins with hym in prison halfe a yeare. Duryng which tyme the sayd Bishop was so rigorous vnto hym, that he beat hym bitterly about the face, whereby his face was swelled. Where vpon the Bish. caused hys beard to be shauen, and gaue the Barbour xii.d " (1533). The text repeats, "But Boner in fine sent for the Barber, & caused his beard to be shauen of. The very cause was for that Boner had pluckt of a peece of his beard before" (1533), drawing attention to the bishop's attempt to humiliate and emasculate the weaver. If the weaver will violate hierarchy, the bishop will respond in kind.

At this point in the story, the Bishop falls into a great rage at what he sees as the ignorant commoner's insolent refusal to submit:

> The rage of this bishop was not so great against him, but the constancie of the partie was much greater with pacience to beare it: who although he had not the learning as the other haue, yet hee was so endued with Gods mighty spirite, and so constantly planted in the perfect knowledge of Gods truth, that by no meanes he could be remooued from the confession of truth, to impietie and error. Whereuppon Boner the Byshop being greatly vexed agaynste the poore man, when he sawe that by no perswasions he could preueaile with him, deuised an other practise not so straunge as cruel, further to try his constancie, to the intent, that seeing he could not other wise conuince him by doctrine of Scriptures, yet he might ouerthrow him by some forefeeling and terror of death … [T]he bishop fel from beating to burning. Who hauing there a taper or waxe candle of three or foure wikes standing vpon the table, thought there to represent vnto vs, as it were, the olde Image of King *Porsenna*. For as he burned the hand of *Scaeuola*, so this Catholike bishop tooke Tomkins by the fingers, and held his hand directly ouer the flame, supposing that by the smart and pain of the fire being terrified, he wold leaue off the defence of his doctrine, which he had receiued. (1234)

When teaching doctrine fails, rage takes over, much as in the case of Malchus, Buchanan's allegory for the Catholic hierarchy. Indeed, in Tomkins's story we see the fulfilment of Tyndale's plan as described in Foxe: "if the Scripture were turned into the vulgar speech, that the poore people might also reade and see the simple plaine word of God" and thus be able to challenge "abhominable doings and idolatries maintained by the Pharisaicall Clergie" (1076).[35] Tyndale has unleashed a revolution, and Bonner can only respond by impotently attempting to force the conscience to submit to pain. However, "Gods mighty spirite" allows the uneducated man to withstand not only the bishop's greater learning but his violent rage. The flame symbolizes both the Bishop's rage and the flames that face the men and women he condemns as heretics. The writer here then reads Bonner in a typology of tyranny, even claiming that the bishop actively sought to show himself playing the role of the original type, that he "thought there to represent vnto vs, as it were, the olde Image of King *Porsenna*." In Livy, the Etruscan King Porsinna, "at the same time hot with anger and terrified by the danger," orders Gaius Mucius Scaevola thrown into the flames, but when the youth thrusts his own hand into the flames in a display of defiance, he is so amazed at his bravery and republican piety that he sets him free.[36]

This tyrannical Bishop's fiery rage cannot be sated or quenched, the text tells us, surpassing even Porsinna's royal rage, which dissipates in the presence of this model of pious bravery; the Roman youth's stoicism, "his soul seeming alienated from feeling," becomes a type for the weaver's stoic calm, supported by love of God instead of love of country:

> Tomkins thinking no otherwise, but there presently to die, began to commend him selfe vnto the Lord, saying: *O Lorde into thy handes I commend my spirite. &c.* In the time that hys hand was in burning, the sayde Tomkins afterwarde reported to one James Hinse, that hys spirite was so rapte vp, that he fealt no paine. In the which burning he neuer shronke, till the vaines shronke, and the sinews braste, and the water did spirte into maister Harpsfieldes face: In so much that the sayd maister Harpsfield mooued with pitie, desired the Byshop to stay, saying, that he had tried hym enough. (1534)

Tomkins follows his martyr's script in word and deed right till the end, impassive and unyielding even as his flesh breaks. Likewise, the bishop follows the path of his fiery rage, "hitherto not contented with the burning of hys hande, rested not vntill he had consumed his whole body into ashes" (1534). Bonner's tyrannical rage cannot be stemmed and destroys all – except for the martyr's conscience.

We should not overlook Harpsfield's small moment in this story, where he is struck by the burning fluids spurting from the burning hand and then "mooued with pitie" so that he tells the bishop he has "tried hym enough." Whereas Bonner intends his violent act as a glimpse of the purging fire in which he will sacrifice the heretic, even Harpsfield, himself an energetic persecutor of Protestants, responds with pity. In his excess of cruelty, the torturer loses control over the meaning of his violence to the witnesses who see and feel the blood. The woodcuts sometimes show witnesses who join in the torture with pleasure, but frequently they show the conflicting responses of those who themselves are participating, willingly or unwillingly, in the cruelty.[37] This woodcut portrays one layman at the edge of the frame who turns his head in sympathy, though he does not intervene, very much in the position of those readers looking at the picture.[38] Like Harpsfield, splattered with gore, the readers are stained and implicated as witnesses to cruelty. Moved to pity, they are called to act. These small acts of resistance, or near-resistance, stand alongside the martyrs' obvious heroism to provide mirrors for the readers to learn from.

Often, though, Bonner serves as a pattern for petty tyrants to follow. For instance, Edmund Tyrrell, a justice of the peace acting on Bonner's orders, imitates the bishop's candle torture:

> Then that cruell Tyrill taking the candell from her, held her wrest, and the burning candell vnder her hande, burning crosse wise ouer the backe thereof, so long till the very sinowes crackt a sunder …
>
> In which time of his tyranny, he sayd often to her: why whore wilt thou not cry? Thou young whoore, wilt thou not cry? &c. Unto which always she aunswered, that she had no cause, she thanked God, but rather to reioyce. Hee had, she sayd more cause to weepe then she, if he considered the matter well. (2007)

The integrity and stoic resistance of this young woman, Rose Allin, sharply contrasts with the tyrant's enraged loss of control over his passions and body. As he loses control over his anger, he gets ever further from controlling the victim's conscience. Likewise, he loses linguistic control, yelling at her that she's a whore, though his false accusations have no power to make her one or in any way touch her conscience. Although torture seeks to control the conscience through pain, these stories repeatedly show the impassive victim's mind untouched by the physical pain inflicted upon the body.

Figure 10.2 "The burning of Rose Allins hand, by Edmund Tyrrell, as she was going to fetch drink for her Mother, lying sicke in her bedde." In John Foxe, *Actes and Monuments of matters most speciall and memorable …*, 4th ed. (London, 1583), 2006. Beinecke Rare Book and Manuscript Library, Yale University.

In the woodcut, Rose Allin stands in a classical pose, firm and unyielding as the officer burns her hand (see fig. 10.2). This is in many ways a companion piece to the burning of the weaver Tomkins's hand, and, as Marsha Robinson argues, the book consistently links the resisting female martyr to other popular voices from the lower orders of the social hierarchy.[39] Even as she upends the religious hierarchy, Allin, like the honest and hard-working Tomkins, plays her traditional role in the social order, here portrayed still holding the drink she went to get her mother, a symbol of her filial piety that matches her godly religious piety. The officers have invaded the world of domestic duties and private conscience in an act of tyranny. Behind her appears an image of martyrs burning at the stake, perhaps a broadside hung on the wall, which serves both as the model for her constancy and as a prophecy of her death by burning.[40] She becomes an emblem of integrity of conscience, while Tyrrell joins Bonner as an emblem of tyranny.

The Conscience and Resistance to Torture, Tyranny, and Injustice

In all of these examples from Foxe, the torturer makes a mockery of the forms of justice that were supposed to structure the torture regime. Torture begins with *quaestio*, the question, a search for intelligence, but rapidly degenerates into boundless rage. Seneca usefully defines anger, "the most hideous and frenzied of all the emotions," as "wholly violent, raging with a most inhuman lust for weapons, blood, and punishment."[41] Anger here expresses a desire for power and tyranny over the other, yet it paradoxically involves a loss of power over oneself in "temporary madness."[42] By contrast, the stoic self-possession of the men and women under torture allows them to seize control of their stories by remaining faithful to their consciences. Braden notes that "The essential Stoic strategy for dealing with a tyrant is not interference but indifference."[43] However, in Foxe's narratives, the confrontation between the Christian stoic self-possession of the martyr and the insane, uncontrollable rage of the torturer generates resistance to tyranny. In naming the tyrant and revealing his ineffectiveness in breaking consciences even as he breaks bodies, Foxe's narratives destroy his authority. Elizabeth's government recognized the threat posed by such a power of naming. Under the treason act of 1571, developed in response to the Northern Rebellion and the papal bull of excommunication against Elizabeth, it was treasonable to "publish, set forth, and affirm that the Queen our said sovereign lady Queen Elizabeth is an heretic, schismatic, tyrant, infidel or an usurper of the crown."[44] To name the tyrant is to commit treason.

As Elizabeth's government turned to the rack with increasing frequency to combat threats to its existence, it did so in defiance of the common law whereby torture was an alien practice. It also implicitly confronted the narrative established by Foxe's *Actes and Monuments*, which identified torture as the cruel practice of Catholic tyrants. Although the old story that Foxe's book was placed in every parish church does not appear to be true, it *was* ordered to be displayed prominently in cathedrals and in the house of every archbishop and bishop.[45] It serves as a warning against the powerful, a rebuke against their potential for tyranny. The bishops, lords, and monarch can see their reflections in the images of cruel tyrants. Foxe encourages kings and princes to read the lives of the martyrs to learn the nature of true heroism, "not that kill one an other with a weapon, but they which being rather killed in Gods cause, do retayne an inuincible constancie agaynst the threates of tyrantes and violence of tormentours" ("The vtilitie of this Story," fol. *vir). The people, moreover, can see their positions reflected in the stoic resistance of weavers and common women – or in the reactions of the witnesses to torture who have to choose whether to aid or resist the tyrant.

Elizabeth's government found itself in a paradox of its own creation: it tortured because, as a regime whose legitimacy was under threat, it found it necessary to use force to combat subversion, and yet those very acts of torture could become the signs that the regime was an unjust and illegitimate tyranny. Of the nearly five dozen surviving torture warrants, around half of which cover multiple suspects, the vast majority are for sedition, treason, and religion, with the numbers peaking during the crises surrounding Mary Stewart, the Jesuit mission, and the succession.[46] Threatened with Mary in prison and Jesuits in the houses of recusants, for instance, the Council issued three warrants to torture Edmund Campion and other priests between July and October 1581. Months later, in *A Briefe Historie of the Glorious Martyrdom of XII. Reverend Priests*, Cardinal Allen returns again and again to the cruelty of the rack: "they sticke not now without pitie to use al kind of torture, often, rather for a punishment of them, or to make them by paines to forsake their faith, or of malice and despite of the Catholike faith, then for any matter they looke to be opened by them." Blasphemously, they especially enjoy racking priests on Sundays and holy days.[47] At his trial, Allen claims, Campion could not even raise his hand to swear, "being pitifully by his often cruel racking benumbed before of bothe his armes."[48] Burghley and others would rush to answer the charge that the government's actions showed it to be an "Antichristian tyranny,"[49] but by responding to threats to its authority with torture, Elizabeth's Council had essentially taken up the role of Foxe's inquisitors and allowed the Catholic priests to assume the role of the persecuted men of conscience.

In Catholic exposés of Tudor cruelty like Verstegan's "Descriptions of the English Inquisition and the cruel Machiavellian crimes carried out in England and Ireland by Calvinist Protestants, under Elizabeth,

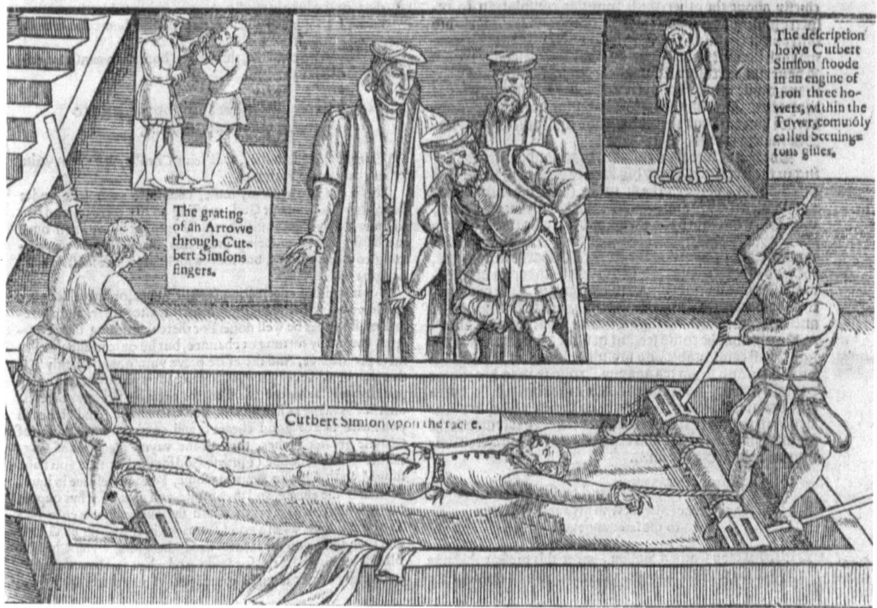

Figure 10.3 "A true description of the racking and cruell handeling of Cutbert Simson in the Tower." In John Foxe, *Actes and Monuments of matters most speciall and memorable …*, 4th ed. (London, 1583), 2032. Beinecke Rare Book and Manuscript Library, Yale University.

still reigning," the opposition would exploit the connection Foxe forged between torture and a tyrant's irrational and hence illegitimate authority.[50] Verstegan sets out to show how priests and other Catholics "are subjected to cruel and unusual tortures in the Tower of London" through stories centred on engravings that bear many similarities to those found in Foxe (see figs. 10.3 and 10.4). Both books bring their readers into the secret torture chamber to witness and experience the cruelty of the physical attack upon the body. In both, the well-dressed inquisitors in the centre of the frame compete with the tormented bodies for the viewers' attention, while other images of the horrors of prison encircle them. Both present vivid images of martyrs and tyrants.

Figure 10.4 "Persecutiones aduersus Catholicos à Protestantibus Caluinistis excitae in Anglia." In Richard Verstegan, *Theatrum Crudelitatem Haereticorum Nostri Temporis* (Antwerp, 1587), 73. Beinecke Rare Book and Manuscript Library, Yale University.

Despite such similarities, however, Verstegan's images work differently.[51] The witnesses to his horrors are all zealous, cruel Protestants who actively participate in the persecution of passive Catholic victims; none of them ever manifests a hint of pity regarding the horrors they witness and participate in. Indeed, they are never given the individuality that Foxe's tyrants attain. They are merely Protestants and Calvinists, undifferentiated personages defined by heresy and Machiavellian cruelty, alien others upon whom the Catholic reader is called to inflict revenge. While Foxe includes ambivalent witnesses whose conflicting emotional responses serve to push them, and the reader, to embrace a Protestant identity, Verstegan positions his believers either in the centre of the spectacle embracing martyrdom or outside the frame reading the image in veneration, meditating upon the call for revenge: "Indeed, [the heretics] know that it is proper that equity and truth are keeping watch in order to avenge their wicked acts" ("Sciant enim oportet, aequitatem vertatemque excubare, vt iniquas eorum actions patefaciant & vlciscantur").[52] In fact, the images were copied in a large format and hung in St Séverin and Nôtre Dame de Paris to incite Catholic believers during the Catholic League's rebellion against the French crown, a revolt that forced the King from Paris.[53] These images of tyranny and martyrdom could pose real dangers to governments.

When called to answer attacks upon his government's suppression of the Catholic resistance, Burghley's convoluted defence begins by claiming that Campion and others were not tortured, or at least not tortured too cruelly, but then concludes that it all doesn't matter since their treason justifies any treatment. Only the guilty are tortured, men whose actions and character place them outside the bounds of charity:

> yet euen in that necessarie vse of such proceeding [i.e., torture], enforced by ye offenders notorious obstinacie, is neverthelesse to be acknowledged the sweete temperature of her Majesties milde and gratious clemencie, & their slaunderous lewdenes to be the more condemned, that haue in favour of haynous malefactours, and stubborne traytors, spred vntrue rumors and slaunders, to make her mercifull gouernment disliked vnder false pretense, & rumors of sharpenesse and crueltie, to those against whome nothing can be cruel, and yet vpon whome nothing hath bene done, but gentle and mercifull.[54]

Burghley has to deny that Elizabeth's use of the rack counts as cruel torture since acts of torture have come to be associated with tyranny. Ironically, Burghley then accuses Catholics of treason on the grounds that they have called Elizabeth a tyrant for torturing men accused of crimes of conscience. Moreover, he attempts to distinguish their tortures from the cruelty described by Foxe. Unlike victims like Askew, who had to be carried from the rack, Campion "was charitably vsed, was neuer so racked, but [that] he was presently able to walke, & to write, & did presently write & subscribe al his confessions, as by the originals may appeare."[55] Apparently, a little torture is not to be considered as crossing the line into cruelty – not a terribly effective rhetorical position to have to be taking. Significantly, Foxe himself risked his position with Elizabeth's government by opposing Campion's execution, perhaps recognizing that forcing conscience through spectacles of pain was more destructive than productive in the battle against Catholics.[56]

Foxe's religious vision had come to embrace a form of toleration that would avoid using cruelty and physical coercion to enforce a uniformity of belief, a position that was, to say the least, out of step with the times.[57] Indeed, the stories of *Actes and Monuments* identify the tyrants to be opposed and call upon the faithful to convert and resist, but, unlike those in *Theatrum Crudelitatem*, they avoid direct calls for revenge.

Elizabeth and her government, however, would continue to use the rack against the Catholic threat, despite the propaganda advantage the policy gave to the Catholic opposition.[58] Moreover, once they had gotten into that habit, they would use the practice against all opposition, as when they issued warrants to use torture to find the identity of the writers of the Marprelate tracts. To call the Queen a tyrant would be too obvious an act of treason, but the Marprelate tracts happily identify the bishops by that name, at one point warning John Whitgift, Archbishop of Canterbury, "play not the tyrant as you do, in God's Church," and at another time directly comparing the current Bishop of London to his infamous predecessor, calling him "worse than Bonner in regard of the time" for "tyrannizing" people during the search for the Marprelate publishers.[59] Marprelate gets even freer with the term in the later pamphlets, as the bishops' hunt gets more intense: "For indeed thine uncle Canter. is not less than a most vile and cursed tyrant in the church."[60] Torture becomes a great source of fear for the Puritan opposition and a great source of their anger: "The reason why we must not know our father is, that I fear lest some of us should fall in John Canterbury his hand, and then he'll threaten us with the rack unless we bewray all we know."[61] Although no Puritans would burn, the rack could only increase the sense that this church, and the state that backed it, was an unjust tyrant.

As in Foxe's stories about Bishop Bonner, the recourse to torture is a sign of the failure of political authority. The sovereign power can no longer force its will on the subject's conscience, and, in a mad rage, it attempts to inflict pain on the body to such a degree that the conscience will submit. Rather than triumphantly unveiling the hidden truth, torture reflects the authority's frustration with his or her inability to touch the true conscience of the victim. The only truth that is being generated is the public revelation that the sovereign will is unjust and tyrannical. The narrative of torture thereby renders the sovereign power impotent.

In *King Lear* we can see this dynamic play out in the character of Cornwall, who, in partnership with Regan, is the archetypal tyrant.

"[T]he fiery quality of the Duke" (2.2.28) makes him prone to rage, incapable of any control, a fact that (Gloucester says) "all the world well knows" (2.2.151). Although he gains the unchecked authority of an absolute monarch, he loses all self-control the moment he is challenged, shouting like a Senecan tyrant, "I will have my revenge" (3.5.1). In place of a public trial and execution, his vengeance upon Gloucester will take place in a private home he has turned into a secret torture chamber: "Leave him to my displeasure ... the revenges we are bound to take upon your traitorous father are not fit for your beholding" (3.7.7–9). He is "bound," passively under control of his anger as he paradoxically tries to assert his absolute power.

The infliction of pain is a pure expression of Cornwall's tyrannical power:

> Though well we may not pass upon his life
> Without the form of justice, yet our power
> Shall do a courtesy to our wrath, which men
> May blame but not control. (3.7.24–7)

The tyrant sees his power as existing to serve his passions, ironically, in contrast to the courteous pity that Gloucester's conscience has shown Lear: "When I desired leave that I might pity him, they took from me the use of mine own house" (3.3.2–4).[62] The tyrant's invasion of the domestic space, his overthrowing of the father's legitimate rule, which includes piety and pity, recalls the intrusions of Bonner's agents into homes like the Allins' – and, for that matter, the pursuivants who searched Catholic homes for hidden priests or the officers who searched for the hidden presses of Martin Marprelate.

Like Bonner's agent, Cornwall perverts the privacy of the home by turning it into the secrecy of the torture chamber. Regan plucks Gloucester's beard – "So white, and such a traitor" (3.7.37) – mocking his male authority much as Bishop Bonner humiliated Tomkins by plucking and shaving his beard. Cornwall and Regan's *quaestio* is a parody of an interrogation that goes through the form of asking questions while always really being about humiliating and punishing Gloucester – which is, of course, one of the primary functions of torture in a legal system where the intelligence gathered under torture cannot be used at trial. "Be simple answered, for we know the truth," Regan says, confirming that the questioning serves no other function than to make Gloucester submit to their authority. Nonetheless, much like Foxe's martyrs standing up for their consciences, Gloucester refuses to acknowledge their power: "Because I would not see thy cruel nails / Pluck out his poor old eyes ... / ... but I shall see / The winged vengeance overtake such children" (55–65). In refusing to see their power and prophesying that he will see their power destroyed, Gloucester brings the play's obsession with sight and recognition to its horrific climax.[63] Just as Bonner would fall into a rage when his authority was challenged by the man or woman under the *quaestio*, so Cornwall explodes at Gloucester's defiance: "See't shalt thou never" (66). There is a mad symbolic logic to the expunging of Gloucester's eyes, growing out of his own words here and elsewhere, just as the bishop's acts of burning had their own cruel logic as tools of discipline.

As Cornwall shouts furiously, "Fellows, hold the chair; / Upon these eyes of thine I'll see my foot," the servants are called in as "fellows," partners in the cruelty (3.7.66–7). They play the roles assigned to them in Foxe, binding Gloucester to a chair, seeing and participating in the brutality. Likewise, the audience in the theatre plays the role assigned to the reader of Foxe's book, horrified witnesses who can only stand and watch. As he moves to take the second eye, however, a servant breaks out of this role and rebels. His conscience urges him to an act of resistance that the audience sympathizes with and even cheers on. He sees that Cornwall is a tyrant – that he has become Bishop Bonner – and not only blames but attempts to control him. In speaking and acting against his lord, the servant goes beyond the pained and shamed faces of the men who participated in Bonner's tortures despite their qualms. Although Robert Matz, among others, sees the servant as reaffirming Gloucester's patriarchal authority, it is important to recognize that in claiming the right and responsibility to judge his lord's actions according to the dictates of conscience, commanding him to stop ("Hold your hand, my lord" [3.7.71]), and finally committing tyrannicide, the servant follows a very different ideology.[64] Like Buchanan's, it empowers any member of the commonwealth, not just the patriarchal heads, to think and judge. Indeed, as with so many of Foxe's narratives, the scene bristles with conflict between social orders as the world is turned upside down. Cornwall and Regan, stunned by his rebellion, attempt to reassert authority verbally, calling him "dog," "my villein," "peasant," and "slave" (3.7.74, 3.7.77, 3.7.79, 3.7.95). The servant then evokes the confusions of gender hierarchy by calling again upon the beard as symbol of authority: "If you did wear a beard upon your chin, / I'd shake it on this quarrel" (3.7.75–6). That Regan has to seize a sword from one of the servants, who has been standing by passively in a pose out of a Foxean tableau, shows how much Cornwall's tyrannical rage has unmanned him.[65] He will soon be in the ultimate impotency of the grave.

Admittedly, the rebellion is, to a large extent, put forth in the conservative language of service,[66] and the same can be said of Foxe's narratives. On one hand, his Protestant martyrs are the radical voices of a new interpretive community created and authorized by their own interpretations of the scriptural text and by their faith that they *should* judge and resist those who would suppress them; on the other, Foxe often presents them as idealized embodiments of their social orders – the good, charitable weaver or the pious daughter – as if they were perfect social types like the ideal plowman in a medieval estates satire. Foxe often implies that Bonner's tyranny is an affront against the traditional social hierarchy and the reformed religion is its defender. Those conservative grounds, however, do not nullify the ultimately radical directions taken by those theories and by those who absorbed and put them into action. When Cornwall's servant rebels, he lends a public voice to resistance theory, even if it is one dressed up in the traditional language of service and hierarchy. A political revolution is occurring. Gloucester has called upon the gods to fight for him, but they do not answer. An unnamed servant does. Cornwall and Regan, Machiavellian tyrants, are radically secular, like Edmund, who scoffs at Gloucester's superstitions. The only way to destroy such a tyrant is not to pray for relief but to take arms. Therefore, it would be a mistake to dismiss this rebellion as merely reinforcing the old value systems. The servant has exercised his moral reasoning to defend his sense of right. In doing so, his conscience acts on behalf of the audience members, who have made their own judgments against Cornwall and Regan's tyranny. In that sense, he has led the entire audience to open resistance, and, in the Quarto text at least, his rebellion spreads to other servants. This is the logical conclusion of the political and religious thought of Foxe's *Actes and Monuments.* Lear's realm is thus well on the way to the world where the ideas of *Vindiciae contra Tyrannos* and Buchanan's secularized resistance theories are put into practice.

Shakespeare, moreover, does not treat the martyrologies with reverence here. Like the martyrs, Gloucester calls upon his gods, and upon the son he foolishly trusted, but hears and sees nothing: "All dark and comfortless?" (3.7.84).[67] Albany's attempt to find divine justice in the events ironically emphasizes this emptiness: "This shows you are above, / You justicers, that these our nether crimes / So speedily can venge" (4.2.79–81). The search for signs of divine providence in the death of a tyrant leads to this pathetic exchange: "But, O, poor Gloucester, / Lost he his other eye?" "Both, both, my lord" (81–2). So much for Foxe calling upon "Gods great mercies and iudgmentes in preseruing his Church, in ouerthrowing tyrauntes, in confounding pride, in altering states & kingdomes." It is up to men and women to act for justice, even if, in a tragic world, that justice may never be perfected. Edgar (or Albany, in the Quarto) ends the play saying, "The weight of this sad time we must obey, / Speak what we feel, not what we ought to say" (5.3.322–3). He uses not the royal "we' but the collective "we," speaking for all the witnesses, from servants to noblemen, who feel, speak, and act according to how their consciences judge the time, rather than according to how law or custom says they ought to.[68]

Foxe would be reprinted in the campaigns against King Charles and become part of the dissenter's identity, embraced by John Bunyan, among others.[69] Likewise, *Vindiciae contra Tyrannos* and Buchanan's tracts would be translated and printed to justify the tyrant's execution. Torture, however, would not be one of the charges levied against Charles, who rarely used it. Why torture disappeared so quickly remains a mystery, though I'd suggest that one reason is that for a century writers had been identifying torture with tyranny. Without the exigencies of an immediate Catholic threat to overthrow the government, as during the Guy Fawkes crisis, the rack quietly fell into disuse. Significantly, the last of the only two torture warrants from Charles's reign was to investigate a 1640 attack upon Archbishop Laud's palace. With the regime tottering, Charles personally ordered it, a desperate act that ironically serves as a sign of his faltering authority; by contrast, in 1628 his council had considered torturing the Duke of Buckingham's assassin but decided it did not need to do so.[70] The discourse of torture and tyranny not only helped make the practice an unsuitable option for the English monarchy, but it contributed to the questioning of authority that would ultimately make thinkable the overthrow of Charles as a tyrant against conscience. Foxe and his martyrs, tyrants, and conflicted witnesses had helped to prepare the way for the end of torture in England and the start of revolution.

NOTES

1 John H. Langbein, *Torture and the Law of Proof: Europe and England in the Ancien Régime*, pp. 73–139. Other essential studies of torture in England include David Jardine, *A Reading on the Use of Torture in the Criminal Law of*

England Previously to the Commonwealth; Edward Peters, *Torture*; L.A. Parry, *The History of Torture in England*; Henry Charles Lea, *Torture*; James Heath, *Torture and English Law: An Administrative and Legal History from the Plantagenets to the Stuarts*.

2 Thomas Smith, *De Repvblica Anglorvm. The maner of Gouernment or policie of the Realme of England*, 2.24.

3 Michel Foucault, *Discipline and Punish: The Birth of the Prison*; Paige duBois, *Torture and Truth*. For an application of Foucault's ideas about torture and truth to the epistemology of English treason investigations, see Elizabeth Hanson, "Torture and Truth in Renaissance England."

4 Langbein, *Torture and the Law of Proof*, p. 139.

5 Using Girard's theory of the sacrificial crisis, David K. Anderson examines *Actes and Monuments* and *King Lear* as texts that respond to the sixteenth-century crisis over the meaning of violence, convincingly seeing Foxe as a formative writer against cruelty. See "The Tragedy of Good Friday: Sacrificial Violence in *King Lear*."

6 Ayanna Thompson has shown how English Restoration plays establish both the torturer and the torture victim as national and racial others, and we can see the origins of some of that conceptualization in the Tudor period. Thompson, *Representing Race and Torture on the Early Modern Stage*.

7 Citations from Foxe will be from the fourth edition: Foxe, *Actes and Monuments of matters most speciall and memorable*.

8 Rebecca Bushnell, *Tragedies of Tyrants: Political Thought and Theater in the English Renaissance*, pp. 1–36.

9 [Philippe du Plessis Mornay], *Vindiciae contra Tyrannos: A Defence of Liberty against Tyrants*. References are to this edition and appear in the text parenthetically. I am quoting from the first English translation, published to justify the tyrannicide of Charles I and draw connections to that earlier generation of Protestant resistance theorists.

10 In ascribing *Vindiciae contra tyrannos* to Mornay instead of Hubert Languet, I am following Quentin Skinner, *The Foundations of Modern Political Thought*, p. 305.

11 Skinner, *Foundations of Modern Political Thought*, p. 320.

12 On resistance theory as a response to absolutism, see Skinner, *Foundations of Modern Political Thought*, pp. 251–301.

13 George Buchanan, *Tragedies*. References, which appear in the text, refer to the page of the translation and the line number of the original Latin.

14 See Buchanan, *A Dialogue on the Law of Kingship among the Scots*, pp. 155–7. For useful accounts of Buchanan's theories, see Skinner, *Foundations of*

Modern Political Thought, pp. 338–48; Roger A. Mason, "Introduction" to Buchanan, *Dialogue*, pp. xv–lxxi; J.H. Burns, "The Political Ideas of the Scottish Reformation" and "The Political Ideas of George Buchanan."

15 Bushnell, *Tragedies of Tyrants*, p. 46.

16 On Buchanan's uses of narrative to express his theories, see John D. Staines, *The Tragic Histories of Mary Queen of Scots: Rhetoric, Passions, and Political Literature*, pp. 27–50.

17 Gordon Braden, *Renaissance Tragedy and the Senecan Tradition: Anger's Privilege*, p. 15. On Buchanan's ideal of the *rex stoicus*, see Roger A. Mason, "*Rex Stoicus*: George Buchanan, James VI and the Scottish Polity."

18 Elaine Scarry, *The Body in Pain: The Making and Unmaking of the World*, p. 38.

19 As John R. Knott argues, Foxe's martyr is not miraculously delivered from suffering like many medieval saints; rather, his conscience is supported – "rapt up" – by a God-given faith that sustains him. Knott uses Tompkins's endurance to make a similar contrast to Scarry's account of the destructive power of pain. Knott, "John Foxe and the Joy of Suffering."

20 Jardine, *Reading on the Use of Torture*, p. 68.

21 Lorna Hutson, "Rethinking the 'Spectacle of the Scaffold': Juridical Epistemologies and English Revenge Tragedy." In a different way, James C.W. Truman explores how "martyrdom inverts the Foucauldian model of disciplinary suffering," turning the public display against the sovereign power. Truman, "John Foxe and the Desires of Reformation Martyrology."

22 Smith, *De Republica Anglorum*, 2.24.85.

23 Seneca, *De ira*, III.xviii I have silently emended Basore's translation.

24 Seneca, *De ira*, III.xvii.

25 Peters, *Torture*, pp. 11–18.

26 On treason as a crime of the imagination, see Karen Cunningham, *Imaginary Betrayals: Subjectivity and the Discourses of Treason in Early Modern England*, pp. 1–22. On the place of torture in the investigation of treason, see John Bellamy, *The Tudor Law of Treason: An Introduction*, pp. 108–21.

27 John Bale, ed., *The latter examinacyon of Anne Askewe*, p. 129.

28 Jardine could not find a torture warrant for this case, leading him to conclude that the story was one of the "fables" of the martyologists (*Reading on the Use of Torture*, pp. 65–6). However, Foxe seems to have been careful to document this case, seeking out evidence beyond that offered by Bale. Parry, for one, finds the story credible, pointing out that torture warrants rarely survive in the earlier records (*Torture*, pp. 43–4). The lack of a warrant, in any case, might also point to the circumvention of common law in these early Tudor cases.

29 This additional account of her racking does not appear in Bale's original version or in the *Actes and Monuments* of 1563, but was added by Foxe in 1570. See Askew, *Examinations*, pp. liv, 132, 188.
30 Deborah G. Burks reads Foxe's stories as part of a "rhetoric of violation" that early modern writers used "to mobilize powerful, real political action." *Horrid Spectacle: Violation in the Theater of Early Modern England*, p. 12.
31 Tacitus, *Annales*, trans. Church and Brodribb, XV.57. See Peters, *Torture*, p. 24.
32 On the function of these woodcuts within the larger project of *Acts and Monuments*, see Andrew Pettegree, "Illustrating the Book: A Protestant Dilemma."
33 For example, in the new edition of the *Dictionary of National Biography*, Kenneth Carleton laments that "his reputation for cruelty has come to overshadow many years of valued service to both church and state" even as he includes the woodcut from Foxe of Bonner burning the hand of Thomas Tomkins (see *fig. 10.1*). Carleton, "Bonner, Edmund," p. 556. The woodcut appears there on p. 553.
34 Cynthia Wittman Zollinger, "'The booke, the leafe, yea and the very sentence': Sixteenth-Century Literacy in Text and Context," p. 106. On the ways that Foxe's book itself responded to and shaped the experience of reading and interpretation during the Reformation, see Susan Felch, "Shaping the Reader in the *Acts and Monuments*."
35 On Tyndale and Foxe, see Felch,"Shaping the Reader in the *Acts and Monuments*," pp. 52–5.
36 Livy, *Ab urbe condita*, II.xii. I have used the text from Livy, *History of Rome*, ed. and trans. B.O. Foster, but given my own translation.
37 On the centrality of witnesses to the woodcuts, see Margaret Aston and Elizabeth Ingram, "The Iconography of the *Acts and Monuments*," pp. 87–9.
38 Deborah Burks helpfully describes such figures in Foxe as "surrogates within the illustration for the sympathetic viewer beyond the frame." "Polemical Potency: The Witness of Word and Woodcut," p. 266.
39 Marsha S. Robinson, "Doctors, Silly Poor Women, and Rebel Whores: The Gendering of Conscience in Foxe's *Acts and Monuments*."
40 Tessa Watt sees Foxe's woodcuts as having a strong influence on the iconography of anti-Catholic broadside prints, especially in the seventeenth century, when some of his woodcuts would be produced as broadsides. *Cheap Print and Popular Piety 1550–1640*, pp. 158–9.
41 Seneca, *De ira*, III.i.1.
42 Seneca, *De ira*, III.i.1.
43 Braden, *Renaissance Tragedy*, p. 17.
44 "An Act whereby certain offences be made treasons," p. 74.

45 See David Scott Kasten, "Little Foxes," pp. 118–19.

46 See the list of torture warrants compiled by Langbein, *Torture and the Law of Proof*, pp. 100–19.

47 William Allen, *A Briefe Historie of the Glorious Martyrdom of XII. Reverend Priests, executed within these twelve monethes for confession and defence of the Catholike Faith. But under the false pretence of Treason*, sigs biiv–biiir.

48 Allen, *Briefe Historie of the Glorious Martyrdom of XII. Reverend Priests*, sig. d8r.

49 Allen, *Briefe Historie of the Glorious Martyrdom of XII. Reverend Priests*, sig. ciiir.

50 Richard Verstegan, "Inqvisitionis Anglicanae," *Theatrum*, p. 69. Translations from Verstegan are my own.

51 See Christopher Highley's useful account of Verstegan's responses to Foxe in "Richard Verstegan's Book of Martyrs."

52 Verstegan, *Theatrum*, p. 95.

53 See Alexander S. Wilkinson, *Mary Queen of Scots and French Public Opinion, 1542–1600*, pp. 106–9; Anne Dillon, *The Construction of Martyrdom in the English Catholic Community, 1535–1603*, pp. 163–70.

54 [William Cecil, Lord Burghley], *A Declaration of the favourable Dealing of her Majestie's Commissioners*, sigs Aiiiir–Aiiiiv. This anonymous pamphlet would be later published together with Burghley's *Execution of Justice in England*, leading to the probability that he wrote it or at least oversaw its production. See Robert M. Kingdon, "Introduction" to "*The Execution of Justice in England*," pp. xii–xxxvii.

55 Cecil, *Declaration*, sig. Aiiv.

56 See Glyn Parry, "John Foxe, 'Father of Lyes,' and the Papists."

57 Viggo N. Olsen, *John Foxe and the Elizabethan Church*, pp. 212–19.

58 On the public debates between Elizabethan Catholics and Protestants over the binaries of persecution, tyrant, and error versus martyrdom, truth, and virtue, see Peter Lake with Michael Questier, *The Antichrist's Lewd Hat: Protestants, Papists, and Players in Post-Reformation England*, pp. 229–80.

59 *Theses Martinianae*, p. 162; *Hay any Work for Cooper*, p. 134.

60 *The Just Censure and Reproof of Martin Junior*, p. 177.

61 *Just Censure*, p. 189.

62 On the relationship between pity and courtesy, see John D. Staines, "Pity and the Authority of Feminine Passions in Books V and VI of *The Faerie Queene*."

63 Robert Bechtold Heilman gives the classic humanist account of the so-called "sight pattern" in *This Great Stage: Image and Structure in "King Lear,"* p. 50. Paul Alpers attacks the idea of blind insight in "*King Lear* and the Theory of the Sight Pattern." Stanley Cavell attempts to resurrect the sight

pattern to serve his argument about recognition in the play in *Disowning Knowledge in Six Plays of Shakespeare*, pp. 44–57.

64 Robert Matz, "Speaking What We Feel: Torture and Political Authority in *King Lear*." Jonathan Dollimore sees the rebellions of pity and empathy in the play as woefully inadequate to the task of justice (*Radical Tragedy: Religion, Ideology and Power in the Drama of Shakespeare and his Contemporaries*, pp. 191–203), while Richard Strier sees the play supporting the ethics and politics of being moved to action ("Against the Rule of Reason: Praise of Passion from Petrarch and Luther to Shakespeare and Herbert."). See also Strier, *Resistant Structures: Particularity, Radicalism, and Renaissance Texts*, pp. 165–202. In "Tragedy of Good Friday," Anderson defends pity in the play using theological writings from both the Reformation and modern Christianity.

65 On the effeminate tyrant, see Bushnell, *Tragedies of Tyrants*, pp. 20–5.

66 See Matz, "Speaking What We Feel," pp. 36–9.

67 As Anderson argues, these sentiments belong to the Good Friday story, where even the crucified Jesus asks why God has abandoned him, rather than to stories of martyrs, who are not allowed to express such tragic despair because of their hope in Easter ("Tragedy of Good Friday," p. 280).

68 R.A. Foakes, in his notes to line 322, insists that Edgar is speaking the royal plural to signal his taking up of the crown, which is possible, but it seems clear that by the next line, "we that are young" (324), Edgar is speaking collectively about the play's survivors.

69 Damian Nussbaum notes that the 1632 edition appears in the context of renewed fears of religious persecution and contains editorial changes and additions that make the first explicit calls for resistance in an edition of *Actes and Monuments* ("Appropriating Martyrdom: Fears of Renewed Persecution and the 1632 Edition of *Acts and Monuments*").

70 Langbein, *Torture and the Law of Proof*, p. 135–9. As Jardine first showed, and Langbein confirmed (211–13n63), the Council decided it was unnecessary to torture the assassin John Felton but (contrary to a legend based on a misreading of the sources) did not rule that torture was against the laws of England. Charles's Council had in fact tortured a suspect under warrant two years earlier.

BIBLIOGRAPHY

"An Act whereby certain offences be made treasons (Second Treasons Act of Elizabeth, 1571: 13 Eliz. I, c. 1)." *The Tudor Constitution*. Ed. G.R. Elton. Cambridge: Cambridge UP, 1982. 73–7.

Allen, William. *A Briefe Historie of the Glorious Martyrdom of XII. Reverend Priests, executed within these twelve monethes for confession and defence of the Catholike Faith. But under the false pretence of Treason.* [Rheims], 1582.

Alpers, Paul. "*King Lear* and the Theory of the Sight Pattern." In *In Defense of Reading*. Ed. Reuben A. Brower and Richard Poirier. New York: Dutton, 1963. 133–52.

Anderson, David K. "The Tragedy of Good Friday: Sacrificial Violence in *King Lear*." *ELH* 78 (2011): 259–86.

Askew, Anne. *The Examinations of Anne Askew*. Ed. Elaine V. Beilin. New York and Oxford: Oxford UP, 1996.

Aston, Margaret, and Elizabeth Ingram. "The Iconography of the *Acts and Monuments*." *John Foxe and the English Reformation*. Ed. Loades. Aldershot: Scholar Press, 1997. 66–142.

Bale, John, ed. *The lattre examinacyon of Anne Askew. The Examinations of Anne Askew*. Ed. Elaine V. Beilin. New York and Oxford: Oxford UP, 1996. 73–162.

Bellamy, John. *The Tudor Law of Treason: An Introduction*. London: Routledge & Keegan Paul, 1979.

Braden, Gordon. *Renaissance Tragedy and the Senecan Tradition: Anger's Privilege*. New Haven, CT: Yale UP, 1985.

Buchanan, George. *A Dialogue on the Law of Kingship among the Scots: A Critical Edition and Translation of George Buchanan's "De Iure Regni apud Scotos Dialogus."* Ed. and trans. Roger A. Mason and Martin S. Smith. Aldershot: Ashgate, 2004.

– *Tragedies*. Ed. and trans. P. Sharratt and P.G. Walsh. Edinburgh: Scottish Academic Press, 1983.

Burks, Deborah G. *Horrid Spectacle: Violation in the Theater of Early Modern England*. Pittsburgh: Duquesne UP, 2003.

– "Polemical Potency: The Witness of Word and Woodcut." In *John Foxe and His World*. Ed. Highley and King, 263–76.

Burns, J.H. "The Political Ideas of George Buchanan." *Scottish Historical Review* 10 (1951): 60–8.

– "The Political Ideas of the Scottish Reformation." *Aberdeen University Review* 36 (1956): 251–68.

Bushnell, Rebecca. *Tragedies of Tyrants: Political Thought and Theater in the English Renaissance*. Ithaca, NY: Cornell UP, 1990.

Carleton, Kenneth. "Bonner, Edmund." *Oxford Dictionary of National Biography*, vol. 6. Oxford: Oxford UP, 2004. 552–6.

Cavell, Stanley. *Disowning Knowledge in Six Plays of Shakespeare*. Cambridge: Cambridge UP, 1987.

[Cecil, William, Lord Burghley]. *A Declaration of the favourable Dealing of her Majestie's Commissioners, appointed for the Examination of certaine Traitours, and of Tortures unjustly reported to be done upon them for Matters of Religion.* London, 1583.

Coke, Edward. *The Third Part of the Institutes of the Laws of England: Concerning High Treason, and other Pleas of the Crown, and Criminal Causes.* 4th ed. London, 1669.

Cunningham, Karen. *Imaginary Betrayals: Subjectivity and the Discourses of Treason in Early Modern England.* Philadelphia: U of Pennsylvania P, 2002.

Dillon, Anne. *The Construction of Martyrdom in the English Catholic Community, 1535–1603.* Aldershot: Ashgate, 2002.

Dollimore, Jonathan. *Radical Tragedy: Religion, Ideology and Power in the Drama of Shakespeare and his Contemporaries.* Chicago: U of Chicago P, 1984.

duBois, Paige. *Torture and Truth.* London: Routledge, 1991.

Felch, Susan. "Shaping the Reader in the *Acts and Monuments.*" In *John Foxe and the English Reformation.* Ed. Loades. Aldershot: Scholar Press, 1997. 52–65.

Foucault, Michel. *Discipline and Punish: The Birth of the Prison.* Trans. Alan Sheridan. New York: Vintage, 1995.

Foxe, John. *Actes and Monuments of matters most speciall and memorable ...* 4th ed. London, 1583.

Hanson, Elizabeth. "Torture and Truth in Renaissance England." *Representations* 34 (1991): 53–84.

Heath, James. *Torture and English Law: An Administrative and Legal History from the Plantagenets to the Stuarts.* Westport, CT: Greenwood, 1982.

Heilman, Robert Bechtold. *This Great Stage: Image and Structure in "King Lear."* N.p.: Louisiana State UP, 1948.

Highley, Christopher. "Richard Verstegan's Book of Martyrs." *John Foxe and His World.* Ed. Highley and King, 183–97.

Highley, Christopher, and John N. King, eds. *John Foxe and His World.* Aldershot: Ashgate, 2002.

Hutson, Lorna. "Rethinking the 'Spectacle of the Scaffold': Juridical Epistemologies and English Revenge Tragedy." *Representations* 89 (Winter 2005): 30–58.

Jardine, David. *A Reading on the Use of Torture in the Criminal Law of England Previously to the Commonwealth.* London, 1837.

Kasten, David Scott. "Little Foxes." In *John Foxe and His World.* Ed. Highley and King, 117–29.

King, John N. *English Reformation Literature: The Tudor Origins of the Protestant Tradition.* Princeton, NJ: Princeton UP, 1982.

Kingdon, Robert M. Introduction to *"The Execution of Justice in England" by William Cecil and "A True, Sincere, and Modest Defense of English Catholics" by William Allen*. Ithaca, NY: Cornell UP, 1965.

Knott, John R. "John Foxe and the Joy of Suffering." *Sixteenth Century Journal* 27 (1996): 721–34.

Lake, Peter, with Michael Questier. *The Antichrist's Lewd Hat: Protestants, Papists, and Players in Post-Reformation England*. New Haven, CT: Yale UP, 2002.

Langbein, John H. *Torture and the Law of Proof: Europe and England in the Ancien Régime*. Chicago and London: U of Chicago P, 1976.

Lea, Henry Charles. *Torture*. 1866. Philadelphia: U of Pennsylvania P, 1973.

Livy. *History of Rome*. Ed. and trans. B.O. Foster. Cambridge, MA: Harvard UP, 1919.

Loades, David, ed. *John Foxe and the English Reformation*. Aldershot: Scolar Press, 1997.

Martin Junior. *Theses Martinianae. The Martin Marprelate Tracts*. Ed. Joseph Black. Cambridge: Cambridge UP, 2008. 141–63.

Martin the Metropolitan. *Hay any Work for Cooper. The Martin Marprelate Tracts*. Ed. Joseph Black. Cambridge: Cambridge UP, 2008. 95–139.

Martin Senior. *The Just Censure and Reproof of Martin Junior. The Martin Marprelate Tracts*. Ed. Joseph Black. Cambridge: Cambridge UP, 2008. 165–89.

Mason, Roger A. Introduction to *A Dialogue on the Law of Kingship among the Scots: A Critical Edition and Translation of George Buchanan's "De Iure Regni apud Scotos Dialogus."* Ed. and trans. Mason and Martin S. Smith. Burlington, VT: Ashgate, 2004. xv–lxxi.

– "*Rex Stoicus:* George Buchanan, James VI and the Scottish Polity." In *New Perspectives on the Politics and Culture of Early Modern Scotland*. Ed. John Dwyer, Roger A. Mason, and Alexander Murdoch. Edinburgh: John Donald, n.d. 9–33.

Matz, Robert. "Speaking What We Feel: Torture and Political Authority in *King Lear*." *Exemplaria* 6 (1994): 223–41.

[Mornay, Philippe du Plessis]. *Vindiciae contra Tyrannos: A Defence of Liberty against Tyrants. Or, Of the lawfull power of the Prince over the people, and of the people over the Prince*. London, 1648.

Nussbaum, Damian. "Appropriating Martyrdom: Fears of Renewed Persecution and the 1632 Edition of *Acts and Monuments*." *John Foxe and the English Revolution*. Ed. Loades, 178–91.

Olsen, Viggo N. *John Foxe and the Elizabethan Church*. Berkeley: U of California P, 1973.

Parry, Glyn. "John Foxe, 'Father of Lyes,' and the Papists." In *John Foxe and the English Reformation*. Ed. Loades, 295–305.

Parry, L.A. *The History of Torture in England*. 1934. Montclair, NJ: Patterson Smith, 1975.

Peters, Edward. *Torture*. Oxford: Basil Blackwell, 1985.

Pettegree, Andrew. "Illustrating the Book: A Protestant Dilemma." In *John Foxe and His World*. Ed. Highley and King, 133–44.

Robinson, Marsha S. "Doctors, Silly Poor Women, and Rebel Whores: The Gendering of Conscience in Foxe's *Acts and Monuments*." In *John Foxe and His World*. Ed. Highley and King, 235–48.

Scarry, Elaine. *The Body in Pain: The Making and Unmaking of the World*. Oxford: Oxford UP, 1985.

Seneca. *De ira*. *Moral Essays*. Vol. 1. Ed. and trans. John W. Basore. Cambridge, MA: Harvard UP, 1928.

Shakespeare, William. *King Lear*. Ed. R.A. Foakes. Arden Shakespeare, 3rd ser. Walton-on-Thames, Surrey: Thomas Nelson, 1997.

Skinner, Quentin. *The Foundations of Modern Political Thought*. 2 vols. Cambridge: Cambridge UP, 1978.

Smith, Thomas. *De Repvblica Anglorvm. The maner of Gouernment or policie of the Realme of England*. London, 1583.

Staines, John D. "Pity and the Authority of Feminine Passions in Books V and VI of *The Faerie Queene*." *Spenser Studies* 25 (2010): 129–61.

– *The Tragic Histories of Mary Queen of Scots 1560–1690: Rhetoric, Passions, and Political Literature*. Aldershot: Ashgate, 2009.

Strier, Richard. "Against the Rule of Reason: Praise of Passion from Petrarch and Luther to Shakespeare and Herbert." In *Reading the Early Modern Passions: Essays in the Cultural History of Emotion*. Ed. Gail Kern Paster, Katherine Rowe, and Mary Floyd-Wilson. Philadelphia: U of Pennsylvania P, 2004. 23–42.

– *Resistant Structures: Particularity, Radicalism, and Renaissance Texts*. Berkeley: U of California P, 1995.

Tacitus. *Annales*. Trans. Alfred John Church and William Jackson Brodribb. London: Macmillan, 1906.

Thompson, Ayanna. *Representing Race and Torture on the Early Modern Stage*. London: Routledge, 2009.

Truman, James C.W. "John Foxe and the Desires of Reformation Martyrology." *ELH* 70 (2003): 35–66.

The Tudor Constitution. 2nd ed. Ed. G.R. Elton. Cambridge: Cambridge UP, 1982.

Verstegan, Richard. *Theatrum Crudelitatem Haereticorum Nostri Temporis*. Antwerp, 1587.

Watt, Tessa. *Cheap Print and Popular Piety 1550–1640*. Cambridge: Cambridge UP, 1991.

Wilkinson, Alexander S. *Mary Queen of Scots and French Public Opinion, 1542–1600*. Basingstoke: Palgrave Macmillan, 2004.
Zollinger, Cynthia Wittman. "'The booke, the leafe, yea and the very sentence': Sixteenth-Century Literacy in Text and Context." In *John Foxe and His World*. Ed. Highley and King, 102–16.

11 The Literatures of Toleration and Civil Religion in Post-Revolutionary England

ELLIOTT VISCONSI

In 1967 the sociologist Robert Bellah published his foundational article "Civil Religion in America."[1] In this deeply influential essay, Bellah sketched out a non-sectarian pattern of beliefs, rituals, customs, and symbols – a shared public language for the expression of a collective religiosity – which he described as American civil religion. Bellah's account was intended to remedy two popular but largely antithetical misapprehensions about the function of religion in American public life. On the one hand, he sought to refute the historically dubious proposition that the American republic was fundamentally Christian in character and intention; on the other, he hoped to remedy the colourless resort to "faith-in-faith," the view that religiosity of any decent sort was sufficient but best kept out of sight. By seeing American civil religion as a language of collective self-expression at work in the speeches of high constitutional actors and in the historical sensibility of everyday folks, Bellah asserted the view that even while church and state were functionally and constitutionally separate, the language of American politics and history was fundamentally religious if non-sectarian in character.

The elements of American civil religion as Bellah described them are still very much with us at this hour. Americans enjoy natural rights endowed by God; "we the people" are sovereign but nonetheless subordinate to God; we are citizens of an elect nation whose history unfolds providentially and with God's especial attention. We are the heirs of generations of latter-day Israelites who fled from bondage in the Old World to realize their God-given liberty in the New World. Indeed, this last point – the trope of American Israel – has been enormously influential in the twentieth-century jurisprudence that has constitutionalized the separation of church and state. Decisions such as *Everson v Board of Education* and *Engel v Vitale*, for example, which are intended to keep religion and government functionally separate in the best interests of both spheres, must and do use the figure of the American Israel and other aspects of American civil religion to locate their constitutional utterances firmly within the context of such a historical and religious self-understanding. Bellah's article, and the sociological program it generated, has not been uncontroversial. Bellah identified what he saw as a constitutive but fluid language – a set of accessible beliefs, figures, customs, and symbols that structured American religious and political life and that emerged not from the needs of the state but instead from the shared expressive practices of its citizens. Put another way, even though it is chiefly visible at the highest levels of civic ritual and political utterance (think for instance of the profession that we are "one nation, under God," added to the Pledge of Allegiance in 1952), Bellah's American civil religion emerges from the bottom up (in the domains of culture) as well as from the top down.

In the historiography of early modern England, by contrast, the category of "civil religion" has typically been understood, in Mark Goldie's terms, as "a Faustian and totalitarian device to secure blind obedience to the state by the exploitation of human aspirations to spiritual fulfillment."[2] In this essay, part of my aim is to demonstrate that Bellah's more capacious model of civil religion as a collective language of religious and historical self-understanding can help us to see beyond pat narratives about early modern secularization. But my goal is not to export a congenial methodology to a distant and unrelated period. Rather, it is to demonstrate that the language of American civil religion has its origins in late Stuart England, a period which was clearly felt and understood as the proximate past of the American revolutionary generation. Constitutional actors such as James Madison and John Adams imagined themselves not only as the heirs of the English constitution that had degenerated at home but thrived in the colonies, but also they saw themselves as warriors combating an enduring Stuart-style tyranny over property and liberty of conscience. It is in that struggle, that moment of contested identity and constitutional foundation, that the language of American civil religion emerges most fully, not *sui generis*, but as a clarifying extension of the liberal civil religion in England in the late seventeenth century. The functionalist language of these emerging values was the common language of the revolutionary generation, and it appears vividly in the writings and public utterances of key figures from Benjamin Franklin and Madison to Washington and Jefferson. To go a bit farther, if we wish to understand the religion clauses in the First Amendment and the constitutional principle of separation of church and state developed therein, we need to understand not only the utterances, opinions, and intentions of the framers but also – and indeed perhaps more so – the English civil religion out of which that fundamental law emerged.

Accordingly, I think of civil religion as a *shared language* rather than a *program* of particular belief. And in the later seventeenth century, the preferred medium of the English people's historical and religious self-understanding was literature, where language, symbol, history, and ritual took on their most durable affective force. This language is the work of many hands; it appears in all major forms of mediation, from tragedy and satirical poetry to printed sermon, parliamentary debate, and the theoretical essay. Later Stuart civil religion flourishes as a language of collective religious and historical self-understanding in part because it is the expression of a deeply heterogeneous group of intellectual actors, a cast that includes predictable writers such as Marvell, Milton, and Locke, but also characters like William Sancroft, the Archbishop of Canterbury, and Lord Chief Justice Sir Matthew Hale, the freethinker John Toland, the influential Presbyterian Richard Baxter, and the Stuart loyalist John Dryden. These writers are practitioners of what has been termed "popular constitutionalism," or the deliberative public contestation of constitutional norms – the life of the constitution outside the courts.[3] In this case, the constitution under popular debate is the unwritten English constitution, which is itself a language, a style of remembering rights, liberties, and immemorial customs; that unwritten and customary constitution is a widely popular version of collective "rights-talk," rather than what obtains in the United States, a written fundamental law outfitted with a charismatic foundation myth.

Between 1660 and 1688, the scope, character, and institutional function of English religious practice underwent a radical transformation. With the return of Charles II, the Church of England was re-established on a seemingly durable foundation as a national church; every subject was to be encompassed within the true faith as shaped by the ecclesiastical hierarchy and underwritten by the benevolence of the restored sovereign. Uniformity was to be the path to stability, and the suppression of sectarian dissent became the banner behind which there rallied a generation of restored divines. Out of chaos, order; out of licence, obedience. But the established Church squandered its advantageous position, largely by appealing again and again to the civil power (the state) to compel uniformity of worship and belief. Such a tight bond between church and state was a source of enviable political leverage, but it was also potentially disastrous. Having relied upon the civil sword to enforce a national religious policy, the Church establishment beat a hasty retreat from its cosy political position when the accession of the tendentious, Cheneyesque, Roman Catholic James II became increasingly inevitable. In 1682, for instance, William Sancroft, Archbishop of Canterbury, wrote privately that he hoped church and state might be disentangled successfully.[4] James II was interested in centralizing state authority, and his version of absolute sovereignty was a robust form of Gallicanism; he saw the Church of England as a rival rather than an asset and as such, he blundered into putting Sancroft and six other prominent bishops on trial for failing to read his Declaration of Indulgence (ostensibly a decree in favour of religious toleration) from their pulpits. The Trial of the Seven Bishops made heroes out of the churchmen, but it also led to James's ouster, and by 1689 the last vestiges of a truly *national* Church had been swept away by the Act of Toleration. The Church of England was still established by law (as it is to this day), but it could no longer purport to be the national faith of the English people.

Is this a narrative of secularization? Perhaps, but only in a limited and institutional sense. The later Stuart period certainly witnessed a decline in the political efficacy and the systematic authority of the Church of England – which was in part a victim of its own political strategy but which was also a casualty of the rising tide of political economy and the flourishing language of national interest. As Steve Pincus has demonstrated, beginning in the 1650s, the language of English politics and foreign policy underwent a radical transformation. Appeals to the universal cause of Protestant internationalism or assertions of crusade against the infidel were abandoned; the new political-economic idiom was rooted in the calculation of a national interest based firmly in trade. As such, geopolitical questions were increasingly strategic rather than confessional; the state's controlling interest was no longer to promote the one true faith against the ungodly, but rather to cultivate and defend the economic hence political interests of the English state and its corporate affiliates.[5] Building upon these grounds, Blair Worden has proposed that the later Stuart period is marked by the domestic exhaustion of theological controversy and a broad-spectrum shift towards the view that the "test of Christianity became good conduct, not right belief."[6] Worden's aim is to insist upon the relative interiorization of religious experience – or what Michael McKeon thinks of as the privatization of belief – as a shared response to the violent and coercive dogmatism of the proximate past.

Despite this transformation of political language, there was, I propose, little in the way of a full-scale attitudinal secularization or a decline in individual religious practice. English subjects did not, despite the hand-wringing of some clergymen, devolve en masse into a horde of atheistical, blasphemous libertines who scoffed at religion. The question of toleration was increasingly seen not through the lens of theological or doctrinal correctness, but rather through a functionalist lens. Religious pluralism became increasingly tolerable whenever the members of a minority sect could pass a political sociability test – that is, as long as the beliefs and practices of the group were peaceable and did not by their exercise create riots, factions, insurrections, or other threats to the social fabric. Under those circumstances, they might be tolerated within an increasingly outward-looking and recognizably modern state.

A civil religion so deeply indexed to functional social norms must be understood as "assimilationist." Under such conditions, the individual's right to free exercise is controlled when it scandalizes the common peace or threatens to agitate the general public into violence. The magistrate is tasked with distinguishing between religion and irreligion, not for sectarian ends but in order to preserve social cohesion and the tranquillity of the kingdom. Irreligion – popery, idolatry, superstition, atheism, and priestcraft too – is to be suppressed by civil power because it causes popular discord tending towards treason, not because it contains errors of belief. It is with such a secular purpose – the preservation of the social fabric – that in 1676 Matthew Hale acquires common law jurisdiction over blasphemy in the case of *Rex v Taylor*, and indeed it was in such terms that eighteenth- and nineteenth-century American jurisprudence upheld convictions for blasphemy and other crimes of religious expression.[7]

Until 2008, such an assimilationist paradigm was the norm in English religious-liberty jurisprudence (if not in social practice); the cherished feelings and religious viewpoints of the Christian community were protected from the inflammatory speech and incitements of individuals. In March 2008 the Lords, and then in May the Commons, overturned the blasphemy laws laid down in *Rex v Taylor*, chiefly in order to prevent the establishment of new blasphemy laws for Islam, Hinduism, Judaism and other well-populated faiths in contemporary Britain.

These new overlapping jurisdictions would have extended protections against religious incitement and "hate speech" aimed at the United Kingdom's minority faiths, protections heretofore reserved by law for Christianity alone. The path forward was a secular one, however; the blasphemy laws were abolished and for many commentators in the debates, this seemed like a step in the direction of the individualist model on offer in the United States. In U.S. constitutional law it was not until the major First Amendment cases of the 1940s that the assimilationist paradigm withered in preference for a strong assertion of "intellectual individualism." The key case here is *West Virginia State Board of Education v. Barnette* (1943); this landmark decision overturned a compulsory flag salute in public schools at the appeal of Jehovah's Witnesses, for whom the ritual was an act of false worship, the idolatry of a secular object. Justice Jackson's famous affirmative opinion in the case protected the individual from compulsory professions of civic or patriotic belief; national unity might be achieved through persuasion and example, but not through force. Justice Felix Frankfurter, writing in dissent, was not troubled by such civic rituals, for in his view they insisted on a stronger secular rule of law; the individualist position would lead inevitably to anti-sociability, to a personal sense of civic immunity, in which religious belief might excuse a citizen from obeying any law or obligation that she or he found invasive. Channelling Rousseau, Frankfurter argued that compulsory civic rituals such as the flag salute were ethically and politically useful, for they called into being a horizontal and coherent moral community of citizens instead of what promised to be a mere aggregation of individuals. The constitutionalization of intellectual individualism in *Barnette* represents a notional end point of an assimilationist genealogy that begins in the domains of later seventeenth-century culture as English civil religion and becomes the foundation of the religion and speech clauses in the First Amendment.

My story about the seventeenth century proper begins in 1644. Roger Williams, a transatlantic fugitive from the stifling church discipline of the Massachusetts Bay Colony, synthesized a program of comprehensive religious toleration in two influential works – the *Bloudy Tenet of Persecution for Cause of Conscience* and *Mr Cotton's Letter Examined and Answered*, both published in London in 1644. Williams was a charismatic and highly motivated labourer in the cause of liberty of conscience, part of what John Coffey has described as a "chorus of godly voices calling for the toleration of false religions."[8] Among the other choristers in this song were Sir Henry Vane, William Walwyn, and John Saltmarsh, and their objective was, as Coffey puts it, "to untie the Constantinian knot and recover the distinction between church and world."[9] The *Bloudy Tenent* in particular was quickly notorious because Williams called for the toleration of not just godly dissent but also of all false religions: "It is the will and command of God, that (since the comming of his Sonne the Lord Jesus) a permission of the most Paganish, Jewish, Turkish, or Antichristian consciences and worships, bee granted to all men in all Nations and Countries: and they are onely to bee fought against with that Sword which is only (in Soule matters) able to conquer, to wit, the Sword of Gods Spirit, the Word of God."[10] The notion that a civil state ought to tolerate infidels in its bosom was certainly inflammatory, but Williams imagined such toleration as an occasion to evangelize; only persuasion could lead a paganish soul to God, and Williams looked forward to the day when the divine reaper separated the wheat from the tares, the saved from the damned.

But Williams was no millenarian anarchist; he saw that liberty of conscience had to be limited by the civil power when its free exercise was a direct threat to the civil peace of the Commonwealth. His letter of January 1655 to the Town of Providence outlines the limits of toleration and the fundamental need for the civil power to distinguish between religion and irreligion:

> That ever I should speak or write a tittle, that tends to such an infinite liberty of conscience, is a mistake, and which I have ever disclaimed and abhorred. To prevent such mistakes, I shall at present only propose this case: There goes many a ship to sea, with many hundred souls in one ship, whose weal and woe is common, and is a true picture of a commonwealth, or a human combination or society. It hath fallen out sometimes, that both papists and protestants, Jews and Turks, may be embarked in one ship; upon which supposal I affirm, that all the liberty of conscience, that ever I pleaded for, turns upon these two hinges – that none of the papists, protestants, Jews, or Turks, be forced to come to the ship's prayers of worship, nor compelled from their own particular prayers or worship, if they practice any. I further add, that I never denied, that notwithstanding this liberty, the commander of this ship ought to command the ship's course, yea, and also command that justice, peace and sobriety, be kept and practiced, both among the seamen and all the passengers. If any of the seamen refuse to perform their services, or passengers to pay their freight; if any refuse to help, in person or purse, towards the common charges or defence; if any refuse to obey the common laws and orders of the ship, concerning their

> common peace or preservation; if any shall mutiny and rise up against their commanders and officers; if any should preach or write that there ought to be no commanders or officers, because all are equal in Christ, therefore no masters nor officers, no laws nor orders, nor corrections nor punishments ... the commander or commanders may judge, resist, compel and punish such transgressors, according to their deserts and merits.[11]

The appeal here is plainly secular, for Williams refutes charges of his support for promiscuous or "infinite liberty of conscience" by reiterating the point (plain enough in the *Bloudy Tenent*) that the free exercise of religious belief is permitted only insofar as believers comport themselves with "justice, peace, and sobriety" as they "obey the common laws and orders ... concerning their common peace and preservation." In such a system, confessional distinctions and professions of right belief are of little functional value; the state's task of distinguishing between religion and irreligion must be conducted chiefly with reference to the durable social norms of the community.

Moreover, it was this language of sobriety, of peaceable obedience and sober cultivation of individual belief, that became a core component of the King's 1663 Charter granted to Rhode Island and Providence Plantations. Charles (acting through the Committee on Foreign Plantations), recognizing the "peaceable mindes and loyal subiection" of the distant colonists and proposing that "true pietye rightly grounded upon gospell principles, will give the best and greatest security to sovereignetye," granted to the distant colonist a remarkably broad latitude:

> noe person within the sayd colonye, at any tyme hereafter, shall bee any wise molested, punished, disquieted, or called in question, for any differences in opinione in matters of religion, and doe not actually disturb the civill peace of our sayd colony; but that all and everye person and persons may, from tyme to tyme, and at all tymes hereafter, freelye and fullye have and enjoye his and theire owne judgments and consciences, in matters of religious concernments, throughout the tract of lance hereafter mentioned; they behaving themselves peaceablie and quietlie, and not useing this libertie to lycentiousnesse and profanenesse, nor to the civill injurye or outward disturbeance of others.[12]

We are not yet at the point of a civil religion here, though this charter is surely evidence of the Crown's willingness to use the once-controversial language of comprehensive toleration – at least as it might apply to the safely distant American colonies. The royal grant is at once utilitarian – true piety grounded on the gospel is the prop of sovereignty – and emblematic of the political sociability test: an expansive religious liberty is permitted so long as it is exercised "peaceablie and quietlie, and not [in the cause of] lycentiousnesse and profanenesse, nor to the civill injurye or outward disturbeance of others." But such a manoeuvre, especially one descending from the Crown, was only possible across the sea where "by reason of the remote distances … will (as wee hope) bee noe breach of the unitie and uniformitie established in this nation."

Like his friend and fellow-traveller Roger Williams, John Milton enjoyed a high profile as a tolerationist and a strong advocate for the functional separation of church and state; such sentiments are clearly on display in poems such as "On the New Forcers of Conscience Under the Long Parliament" and the 1652 sonnets to Cromwell and Henry Vane. Like "On the New Forces of Conscience," the "Sonnet to Cromwell" worries about the persistence of priestcraft, for as that earlier poem has it, "New Presbyter is but Old Priest writ Large."[13] Most of the sonnet is preamble to a direct appeal: that Cromwell resist the threat of "new foes" who threaten "to bind our souls with secular chains" and that he "Help us to save free Conscience from the paw / Of hireling wolves whose Gospel is their maw."[14] This will not be the last time Milton imagines overreaching prelates as "hireling wolves" who solicit the aid of the secular magistrate to crack down on liberty of conscience; we can jump forward to Book XII of *Paradise Lost,* in which Milton provides a vigorous jeremiad against the "grievous wolves" who pollute the true church in its early years. The sonnet to Vane is more hagiographic than topical, for it is addressed to a fellow-traveller rather than a dubious but still potentially sympathetic Protector; Vane is nonetheless singled out for his knowledge of – and in the Trinity Manuscript version of that poem – his public teaching of the limits of spiritual and civil power.[15]

These short poems anticipate, both in their language and in their theoretical underpinnings, Milton's most judicious prose tract on toleration and the church-state nexus – *A Treatise of Civil Power in Ecclesiastical Causes* – published in or around late February 1659 as part of a campaign to equip the new Parliament with an anti-Erastian and tolerationist language to use in the "defense of true religion and our civil rights."[16] In *Civil Power,* Milton expands upon Christ's teaching to tolerate the tares among the wheat during the secular age by rejecting the jurisdiction of the civil magistrate over individual conscience or private religious belief, for to impose religious uniformity is to imply that the Gospel is both fragile and publicly demonstrative. It is to "show us the divine excellencies of his spiritual kingdom, able without worldly force to subdue all the powers and kingdoms of this world" that Christ rejects absolutely the jurisdiction of civil magistrates over conscience. No offices, Milton writes, are "more different than state and church government" (*CP*, 844). To engineer an Erastian solution to the church-state problem is an act of profane slavishness that rejects the freedom from fear offered by the gospel; by subordinating the church to the civil sovereign, we are "now servile towards the magistrate: who by subjecting us to his punishment ... brings back into religion that law of terror and satisfaction belonging now only to civil crimes: thereby in effect abolishes the gospel, by establishing again the law to a far worse yoke of servitude upon us than before" (*CP*, 851). The separation of church and state is both a secular necessity and a divinely authored decree. For Milton, to organize the Commonwealth otherwise is profane: "If church and state be made one flesh again as under the law, let it be withal considered that God, who then joined them, hath now severed them; that which, he so ordaining, was then a lawful conjunction, to such on either side as join again what he hath severed would be nothing now but their own presumptuous fornication" (*CP*, 849). That the fusion of church and state should form "one flesh" bound together in "presumptuous fornication" is an unusually carnal figure, which we will see again in *Paradise Lost*, when the first parents are not joined as, but at the fall divided from being "one flesh." In each case, fornicators elevate their own historically insensitive pleasure over divine decree. But if indeed Milton resists the forcing of conscience as a profane presumption, why then does he seem unwilling to travel as far down the path of comprehensive toleration as Roger Williams?

The sticking point for Milton is the question of what to do about Roman Catholics; as scholars have long observed, popery seems to be beyond the pale of toleration. His objection is conventionally Protestant. Catholicism is idolatrous as it venerates men, ceremonies, rituals, and images; it is improbable as it lacks a basis in scripture; it is tyrannical as it pretends to universal political dominion and "punishes them who believe not as the church believes though against scripture" (*CP*, 846). In *Civil Power*, Milton has stronger words for Protestant persecutors – who should know better insofar as they should welcome the spirited interpretive debate over scripture – than he does for papists, though he seems to reject the cause of Catholic toleration: "As for popery and idolatry, why they also may not hence plead to be tolerated, I have much less to say. Their religion, the more considered, the less can be acknowledged a religion, but a Roman principality rather ... more rightly named a catholic heresy against the scripture, supported mainly by a civil, and except in Rome, a foreign power; justly therefore to be suspected, not tolerated, by the magistrate of another country." Since the conscience of the papist is enthralled to man instead of God, and to a foreign power, Milton proposes that "they ought not to be tolerated for just reason of state more than of religion" (*CP*, 846). He continues, harping on the string of idolatry, which is nothing more than an impiety "evidently against all scripture, both of the Old and New Testament ... the works thereof so manifest than a magistrate can hardly err in prohibiting and quite removing at least the public and scandalous use thereof" (*CP*, 846). When compounded with the shrill and venomous anti-Catholicism on display in *Of True Religion*, these kinds of arguments seem to be plain evidence of Milton's illiberal unwillingness to tolerate Catholicism; idolatry in particular is the antithesis of the Christian liberty that Milton's work always hopes to cultivate.[17]

These findings in *Civil Power* are part of the rising tide of a later Stuart civil religion. The limits of toleration are not to be drawn by the will of a magistrate who distinguishes between religion and irreligion however he may wish, but rather with reference to the broad social norms of the Commonwealth, which the magistrate is tasked with defending from carnal and spiritual licentiousness. It is necessary, in Milton's view, to leave the magistrate to his civil jurisdiction and allow that "things religious [be] settled by the churches within themselves; and the repressing of their contraries determinable by the common light of nature" (*CP*, 848). It is this last point – that a contingent definition of irreligion is to be socially determined by the common light of nature rather than imposed by private will – that links him deeply to the language of civil religion. In England, popery is to be controlled by the civil sword insofar as it threatens criminally the peace and security of the Commonwealth and insofar as it threatens to tear the social fabric by soliciting public scandals. Milton sees neither of the two prongs of his argument against Catholicism as theological or confessional, and indeed, he goes out of his way in the section above to distinguish between popery and idolatry, the former being an explicitly political threat to be suppressed for "just reason of state more than of religion" and the latter being an impious cause of "given" public scandal that stirs up tumult. In each case, Milton sees Catholicism – as the majority of the English people would have – as an irreligious imposition on right social order, a disloyal fifth column whose loyalty was attached indelibly to a foreign power.

For Milton, the only charitable and Christian remedies for irreligion are persuasive. As he grumbles in *Of True Religion* when facing the potential threat of a Catholic ascendancy, "I suppose it stands not with the clemency of the gospel, more than what appertains to the security of the state" to sanction papists with corporal punishments, fines, and penal restrictions.[18] Here again the objection to idolatry is both scriptural and civil, for it offends God and causes "grievous and unsufferable scandal [to be] given to all conscientious beholders." Idolatry is a secular problem and not a doctrinal one; it is an irreligious practice that scandalizes the community, incites a violent response, and tears the social fabric of the kingdom. Criminal treason falls under the jurisdiction of the civil sword, but as an irreligious practice, popery must be controlled only through persuasion or "force inward and spiritual, not outward and corporeal" (*CP*, 852).

Even in Milton's late tract, *Of True Religion*, which seems to give no quarter to popery, Milton's remedies are persuasive rather than compulsory.[19] He leaves it "to the consideration of all magistrates, who are best able to provide for their own and the public safety" whether or not to tolerate the presence of traitors in league with a foreign power, but when it comes to the removal of popery from the English body politic, Milton never calls for the assistance of the civil sword. How then to suppress popery in "our natives"? *Sola scriptura*. "Even an ordinary English protestant, well-read in the Bible" can repudiate "their idolatries," and it is in such public disputation, underwritten by the free circulation of heterodox religious writings including "the idolatrous books of papists," that the gospel will win out. Beyond such a deliberative process, Milton calls for the patient hearing and reading of the gospel in public – civic education organized on broadly Protestant lines – and true to form he also calls for the national improvement of moral conduct.

But Milton's anti-Erastian arguments in *Civil Power* failed to persuade, and in the Restoration settlement, the Church of England roared back with its full fury.[20] Where Charles II had offered in his Declaration from Breda "a liberty for tender consciences" such that "no man shall be disquieted or called in question for differences of opinion in matter of religion which do not disturb the peace of the kingdom," the churchmen, aided by a pliable Parliament, insisted upon the uniformity of worship and the supremacy of the national church. In February 1663, for instance, the Commons advised the King that his offer of "liberty for tender consciences" was not a binding legal promise but was rather only a declaration of his legislative intention, an outline of a plan he hoped to implement with the advice of his Parliament. That same Parliament passed instead the Act of Uniformity and other such blunt instruments, and indeed the Commons used a familiar language as they rebuked the King for his Indulgence, his interest in toleration:

> it is humbly conceived, that the Indulgence proposed will be so far from tending to the Peace of the Kingdom, that it is likely rather to occasion great Disturbance: And, on the contrary, that the Asserting of the Laws, and the Religion established, according to the Act of Uniformity, is the most probable Means to produce a settled Peace and Obedience through the Kingdom; because the Variety of Professions in Religion, when openly indulged, doth directly distinguish Men into Parties, and, withal gives them Opportunity to count their Numbers; which, considering the Animosities that, out of a religious Pride, will be kept on Foot by the several Factions, doth tend, directly and inevitably, to open Disturbance: Nor can Your Majesty have any Security, that the Doctrine or Worship of the several Factions, which are all governed by a several Rule, shall be consistent with the Peace of Your Kingdom.[21]

The argument for uniformity and supremacy is, like the corresponding claims for liberty of conscience, linked to the maintenance of civil peace and social order. Sects devolve into factions and parties that inevitably create "great Disturbance" in both social and political terms. By atomizing the kingdom into rival factions, dissent weakens the moral and political authority of the Crown, while the heterodox practices of those sects cultivate only rivalry, animosity, and violence. Here we see the Commons co-opting the language of sociability and civil peace in stating that the ends of stability and tranquillity are only to be achieved through the uniformity and supremacy of the established church. The crucial distinction to note here, however, is that the Commons' advice to the King is entirely devoid of theological content or the expression of doctrinal orthodoxy. The Church of England is nowhere here the one true faith or the single path to salvation. It is instead just the "religion established," its supremacy linked by a sympathetic Parliament chiefly to the functional or instrumental ends of a "settled peace and obedience." Perhaps because assertions of orthodox belief no longer held sway in the chaotic and high-velocity marketplace of ideas spawned by the explosion of print culture and the decentralization of religious authority in the 1640s and 50s, advocates of a supreme and compulsory national church – men like Roger L'Estrange, Samuel Parker, and Archbishop Sheldon – were forced to enter a public conversation they had not created, where they had no choice but to use the language of "political sociability" first outlined in the mid-seventeenth century by tolerationists like Milton, Williams, and Henry Vane.

It is within such a tradition that we must view John Dryden, whose limitless hatred of priestcraft usually put him at odds with the High Church party and their scribbling creatures.[22] Dryden took a utilitarian view of religious liberty, and his version of the political sociability test was quite capacious, as we can see in, for instance, his affirmative portraits of natural religion as exercised by infidel princes in his heroic plays. Political stability and civil peace were for Dryden of the highest significance, and he was scarcely if at all interested in questions of controversial theology. Because his commitment to the Stuart kings was so durable (and occasionally puzzling), Dryden has often been understood as an uncomplicated apologist for church and king eager to squash religious and political dissenters. Deeply sceptical of the intermeddling of wicked priests in temporal affairs (a recurring figure in most of his serious plays), Dryden was usually at odds with the Establishment. His writings – from the early heroic plays to later tragedies like *The Duke of Guise* and from *Absalom and Achitophel* to *The Hind and the Panther* – are marked by a series of structuring oppositions. Dryden valued tradition and custom over innovation, a stable social order over radical social change, inner piety over religious uniformity, civil peace over individual liberty. He valued especially the mixed English constitution, understanding the liberties and rights of the subject to have been transmitted by posterity and expressed in the formula of the King-in-Parliament. His sovereign was to be the custodian of the people's timeless rights when the work of demagogues and enthusiasts seduced them into rebellion, and such a prince had to sit above the law in order to control a wayward people.

Dryden saw in his opponents the rising spirit of raw appetite – naked self-interest gussied up seductively to mislead the people. The stable English constitutional tradition was for Dryden threatened not by the ideas contained within dissent or classical republicanism – it was indeed quite flexible and accommodating – but rather by bad actors like the Earl of Shaftesbury or the Duke of Monmouth, who sought to aggrandize themselves at the expense of the Commonwealth and its enduring constitution. Enthusiasm, superstition, sectarian division, and priestcraft of all kinds were the most noxious forms of malevolent appetite; here Dryden saw interest and ambition as the demonic antitypes of inner piety and the peaceable searching after grace. Dryden cast his lot with the secular state even though he was deeply critical of the more cynical forms of Erastianism. His suspicion of excessive religious appetite of all kinds (from Anglican priestcraft to village Ranterism), his appeal to assimilationist legal and religious norms of the English nation, and his utilitarian view of religious pluralism put Dryden squarely at the centre of the flourishing language of English civil religion. Dryden is not the most affirmative writer in this period – he is in many ways a conservative crank whose writing is usually corrosive, venomous, and bitterly dismissive of his opponents – but his work is a crucial and influential pathway through which the language of civil religion moves into the contested space of the popular imagination.

In 1684, as the Church of England increasingly sought to disentangle itself from the Crown, Dryden began to heal his own breach with the "reverend divines" whom he had, so often before, gleefully accused of priestcraft. The instrument of this gesture was *Religio Laici*, a poem that asserts the supremacy of tradition over enthusiasm in the charged work of scriptural interpretation. Although the poem was not a popular success in the way that *Absalom and Achitophel* had been, Dryden nonetheless saw it as an instrument of public political education rather than a profession of faith: he described the poem as written in "the legislative style ... since a man is to be cheated into passion but to be reasoned into truth." And he supplemented his reasoned appeal to tradition and custom with a strong claim to see religion as a question of political sociability:

> Faith is not built on disquisitions vain;
> The things we must believe are few and plain:
> But since men will believe more than they need,
> And every man will make himself a creed;
> In doubtful questions 'tis the safest way
> To learn what unsuspected ancients say:
> For 'tis not likely we should higher soar
> In search of heaven, than all the Church before:
> ...
>
> And after hearing what our Church can say,
> If still our reason runs another way,

That private reason 'tis more just to curb,
Than by disputes the public peace disturb.
For points obscure are of small use to learn:
But common quiet is mankind's concern. (431–8, 445–50)

Dryden takes individual searching – liberty of inward conscience – as a given here: "every man will make himself a creed." Because the uniformity of religious belief was impossible, and because the national church had declined in its utility, the remedy for religious pluralism had to be purely functional. Tradition is the best guide because it is vetted by time and long experience (rather like the English constitution), though not because it has a monopoly on salvation or a verifiable claim of right belief. And even if the claims of conscience lead a subject to reject tradition, they must curb their enthusiasm, subordinating their individual right of free exercise to the controlling interests of the community. Dryden is here strategically conflating "private reason" or individual conscience with "points obscure ... of small use" in order to move past the evaluative language of toleration, which is a category predicated upon first the content and second the exercise of belief. The essential qualities of later Stuart civil religion are vividly on display in the last axiomatic line of this verse paragraph: "common quiet is mankind's concern." We are well on our way here to an understanding (no doubt influenced by Hobbes) of religion as an anthropological phenomenon, a set of practices to be understood with analytical tools; these same years witness the rise of disciplines and the first systematic blossoming of the study of idolatry under the sign of comparative religion.[23]

At this point, I circle back to Milton, thinking about *Samson Agonistes* as an exceptional case in his late works, considering the late verse tragedy as an example of Milton's descriptive anthropology of religion – as a study of idolatry through the lens of comparative religion rather than as a work designed chiefly for normative persuasion. *Paradise Lost* and the "brief epic" of Christ's temptation, *Paradise Regained*, are both understood widely as works designed to cultivate godly virtue and individual excellence in their readers. Those poems are in the end aimed at the therapeutic transformation of the English people; they are doing the work of evangelical persuasion that Milton so values. *Samson* is another matter entirely. The play – a closet tragedy modelled on Aristotelian principles – is often understood in relation to its double, *Paradise Regained*, with which it was published in 1671; *Samson*, by many accounts, is Milton's sketch of the normative world of the Hebrew Scriptures, what he would have called the severe "old law" uttered by a vengeful and jealous God. In describing Samson's humiliation in Gaza at the hands of the idolatrous Philistines and then his enthusiastic and self-consuming retaliation, Milton begins the typological arc that bends towards the merciful dispensation of the Gospel, that new law expressed by Christ and vividly on display in *Paradise Regained*. Compelled to attend the feast of Dagon, Samson acquiesces; he serves the Philistines "not in thir Idol-Worship, but [rather] by labor / Honest and lawful to deserve my food / Of those that have me in thir civil power."[24] When Samson feels within the "rousing motions" that compel him forward to "some great act" (ll. 1382, 28), his therapeutic reclamation has been achieved; his self-lacerating doubt gives way before an enthusiastic but vacant purposiveness. The consequence is what some have called, intemperately, a "martyrdom operation." He pulls the temple of the Philistines down, destroying himself along with a Philistine aristocracy "drunk with idolatry" that had called "in haste for thir destroyer" (ll. 1670, 1678).

In the aftermath of this final act, Samson's father Manoa is pleased to erect a shrine – if not an idol – to Samson at his home:

> there will I build him
> A Monument, and plant it round with shade
> Of Laurel ever green, and branching Palm,
> With all his trophies hung, and Acts enrolled
> In copious legend, or sweet lyric song.
> Thither shall all the valiant youth resort,
> And from his memory inflame their breasts
> To matchless valor and adventures high. (ll. 1733–40)

As is often the case in Milton, this account is notable for what it omits; in his long speech of praise, Manoa largely avoids the angry God of the Israelites who has just used Samson as the instrument of "wrath divine" (ll. 1683). Manoa's monument is not a profane idol as some have proposed, but rather it is the material premise for a complete symbolic language that will give the Israelites a spur "to matchless valor and adventures high," and a charge for "that band … to resist" their Philistine oppressors (ll. 1740, 1753). The monument has little to say about right belief or godliness; it commemorates Samson and in so doing calls into being a fund of language – those legends and sweet lyric songs – that give to the Israelites identity and inspiration. Put another way, Manoa frames a set of durable secular rituals that firm up the horizontal bonds of national belonging. As readers of Milton's epics, somewhere around here we ought to expect an appeal to the consolations of the inviolable conscience or of the buffered self; despite a corrupt age, the argument goes, the godly can remain unpolluted as long as they cultivate the "paradise within, happier far." But as *Samson Agonistes* winds towards its conclusion, instead Milton provides only an uncharacteristic appeal to a purely inscrutable God: "All is best, though we oft doubt, / What th'unsearchable dispose / Of highest wisdom bring about, / And ever best found in the close" (ll. 1745–8). The final appeal in the play is to the consolations of experience: "this great event" will have taught God's servants "peace and consolation ... and calm of mind, all passion spent" (ll. 1756–8). Milton's play describes enthusiastic violence and idolatry just as it describes the formation of a crude style of Israelite civil religion around the memory of Samson.

But the play's denouement, I would propose, is Milton's searching analysis of the attractions and the demerits of the theory of civil religion. Religious violence is exhausted, the antisocial passions are liquidated, and the consolations of peace are to have been demonstrated. But secular violence remains, and indeed the "adventures high" and "matchless valor" of the young Israelite heroes seem to promise an energetic commitment to armed national resistance. So too in later Stuart England did the language of civil religion seem at once like a rational remedy for the problem of sectarian violence and a potentially coercive imposition of the nation as the new measure of political belonging. Because the common peace of the many is valued over the religious rights of the few, and because functional or utilitarian interest outweighs truth claims, and especially because that common peace is attached so firmly to the racial and legal constitution of the English people, the rise of the language of civil religion in later Stuart England may mark a secularizing trend, but it is also an augury of consolidation around the more durable abstraction of the nation.

NOTES

1 Robert Bellah, "Civil Religion in America," passim.
2 Mark Goldie, "The Civil Religion of James Harrington," p. 197.
3 Larry Kramer, *The People Themselves: Popular Constitutionalism and Judicial Review in America*, pp. 9–14.

4 John Spurr, *The Restoration Church of England*, p. 78.
5 Steven Pincus, "From Holy Cause to Economic Interest," passim; on the rising language of political economy, see also Blair Hoxby, *Mammon's Music: Literature and Economics in the Age of Milton*, pp. 1–61.
6 Blair Worden, "The Question of Secularization," in *A Nation Transformed*, p. 39.
7 On the disputes between assimiliationist and individualist approaches to the regulation of religious speech, and the secular control of inflammatory religious speech more generally, see Robert Post, "Cultural Heterogeneity and Law: Blasphemy, Pornography, and the First Amendment"; Sarah Barringer Gordon, "Blasphemy and the Law of Religious Liberty in Nineteenth-Century America"; Stuart Banner, "When Christianity Was Part of the Common Law"; and my article, "The Invention of Criminal Blasphemy," pp. 30–54.
8 John Coffey, "Liberty and Property Revisited: The Question of Toleration in the English Revolution," p. 965.
9 Coffey, "Liberty and Property Revisited," p. 975.
10 Roger Williams, *The Bloudy Tenent of Persecution for Cause of Conscience*, p. 3.
11 Roger Williams, "A Letter to Providence Plantation, January 1655," in *The Correspondence of Roger Williams*, vol. II, pp. 424–5.
12 *Charter of Rhode Island and Providence Plantation, June 15, 1663*. The second full paragraph of the charter outlines the grant of religious liberty: "And whereas, in theire humble addresse, they have ffreely declared, that it is much on their hearts (if they may be permitted), to hold forth a livlie experiment, that a most flourishing civill state may stand and best bee maintained, and that among our English subjects. with a full libertie in religious concernements; and that true pietye rightly grounded upon gospell principles, will give the best and greatest security to sovereignetye, and will lay in the hearts of men the strongest obligations to true loyaltye: Now know bee, that wee beinge willinge to encourage the hopefull undertakeinge of oure sayd lovall and loveinge subjects, and to secure them in the free exercise and enjovment of all theire civill and religious rights, appertaining to them, as our loveing subjects; and to preserve unto them that libertye, in the true Christian ffaith and worshipp of God, which they have sought with soe much travaill, and with peaceable myndes, and lovall subjectione to our royall progenitors and ourselves, to enjoye; and because some of the people and inhabitants of the same colonie cannot, in theire private opinions, conforms to the publique exercise of religion, according to the litturgy, formes and ceremonyes of the Church of England, or take or subscribe the oaths and articles made and established in that

behalfe; and for that the same, by reason of the remote distances of those places, will (as wee hope) bee noe breach of the unitie and unifformitie established in this nation: Have therefore thought ffit, and doe hereby publish, graunt, ordeyne and declare, That our royall will and pleasure is, that noe person within the sayd colonye, at any tyme hereafter, shall bee any wise molested, punished, disquieted, or called in question, for any differences in opinione in matters of religion, and doe not actually disturb the civill peace of our sayd colony; but that all and everye person and persons may, from tyme to tyme, and at all tymes hereafter, freelye and fullye have and enjoye his and theire owne judgments and consciences, in matters of religious concernments, throughout the tract of lance hereafter mentioned; they behaving themselves peaceablie and quietlie, and not useing this libertie to lycentiousnesse and profanenesse, nor to the civill injurye or outward disturbeance of others; any lawe, statute, or clause, therein contayned, or to bee contayned, usage or custome of this realme, to the contrary hereof, in any wise, notwithstanding. And that they may bee in the better capacity to defend themselves, in theire just rights and libertyes against all the enemies of the Christian ffaith, and others, in all respects, wee have further thought fit, and at the humble petition of the persons aforesayd are gratiously pleased to declare, That they shall have and enjoye the benefist of our late act of indempnity and ffree pardon, as the rest of our subjects in other our dominions and territoryes have; and to create and make them a bodye politique or corporate, with the powers and priviledges hereinafter mentioned."

13 Milton, "On the New Forcers of Conscience Under the Long Parliament," *Complete Poems and Major Prose*, p. 145.

14 Milton, "Sonnet XVI," *Complete Poems*, pp. 160–1.

15 My discussion here is indebted generally to Martin Dzelzainis, "Milton and Antitrinitarianism."

16 Milton, *Complete Poems*, p. 839. Subsequent references are to this edition and will appear parenthetically in the text following the abbreviation *CP*.

17 Barbara Lewalski, "Milton and Idolatry," pp. 218–20.

18 John Milton, "Of True Religion, Haeresie, Schism, Toleration And What Best Means May Be Used Against the Growth of Popery," p. 11.

19 Nicholas von Maltzahn, "Milton, Marvell, and Toleration," pp. 97–8.

20 It is easy enough to find proponents of an Erastian civil religion – both Hobbes and Harrington fit the bill here, though the former is far less tolerant of a mixed church-state than the latter, who in *Oceana* sees an established and rationalized church as a crucial component of his republican political machinery. As Goldie has pointed out, for Harrington, a religious

establishment is in the end devoted to the service of the state – it is one of many technical solutions to the political problem. But Hobbes had been, true to form, less temperate in *Leviathan*. Hobbes repeatedly goes out of his way to emphasize the dangers of priestcraft in all its forms, including the cynical manipulation of popular fear or longing and the cultivation of divided loyalties between temporal and spiritual lords. He rejects any political arrangement in which the "ghostly authority" of the church (especially as expressed in the excommunicating power) rivals the authority of the civil sovereign. The sovereign might for reasons of state establish a national church or tolerate denominational pluralism. So too could the sovereign subcontract out the pastoral care of his subjects to a pope or a disciplinary committee of presbyters, but in no case did individual religious belief or confessional membership authorize armed resistance to the sovereign. The plain effect of such confusion was "civil war and dissolution" of the Commonwealth: "Temporal and spiritual government are but two words brought into the world to make men see double and mistake their lawful sovereign … There is, therefore, no other government in this life, neither of state nor religion, but temporal; nor teaching of any doctrine, lawful to any subject, which the governor, both of the state and of the religion, forbiddeth to be taught. And that governor must be one, or else there must needs follow faction and civil war in the commonwealth; between the Church and the State; between spiritualists and temporalists; between the sword of justice and the shield of faith; and (which is more) in every Christian man's own breast, between the Christian and the man," p. 216. From this Erastian stance, liberty of conscience is a possible (and often desirable) manifestation of the civil sovereign's will, but the subject has no natural right to religious liberty and the sovereign is not obliged to provide it. Thomas Hobbes, *Leviathan*.

21 *House of Commons Journal*, vol. 8, no. 27 (February 1663), pp. 421–3.

22 Oscar Kenshur, "Scriptural Deism and the Politics of Dryden's *Religio Laici*."

23 Jonathan Sheehan, "Sacred and Profane: Idolatry, Antiquarianism, and the Polemics of Distinction in the Seventeenth Century," p. 38.

24 Milton, *Samson Agonistes*, in *Collected Poems*, ll. 1365–7. All subsequent references are to this edition and appear parenthetically in the text.

BIBLIOGRAPHY

Banner, Stuart. "When Christianity Was Part of the Common Law." *Law and History Review* 16 (1988): 27–62.

Bellah, Robert. "Civil Religion in America." *Daedalus* 134, no. 4 (1967): 40–55.

Charter of Rhode Island and Providence Plantation, 15 June, 1663. *The Avalon Project*. http://avalon.law.yale.edu/17th_century/ri04.asp. 18 June 2012.

Coffey, John. "Liberty and Property Revisited: The Question of Toleration in the English Revolution." *Historical Journal* 41, no. 4 (1998): 961–85.

Dzelzainis, Martin. "Milton and Antitrinitarianism." In *Milton and Toleration*. Ed. Sharon Achinstein and Elizabeth Sauer. Oxford: Oxford UP, 2007. 171–85.

Goldie, Mark. "The Civil Religion of James Harrington." In *The Languages of Political Theory in Early Modern Europe*. Ed. Anthony Pagden. Cambridge: Cambridge UP, 1987. 197–222.

Gordon, Sarah Barringer. "Blasphemy and the Law of Religious Liberty in Nineteenth- Century America." *American Quarterly* 52 (2000): 682–719.

Hobbes, Thomas. *Leviathan*. Ed. Edwin Curley. Indianapolis: Hackett, 1994.

House of Commons Journal. 8.27 (February 1663): 441–3. *British History Online*. http://www.british-history.ac.uk/report.aspx?compid=26531. 18 June 2012.

Hoxby, Blair. *Mammon's Music: Literature and Economics in the Age of Milton*. New Haven, CT: Yale UP, 2004.

Kenshur, Oscar. "Scriptural Deism and the Politics of Dryden's *Religio Laici*." *ELH* 54 (1987): 869–92.

Kramer, Larry. *The People Themselves: Popular Constitutionalism and Judicial Review in America*. New York: Oxford UP, 2004.

Lewalski, Barbara. "Milton and Idolatry." *SEL* 43 (2003): 213–32.

Milton, John. *Complete Poems and Major Prose*. Ed. Merritt Y. Hughes. New York: Macmillan, 1957.

– *Of True Religion, Haeresie, Schism & Toleration*. London, 1673.

Pincus, Steven. "From Holy Cause to Economic Interest." In *A Nation Transformed*. Ed. Alan Houston and Steve Pincus. New York: Cambridge UP, 2001. 272–98.

Post, Robert. "Cultural Heterogeneity and Law: Blasphemy, Pornography, and the First Amendment." *California Law Review* 76, no. 2 (1988): 297–335.

Sheehan, Jonathan. "Sacred and Profane: Idolatry, Antiquarianism, and the Polemics of Distinction in the Seventeenth Century." *Past and Present* 192, no. 1 (2006): 35–66.

Spurr, John. *The Restoration Church of England*. New Haven, CT: Yale UP, 1991.

Visconsi, Elliott. "The Invention of Criminal Blasphemy." *Representations* 103 (2008): 30–52.

Von Maltzahn, Nicholas. "Milton, Marvell, and Tolerations." In *Milton and Toleration*. Ed. Sharon Achinstein and Elizabeth Sauer. New York: Oxford UP, 2007. 86–106.

Williams, Roger. *The Bloudy Tenent of Persecution for cause of conscience*. London, 1644.

– "Letter to Providence January 1655/6." In *The Correspondence of Roger Williams*. Ed. Glenn LeFantasie. 2 vols. Hanover, NH: UP of New England, 1988. 424.

Worden, Blair. "The Question of Secularization." In *A Nation Transformed*. Ed. Alan Houston and Steve Pincus. New York: Cambridge UP, 2001. 20–40.

12 Obnoxious Satan: Milton, Neo-Roman Justice, and the Burden of Grace

PAUL STEVENS

In memoriam Marshall Grossman

In the final essay of his influential 1998 collection *Liberty before Liberalism*, Quentin Skinner reflects on his practice as an historian. He thinks of his work, so he says, as that of an archaeologist, a digger unearthing long-forgotten and disused artefacts, bringing them back to the surface, dusting them down, and so enabling us to reconsider what we think of them. In his case, the artefacts are political theories, ideas, or systems of ideas, and what is remarkable about them is their obsolescence: the artefacts that most interest him constitute "a repository of values we no longer endorse, of questions we no longer ask."[1] While Skinner is conventional in seeing the relationship between past and present as an intertwining of continuities and discontinuities, he is unusual in acknowledging that his interest always tends to fall on the discontinuities, on the things that got thrown away, on the dead ends of history. But he is no roving, maggoty-headed Aubrey, no collector of idle curiosities. He bristles at the charge of antiquarianism, and his defence of a practice that might seem at first sight so self-indulgent or useless is not only that the discontinuities make us look at the continuities in a fresh light but that in defamiliarizing the present they allow us to see alternatives to it. While we might say that their otherness is liberating, Skinner is more conservative and simply wants to understand more clearly the choices he claims our culture has made in the process of creating the present. This, then, is why he is so interested in what he considers the long-forgotten neo-Roman theory of free states. Much in this theory seems familiar. Individual liberty is inseparable from the liberty of the state, polity, or nation: that is, only in free states can a citizen be truly free, and what makes a state free or a *civitas libera* is sovereignty or independence from without, equal subjection of every citizen to the rule of law, and consensual, if not democratic, government from within. What makes neo-Roman theory so distinctive, however, is not the relation between individual liberty and the liberty of the state so much as its now obsolete understanding of what Skinner calls "un-freedom" as something close to the condition of slavery.[2] Lack of freedom and the injustice it entails is not understood as the effect of coercion but much more radically as that of dependence, and dependence is frequently figured in terms of slavery. It is a key assumption of modern, mainstream liberalism, Skinner explains, "that force or the coercive threat of it constitute the only forms of constraint that interfere with individual liberty."[3] For neo-Roman writers like Marchamont Nedham or James Harrington, however, "to live in a condition of dependence is in itself a source or form of constraint,"[4] the full pain of which can only be expressed by likening it to a state of slavery.[5] That is, individual liberty is felt to be violated by what might seem to us relatively innocuous or necessary forms of legal or political dependency. Executive privilege or the routine prerogative power of any current president or prime minister, for instance, might be considered arbitrary and inimical to neo-Roman liberty. Such a conviction argues an extraordinarily aggressive or heightened sense of individual agency or personal virtue. Dependency saps virtue, the specific quality of *virtus* that makes a man a man and truly free, or in Latin, a *vir*. What I want to suggest in this chapter is that Skinner's insight, the fruit of his apparently pointless archaeological work, has dramatic implications for Milton's understanding of grace and its relation to justice. That is, Milton's increasingly neo-Roman conception of justice draws attention to the degree to which God's grace might feel anything but liberating.

My argument falls into three parts. First, I want to focus on *Samson Agonistes* in order to rethink the dangers implicit in such an undertaking, that is, the limitations of a critical practice that encourages us to apply unmediated political theory, no matter how historically specific, too directly to literature, flattening out formal distinctions and happily turning poems into pamphlets, making, as the late Marshall Grossman put it, "art [merely] documentary."[6] Second, I want to use this caveat to focus on Satan and begin an exploration of what Milton understands by grace, most importantly, by suggesting how Skinner's insight helps us see just how neo-Roman antipathy to dependence creates problems for Milton's biblical understanding of grace and its transformative sense of justice. And third,

I want to suggest that these problems reveal a profound fissure between seventeenth-century habits of thinking about contingency and our own, a fissure between what we might provisionally call a culture of grace and one of growth. Let me begin with neo-Roman theory and *Samson Agonistes*.

I

In a very fine recent essay, one of Skinner's admirers, Rosanna Cox, provides an impressively succinct and lucid example of just how useful applying neo-Roman theory to Milton can be.[7] She is very effective in showing how *Samson Agonistes* illustrates the misery of unfreedom as dependency, the mental anguish of being *in potestate alieni*, that is, the debilitating effect of being in the power of others. Being in such a base condition, being a dependent in law, is the defining condition not only of slaves, but of children before they come of age and women in the context of family or household. All this is made clear, she indicates following Skinner, in one of the principal classical sources for neo-Roman legal theory, the *Corpus Juris Civilis* of the sixth-century Emperor Justinian, a set of texts to which Milton refers directly in his *Commonplace Book* (*CPW* 1:470).[8] Accordingly, she is entirely persuasive in showing how Samson is "thrice enslaved"[9] – servile, effeminate, and childish. In many respects, her case is even stronger than she claims, for Samson actually refers to himself as being *in potestate alieni* when he confesses himself to be quite literally in the "power of others, never in my own" (*Samson Agonistes*, 78) – his blindness being imagined as a synecdoche for his legal status. He sees himself as being "obnoxious" (106), precisely the term used by Sallust and Tacitus to articulate the contemptible nature or slavishness of being at the mercy of others, of being liable to harm or punishment.[10] At its most effective, Cox's essay is compelling in bringing home just how dangerous all forms of dependency are in habituating both individual and nation to slavery. The famous passage in *Eikonoklastes* where the English forsake their true nature, their "old English fortitude and love of Freedom" (*CPW* 3:344), indeed their very agency, for a kind of self-abnegation before the King's image is made to explain how nations grow corrupt and the English in the shape of Samson's Israelites have come to love their bondage (*Samson Agonistes*, 6–7). The fact that Samson hates his bondage is the most immediate indication that his virtue, his independence, manliness, and maturity are still, to some extent at least, intact. His condition may be slavish but his mind is not. Cox's essay is at its least effective, however, in its account of Dalila, and the tenaciously programmatic quality of that account is central to my argument.

Because Dalila is judged according to the precepts of Roman law with such single-mindedness, all kinds of troubling details get obscured and the text is made to appear far more stable than it quite evidently is. According to Roman law, says Cox, Dalila turns out to be "a monstrous perversion of masculinity."[11] Her appeal to civic virtue, to the "grounded maxim" that "to the public good / Private respects must yield" (*Samson Agonistes*, 865–8), is perverse because as a wife she has no right to make such an appeal in the context of her marriage. Since Dalila is legally within the power of her husband, her sacrifice of Samson to the authorities is anything but an act of civic virtue: "in overstepping the bounds of appropriate female behavior," says Cox, "she has not displayed *virtus* because, as a woman, it is simply not available to her. In fact, in her failure to privilege 'the faith of wedlock-bands"'(*Samson Agonistes*, 986), she exemplifies the utter perversion of the natural order."[12] Dalila's parody of civic virtue, so Cox feels, is the last act in a marriage notorious for the unnatural dominance of the wife and the highly sexual uxoriousness of her husband, characteristics quite alien to the ideal of marriage imagined in Roman law and indeed in Milton's own divorce tracts, a set of texts where marriage is idealized as a companionate union of "meet and happy conversation."[13]

Strong as this reading is, two problems immediately come to mind, both of them rooted in an unwillingness to come to terms with one of the most important formal or artistic decisions Milton has made in the creation of his dramatic poem, that is, his decision to express the horror of contemporary internal, civil subjection in the biblical figure of external, national oppression. By doing so, I want to suggest, Milton renders whatever political purpose he has overdetermined. By mapping the English people's willing acceptance of a corrupt government onto ancient Israel's conquest by an alien and irredeemably impure nation, he renders it extremely difficult to produce any kind of comprehensive interpretation of the poem in terms of neo-Roman law. The biblical story comes with its own set of protocols, and these don't always jibe with neo-Roman theory. However satisfying from an emotional, expressive, or aesthetic point of view this radical move to figure civil subjection in terms of external Philistine oppression might be, from a pragmatic perspective, as a call to political action, it is a source of considerable confusion – as the record of the poem's reception continues to demonstrate.[14]

The first problem is that because of the biblical quality of their national differences, the marriage of Samson and Dalila is vitiated from the outset. It is hardly the good faith union imagined in either Roman law or the divorce tracts. There is no evidence to suggest, for instance, that Milton married Mary Powell to deliver England from bondage or to oppress Oxfordshire's minor gentry – no matter how laudable many of us might feel such a venture to be. Despite the very real impact of Dalila's beauty, Samson makes it clear over and again that his prime or ideal motive for marrying Dalila was exactly the same as that of the biblical Samson for marrying the woman of Timnath; that is, as the Book of Judges puts it, "he sought occasion against the Philistines" (14:4). In *Samson Agonistes*, sanctioned by the "Divine impulsion" of his first marriage (422), he marries Dalila in order to do harm to her people – "watching to oppress / Israel's oppressors" (232–3). Despite his protestation to the Philistine Harapha that his first marriage "argued me no foe" (1193), his final justification for entering into both unions was, as his father concedes and Scripture confirms, to find "some occasion to infest our foes" (423). Although Dalila knows from the beginning, so Samson claims, that he was her "country's foe professed" (884), she does not know that oppressing her country was his principal purpose for marrying her. Samson's appeals to the sanctity of marriage thus seem more than a little disingenuous – whether Milton intended it or not. If this is the case, then, it also seems unclear why Dalila's final tortured appeal to the authority of her religion, the well-being of her civic community, should be dismissed *tout court* as "a perversion of the natural order." It may be hateful to Samson, but since the marriage has been compromised from the outset, even by Roman standards, it is hardly unnatural. My point is that Milton's poem is written in such a way that its relativism, whether deliberately or inadvertently, is substantial, not a straw man or painted figure, but a deeply embedded cause for concern. In a political pamphlet where the text's pragmatic purpose might need to be more direct, he may well have tried harder to control his relativism, what the chorus calls his "wandering thought" (302), but in his poetry the often subversive fertility of his imagination seems to have been given a much freer rein. One of the marks of Milton's greatness as an artist, as a dramatist schooled in what he calls at the beginning of *Paradise Lost* "our best English tragedies" (note on "The Verse"), is that in his poetry he is willing to reach deep within himself and give his enemies – Comus, Dalila, Satan – an authentic voice, sometimes indeed, his own voice.

Thus Dalila's identification of herself with the Israelite heroine Jael is not to be taken lightly (988–90). It may be specious from Samson's and Manoa's ancient Hebrew point of view, but from that of Milton the many-minded poet and international humanist, the admirer of Cardinal Francesco Barberini and Protestant apostates like Lucas Holst, the problem seems much more difficult.[15] And perhaps it has to be if Milton's poem is to aspire to the greatness of a critically important biblical model like the Book of Job.[16] In what exactly do the two female heroines differ? We are made to wonder. Jael is not her victim's wife, it is true, but her act of betrayal is every bit as brutal, bloody, and deceitful as Dalila's, and its morality can only be distinguished from the Philistine's not by an appeal to reason or Roman law but by revelation, by the scriptural assurance that while Jael serves God, Dalila does not. But if this is the case, then the biblical example of Jael makes it clear that in certain circumstances it is perfectly appropriate for a woman to behave like a man and *virtus* certainly is available to her. In fact, according to Scripture, Jael is a model of civic, or more accurately, national virtue, because unlike the fence-sitting Israelites of Meroz, the "cold neuters" against whom Milton rails in his 1642 *Apology* (*CPW* 1: 68), Jael acts.[17] She may only be a Kenite ally of Israel, but unlike the Hebrew natives of Meroz she doesn't hesitate to deceive the defeated Canaanite general Sisera, break the good faith bonds of hospitality, and drive a stake through the poor man's sleeping skull. "Most blessed of women be Jael," the prophet Deborah exults. "So perish all your enemies, O Lord! But may your friends be like the sun as it rises in its might" (Judges 5:24, 5:31). But even Deborah knows there's an issue here, and Milton's relativism may have been encouraged by the female prophet's fleeting and conflicted memory for Sisera's mother: "The mother of Sisera looked out of her window," Deborah says, "and cried through the lattice, Why is his chariot so long in coming? why tarry the wheels of his chariots?" (Judges 5:28–30). The second problem brings us to the heart of the matter.

For Cox what matters in *Samson Agonistes* is not the outcome but the process by which Samson arrives at his final act of heroic resistance. The problem is that she sees that process quite specifically as the story of a Roman recovery. That's the point of her essay. But for Milton "a Roman recovery" is, as he explains in *Areopagitica,* one that occurs explicitly without "the strong assistance of God our deliverer" (*CPW* 2:487). According to Cox, Samson's resistance "is all the more significant because it rises from within himself: no longer does he expect God to appear to act or to inspire; nor does he impugn God for his absence and failure to intervene. Instead, Samson is now able to reason, to accept blame, and to act for himself."[18] He is free, in no one's power, and able to act for himself. Although her carefully placed phrase "appear to" allows some room for God's grace should we wish to see it, Cox's strong neo-Roman reading encourages us to forget about God's role and the work of grace. This is hardly the intent of the poem and in its indifference to the work of prevenient grace, her reading of *Samson* for all its topspin is ultimately as misleading as that of Dalila. Having said this, however, it needs to be emphasized that Cox's analysis is of enormous value, because in demonstrating how easy it is to produce a neo-Roman reading, it inadvertently reveals the degree to which Skinner's original insight suggests a deep-rooted emotional ambivalence on Milton's part to the Christian doctrine of grace. When he thinks of grace as liberation, most importantly from the law, the letter, and all its works, his joy is palpable, but when he gives rein to his wandering thoughts, as he does so often in his poetry, and thinks of grace as dependency, he is perfectly capable of entering into the spirit of Satan's proud imaginations and seeing it as "obnoxious," that is, as a state of being quite literally *ob / noxia*, liable to harm or punishment, as a state of abjection similar to the one he has struggled against all his life. He knows only too well what Satan feels like, merit impaired and the feet of those in power on your neck.[19] This temperamental disposition is exacerbated by his humanist education in general and by his attraction to neo-Roman theory in particular. It is worth remembering that for so many of the classical authorities responsible for early modern neo-Roman theory – authorities Milton loved – Christianity, with what Pliny calls its "cult-superstition" and emphasis on absolute self-abnegation before God's grace, is the religion of slaves or, as Tacitus puts it, of "a class hated for their abominations," of criminals "who deserve extreme and exemplary punishment."[20] Skinner makes the point in a striking aside: "According to the New Testament, drawing as it so often does on the assumptions of Roman moral philosophy," he says, "this [dependence, the dependence of slaves on the will or goodwill of others] describes the nature of our relationship with God: we depend entirely on His benevolence."[21] From a neo-Roman perspective, the Christian doctrine of grace renders us obnoxious.

What I want to suggest then is that when grace is thought of in terms of absolute dependency, it is a source of considerable anxiety for Milton, it throws the precariousness of the doctrine itself into relief, and to some extent explains why scholars as acute and painstaking as Stephen Fallon are tempted to claim, quite mistakenly in my view, that Milton is not a religious writer.[22] Most importantly, it foregrounds a problem for the neo-Roman Milton with the Scriptural representation of grace. It suggests why he has such difficulty containing Satan and why he increasingly moves to reimagine grace as a matter of growth.

II

In one of his most recent books, Terry Eagleton, in a move worthy of Skinner's archaeologist, recaptures the long-forgotten centrality of God's freedom. God "created the world out of love, not need," he says. "There was nothing in it for him. The Creation is the original *acte gratuit*," the original act of gratuitousness or graciousness.[23] One can hear the influence of Charles Taylor in Eagleton's insistence on the fact that it is entirely, absolutely non-instrumental.[24] For Eagleton, the chief value of God himself is that he stands as "a kind of perpetual critique of instrumental reason."[25] While there is, of course, no single issue that dominates early modern English culture, if there were, it might well be this – the question of grace and God's freedom. The question is not simply a matter of religion, but, to use Debora Shuger's term, it is "a habit of thought" for the whole culture; it is a way of thinking that permeates to some degree or other every aspect of English life.[26] In his important book *The Literary Culture of the Reformation*, Brian Cummings makes it clear just how problematic this way of thinking is: "grace was at once the transcendent, incomprehensible gift of God, and yet the inevitable locus of religion," that is, of everyday religious practice.[27] It was so, because without grace, "there could be no God," that is, "God was only in the world through grace, and could only be apprehended by grace."[28] All meaning, religious, civil, and domestic, to a degree that is almost completely alien to our twenty-first-century culture of economic, social, and personal growth, turned on the contingency of grace.[29] Unlike growth, God's grace, especially in its more radical Protestant articulations, was not only unknowable – it was completely unobtainable by any kind of independent human agency, education, effort, or ingenuity. It was essential but profoundly uncertain. The question that tortured so many became how is grace to be facilitated – that is, "how is it possible to bring forth the completely gratuitous?"[30] The answer is, of course, faith, but the ways of faith are difficult to understand and always fraught with doubt. Doubt may be the condition of a servile mind for the neo-Roman theorist, as Cox contends, but it is the daily bread, the existential reality of the warfaring Christian. And Milton is, of course, both; that is, his way of being in the world is profoundly conflicted.

In order to capture the precariousness of the doctrine, Cummings offers an economic metaphor: "Rather than purchasing grace through works, or else mortgaging grace and surrendering works in repayment," he says, "the Christian offers them from an apparently supplementary credit."[31] The credit value of this supplement is in reality an illusion, because it can never be repaid. If taken at face value, it backfires, producing the spectre of a debt crisis that quite literally drives Marlowe's Faustus and Milton's Satan to despair – Satan rebels against God precisely in order to quit "The debt immense of endless gratitude, / So burdensome still paying, still to owe" (*Paradise Lost* 4.52–3). His sense of dependency is unbearable. He feels himself quite literally *in potestate domini*, in the power of his master, "obnoxious," liable to harm, impaired and injured, a debtor only worthy of contempt. He disdains subjection and, as generations of readers have indicated, it is hard not to feel the horror of his spiralling abjection:

> Me miserable! Which way shall I fly
> Infinite wrath and infinite despair?
> Which way I fly is hell; myself am hell;
> And in the lowest deep a lower deep
> Still threatening to devour me opens wide,
> To which the hell I suffer seems a heaven. (4.73–8)

If taken spiritually or figuratively, however, the supplementary credit of grace allows one the freedom to believe and act in the world. Satan knows this but still can't believe it. He knows that redemption turns on a simple *acte gratuit*, on his ability to believe in the paradox that this supplementary credit can be paid off simply by drawing on it in order to acknowledge it: he knows that "a grateful mind / By owing owes not, but still pays, at once / Indebted and discharged" of that debt (4.55–7). Exactly why he can't believe is of critical importance, and Milton's own act of belief in his blindness sonnet helps clarify, if not fully resolve, the issue.

According to Fallon, Satan can't believe for the same reason Milton himself can't believe: Milton may be a theological poet, but he is not really a believing or religious one.[32] For Fallon, the distinction between "theological" and "religious" turns on a person's absolute conviction of his or her sinfulness. For without that sense of one's own fallenness or depravity the experience of grace, that is, the immediate presence of God in one's life, can only be very limited and the doctrine itself becomes so much background noise. In all Milton's self-representations, Fallon claims, there is no record of "any sudden, blinding infusion of divine grace" and this failure, so he feels, is "a function of the apparent absence of a conviction of sin."[33] Although there is clearly something in Fallon's argument, in this particular formulation it is less than compelling. This is so, it seems to me, because redemption is not simply a matter of one's conviction of sin but of something infinitely larger. Conviction of sin, the "self-deploring and despairing," that thinkers like Luther dwell on is itself merely a part of a much greater recognition of God's freedom.[34] Consider the case of Job, a man without sin, a man who was "perfect and upright," "feared God," and "eschewed evil" (Job 1:1). Job is finally redeemed not so much by a sense of his unworthiness, though he certainly comes to feel that, but by the sudden, overwhelming, unmediated experience of God's freedom, the sublimity and sheer gratuitousness of his power and glory. When Yahweh finally speaks out of the whirlwind, the defiant Job cracks: "I know [now] that canst do every thing," he says, "and no thought can be witholden from thee ... therefore have I uttered that I understood not; things too wonderful for me, which I knew not ... Wherefore I abhor myself and repent in dust and ashes" (Job 42:2–6). The sense of wonder here marks the experience of transcendence. Fallon's assertion that there is no such moment in Milton, no record of a "sudden, blinding infusion of divine grace," is singularly inappropriate, since unlike so many of the endlessly self-confessing Puritans we are invited to admire, Milton actually was struck blind. And in that blindness, as the interregnum poetry records, he reveals a sensitivity to the various, daily workings of grace infinitely more painstaking and subtle than one finds in so many contemporary conversion narratives – a sensitivity impossible to dismiss as less than religious. During August 1653, for instance, Milton translated Psalms 1–8 and in these it requires a real effort not to hear the Job-like authenticity of his struggle with God's will over his blindness: "Lord in thine anger do not reprehend me / Nor in thy hot displeasure me correct; / Pity me Lord for I am much deject," he cries. Consider how "mine eye / Through grief consumes, is waxen old and dark" (Ps 6 ll. 1–3, 13–14).

For Milton, it needs to be emphasized, grace is not confined to the road to Damascus, but appears everywhere, most movingly, especially in his youth, in his experience of music. In the Ludlow Maske, for instance, God's action and our reaction are reproduced in the experience of the Lady's echo song, giving "resounding grace to all heaven's harmonies" (243). It is in the figure of echo that Milton at his most optimistic comes to see how God's absolute freedom and our relative freedom might coexist. In his maturity, he comes to understand the echoic function of grace not only in voice but in verse, where over and again imitation creates originality. In this he produces his own unique understanding of Luther's insistence on the relation between grammar and grace. As Cummings explains, Luther came to realize that the recurring phrase "Iustitia dei" in the Epistle to the Romans might be read not as an active but as a passive construction, and as it is repeated passively, "Iustitia" is transformed from the "justice which judges man" into "that by which man is justified"[35] – judgment becomes justification. In this single grammatical turn, the scales fall from his eyes and Luther experiences the liberation of God's grace. "It is in language that he locates his conversion," says Cummings, "in an epiphany of reading, a loving act of interpretation,"[36] not unlike the collaborative act of interpretation that Adam and Eve perform in Book X of *Paradise Lost*. As Job is justified by experiencing the actual appearance of God, so here, in the Epistle to the Romans, Luther is justified, so he feels, by reading Paul's explanation of the event of God's own redemptive sacrifice. It is a function of God's justice that he who was delivered for our offences, says Paul, "was raised again for our justification" (Romans 4:25). This manifestation of God's absolute freedom is what Alain Badiou calls a truth-event, that is, an event not immediately experienced but so remarkable that it opens up a conviction of extraordinary, unforeseen, and compelling possibility.[37] This is what animates both Paul and Luther, and something similar, but not quite, appears to happen in Milton's sonnet 16, "On his Blindness."

The full power of this poem can only be apprehended as a gracious echo of God's word, that is, in the poem's intertextual response to both the parable of the talents and, more importantly, the incident at Siloa's Brook. As Milton struggles with the immediate reality of his blindness in the winter of 1651–2, a test of faith more than a little hard to fake, he is reassured by the story of the blind man in John 9. The man's blindness is not so much a judgment, Milton learns, as an occasion of justification – not so much a consequence of sin in him or his parents as the occasion by which "the works of God should be made manifest" in Christ, says John (9:3). This reassurance is immediately dashed in the Gospel's story by Christ's urgent outburst: "I must work the works of him that sent me, while it is day; the night cometh, when no man can work" (John 9:4). It is this that precipitates Milton's downward spiral towards despair – for in his self-absorption he now identifies not with the blind man but with Christ, and in Milton's blindness it is already night. As he turns Christ's outburst into the terrified question, "Doth God exact day-labor, light denied" (7), he reveals the degree to which Christ's concern, if applied literally to himself, John Milton, is profoundly "fond" or foolish in that it inhibits God's freedom. The talent lodged with Milton is not "useless" or "death to hide" (3) if God does not want it to be. God's peculiar grace is beyond restraint and prevenient grace in the form of patience comes before "to prevent / That murmur" (8–9), insisting on God's own liberating freedom, the justice that justifies: "God doth not need / Either man's work or his own gifts" (9–10). In that simple turn, Milton is liberated not only from his terrible doubts but from the burden of his own responsibility or agency. For grace does not encourage him to resume his isolated prophetic stance; it insists that he is simply one of many: "They also serve who only stand and wait" (14). There is no question that Milton means what he says and that the poem is a performative utterance – it acts out the descent of grace it describes. Even so, the consolation the final courtly metaphor affords remains troubling; the conviction of possibility seems anticlimactic and limited, and it bears directly on Satan's inability to believe.

From Satan's neo-Roman perspective, a new and intensely nonbiblical perspective, what Milton has achieved is not liberation or a balance between God's freedom and his own but a renewed form of subjection. As the poet acknowledges God's "kingly" state and learns to bear his yoke, however "mild," he has learned to love his bondage. At the heart of the problem lies the degree to which grace and its justice cannot be separated from the biblical metaphor of divine kingship. According to the logic of this metaphor, Milton has become a courtier and not a very important one at that. As the poem's anticlimactic ending suggests, he seems to have given up all claim to agency, that is, to virtue or *virtus* in its original Latin sense. Even though he has done this in a way that is paradoxically not true of the poem's gracious process of interpretation, from Satan's neo-Roman perspective all he has done is demonstrate the bondage of the will and the tyranny of grace. To pursue this line of reasoning is, of course, as any freshman might object, to mire oneself in a category error. God is no earthly king, and although Milton routinely represents him as such, the poet, especially when he writes prose, is emphatic about the difference. In *The Ready and Easy Way*, for instance, he insists that the English people never covenanted with Charles I as though there were "no difference between a king and a god," and they never "promised him, as Job did to the Almightie, 'to trust in him though he slay us'"

(*CPW* 7:411). Having said this, the emotional force of subjection or dependency implicit in the metaphor's vehicle cannot so easily be separated from its tenor, and Milton is caught by his own scripturalism. All poetry is by definition a series of category errors – that's what metaphors are. And Milton has to use this particular metaphor because, as he explains in *De Doctrina Christiana*, he has to represent God as he represents himself in Scripture.[38] Nowhere is the difficulty of the metaphor more evident than in a text like Psalm 2, where God anoints David king in such a way that it dramatically undermines the familiar critique of monarchy in texts like I Samuel 8. More importantly, the absolute discontinuity between earthly and divine collapses as the psalm represents the human King David as Yahweh's only begotten son, Messiah: "Yet have I set my king upon my holy hill of Zion," declares Yahweh, and then addressing David directly, he says, "Thou art my Son; this day have I begotten thee. Ask of me and I will give thee the heathen [and all those who rebel against you] for thine inheritance, and the uttermost parts of the earth for thy possession. Thou shall break them with a rod of iron; thou shalt dash them in pieces like a potter's vessel" (Ps 2:6–9). They should look on you with fear and trembling. In his classic book *Writing the English Republic*, David Norbrook seizes on Milton's use of Psalm 2 in *Paradise Lost* to break the impasse between neo-Roman and biblical perspectives I have been describing.[39]

In Raphael's angelic epic, God somewhat confusingly initiates the master narrative of his charity not with what appears to be an act of grace but with Psalm 2's brutal assertion of monarchal power – an assertion that appears to be anything but Eagleton's *acte gratuit*. "This day I have begot whom I declare / My only Son, and on this holy hill / Him have anointed," declares God the Father. And then addressing the angelic host as though they were the heathens and rebels whom the psalm's Yahweh would "vex in his sore displeasure," he continues, "All knees in heaven" shall bow to the Son and "confess him Lord" – those who disobey shall be cast out "Into utter darkness, deep engulfed ... without redemption, without end" (*Paradise Lost* 5.603–15). As Abdiel's later imitation of Job's friends suggests,[40] the intention here may have been to reproduce the power and glory, the freedom of Job's Yahweh. But the effect is something less. The defensive tone, insistence on liability, and demand for subjection not from rebels but from the already zealous and loving heavenly host is startling. Even for the most loyal angel, it would be difficult not to feel impaired or obnoxious. What is critical to Norbrook is Abdiel's interpretation of God's declaration, that "God's creation of the Son epitomizes the principle of divine reduction."[41] As Abdiel explains to Satan, in begetting the Son, God the Father is in fact reducing himself and raising us up so that we might become in the Father's own words "one individual soul" (*Paradise Lost* 5.610): "nor by his reign," says Abdiel, is our virtue obscured, our being diminished, "But more illustrious made, since he the head / One of our number thus reduced becomes, / His laws our laws, all honour to him done / Returns our own" (5.841–5). This act of reduction, so Abdiel implies, is the beginning and end, the first and final act of God's charity, the still point where "God shall be all in all" (3.341). Norbrook's key move is to identify this act of reduction or grace with neo-Roman or republican traditions of self-sacrifice, to suggest that in the prime example of Lucius Junius Brutus calling for the death sentence on his own unpatriotic sons Roman virtue endorses a form of reduction or subjection entirely compatible with the Christian argument of grace, that is, with God willingly accepting the death sentence on his Son (97, 476–7). And indeed, the rhetoric of being raised up by another's gracious self-reduction or condescension is a constant in Milton's writings – not only here, as Norbrook emphasizes, but in *Defensio Secunda,* where in refusing the crown Cromwell reduces himself to raise up the English people,[42] or in Milton' s 1639 letter to Lucas Holst, where in his urbanity and modesty Cardinal Barberini effectively reduces himself to raise up his guests: not only does the Cardinal in his "submissive loftiness of mind ... raise himself by self-depression" but he also raises the young English poet (*CW* 12:45).

The question now becomes, if Abdiel and Norbrook can figure all this out so elegantly, why can't Satan? Although it's hard to believe, Satan is actually smarter than Norbrook – his angelic reason, so we are told, is "intuitive," whereas Norbrook's is only "discursive" (5.487–90). The poem's Augustinian answer is emphatic – it's Satan's pride, stupid; it's the kind of solipsism to which we're all prone, the narcissism or self-absorption that renders us incapable of reading difficult texts spiritually or graciously. My own answer is more sceptical or at least historicist, and it is central to my argument that the Augustinian solution is not quite as straightforward or disinterested as it sounds.

III

When Milton listens to Augustine, as C.S. Lewis and innumerable others insist he does, he is listening to the most inveterate enemy of Roman virtue.[43] "Augustine" is not a universal truth, but a historically specific writer, a man of his time, who defines Christianity's City of God in opposition to the City of Rome. Milton's fascination with that historical city and what it might mean is evident from his school days. In a work as early as Prolusion V (1628–9), for instance, the defence of the city signifies the mission of humanist education, cultivation, and civility, its destruction the triumph of barbarism and the victory of error over truth.[44] Unlike Augustine in *De Civitas Dei*, young Milton perceives the fall of Rome as an unmitigated disaster. Augustine glories in the way the barbarian triumph of 410 humbles the city, demonstrating that the great task Virgil assigns to Rome in the *Aeneid*, Anchises's imperative "To spare the conquered, and beat down the proud," is vacuous, merely an empty arrogation of God's power (1.Preface [5]).[45] For young Milton, there is no such satisfaction. No event "in fact or fable could be more remarkable" in its shamefulness than the fall of Rome, he says (*CPW* 1:258). The struggle to preserve the city is eternal: it is the struggle to rescue the citadel of truth from "the inroads which the vile horde of errors daily makes upon every branch of learning" (258), and the mission of education is every bit as heroic as that of Aeneas. Augustine is no lightweight and he is perfectly capable of appreciating the very real intelligence of Milton's Roman heroes, especially heroes like Cicero and Sallust who were once his own, but he despises their emphasis on a virtue that has no end but itself and the public good. He sees it as an idealization of human agency or will, the independence of which from God has precipitated the crisis in which the civilized world at the beginning of the fifth century finds itself. He is in fact not unlike Badiou in as much as he apprehends the truth-event of God's self-sacrifice as a means of seeing a new possibility, a city not of this world but of the next. When he explains the fall of Adam and Eve in terms of the fallibility of the creaturely will idealized by Cicero, he is formidably persuasive: when man "had turned towards himself," he says, "his being was less real than when he adhered to him who exists in a supreme degree. And so, to abandon God and to exist in oneself [*esse in semet ipso*], that is, to please oneself, is not immediately to lose all being; but it is to come nearer to nothingness" (14.13 [572]). But when Augustine turns to our particular question and tries to explain Satan's fall in the same terms, he encounters considerable difficulty. Although he insists it's all a matter of the "Devil's pride" (11.16 [447]), he cannot understand any more than we can why a creature born into beatitude – that is, into "the untroubled enjoyment of the changeless Good, which is God, together with the certainty of remaining with him for eternity, a certainty that admits no doubt or hesitation" (11.13 [444]) – should decide to turn away and live unto himself alone. He goes on to speculate that perhaps Satan and the apostate angels were created separately from the good angels, that they had no certainty, and that in this sense they were made vulnerable, doomed to fall, condemned to serve the greater good like the organ-donating clones in Kazuo Ishiguro's novel *Never Let Me Go*.[46] This thought that their merit might have been injured from the outset may be "intolerable," as Augustine concedes, but he can't come up with anything better (11.13 [444]).

My point is that Milton demonstrates his independence from Augustine and suggests the atavistic persistence of his neo-Roman sensibility in the degree to which his representation of Satan problematizes the Christian doctrine of grace as supplementary credit or as a doctrine that insists, as it does so vehemently in Luther's *De Servo Arbitrio*, on the absolute negation of human agency. In Milton's fiction, Satan has not now and never has had the beatific certainty of Augustine's good angels, and, most importantly, he experiences the endless burden of a love that can never be requited as an assault on his freedom, on his identity, on the very point of being – as something that is radically unjust. As Milton records it, he is made to feel obnoxious. In this, not only is he like Samson, but he is also curiously like Milton himself as the poet struggles with the burden of his own father's overwhelming love. The same expressive pattern is evident in all three representations. In *Ad Patrem*, young Milton recognizes the immense debt of endless gratitude: "I know not what offerings from me can better repay your gifts," he says to his father as he offers him his poem; indeed, "not even the greatest can repay them, nor can any gratitude expressed by the vain return of empty words be equal to the obligation" (8–11).[47] Even so, he persists not only in offering his poem but in preferring his own will to that of his father. He will not be in the power of another. "Do not persist, I pray you, in contemning the muses," he rebukes his father (52). But as he does so, he reinterprets him, transforming his grace into a power that allows him to grow. "Although you pretend to hate the gentle muses, I don't believe you do" (67–8), he says. I don't believe you do, because you did not command me to take another path, to become a banker or a lawyer. "But, wishing my nurtured mind to grow more rich, you permit me in deep retreats, far from the city's uproar, to pass my pleasant leisure by the Aonian stream, and to go a happy companion by Apollo's side" (74–7). This wilful reinterpretation of his father reproduces itself at its most sublime in Book III of *Paradise Lost* when the Son intercedes and reinterprets God the Father's justice as a form of grace.[48] Grace appears here not as a supplementary credit or a declaration that produces fear and trembling but as something that grows in the human heart. Only after the Son has rebuked the Father does God explain how he will nurture the fallen, "clear their senses dark, / What may suffice, and soften stony hearts" (3.188–9). This revelation of grace as growth is only precipitated by the Son's act of will: "For should man finally be lost," he admonishes his father, "So should thy goodness and thy greatness both / Be questioned and blasphemed without defence" (3.150–66). In very carefully making this challenge in the words of Abraham and Moses,[49] the Son validates human agency in a way that the neo-Roman Satan would surely have welcomed had he heard it.

What is most striking about *Ad Patrem* is the young poet's self-confidence. As Milton's self-portraits in both his poetry and his prose suggest, this self-confidence seems to have been there from the beginning. It is the result of his own gifts, his father's nurture, and an extraordinarily enabling education, a system that makes him receptive to neo-Roman theory, sure that any educated and virtuous citizen is the equal of a king, and convinced that education is of such potency that it may play a major role in repairing the ruin of our first parents. It is his life in education, his humanist commitment to agency and the cultivation of the mind, that leads him not to abandon religion and the radical doctrine of grace but to want to naturalize it, increasingly to re-present it as a matter of growth, of removing the stony from our hearts and making "new flesh Regenerate / Grow instead" (11.1–5).[50] What I'm trying to suggest then is that this turn to grace as growth is not unrelated to Milton's controversial representation of Satan. Satan in his refusal to believe functions as a kind of atavism of the idealization of human agency in Cicero and Sallust and so, however inadvertently, suggests the cultural relativism or historicity of the doctrine of grace. "Once this consideration is given due weight," once Satan's neo-Roman sense of justice is thought through, Skinner argues in a recent article, "it becomes more difficult to dismiss with complete assurance the suggestion that, as William Blake wonderfully expressed it, Milton may have been of the devil's party without knowing it."[51] I would put it more like this: the Christian argument of grace with its emphasis on self-abnegation and the neo-Roman theory of liberty with its emphasis on personal virtue, despite Milton's best efforts and to the degree that the one encourages the surrender of agency and the other the cultivation of it, are ultimately doomed to confusion and conflict. It's not that Milton is not committed to both ways of thinking or being in the world; he clearly is, and the register of the divided and distinguished worlds in which he lives at its most intractable is obnoxious Satan. Most importantly, for the present argument, Skinner's archaeology enables us to see how Milton's Satan marks the fault line between a culture of grace and one of growth.

NOTES

1 Quentin Skinner, *Liberty*, p. 112.
2 Skinner, *Liberty*, p. 83.
3 Skinner, *Liberty*, p. 84.
4 Skinner, *Liberty*, p. 84.
5 This is what Mary Nyquist calls "figurative" slavery ("Slavery, Resistance, and Nation," pp. 356–97).
6 Marshall Grossman, "Limiting History." See also Paul Stevens, "Intolerance," pp. 243–67.
7 Rosanna Cox, "Neo-Roman," pp. 1–22.
8 Milton, *The Complete Prose Works of John Milton*, cited as *CPW*, and from *The Works of John Milton*, cited as *CW*. His poetry is quoted from *The Poems of John Milton*. All citations are to this edition and can be found parenthetically in the text..
9 Cox, "Neo-Roman," p. 3.
10 See Skinner, *Liberty*, pp. 42–4.
11 Cox, "Neo-Roman," p. 13.
12 Cox, "Neo-Roman," p. 13.
13 Cox, "Neo-Roman," p. 11.
14 Feisal G. Mohamed's fine essay, "Confronting Religious Violence," pp. 327–40, provides a valuable point of entry into the current debate. See also Stevens, "Intolerance," esp. pp. 243–9.
15 See Milton's fascinating letter to Lucas Holst, 30 March 1639, in *CW* 12: 39–45.
16 I mean Job not Judges. While the Book of Judges is obviously the immediate source of Milton's story, the mood of the Book of Job is recurrently invoked in *Samson Agonistes*, as it is in *Paradise Regained*, the poem with which it was first published. Cf. the Chorus's invocation of Job's parody (7:17) of Psalm 8:4–9: "what is man! / That thou towards him with hand so various, / Or might I say contrarious" (pp. 667–9).

17 On Meroz, see Stevens, "Intolerance," esp. pp. 256–62.

18 Cox, "Neo-Roman," p. 8.

19 Cf., for instance, *Of Reformation*, *CPW* 1:571, pp. 547–8.

20 Tacitus, *Annals* XV: 44. See also Pliny, *Epistles* X: pp. 96–7, on Christianity as a religion that flourished among slaves: "I thought at this point," he says reporting to the emperor Trajan, "that it was necessary to get information from two slave women, whom they call Deaconesses (*ministrae*) about the actual truth [of what it meant to be a Christian], by means of torture. I found nothing worthy of blame other than the blind and over-wrought nature of their cult-superstition."

21 Skinner, *Liberty*, pp. 42–3.

22 See Stephen M. Fallon, *Milton's Peculiar Grace*.

23 Terry Eagleton, *Reason, Faith, & Revolution*, p. 8.

24 For instrumental reason as the antithesis of life-giving "enchantment," see Charles Taylor, *A Secular Age* and *The Malaise of Modernity*.

25 Eagleton, *Reason, Faith, & Revolution*, p. 10.

26 Debora Shuger, *Habits of Thought*.

27 Brian Cummings, *Literary Culture*, p. 49.

28 Cummings, *Literary Culture*, p. 49.

29 On growth as an "organizing principle" of modernity, see, for instance, Liah Greenfeld, "Is Modernity Possible without Nationalism?," pp. 38–50.

30 Cummings, *Literary Culture*, p. 50.

31 Cummings, *Literary Culture*, p. 50.

32 Fallon, *Milton's Peculiar Grace*, pp. x, 38. For Fallon's gracious and thoughtful response to my critique, see Stephen Fallon, "Is Milton a Religious Writer?" *Religion & Literature* 45:1 (2013): 207–8.

33 Fallon, *Milton's Peculiar Grace*, p. 38.

34 On Luther's call to absolute dependency, see his 1525 *De Servo Arbitrio*: "God has promised certainly His grace to the humbled; that is, to the self-deploring and despairing," says the vehement Luther. "But a man cannot be thoroughly humbled until he comes to know that his salvation is utterly beyond his own powers, counsel, endeavours, will, and works, and absolutely depending on the will, counsel, pleasure, and work of another, that is, of God only" (Luther, "The Bondage of the Will," pp. 700–1).

35 Cummings, *Literature Culture*, pp. 51–2.

36 Cummings, *Literature Culture*, p. 52.

37 Cf. Alain Badiou: "the Resurrection ... is not, in Paul's own eyes, of the order of fact, falsifiable or demonstrable. It is pure event, opening of an epoch, transformation of the relations between the possible and the impossible ... Its genuine meaning is that it testifies to the possible victory over death ...

The apostle is then he who names this possibility (the Gospels, the Good News, comes down to this: we can vanquish death). His discourse is one of pure fidelity to the possibility opened by the event" (*Saint Paul*, p. 45).

38 Cf. *CPW* 6:133: "God as he really is, is far beyond man's imagination, let alone his understanding ... It is safest for us to form an image of God in our minds which corresponds to his representation and description of himself in the sacred writings."

39 David Norbrook, *Writing the English Republic*, esp. pp. 467–80.

40 Abdiel's admonition, "Shalt thou give law to God" (5.822) echoes Eliphaz's question, "Shall mortal man be more just than God?" (Job 4:17) and, of course, Yahweh's own demand, "wilt thou condemn me, that thou mayest be righteous" (Job 40:8).

41 Norbrook, *Writing the English Republic*, p. 474.

42 See Paul Stevens, "Milton and National Identity," esp. pp. 358–62.

43 C.S. Lewis, *A Preface to Paradise Lost*, esp. pp. 66–72.

44 For the dating of the Prolusions, see Gordon Campbell and Thomas N. Corns, *John Milton*, pp. 41–2.

45 Augustine, *The City of God*.

46 Kazuo Ishiguro, *Never Let Me Go*.

47 The translation of *Ad Patrem* is quoted from *John Milton*, ed. Stephen Orgel and Jonathan Goldberg, pp. 135–41.

48 See Paul Stevens, *Imagination*, esp. pp. 145–77.

49 See Michael Leib, "*Paradise Lost*," pp. 39–50.

50 Grace as growth is, of course, entirely biblical. But it's the emphasis in Milton that seems remarkable, especially, one might add, in the light of Paul's attempt to limit the naturalizing force of the metaphor in I Corinthians 6-7: "I have planted [the belief], Apollos watered; but God gave the increase. So then neither is he that planteth anything, neither is he that watereth; but God hath given the increase."

51 Quentin Skinner, "What does it mean to be a Free Person?" pp. 16–18.

BIBLIOGRAPHY

Augustine. *The City of God*. Trans. Henry Bettenson. Intro. G.R. Evans. London: Penguin, 2003.

Badiou, Alain. *Saint Paul: The Foundation of Universalism*. Trans. Ray Brassier. Stanford, CA: Stanford UP, 2003.

Campbell, Gordon, and Thomas N. Corns. *John Milton: Life, Work, and Thought*. Oxford: Oxford UP, 2008.

Cox, Rosanna. "Neo-Roman Terms of Slavery in *Samson Agonistes.*" *Milton Quarterly* 44, no. 1 (2010): 1–22.

Cummings, Brian. *The Literary Culture of the Reformation: Grammar and Grace.* 2002; rpt. Oxford: Oxford UP, 2007.

Eagleton, Terry. *Reason, Faith, & Revolution: Reflections on the God Debate.* New Haven, CT: Yale UP, 2009.

Fallon, Stephen M. *Milton's Peculiar Grace: Self-representation and Authority.* Ithaca, NY: Cornell UP, 2007.

Greenfeld, Liah. "Is Modernity Possible without Nationalism?" In *The Fate of the Nation-state.* Montreal and Kingston: McGill-Queen's UP, 2004. 38–50.

Grossman, Marshall. "Limiting History." In *Rethinking Historicism from Shakespeare to Milton.* Ed. Ann Baynes Coiro and Thomas Fulton. Cambridge: Cambridge UP, 2012. 65 84.

Ishiguro, Kazuo. *Never Let me Go.* 2005; rpt. New York: Vintage, 2010.

Leib, Michael. "*Paradise Lost,* book III: the Dialogue in Heaven Reconsidered." In *Renaissance Papers 1974.* Ed. Dennis G. Donovan and A. Leigh Deneef. Durham, NC: SE Renaissance Conference, 1975.

Lewis, C.S. *A Preface to* Paradise Lost. 1942; rpt. London: Oxford UP, 1967.

Luther, Martin, "The Bondage of the Will." In *The Portable Renaissance Reader.* Ed. James Ross and Mary McLaughlin. Harmondsworth: Penguin, 1981. 700–1.

Milton, John. *The Complete Prose Works of John Milton* [*CPW*]. Gen. ed. Don M. Wolfe. 8 vols. New Haven, CT: Yale UP, 1953–82.

– *The Poems of John Milton.* Ed. John Carey and Alastair Fowler. London: Longman, 1968.

– The *Works of John Milton* [*CW*]. Ed. Frank Allen Patterson. 18 vols. New York: Columbia UP, 1931–8.

Mohamed, Feisal G. "Confronting Religious Violence: Milton's *Samson Agonistes.*" *PMLA* 120, no. 2 (2005): 327–40.

Norbrook, David. *Writing the English Republic: Poetry, Rhetoric and Politics, 1627–1660.* 1999; rpt. Cambridge: Cambridge UP, 2000.

Nyquist, Mary. "Slavery, Resistance, and Nation in Milton and Locke." In *Early Modern Nationalism and Milton's England.* Ed. David Loewenstein and Paul Stevens. Toronto: U of Toronto P, 2008. 356–97.

Orgel, Stephen, and Jonathan Goldberg. *John Milton.* Oxford: Oxford UP, 1991. 135–41.

Shuger, Debora. *Habits of Thought in the English Renaissance: Religion, Politics, and the Dominant Culture.* Berkeley: U of California P, 1991.

Skinner, Quentin. *Liberty before Liberalism.* 1998; rpt. Cambridge: Cambridge UP, 2008.

– "What does it mean to be a Free Person?" *London Review of Books* 30, no. 10 (22 May 2008): 16–18.

Stevens, Paul. *Imagination and the Presence of Shakespeare in* Paradise Lost. Madison: U of Wisconsin P, 1985.

– "Intolerance and the Virtues of Sacred Vehemence." In *Milton and Toleration*. Ed. Sharon Achinstein and Elizabeth Sauer. Oxford: Oxford UP, 2007. 243–67.

– "Milton and National Identity." In *The Oxford Handbook of Milton*. Ed. Nicholas McDowell and Nigel Smith. Oxford: Oxford UP, 2009.

Taylor, Charles. *The Malaise of Modernity*. Toronto: Anansi Press, 1991.

– *A Secular Age*. Cambridge, MA: Belknap Press, 2007.

Contributors

Donald Beecher has written on English and Continental theatre, tricksters, witchcraft, lovesickness, memory, Renaissance travel and pharmaceuticals, and literature and the cognitive sciences, as well as edited several of the early English prose fiction writers and some forty-six works of early music including a madrigal comedy. His current projects deal with human nature and imaginative worlds, and the artistic aftermath of the Battle of Lepanto. He is Chancellor's Professor in the Department of English, Carleton University.

Bradin Cormack is a Professor of English at Princeton University. He studies early modern literature as it relates to the law, the bookish disciplines, and intellectual culture more generally. He has written *A Power to Do Justice: Jurisdiction, English Literature, and the Rise of Common Law, 1509–1625* (Chicago, 2007) and, with Richard Strier and Martha Nussbaum, has edited *Shakespeare and the Law: A Conversation among Disciplines and Professions* (Chicago, 2013). With Lorna Hutson, he is co-editor of *The Oxford Handbook of English Law and Literature, 1500–1700*, expected from Oxford UP in 2016.

Travis Decook is an Associate Professor of English at Carleton University. His research interests include early modern literature, religion, and theology; the Bible; and theories of secularity and modernity. He has co-edited the collection *Shakespeare, the Bible, and the Form of the Book* (Routledge, 2011), and has published articles on early modern religious controversy, utopian literature, and the history of the media.

Elizabeth Hanson is a Professor of English at Queen's University. She is the author of *Discovering the Subject in Renaissance England*

(Cambridge, 1998, 2008) and her most recent book project, provisionally entitled *Education and Social Distinction in Early Modern England,* concerns the so-called education revolution in sixteenth-century England.

Barbara Kreps is a Professor of English at the University of Pisa. She works on literature and legal culture in Renaissance Studies and has published, among other venues, in the *Ben Jonson Journal, Shakespeare Survey, Modern Drama, ELH, Renaissance Quarterly,* and *Shakespeare Quarterly.*

Judith Owens is an Associate Professor of English at the University of Manitoba. She works on sixteenth- and seventeenth-century literature with an emphasis on Edmund Spenser. She has written *Enabling Engagements: Edmund Spenser and the Poetics of Patronage* (McGill-Queen's, 2002) and co-edited *City Limits: Perspectives on the Historical European City* (McGill-Queen's, 2010).

Debora Shuger is Distinguished Professor of English at the University of California, Los Angeles. Her areas of interest are many, including devotional poetry, theology and biblical exegesis, legal history, political thought, rhetoric, life writing, and classical heritages. She has written on authors from Spenser to Milton, and has held a number of important awards including Guggenheim, NEH, and UC President's fellowships. She is the author of *Censorship and Cultural Sensibility: The Regulation of Language in Tudor-Stuart England* (Pennsylvania, 2006), preceded by *Political Theologies in Shakespeare's England* (Palgrave Macmillan, 2001). Her most recent book is *Religion in Early Stuart England, 1603–1638* (Baylor, 2012).

John D. Staines is an Associate Professor of English at John Jay College of Criminal Justice at the City University of New York. He is the author of *The Tragic Histories of Mary Queen of Scots, 1560–1690: Rhetoric, Passions, and Political Literature* (Ashgate, 2009), a study of how political rhetoric uses tragic stories to sway the passions of the public. He is currently researching early modern responses to religious violence.

Paul Stevens is Canada Research Chair in Early Modern Literature & Culture at the University of Toronto. A former President of the Milton Society of America and Visiting Fellow at All Souls College, Oxford, he was elected a Fellow of the Royal Society of Canada in 2012. His recent publications include *Early Modern Nationalism and Milton's England,* co-edited with David Loewenstein, which was awarded the 2009 Irene Samuel Prize, and he is currently working on a new book, *Sola Gratia: English Literature and the Secular Ways of Grace,* for which he was recently awarded a Guggenheim Fellowship

Virginia Lee Strain is an Assistant Professor of English at Loyola University. Her research interests include early modern literature and legal culture, and Shakespeare and the Law. She is working on a book project provisionally entitled "Perfecting the Law: Literature and Law Reform in Early Modern England."

Tim Stretton is a Professor of History at Saint Mary's University, Halifax. He specializes in the social history of law and litigation in Britain, as well as the links between law and literature. His current research examines the history of coverture (the legal condition of married women) from the sixteenth century through to the early twentieth century. He is the author of *Women Waging Law in Elizabethan England* (Cambridge, 1998, 2005).

David Stymeist teaches in the English Department at Carleton University. His research focuses on Renaissance literature and questions of historiography and criminality. His recent work appears in *Cahiers Elizabethains, Studies in English Literature,* and *Genre: Forms of Discourse and Culture.*

Elliott Visconsi is concurrently Associate Professor of English and Associate Professor of Law at Notre Dame University. He works on literature, law, and political thought in the early modern period, from Shakespeare and Milton to the Restoration period as well as early American literature. He is the author of *Lines of Equity: Literature and the Origins of Law in Later Stuart England* (Cornell, 2008) and is currently working on First Amendment doctrine and the future of free expression in the digital age.

Andrew Wallace is an Associate Professor of English at Carleton University and has a particular interest in the reception of classical texts in the English Renaissance. His most recent book, *Virgil's Schoolboys: The Poetics of Pedagogy in Renaissance England* (Oxford, 2010), deals with the triangular conversation between schoolmaster, schoolboy, and schoolbook in the early grammar school, and the conditions of a humanist education. He is currently working on a study of tragedy in its ancient and Renaissance settings.

Grant Williams is an Associate Professor of English at Carleton University. He has co-edited two collections: *Forgetting in Early Modern English Literature and Culture: Lethe's Legacies* (Routledge, 2004) and *Ars Reminiscendi: Mind and Memory in Renaissance Culture* (CRRS, 2009). He works on rhetoric, the imagination, and the memory arts in early modern literature and culture.

Index

www.ingramcontent.com/pod-product-compliance
Lightning Source LLC
LaVergne TN
LVHW090151080826
844660LV00013B/759/J
* 9 7 8 1 4 4 2 6 4 2 0 1 0 *